BLIND BAY HOOKERS

The little ships
of early Nelson
and Colonial Times

Fred Westrupp

Text © 2022 Fred Westrupp & Jon Tucker

All rights reserved. No part of this book may be reproduced or transmitted in any form or by any means without the consent of the copyright holders. This includes the illustrations which are reproduced by permission of the *Nelson Provincial Museum*, the *Hocken Library*, the *NZ National Library* and the *Alexander Turnbull Library*, as well as the private collections of Rob Williams, Lynette Wilson and Kerry Miller.

All newspaper extracts are taken from the *Papers Past* collection, courtesy of the National Library of New Zealand: (paperspast.natlib.govt.nz)

Every effort has been made to trace copyright holders of material reproduced in this book. The publishers would be pleased to hear from any we have been unable to contact.

Cover design: Fred Westrupp
Typesetting, layout, proofreading: Pam Gill, APM Publishing +61 428 232 717
Original editing: Carol Dawber
This edition revision and editing: Jon Tucker
Indexing: Carol Dawber, Barbara Tucker, Jon Tucker

ISBN: 978-0-6489157-3-7

Also available as an eBook
eBook ISBN: 978-0-6489157-4-4

First edition published 2007 by River Press

Second edition (revised and expanded) published 2022 by Storm Bay Books

stormbaybooks@gmail.com
www.nzmaid.com

Acknowledgements

THIS BOOK HAS BEEN OUT-OF-PRINT for a number of years since Carol Dauber's encouragement first saw it issued by *River Press* fifteen years ago. Carol has kindly made available to *Storm Bay Books* her original proofs for a timely revision in view of ongoing interest in its content). This edition is thanks to the substantial additional research, illustration and major re-editing carried out by my adventurous daughter Barbara with her author/sailor husband Jon Tucker, who both hold commercial captains' qualifications.

For other members of my family I am also grateful. To my wife Jocelyn who originally encouraged, read sources as well as my many drafts, helping and putting up with my distraction. She and I visited nearly all of the hooker territory and seas. During our coastal voyaging, three younger daughters Litty, Kate and Anna proved at sea they too had their mother's heart. Our son-in-law Gary Christiansen as well as daughter Cris were of great support with my computer skills. The experience of sons Captain Willie Westrupp (ex-crayfisherman on the West Coast) and Red Westrupp (an exceptionally knowledgeable bushman, since deceased), reflects in the text, as does my late brother Allen Westrupp, one of the last 'old-school' shipwright-boatbuilder craftsmen, a lifelong mate who was always loved and respected by my family. His daughter Carol and partner Steve were helpful in their turn, and his grandson maintains the small-boat handling tradition in Cook Strait waters as a qualified member of the water-police team, aboard the Wellington Police Launch *Lady Elizabeth IV*.

I also acknowledge the authors in the Bibliography and others. I read widely, sifting through scarce records to supplement the 'proximity learning' I grew up with; then the writings of hooker-men the late Ted Reed, Manuel Smith and Percy Williams (Motueka), and Russell Ricketts (Nelson). When I was at an impasse, the staff in Takaka Library and individuals with historians' interests; Jenny Askew, Eileen Stewart, Lynette Wilson, Pamela Fry, Carol Thompson, Dennis Gillooly, Howard Williams (who had crewed under my grandfather) and Rob Williams all helped me find the almost lost people of the story. Nelson Provincial Museum held various resources including a few surviving original documents thus bridging the time between then and now.

But no list is complete in these circumstances and since then further authors and the internet have become available. Tony Simpson's recent book *Before Hobson* has provided further insight into the times. Elizabeth French, a descendent of Nelson's first pilot James Cross, sent me welcome details of his *Pilot Deal* boat. Additionally Linda Cross's evocative painting of *Felicity* in frame at Frenchman's Bay now graces the back cover of this edition.

Illustrative records too evolved during the 19th century. From the sketches and watercolours of the first two decades came the occasional introduction of glass plate negatives, with photographers like Nelson's Tyree brothers gaining much status for their expensive equipment when they set up business in 1878. These early photographic archival records are a treasure trove, as it was not until the 1890s that celluloid film and kodak 'box brownie' cameras became available to produce some of the sailing images in the final decades of the hooker era. Since my time-consuming physical searches for First Edition material, the National Library of New Zealand has obligingly made colonial newspaper content readily available for public use through its 'Papers Past' website.

Being reshaped and republished under the Storm Bay Books banner makes this book internationally accessible through modern-day technology (rather ironic for a story rooted in 19th century colonialism and class distinctions) for which the author is grateful. The text and illustrations have been supplemented to accommodate further material and insights which have come to hand during the intervening years.

Contents

Introduction		vii
Chapter 1	A Practical Guide to Hooker Building	1
Chapter 2	The New Zealand Company	15
Chapter 3	Settlement by the Shore	29
Chapter 4	The First Locally-built Hooker	41
Chapter 5	A Struggling Colony	51
Chapter 6	The Winter of Discontent	63
Chapter 7	The Colony Mis-Stays	73
Chapter 8	Nelson's Early Coastal Margins	85
Chapter 9	Livestock Arrives by Sea	99
Chapter 10	Onto a Steady Course	107
Chapter 11	Marlborough via Cook Strait	119
Chapter 12	Nelson's Second Decade	135
Chapter 13	The Wild West Coast	153
Chapter 14	The Charleston Challenge	167
Chapter 15	Timber for the Taking	177
Chapter 16	Shoal Draft Heavyweights	195
Chapter 17	Steamers Near and Far	211
Chapter 18	Changes along the Waterfront	221
Chapter 19	A Perilous Occupation	237
Chapter 20	The Last Hooker-men	251
Appendix 1	Common 19th Century Rigs in Blind Bay Vessels	264
Appendix 2	Conversion from Imperial to Metric	266
Appendix 3	Relevant Maori Words	268
Appendix 4	A Chronology of the Blind Bay Hookers	270
Bibliography		294
Index of Vessels		297
Index		301
Cover Photographs		318

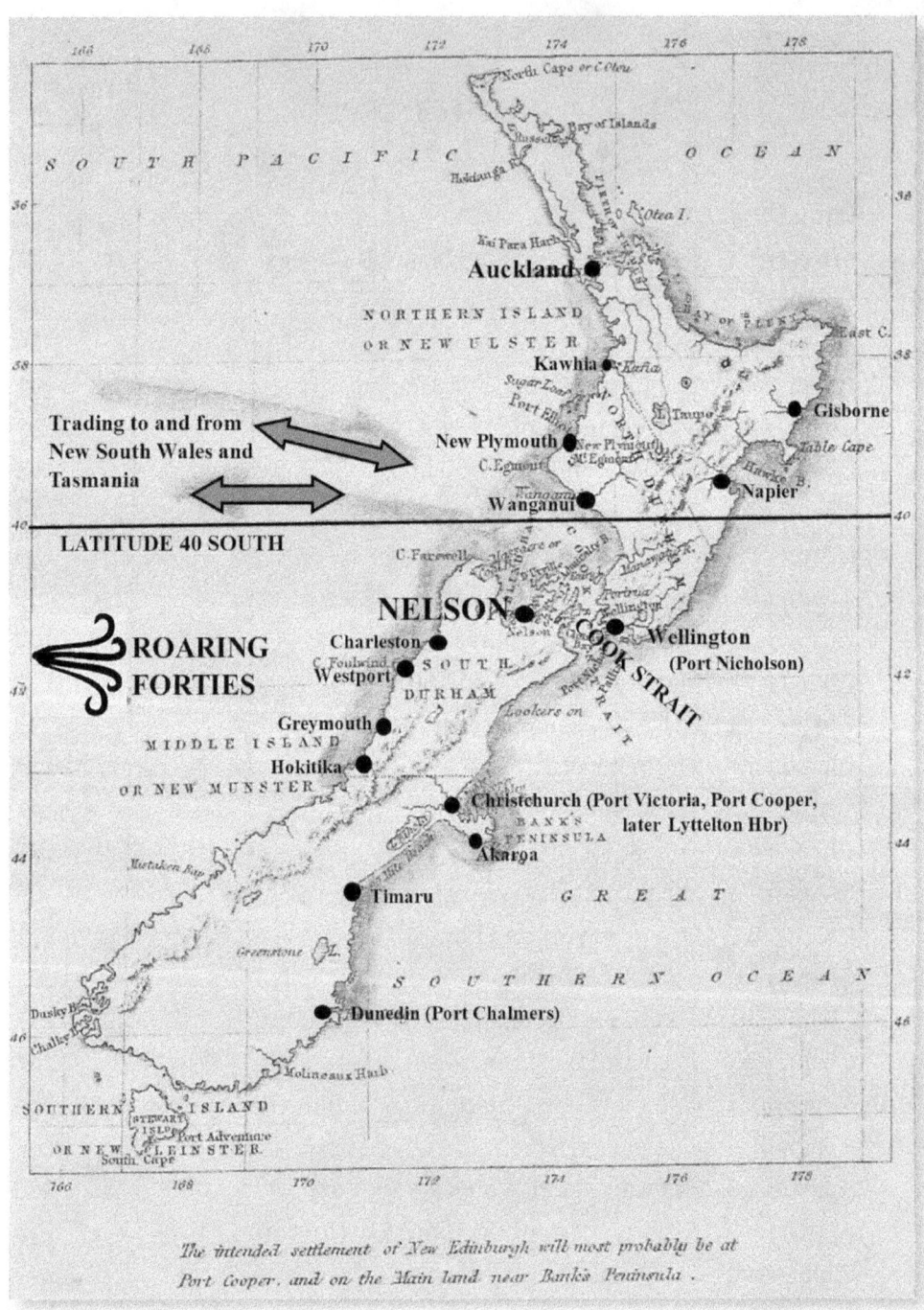

Introduction

NEW ZEALAND HAS ALWAYS BEEN a maritime country, recreationally today more than ever. As a nation we are interested in the sea, and in the ships and boats that sail it. The stories of larger ships and of scows and scow men of the Hauraki Gulf have been written, but there is another important sea story, that of early coasters in the upper South Island which preceded the scows that came on the scene only late in the 19th century, taking over their role of trucks of the sea.

As a boy at Port Nelson in the 1930s with its wharves, old buildings and seafarers' residences redolent of the 19th century, I knew some of the last hooker men, for example, our elderly near neighbour Captain Young, of the *Camellia*. A painting of *Camellia* (featured on the cover of this book) that brought him pleasure in his old age was handed on to my father, and now I have handed this on to my voyaging daughter Barbara and her husband Jon to enjoy too. This lovely hooker provided a precedent seventy years later for them when rigging their own traditional gaff ketch, *New Zealand Maid* (pictured here).

My links with Nelson's colonial maritime history stem initially from the fact that my father was Master of the pilot launch for many years (which made us part of the waterfront *milieu*) and that my grandfather, great-uncles and great-grandfather as well as great-great-grandfather on my mother's side (John Kidson) and his descendants were New Zealand seamen and captains during or after the nineteenth century. During my boyhood, my brother Allen and I helped put Captain Johnny Reeves' cargo-carrying *Neta* on the hard at Haulashore Island to scrub her bottom, and we mixed freely with well-known older waterfront characters like Billy Reed, Captain Sonny Tregidga and Allan McNabb. Two uncles and my father as a youngster had sailed with my grandfather and there was also a cluster of sailor-fishermen I knew.

My grandfather, Captain Sam Westrupp (pictured here at the wheel of the scow *Pearl Kasper*) still visited us, as did other seafarers, and even a lighthouse-keeper, Ivan Anderson, an old shipmate of my father. So most of the two earliest New Zealand generations of my family, and some of the third, were connected with the hookers, from one of the earliest (*Jubilee*) right through to the last vessel plying under sail alone (my Great-uncle's *Lily*). Old-time skippers, including my grandfather seemed to favour a felt hat (their mark of office?), but the harbourmaster-pilot who lived along the road from us, had a uniform and a peaked white cap which better fitted my boyish image of the importance of the position. We were raised to show respect to those whose names carried the prefix 'Captain'.

That original waterfront beside Haven Road is largely gone with reclamation, oil tanks, storage yards and buildings where the tides flowed in our youth, but this story ranges around it and out over the waters adjacent to the long coastlines of the North and South Islands where the Nelson hookers worked. All of the settlers here had come by sea, first the Maori seafarers a millenium ago, and European colonists later. These heroic origins, with their successes and dreams, or adversities and courage are lost in the annals of time. Although a written thread emerges from the European explorers, sealers, whalers and settlers, much grassroots human experience and striving is unrecorded. Even in settler times the importance of a written record was at first discounted, as it was still an era before literacy was for everyone, and its lack judged as though a moral failing. Fortunately others have

recognised this, so another stratum of history has emerged which is needed for a balanced view. These are the people who made New Zealand.

I was ten years old when New Zealand's Centennial celebration began, and I fortunately had a teacher who encouraged our class to research our oral family history. The outcome indicated there were two contrasting versions of early colonisation, and now (over eight decades later) I think this schoolroom experience also awakened a germ of awareness that the *capacity to think* is also an obligation for exactitude in *separating truth from feelings-induced opinions*. Our times are scarred by opinions.

The Nelson colony was shaped by the New Zealand Land Company (which was in the business of selling land for profit). Misleading promotion gave it a veneer of respectable authority, which persisted despite its inevitable failure. Thus, for decades beyond its demise, the Company founders were viewed as heroes (even by some teachers in my primary school). Despite effectively abandoning the early Nelson settlers, the Company unwittingly left, as a legacy, a wide mix of ideas and enterprise in those who had been enticed into emigrating. It put an indelible stamp on the settlement as positive directions emerged from the hardworking settlers who included the skippers and crews of the hookers who had become an economic lifeline.

The hooker-men were a varied lot. As well as being experienced seamen, many Maori also soon became ship-owners (as discussed in chapter 10). The European seafarers' names I had known ranged from English to the Hebrides, and from Scandinavia to the Mediterranean. There were North Americans too. Given my background, I saw myself as custodian of the reality of a colonial maritime enterprise arising from an inauspicious beginning; a balanced view of a history enacted not only on land but its sea links that needed to be recorded before being lost.

Some of our friends were hooker descendants: Ricketts, Williams, Gabrielsens and others. For some of us, unsurprisingly, our lives were boats. Much later, mainly in our own hooker-sized 36 foot ketch *Matuku II* with my wife Jocelyn and our three youngest daughters Litty, Kate and Anna as a staunch crew, we became familiar with the east coast, sailing out of Napier to just below East Cape in the north, and to Wellington, Cook Strait, the Sounds and Blind Bay. I knew the coast from Banks Peninsula, and over into Westhaven across its bar. The deputy harbourmaster and pilot at Gisborne came aboard *Matuku II* a few times, when we were in and out of the port. He paid me the courtesy title of 'Captain', although I lacked the piece of paper and the hat. The commercial titles I had earned paled by comparison. We *had* sailed the same turbulent waters as the hookers probably with the same pleasures and fears; we *had* been tested and felt we earned our place.

And while this is a Nelson story, it runs parallel to the historical record of other hookers which were common around the New Zealand, Australian and Tasmanian coasts. Other shipbuilders, in both Auckland and the Cook Strait area, had preceded those in Nelson by a few years, and by the 1860s, there were

half-a-dozen builders in Akaroa, and others in the Banks Peninsula bays. Dunedin, Port Chalmers and Riverton all had their builders, and a scattering elsewhere in the South Island. With its rugged topography so different from the unreal depiction of it in England, New Zealand had independently developed its own essential coastal transport system to sustain it.

This book is the story of those times.

Fred Westrupp
Nelson 2022

*Sketch from the log: **Matuku II**, in which the author and family sailed the waters of his hooker forebears, learning even greater respect for their seamanship.*

1

A Practical Guide to Hooker Building

WHEN NEXT YOU STAND on an isolated beach, in imagination or reality, imagine yourself landed from a boat with your wife or husband, packages and bundles at your feet. A heavy box of tools and a long pitsaw, probably six feet long (or maybe up to nine feet), have pride of place because you are going to build a boat.

You are hot in your rough serge work suit with the coat open and waistcoat unbuttoned, or equally uncomfortable in a hot, multi-layered dress covering you from your neck to your wrists and ankles, and of course you have heavy leather boots. Most important of all, you are answerable only to yourself and your family. The year is 1842 and there is not a committee in sight.

Felicity in frame on the beach at Frenchman's Bay
Painting by Linda Cross, courtesy Rob Williams collection

How good to bury ourselves in an activity which absorbs us, and lets the world go by for a time! Building our hooker will be such a thing. But somewhere out there, edging on mainly rough coastal land is a settlement. The hinterland, steep and bush-clad, is scarcely touched. How did fresh little town of Nelson come to exist? In a nutshell it is the ill-conceived experiment of Edward Gibbon Wakefield who for years has been seeking an opportunity to fulfil his ambitions. A hard-headed political and business coterie has been eyeing New Zealand since at least 1825, and Wakefield has been supported by those seeking financial gain, as well as enthusiastic devotees. As we will later discover, Wakefield's scheme is not the best of foundations upon which to find oneself stranded 12,000 miles from home.

Company Poster, London C 1839
Source unidentified

The Antipodes were well enough known in Britain by the 1830s, at very least as an idea, in these times of displaced people and colonisation, and as the direction where almost exclusively, the poor were sent because of offences largely against property. A place, too, where land must be for the taking, because Great Britain had already taken Australia, and where a promise of a quick increase in value could be used as a lure for investors. Being judgmental is pointless at this distance in time, but we do need to **understand** *this background. This book revolves around outcomes: how settlers arrived on New Zealand's isolated beaches and how their lack of communication and transportation could be, and was, solved. But first of all, we need to understand what it is like to build a hooker!*

How to build a 'hooker'

The tree-clad slopes behind your beach should be a source of ready timber, and you have chosen a site where launching is practicable, for you need the dream. With a creek to hand, all these surroundings provide a swarm of biting sandflies or, if near dusk, mosquitoes, but those are minor discomforts for such a grand purpose. And you will be sharing it with a working companion or companions, for some of your task needs more than one pair of hands. Pit-sawing trees into planks is not for the faint-hearted, yet even some pioneer women worked one end of the saw. We shall gloss over the vital but mundane problems of shelter and sustenance that you must have confronted already, but you are looking forward to fishing off the headland and maybe even planting a quick garden.

Our sturdy forebears did these things, like selecting potentially suitable tree species. Easy to say, but standing on the bush floor, usually rough, and maybe spongy with mosses growing on the litter of branches and leaves, you study the giant trees, peering up through the broadleafs which form the gloomy lower canopy. How on earth are you to know which ones may suit your purpose? Perhaps you might be able to call then on the experience of other like-minded folk, for you would want to be certain before taking axe and saw to one of these giants. Wood is forgiving, but it needs to dry out and stabilise sufficiently to avoid ongoing problems during your build. A rule of thumb is an inch of thickness per year for finishing work, but obviously this can't be adhered to in pioneering circumstances, nor for structural timbers. Already you face one of the compromises to be made, for time is not on your side, but green timber may well reduce the lifespan of your proposed little ship. You have been told that some green timber immersed may give no problems, but pukatea, for instance, will tend to waterlog, and problems come with drying out, when timbers shrink and boats will leak. So off you go to scour the river edges and beach to see if nature may have delivered you, by flood perhaps, a trunk already seasoned.

The next backbreaking steps involve reducing a tree or log to lumber. Can you fell your tree directly on to bearers placed on the ground, allowing cutting to your lengths? Or maybe you must move it with a timber jack (if you should be so lucky as to have one), digging for bearers and cutting back the bush for saw clearance. Perhaps you will need to trim and float your log to the work-site if it is on the river or beach. A small dinghy, two oars, hard rowing, rollers, levers and patience can shift a large log. Fortunately our central New Zealand coast has sufficient rise and fall of tide – eight feet at neaps and over 12 feet at spring tides – to allow us to float our chosen log onto a structure, and work between tides to cut from it.

Pit-sawing will now be used to shape the sawn frames used internally to shape, strengthen and fasten planking. You may even select rough-hewn grown tree crooks as an early choice. Your decisions will require a balancing of the work needed against what can be moved (and how far), taking account of the desirability

Pit-sawing near Anawhata. What was accomplished by manual work and the skills of the workers, using the simplest of tools, speaks for itself in this picture. The squared baulks of timber would probably be further broken down at a mill. The two men using the pitsaw were traditionally called 'top dog' and 'under dog' (note how he is positioned opposite the saw teeth to avoid much sawdust), and it was such effort and skills that carved out a country.
A P Godber Collection G-822½, Alexander Turnbull Library, Wgtn, NZ

of a particular wood. It will be extremely difficult to move logs, but the terrain will dictate where a saw-pit can be dug. Subsequent planks will be movable.

The Huffams of Bark Bay, who will rejoin the story later, started boat building after settling there, and built several hookers for Nelson folks and for west coasters. Timber was being milled at nearby Awaroa at the time, but some of the timber they cut themselves, with a saw pit close to the high water's edge, sliding the trees down the hills into the tide and floating them to the saw pit.

The skill of splitting is a final woodsman's skill to master: essential as a size-reduction method. You will likely have already seen split planks on the floors of pioneer houses, laid green with the curling edges later smoothed off with an adze. Perhaps you have already practised splitting totara paling fences, held with a couple of twists of wire. Red beech has also been found to be very suitable, and split wood is deemed stronger than sawn. Cut the log to length, drive wedges in the end, the technique being to quarter-split, taking a plank or planks off each of the four faces consecutively to get the grain coinciding with the growth rings. You will now have your planks, to dress further or not. The other splitting technique requires cutting a groove each side of a log and splitting with wedges, the groove necessary to keep the split from wandering off to a side. This will be a technique for big timbers like the keel.

Shipboard companions on the emigrant ships included men of all the practical trades, so that such knowledge was there for the sharing in the watches of the long days and nights. It was not always the talkers from whom one could learn; it was the practical men speaking quietly from their experience; the wise listen. The workmen coming to New Zealand included many artisans, a great cross-section of the knowledge and skills of the trades of the old countries, and doubtless they discussed them.

Likely timber choices

When you have sized up the possibilities in the bush and laboured to get out your timbers, you are likely to have kahikatea (pictured) or matai for planking, and natural bends of rata or matai surface roots that you will work with axe and adze strengthening knees and frames. Grown crooks may be sawn to shape, or combined with ribs steam-bent in place. You may use Titoki, like other 1842 Blind Bay settlers who have observed that its hardness and crooked growth resemble English oak.[1] Your observant eye may have found other timber possibilities in the bush. The keel will require a long straight baulk, beech for choice, perhaps rimu or kahikatea (pictured). The future spars may be kahikatea, too (a decision which you may later regret due to its poor durability).

Kahikatea (White pine)

---

1 Pratt p. 16

In building at Riwaka, Pratt[2] tells of felling a birch [beech] tree, sawing it to size, bringing it up the creek and fixing it to the stocks. The keel is laid! He mentions towing the stem with a small punt and much difficulty, and then abandoning it as unsatisfactory in favour of a rimu one.

You are rather envious of other pioneer boatbuilders in northern New Zealand where the wonderful kauri trees abound, as well as gnarled pohutukawa bends for the knees. Some kauri has found its way here to the Nelson haven – you saw it advertised for sale in the Examiner within the first year of settlement – but you don't have the funds for this luxury planking. Anyway, the golden-blossomed kowhai behind your beach may contribute crooks for your grown knees. You have heard that supplejack can be used as ribs in smaller boats, fixed inside your stringers while it is green and flexible, then drying iron hard. Other woods too may have their place in your hooker hull. Totara especially, as it resists the wood-eating teredo worm which makes vessels leak. But always in mind, for the larger timbers, is that you will have to favour proximity over quality and preferred species.

Of course, wood has been the key resource for crafts at this point in history; woodworking craftsmen included sawyers, builders, joiners and cabinetmakers, shipwrights and boatbuilders, coopers, coachmakers and wheelwrights (the first of the well-known Ricketts boatbuilders was a wheelwright). With the assistance of a blacksmith most trades made their own tools and prepared their own raw materials. If iron were available, nail making for both boats[3] and houses was quite common in earliest circumstances when trade had not brought the products of industry. And while our portrayal is realistic, in more settled places there were other fruits of Europe's industrialisation. Motueka had a sawmill worked by a 20 horsepower waterwheel as early as 1843.

Fastenings and Tools

Your hull structure will need fastening together, and you are considering using the time-honoured trunnels (wooden pegs) due to the expense of metal fastenings. It will take time to find suitably dry wood to split and whittle, but you have an iron plate with a sharp-edged drilled hole in your kit, along with a mallet to drive your whittled pegs through the hole for their final shaping. It would be nice to have some kauri or even Australian bluegum for this, but you will experiment with totara instead, as there are several near your beach.

Traditional builders Jim Persson and Allen Westrupp told me of seeing planks joined to a piece of keel with treenails (trunnels), maybe an inch and more in diameter, picked up on Farewell Spit. An 1894 wreck on the Waimakariri bar, believed to be the remnants of Owake Belle, which was built in 1877 in Southland, where no kauri grows, was uncovered in 1949. The totara timbers and kauri trenails were still quite sound.[4] Trenails, iron bolts and nails were used then; in later times copper and bronze

---

2 Pratt p. 117
3 McGill p. 116
4 *Shipwrecks*, 7th edition, p.154

were the fastenings of choice, although as an impoverished schoolboy I built an eight-footer with battened seams and clinched galvanised nails. I could not afford copper.

In your tool box, as well as your brace and bits, drawknife, spokeshaves and side axe, you will surely have a fine-crafted adze, a beautiful tool to use once you get the heft of it, especially with hardwood. It will dress as well as you were likely to do with a plane, once you have mastered the skill.

There is a nice adze story, that a good man could split a threepenny bit on edge with an adze. My boatbuilder brother Allen, an accomplished user, was working with his adze when a bystander asked if it were true. 'Surely', said Allen 'have you got one?' At which the bystander produced the tiny silver coin from his pocket and asked 'where shall I put it?' 'Don't put it down' said Allen, 'just hold it on this block, between your thumb and finger'. Which of course should be the end of the story, except that the trusting bystander had more faith in Allen's prowess than he had himself, and proffered the thruppence between thumb and finger to be split!

Suitable hull design

In the first edition of this book I referred to the America's Cup contenders' vessels early in the 21st century and the preceding period. The later models may have had functionalism but the simile has run its course and sometimes seamanship has bowed to entertainment values; now, a decade later, comparison with latest foiling developments is hollow.

Our hookers will be simple workers, load carriers with flattish bottoms and rounded bilges for beaching. (We should not confuse these hulls with the later scows which had a square section derived from punts and a rectangular centreboard.) The hookers working in Blind Bay's seaway had bluff bows and wide shoulders well forward – cod head and mackerel tail, a very 18th century look, suitable for the shortish steep waves of the notorious Nor-westers, and there was an easy run from the middle section to the stern no doubt in part to facilitate the run of the planking.

Felicity – a beach-built hooker

They varied in detail at the bow, especially in the straight stem like *Old Jack II* which appears as a rectangle between keel and stem in the photograph below of her grounded on Snapper Rock or Beehive, about 1912 (that being the year her engine is recorded as installed).

There are many similar examples around the world. In Ireland, *Galway Bay*

Old Jack II, *as seen in these two images, demonstrates the plumb bow and knuckle typical of early 19th century hookers.*
FN Jones collection, Box 24, Tasman Bays Heritage collection, Nelson Provincial Museum

hookers up to about 45 feet long are still being sailed. With beam about a quarter of their length, they are rigged quite similar to ours, some having the mainsail fast to the boom only at tack and clew, and no deep keel, just a deadwood underneath. They have black topsides from a creosote compound, and do not

The Galway Bay hooker hull form and rig, as pictured above in 2004, has survived to the present day (although few are originals with a revival having encouraged a racing fleet of replicas). The western Irish coastline offered challenges similar to Blind Bay waters. The cutter rig, straight stem and long bowsprit are very similar to the early hookers operating out of Nelson.
Courtesy Anne and Des Gentleman

differ markedly from the Blind Bay hookers except in detail, such as the curve in their near-vertical stems where they meet the keel, and a more steeply raked transom on which is hung the rudder. Although seagoing, Galway hookers are open boats, with a cockpit and hold. In front of that a foredeck provides limited shelter, under which one could sleep or cook. Their Connemara coastline has the same problems of mountains and bogs as New Zealand would offer, ruling out land transport, and so hookers carried people, products, fuel and all the other requirements. Sailing performance was secondary to their carrying capacity, and when empty or lightly loaded they, too, required ballasting, with hand-loaded rocks. Truth to tell, they seemed not to be easy to handle in a wind, the larger needed two men on the helm, but the style has been faithfully preserved.

Carvel or Clinker?

The Old World hook-and-line fishing vessels and others followed tradition, perhaps an oral set of design proportions handed on, even templates, father to son, skilled builders and numerate, but maybe not literate. There were two methods of cladding a hull: clinker where plank edges overlap like the Viking ships of old, or carvel construction which butts together the planks edges creating

This craftsman-built clinker counter stern demonstrates the versatility of clinker construction. This was one of the earliest such vessels built to accommodate a large propeller and appropriate rudder (meticulously restored by Peter Murton).
Courtesy Barbara Tucker

a flush surface. This, with the traditional use of various jigs and forms, also now largely lost, was the essence of crafts. Available timber sizes could be a limitation. In considering clinker or carvel construction in earliest times, some hookers built here were recorded as having a 'square stern'. In the first edition of this book mention was made of discussing it with older boatbuilders[5] who had never encountered a clinker hull with a counter stern – but in recent times Peter Murton, boatbuilder and restorer found and rebuilt an 18 foot clinker with a 'fantail'counter', so it does not pay to assume too much!

We are accustomed to any boats larger than dinghies being carvel-built, but there were many centuries of lapstrake construction whereby the planks overlap downwards and are each fastened to the preceding one with riveted or clinched fastenings. Some New Zealand hookers over 30 feet long were clinker-built, which may have helped when only partially seasoned wood was used, such as *Calyx* (pictured below). Early in the Chronology too are 1842's clinker-built *Erin* and *Nelson Packet*, existing in an era when photographic records had not yet been conceived. Some had clinker bottoms and carvel topsides. The plank laps on a

Calyx, *an excellent example of a simple clinker-built hooker ketch, seen lying on anchor in Nelson Haven.*
Tyree collection, G178, Alexander Turnbull Library

---

5   Namely Jim Persson, Allen Westrupp and Jack Guard

heavy vessel would be prone to damage, for example against a wharf, so the smooth carvel surface was preferred. Other factors, such as hull flexibility, would come into it as traditional considerations, but they are largely lost nowadays, but simple to suit actual physical conditions but with skilled technique suggests clinker as a first choice, even before the later complication of having to build for a propeller shaft.

Work with wood's qualities

People did not have to design anew in the bush, they built what they knew. The initial choice would point to clinker as requiring fewer facilities, yet yielding pleasing results to those aware of wood's innate qualities, but we do not know. Knowledgeable men could plank up such a hull, requiring just a few moulds, coaxing the planks to yield to visual symmetry. Ships' and boats' shapes are a complex of lines and curves but illustratively think of an earth globe's surface shape as you might quarter an orange; lines of longitude (circumferences) running through the poles yield a shape curved in two directions. A different set of encircling lines at right angles to the longitudes shows discs of decreasing latitudes (parallel to the equator). Peel the strip between any adjacent two latitudes and lay it out flat, it assumes a lengthwise curve because the two sides are of slightly different lengths.

This tendency can be elongated to a boat shape; boatbuilders use a 'spiling' batten to measure from the last plank for the adjoining new plank (you can disregard the theoretical slight curve across the *width* of any one plank). While it can be bent in one direction, twisted, or a combination, it will not lend itself to extreme bending or in two directions (except that a *steam box* can be used to heat and force it to some extent). But, importantly, a curved tree trunk could be utilised; it need not be straight.

Successful boatbuilding requires experience and judgement. I once saw a dinghy (half a dinghy, to be precise) that had been built in a narrow washhouse. When the builder shifted it out to do the other side he faced a problem. The planks he had already fastened to one side were needed as templates for the other side. True clinker construction goes up from the keel, a plank each side at a time, and his boat was irretrievably warped from the unbalanced stresses, but he still finished it. Even now that dinghy might be in the water, forever going around in circles for its frustrated rower.

My last hands-on project was to build a 10ft 6" clinker sailing dinghy (actually glued lapstrake) using scarfed marine ply to get plank lengths. We launched **Weta** *on my eightieth birthday and used it with a small outboard motor on the Picton Clinker and Classic Boat Club's outings for six or so years, until prudence made it clear to Jocelyn and me it was time to 'come ashore'. But I did experience again the wonder of the inanimate materials yielding the pleasing and functional form of a boat.*

Weta, my last hands-on project

What the bush could and could not yield

We leave boatbuilding with a couple of reflections. Fastenings plus the necessary hardware would be brought to the building site, perhaps even forged there. Hookers' essential fittings were of iron. The bush would not yield the more specialist materials. Protective paint or tar, caulking, rope, sails and even wire rigging would have to be bought, or obtained from another vessel. Paint technology had been refined for centuries (just look in an art gallery), although hulls were often black, from coal-derived or pitch mixtures. There was ship chandlery in Port Nicholson across Cook Strait, and soon also in Nelson. Rope was made in Nelson from 1843. Most experienced seamen had some sort of sail-making skill, and for caulking cotton it was possible to make do with old shirts ripped up if nothing better was available. Ballast was stones from the beach. Coal for the forges has been mentioned in some reports. Collingwood had coal, first at West Wanganui, then from close to the base of Farewell Spit, and, later, mined behind Ferntown. Motupipi had coal adjacent. Iron would have to be used for all the stress areas such as the rudder gudgeons; luckily blacksmith's skills were an integral part of any successful colony.

Some of our Hooker builders

Many can rhyme but few are poets and, as in all things, some people's ideas are much more capable of realisation than others. But shipbuilding and boatbuilding are ancient skills, and there are pointers essential to this record, to two people who first became acquainted aboard the *Bolton*. They shared the tedium of emigrant ship conditions, one already a boatbuilder and boatman, John Kidson, who was my great-great-grandfather, and the other wheelwright Ambrose Ricketts. Each founded a seafaring family with an ongoing connection to the hookers. Doubtless there were others aboard ship who would be information sources, not least the ship's carpenter, or *Chips*, as he would be known.

British ship owners by and large had a record of unscrupulousness, and ran a loose downward hierarchy from emigrant ship, to convict ship, to slave ship. We shall hear more of another ship, the infamous *Lloyds*, an emigrant ship to Nelson which had been elevated from carrying convicts on her previous voyage. Life between-decks was not just primitive, but also often exploitative. People were packed in like sardines, and fed food fit only to be thrown away, a major cause of many children's deaths on the voyages. It is said the wealth of Liverpool was founded on slavery, and many eminent people had investments in the companies. Fortunately for some, there were better ships too, but an example of the former, the *John Renwick*, took in 1836 folk to an earlier E G Wakefield-conceived colony in South Australia, soon to become known as 'Port Misery'. The following year she loaded convicts for New South Wales.

Our Nelson boatbuilders did not arrive on convict ships but the slow barque *Bolton*, a condemned ex man-of-war converted to carry emigrants, which sailed from England in October 1841, even before there was a location for this new settlement. She carried 285 steerage passengers, including 130 children, and only four cabin passengers. The marked imbalance between cabin and steerage passengers on *Bolton* in contradiction of Company theory illustrates what would be a growing imbalance between social classes, perceived as employers and employees. The company went ahead, short of emigrating 'capitalists'. On *Bolton*'s crowded lower deck, with two levels of bunks, were John Kidson and his wife Amelia with their three young children (one of whom was my great-grandmother, also named Amelia). Alongside them were William and Maria Ricketts, with William's brother Ambrose and his wife Elizabeth Ricketts in the bunks above. The long, crowded, hungry and gloomy voyage was endured by its passengers in close proximity to each other with daylight from the hatches only when they could be open. There was little else to do but discuss the future which surely would include boats, their building, handling and prospective cargos.

*Charles Heaphy's 1843 painting in the vicinity of Auckland Point captures the styles of all the small ships about at the time. Under the Company crane at right a square-sterned probably clinker-built ship (possibly **Erin**) contrasts in style with the full-bodied hooker grounded out on the mudflat. A Deal boat is seen in the left foreground near a large Maori trading waka.*
Bett Collection 41, Nelson Provincial Museum

By 1843 John Kidson was on record as a Nelson boatman and by the end of that year Ambrose Ricketts was known to be boatbuilding, in all probability spending sea time himself. Wheelwrighting was hardly a trade in the swampy or steep, roadless place at that time. There must have been other shipwrights or boatbuilders whose names are gone now as the records deal only with larger vessels (smaller were not required to be registered) but lightering and fishing called for smaller boats, some of which must have been built in Nelson.

There had been ship-building as well as settlement in the wider Nelson region well before the New Zealand Company. We shall find not only Nelson, but Riwaka, Sandy Bay, Marahau, Torrent Bay, Frenchmans and Awaroa each will have their boatbuilders. Further around, too, Motupipi, and first of all at the Aorere (Collingwood) hookers were built. The Sounds and D'Urville areas were already active in boatbuilding before the 1840s, activity recorded elsewhere and generally outside of our scope. Certainly the shore whaling operations of the 1830s had been served by a small fleet of whaleboats which had been used to scout the coastline of the Marlborough Sounds, D'Urville Island and Blind Bay.

Prior to this, of course too, had been hundreds of years of Maori seafaring in sturdy adze-hewn waka, their trading presence keenly felt in the first decade of settlement. Two of these can be seen in the sketch on the previous page, probably unloading pigs and potatoes or kumara off Green Point.

Not so incredible after all, that determined men, accessing the knowledge of generations of craftsmen, should build, in this case, small ships in a low-tech environment. Using familiar skills and simple tools, they adapted unfamiliar materials, but only inasmuch as not knowing the trees, they recognised the qualities of the woods, looking for similarities. What has just been described was already a fact in various parts of the country, where seafaring men had come ashore. It puts a different perspective on attempts by Wakefield himself, and the Company, to paint him as New Zealand's founding father. Settlement was already ongoing and the question is whether the Company helped or hindered it. To a commercial mind free of the persuasion of Edward Gibbon Wakefield's rhetoric, the most revealing summary must be what happened to all the money that passed through the various hands were it feasible, as a Scotsman would say, to 'follow the bawbies'. The outcomes of Wakefield's schemes differ markedly from the benign message in Company propaganda, yet it did, however incidentally, deliver working people opportunities they did not have in England.

*This extract from the **New Zealand Land Company**'s sales pitch demonstrates the romantic image of a new land opportunity, which bore little resemblance to the reality of settler life.*

This statue of an apprehensive colonist family is located at Wakefield Quay on Nelson's waterfront.

A raft of hollow promises from the New Zealand Company encouraged colonists like these to migrate, but within months the inadequacies of the Wakefield Scheme would lead to disillusionment and hardship.

Edward Gibbon Wakefield spent much of his life embroiled in get-rich-quick schemes. His 'Sufficient Price Theory' was conceived during his three years spent in Newgate Jail, and was to become the foundation principle behind the New Zealand Company's dubious colonisation endeavours in central New Zealand.

ABDUCTED A 15-YEAR-OLD AND FORCED HER TO MARRY HIM

2

The New Zealand Company

WE NEED NOW DIVERT our attention briefly from the hookers, in an attempt to understand their *milieu* – the political, social and physical backstory which helped create the need for transportation far beyond what a bullock wagon could achieve.

When New Zealand's centennial was celebrated in 1940 our primary school teacher took us back into Nelson's history, gleaning from my classmates their grandparents' received information on the starvation years in the settlement. Those recollections were still vivid in some families. I heard of Poorman's Valley (since renamed Marsden Valley with only the creek retaining the original name), where families resorted to digging seed potatoes and trying to eat them[6]. This did not accord with what the 1940 version of 'history' disseminated of the virtues of the New Zealand Company and its settlement theories[7]. This version, derived from the early newspapers of both Wellington and Nelson. The glowing distortion of fact is understandable, given that newspapers were effectively Company organs not impartial sources, and the founding director, E G Wakefield, was well-versed in misdirection. The Company could not afford to have the hardships of its settlers known in England at the time; its profits through land sales were at stake.

Of course as a schoolboy I was curious. My question was how 'The Company' could also be 'The Government' of early Nelson, and, if these hardships had existed then, how could the Company have been as good as the textbooks presented? Such questions, when referred to my locally-born teacher, hung in the air and I came away with impressions which sat uneasily, but with an ongoing curiosity. I was not of an age to sort out underlying motives.

To understand certain tragic events and the unwitting destitution of many working class settlers as early Nelson settlement was developing, we need to dig deeper than the glowing images and accounts published by Company officials. We need to understand how the New Zealand Land Company became the power in the region, simply by filling the semblance of a power vacuum. As we will see, the principal Company personnel were convinced that their connections within the British 'establishment' would allow them to shape events to their advantage, despite having not a shred of title to any land in New Zealand. Nothing happens in isolation, and events in Nelson seemed to be overlaid by the spin of 'alternative truths' until reality began to assert itself.

When older scholarly friends (the late Misses Kath and Nell Dodson of

---

6 Allen chapter XI
7 A view embodied in C B Brewerton's "Vanguard of the South" published 1952

Atawhai) introduced me to literature with wider information (later enhanced by my academic and practical training as a chartered accountant) some of these so-called 'truths' of my school history lessons turned on their heads. My attention was caught by the generous pay-offs to those losing money in the earlier company, and a dividend paid well before a profit could properly be determined. But colourful as they are, the Company's and Wakefield's scarcely credible machinations are not part of this story except where they touch it directly, and it can all be read, especially in *Allan, Burns, Field* and *Temple*. A wider based New Zealand revisionist history now including Tony Simpson's book *'Before Hobson'* has emerged.

I had already come to see that the burden of the Nelson settlement had actually been carried by a host of people, whose part was barely recognised in the records of an era of limited literacy, leaving a distorted historical record which principally reflected a small privileged segment of the population.

In England the entrenched belief that property ownership contained within it the right to govern extended to nationalism too, abetted by the utterances of men-of-letters[8]. As well the 19th century's prominent church presence favoured the class system and the divine right of monarchs, along with of course the wealth that accrued as an outcome. International lawyers[9] offered full justifications of colonialism: the Law of Nature, The Law of God, and other doctrines and laws, including the concept of secular power and empire being God's way of spreading Christianity.

However socio-political change was already in the air. The American Declaration of Independence had been signed in 1776. The French Revolution had occurred soon afterwards in 1789. Land and privilege had been the currency of rulers but *liberty, equality, fraternity* were catch-cries of awakening views; respect the individual without coercion, equality in all its diversity and brotherhood, an overall responsibility towards others. Although still largely unrealised in the mid-nineteenth century of our Nelson settlement, these ideologies were a start for working class individuals to begin looking at themselves and others differently; one of the outcomes was the anti-slavery movement. This was the awakening consciousness that New Zealand's freshly-arrived settlers were bringing. More than just the stresses of the economic and class systems were at work.

Elements of a Pyramid Sales scheme

The core of the New Zealand issue was the Company's unreal expectation that the British Government would sanction Company take-over of the sale of New Zealand land in a revolving scheme requiring no further cash input from them after the first so-called land 'purchase' by E G Wakefield's brother William. The

---

8 Burns chapter 9 discusses this nationalism, of Britain guiding and educating vast areas of the earth.
9 Pre-eminent the ideas of Monsieur Emerick de Vattel whose translated *The Law of Nations* was published in London in 1760. James Stephen of the Colonial Office would not have endeared himself with his 1839 view '… *international jurists … never forget the policy and interests of their own country … to give rapacity and injustice the most decorous veil which legal ingenuity can weave*'.

Directors with E G Wakefield at the helm would *ex officio* become the Governors putting settlers on the land and supplying them with labourers, adjusting Europe's *oversupply* of working class at the same time. They would add value, so that successive waves of settlers would pay higher and higher prices within this colonial class system. The scheme, embellished with a lottery for allocating land blocks to appeal to speculators, raised some money but very few wealthy people were prepared to emigrate. This was the house of cards, precariously dependent on a majority of absentee land-owners, that a very persuasive fraudster, Edward Gibbon Wakefield, had dreamed up while serving time in an English jail. When it inevitably collapsed, it was to leave a group of hopeful but disappointed settlers and a crippling, complicated and challenged land-holding structure with not enough of the promised land. Out of it the real Nelson was slowly forged.

The key players

Among the people involved in the New Zealand Company's scheme there were widely separate aims, ideas and attitudes. The key concept was that New Zealand was perceived as an empty land, ripe for takeover. This flew in the face of the fact that it had been extensively occupied by Maori for a millennium, and by the 1830s there were already 2,000 or so lawless British and others in the North Island, including hundreds of shore-whalers, sealers and former convicts. Acting on the misguided notion that here was a still unplucked plum, a hard-headed business group had formed an earlier 'flash in the pan' colonial company the **1825 New Zealand Company**, and sent settlers to this area on the 62 ton cutter *Lambton* with the 260 ton sloop *Rosanna* to gather flax and kauri. Only six of the 60 prospective settlers disembarked in the far north Hokianga harbour, when these ships sailed on to Sydney, alarmed at missionaries warnings of impending retaliation after the powerful Ngapuhi chief Hongi Hika was wounded in a skirmish.

Over a decade later, in 1837, another group labelling itself the **New Zealand Association** was formed with no less than ten members of parliament in it, as well as entrepreneurs with interests in colonisation who were especially eager to get their hands on New Zealand (by no means the only ones with such thoughts).

These groups of 1825 and 1837 were the core of yet another new grouping two years later. Urgency had now arisen with the leaked news that the British government would be pre-empting land sales to curb land sharks. A dozen men of the 1837 Association, including E G Wakefield, meeting for dinner on 20 March 1839, reckoned that this proposal would increase the price of NZ land by at least 500%, which was anathema to land jobbers. Had colonisation been the true focus, government in the territory would surely have been welcomed by them. So the **New Zealand Land Company**[10] was formalised and Edward's brother William Wakefield was sent off in May, 1839 on the brig *Tory*, defying the colonial office, on a 20 million acre 'land-buying' spree that is still causing

---

10   The word 'Land' was soon dropped from the Company's name.

problems for New Zealand. The Company's Wellington and then Nelson founding settlers were sent in haste, carrying out an injunction of Edward Wakefield at the dinner: *'possess yourselves of the soil and you are secure!'*

Edward Gibbon Wakefield was in fact a convicted con-man. Born in 1796 he had married at the age of 20 by deceptively abducting a girl, but had been later taken into favour by her wealthy family, thereby having an income settled on him, only to lose his wife a few years later, leaving him with two children.

Out of ambition and heightened confidence he had repeated the process in 1826, abducting a suitably wealthy 15 year old girl from her boarding school. She did not know him, but using a tissue of lies about her father, he coerced her into marrying him. Outraged, the father pursued Wakefield to Paris, and ensured that he was brought to justice. Edward Wakefield, his brother William who had conspired with him, along with a servant, were each sentenced to three years in jail.

A man of forceful opinions, Edward Wakefield's was known as as a 'parlour

Newgate Jail, where Edward Gibbon Wakefield conceived his get-rich scheme.
Painting by George Shepherd – public domain

mesmerist' in view of his seemingly hypnotic powers. As well as expecting to acquire an heiress, and her wealth, Wakefield was a frustrated would-be politician, expecting to use her connections as a way to get into the Macclesfield parliamentary seat. While he got a three years sentence, his undeserving victim, 15 year-old Ellen, was likely condemned to a lifetime of whispers and innuendo.

It is ironic that stealing a girl must have been seen by his peers as a less heinous offence than stealing her ribbon or stockings, for which people, even children, were transported to Van Diemen's Land[11]. In fact Wakefield had also demonstrated other facets of a devious mind: his penchant for a *fait accompli*, his

---

11 Elsbeth Hardie, *The Girl Who Stole Stockings*, p28

failure to connect cause with effect, and his disregard for outcomes until they were unavoidable. This unscrupulousness showed also in the way he used people and his viciousness towards any opponents. Governor Hobson and James Stephen of the Colonial Office were both under sustained attack from him well before the Company ships came to New Zealand, because both officials were known to favour government intervention, and properly controlled emigration.

Wakefield was a late convert to the concepts of colonisation and emigration, and not well-versed in the realities. A decade after the first group of businessmen had failed in their 1825 attempt to exploit New Zealand, he made the somewhat arbitrary choice of promoting settlement there while he was still in Newgate prison. He reworked the idea as a vehicle for personal gain and gaining a political foothold, and he strenuously pushed his views as an expert, writing anonymously because of his notoriety. It is interesting that London's *The Times* spoke out about the unscrupulousness of Wakefield's scheme in an editorial on 27 July 1840[12]:

The outcomes had a quite inordinate impact on all aspects of the settlements

'A band of "gentlemen," whose passion for money has unhappily superseded their love of honest fame, have for some time been prosecuting a system of monstrous plunder both in New Zealand and at home ... fingering the money of duped emigrants, of ensnaring their families into a hazardous exile that may involve utter ruin.'

Courtesy archival records, *The Times*, July 27 1840

---

12 Reproduced in Burns, page 146. See her chapter 18.

at both Wellington and Nelson. Because the company over-reached itself at Nelson, the consequences there were more obvious, yet paradoxically these ideas were influential in the migration of nearly 15,000 settlers to New Zealand, as the independent church settlements of Christchurch (Anglican, in Canterbury) and Dunedin (Presbyterian, in Otago) were influenced by Wakefield-promoted ideas. He espoused transplanting Britain without the bad features, but as his basis was advantage-taking and a divisive class-based system, the seeds of dissension already rife in Europe came with the settlers.

The *'Sufficient Price Theory'* behind Wakefield's settlement plans was unashamedly geared towards perpetuating class inequality. His key principle was that land (acquired by the Company for next-to-nothing) would progressively be sold to middle and upper class capitalists at a 'sufficient price', some of which could be spent on supplying labouring class migrants who themselves would be unable to acquire any land for themselves. The scheme would enhance accretion of value and assure the key players of a fortune in profits.

At the bottom of the heap would be the pioneer settlers and the hooker men who served them.

Sowing seeds of conflict

There is one aspect of the glib approach in London that was to prove disastrous for some settlers, and which would disadvantage the Maori occupants of the land, even to the ongoing work of the Waitangi Tribunal today. The seeds of conflict were sown and fostered by Wakefield's (and many others') attitude to land acquisition. He falsely avowed that *'a great proportion of the surface of New Zealand is unoccupied and waste, and ... the natives are strongly disposed to sell land*[13]*'*. It was a convenient lie. His oft-expressed view was that Maori had little right to land that Europeans could use, and that 'the natives' would be sufficiently rewarded for parting with their land, by having a superior civilisation in their midst (the work and customs of which they could emulate). 'Waste' was a euphemism of the times, used to describe land of indigenous peoples not currently under cultivation. Wakefield was expansive in the breadth of his ideas, convinced that even the population of China needed governing by England too!

This 'waste lands' attitude had a marked bearing upon the way much of New Zealand was colonised. In his 1898 history[14], William Pember Reeves could write (and have readers find unremarkable): *'Nothing can justify the magnitude of Colonel [William]*[15] *Wakefield's claims, or the payment of firearms for the land. But at the bottom of the mischief was the attempt of the missionaries and officials at home to act as though a handful of savages – not more, I believe, than sixty-five thousand in all, and rapidly dwindling in numbers – could be allowed to keep a fertile and healthy Archipelago larger than Great Britain.'*

---

13 Temple pages 193, 206, 226/8
14 *The Long White Cloud* page 142
15 William was Edward's brother and co-conspirator in the settlement scheme.

When the well-educated Englishmen (who, one could have hoped, would take a scholarly interest in things Maori) got here, they neglected to recognise the developed indigenous culture, land tenure and codes that existed under their very noses. Especially William Wakefield, who should have learned, as he was given responsibility for negotiating with the Maori. But the New Zealand Company's purpose was better served by non-recognition. Being accustomed to advantage-taking and immured superiority, these key individuals remained blind. It would soon prove fatal[16] for some.

Scrip instead of title

The Company promptly began its land 'sales' in order to circumvent intervention in New Zealand by the British Government. Actively touting the premise that possession was nine tenths of the law (despite the fact that it could not legally issue title to land it didn't own – and had not even located), it issued *scrip*, the pieces of paper commonly called *shares* or land orders, with a disclaimer of legal responsibility in the small print. It says much for the company's persuasive spin that expectant purchasers actually parted with their money for an unsubstantiated paper promise. This lack of not only title to land, but of the greater part of the land itself, would prove a major frustration to the resident scrip holders. Wellington settlement scrip entitled the holder to one town acre and 100 county acres. For Nelson settlement the country allocations were 150 acres, plus an 'accommodation lot' of 50 acres and a town acre, for the price of 300 pounds. This led to the blanket surveying of grids regardless of topography which included cliffs, swamps and impossible slopes. The Wellington and Nelson schemes' viability depended on a significant number of non-emigrant investors (absentee landlords)[17] as well as emigrating capitalists. Insufficient numbers of

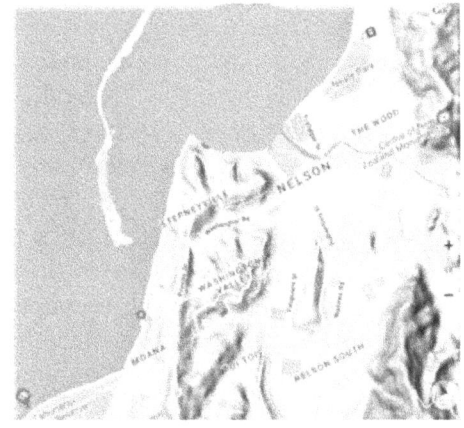

Preliminary survey of Nelson allotments   *Nelson topography*

---

16 See Chapter 10
17 These things are detailed in Turnbull and Burns. Large fare discounts to encourage emigrating capitalists would need compensatory funds from non-emigrants to build the emigration fund.

Maori input into colonial food supplies during Nelson's early years was especially significant. Potatoes (and pigs) had been introduced during Cook's 1769, exploratory voyage) and were a more convenient crop for Maori than traditional kumara tubers, as they had better nutrition for weight, and (requiring less ritual) could be cultivated by women and slaves, freeing the men for other purposes. This 1841 Heaphy painting depicts a large schooner-rigged waka, laden with provisions that probably include potatoes and pigs for the newly arrived colonists, sailing out of Kaiteriteri in western Blind Bay. The use of this lug-sail schooner rig demonstrates innovation probably derived from contact with whaling stations.

B-043-011, Alexander Turnbull Library

either category of investor ultimately led to the Company's collapse in Nelson.

A further example of the Company directors' outrageous over-confidence was its claim to own the Chatham Islands, contracting to sell them to a German company. The Colonial Secretary stamped heavily on that transaction and, under threat of losing its charter the New Zealand Company speedily backtracked[18]. The German settlers later ended up in Nelson district, respected and hard-working.

As an acknowledgement of humanist criticisms of the scheme, the Company set out a policy known as the *Tenths Reserves*, which entitled Rangatira leaders amongst the Maori vendors, (Ngati Rarua, Ngati Koata, Ngati Tama and Te Atiawa iwi) to one-tenth i.e. 22,110 acres, across town, suburban and rural sections, and promised that they should retain any land they specifically used for habitation, cultivation, urupa (burials) and mahinga kai (resource areas). The theory was that Maori would grow rich as the settlement developed and prospered, making the Tenths the true payment for the land. This was later shown to be a rather simplistic gesture, given the hierarchical structure of Maori society, as well as conflicting claims of land ownership through conquest by Ngati Toa and Te Rauparaha's allies. Nor was it honoured, and it took another 170 years for the resulting grievances to be settled.[19]

---

18 Allan, Ruth: Nelson, *A History of Early Settlement*, A H & A W Reed, p300
19 In 2008 the *Waitangi Tribunal* ruled that the Treaty of Waitangi had been breached by the land sale, including failing to set aside 'Native Tenths Reserves. In 2014 the *Te Tau Ihu* compensation settlement was legislated.

The real settlers
There were three types of commitment to the emigration scheme at a personal level. Firstly were the wealthy stay-at-home entrepreneurs expecting to profit for their financial outlay with no further input. Next were the more adventurous investors who intended to travel there for sufficient time to make a substantial profit before returning to the comfort of Mother England.

The third group were the *real* colonists, who comprised a scattering of permanent middle class settlers together with a great over-preponderance of artisans and labourers. Some of these were independent minded, capable men, victims of the British economic and social order, with an eye to making a fortune of their own, or at least a life with self-respect and opportunity for their families.

Our hooker builders were amongst the hundreds of working class migrants garnered by agents who were paid head-money. The offer of a contract for a couple of year's work in a new colony was a considerable inducement in Britain's harsh economic climate.

The arithmetic
The Company's three chartered survey ships (*Will Watch*, *Arrow* and *Whitby*) arrived in November 1841, followed a few weeks later by the first flush of settlers. During 1842 the first 18 colonising ships disembarked 1052 men, 872 women and 1384 children.

They arrived in a settlement where finally only 451 of its 1100 land allotments had been sold to 274 owners. Ominously, the number of resident proprietors in 1843 was never more than 50 or so, when for its survival the Nelson colony needed to be in the hundreds[20]. Fifty capitalists, some short of ready-money, would never employ all these people. This set the scene for disaster as had been forecast by company official Ross Mangles, (an MP friend of E G Wakefield) who had warned that the colony would be swamped with paupers[21].

The Company's scheme called for a ratio of about eight employees to each potential employer, with the labourers' fares paid from part of the land price, but by despatching emigrant labourer families in proportion to the number of allotments sold rather than to the few emigrating capitalists available to employ them, the Company exposed the settlers to the ensuing hardships of unemployment in an under-funded settlement.

The population of the world was 954 million in the year 1800, rising to 1,241 million by 1850 and 1,634 million in 1900. Europe sent about 70 million emigrants (50 million of them permanently) to other continents, mostly to North America although significant numbers went to Siberia, Latin America and Australia. Emigration was big business, and as a destination New Zealand was late on the scene. It was about as far away from Europe as it was possible to get and had a somewhat terrifying reputation as cannibal country. Compared with

---

20 Allan p233, 378
21 Allan, p58

other destinations only a trickle of new settlers came to New Zealand, but as a colourful target for land speculation its remoteness made it admirable.

Edward G. Wakefield, untroubled by regard for the truth, was a master of propaganda and even before 1840 he had enlisted clergymen to his banner. The Times of 13 April 1840 quoted the Reverend Dr Hinds; "… as the highest rates of interest in this country are wholly unequal to the reasonable desires of godly capitalists, the disinterested and philanthropic views of the New Zealand Company … are eminently entitled to Government support." This was a remarkable assertion, considering that the Company secretary was soon to state to a parliamentary select committee in London (on 17 July 1840): "The objects of the company have always been commercial, and no other."[22]

The New Zealand Company's investment deal was packaged to appeal to speculators, promising quick increases in land values, and quite a number of those investors who emigrated as well as the non-emigrant speculators had unreal expectations as a consequence. Wakefield and others presented a glowing picture of central New Zealand before they even knew where the Nelson settlement would be. Having committed the Company to this fictitious 'blueprint', in a bizarre twist the board, led by Wakefield, insisted they adhere to it. So in those earliest years an essential feature of Nelson's history was the Company's insistence on ignoring reality.

The two settlements

The New Zealand Company's first settlement of Wellington, founded two years prior to Nelson, had already been down the road of deceptive land expectations. One Wellington settler, who had migrated with friends who were all land purchasers like himself, wrote: *'With New Zealand we have been partially disappointed, by the New Zealand Company not a little deceived.'*[23]

Instead of the promised plains, the Wellington hills had been a shock, as was the paucity of flat land. Their promised 'town acres' were in a swamp several miles from the town, but even that was nothing to the shock of discovering that their rural farmland was over a hundred miles away, at Wanganui. Wakefield's glowing description of Wellington's hinterland simply did not exist. His description of vast areas of easy arable country to expand the 1,100 100-acre farms clustered around Wellington's 1,100 town acres had been a total fabrication.

Wellington was briefly named *Britannia*, then renamed after the popular hero of the times – The Duke of Wellington – because political patronage was sought. This led to the choice of sea hero Lord Nelson's name for the next settlement. It was to have been called *Molesworth* after British politician Sir William Molesworth, but he already had no confidence in Wakefield and refused to be *"a great decoy-duck to tempt emigrants and in New Zealand as a pigeon for everyone to pluck."*[24]

---

22 Burns p144
23 Burns pp 211–212
24 Burns p 139

This pleasantly civilised rendition of Nelson Haven, as painted by Charles Heaphy in 1841, depicts an image of the proposed settlement location which was likely used as a romantic propaganda image by the New Zealand Company. It presents an apparently flat foreshore in place of the steep terrain above Rocks Road, and the impression of a landscape and copse of trees not unlike that seen in England.
F E Richardson, painted per Heaphy original. Bett Collection: AC809, Nelson Provincial Museum

In 1842 Nelson, the migrant investors had been promised even larger allotments than those in Wellington, with 221,100 acres supposedly available for sale. This comprised a total of 1,100 flat town acres, each with contiguous 50-acre estates, and their 150-acre farms nearby. All this land was expected to lie around Nelson's easy and vast harbour, and an expectation of further adjacent flat land for future expansion. But where *was* Nelson, and where was such land? Yet the company's prowess with propaganda was so effective that, even a century later during my own school history lessons, educated people didn't fully appreciate the deceptive nature of the scheme behind the settlement. But those who had suffered most under it knew, and my wise school-teacher had pointed me to *their* reality.

Blind Bay

The Nelson expedition chose to settle in a coastal wedge backed by mountains, named by James Cook as Blind Bay (now Tasman Bay), on the north end of the South Island. Blame has been cast for the exploratory Nelson party choosing the unsuitably small Blind Bay but Wakefield's injunction had really given these men little choice. They were lucky to have come even marginally close to company land requirements, even if it didn't meet the blueprint. It could scarcely be more different from the propaganda image, but possibly surpassed by the disastrous **Western Australia Company** that Wakefield was also connected with (as well as one in South Australia, one in Canada and one in Central America[25]).

The unfortunate Western Australian settlers had sailed from England on the barque *Parkfield* in December 1840 (prior to the Nelson expedition) and reached Australia in March 1841. Just before they had left, word got back to England that the glowing prospectus description '*It is hardly possible to conceive a finer situation for a Town ...*' was in fact a desert. So the directors of the Western Australian Company had promptly decided to move settlement up the coast to another location, sight unseen. A couple of years later this company ceased, leaving a ghost town, emigrants stranded with no money, and no employment in the Australian bush[26].

Tasman and Golden Bays have been populated since Maori settled there around a millennium earlier. Indigenous occupation had been precarious at times, with vying combative tribes. Abel Tasman, the 1642 explorer, encountered this readiness-to-arms, losing four men in an altercation with a *waka taua* (war canoe) without even landing. Then James Cook in 1770 passed outside the bay from Cape Farewell to Cape Stephens, recognising it was a large, deep bay, but hardly able to see the bottom end of it. The name *Blind Bay* was noted on his chart although he remarked '*but I have reason to believe it to be Tasman's Murderers' Bay*'.[27] The Blind Bay name still appeared on charts well into the 20th century. It was on his second voyage, 1773–74, that Cook recognised it as 'Tasman's bay'.

Dumont d'Urville, 1827, the next explorer to visit, largely completed the charting. He split the two significant bays with his freshly named Separation Point, and concentrated his survey on the part he called Tasman's Bay, under the mistaken impression of this name being bestowed by Cook on his second voyage. As a result Abel Janszoon Tasman received inadvertent acknowledgement. With the three explorers, Nelson had become a well described and charted location by 1840, although its greatest asset – the sheltered haven behind the eight mile long Boulder Bank – had not yet been discovered.

Immediate outcomes

Nelson simply did not have all the land that Wakefield had described. In just two short years the company effectively ceased to function there, abandoning thousands of people like those in Western Australia. With friction in the settlement, through the failure of promised employment, and many families facing near-starvation, labourers demanded redress. When there was not a hope

---

25 Turnbull page 28 and a detailed discussion in Burns
26 Frost
27 Subsequently referred to as Massacre Bay

of work for the majority of the population, five-acre blocks had to be made available (in spite of Edward's Wakefield's opposition) for them to become more self-sufficient.

William Fox, a more enlightened company employee who was able to see the unfolding disaster, was instrumental in this, flying in the face of Company directives. A system of cottier farming had been introduced by Arthur Wakefield, the well-regarded Wakefield brother who was leader of the Nelson settlement.

Nelson was steadily to become a place for agriculture with smaller farms, the antithesis of the Company's land baron ideal, just as had already been done in Wellington to avoid people starving. These early years were bitter and divisive, and while most land-owners had more sense, a few of the wealthier settlers petitioned the government to send a French frigate from Akaroa to put the Nelson labourers in their place, and later (also unsuccessfully) for the governor to send imperial troops.

These snippets from the New Zealand Examiner *during the first years of colonisation are very revealing. We see evidence of one of the early capitalist settlers) already selling up and heading home to Mother England, while the captains of* **Katherine Johnston** *and* **Comet** *are peddling their general cargoes in the hope of a profit. The nature of such cargoes makes fascinating reading.*

Courtesy New Zealand National Library, Papers Past

Maori in the whole region were victims too, swamped by thousands of immigrants when they expected a mere handful coming to assist them. Let it not be overlooked just how helpful and welcoming the Maori were in most cases, at this time. For many settlers, Maori supplies and knowledge saved the day.

An astounding mix of elements had come into play to create the Nelson settlement. The Company's blundering contribution was to commit a large number of people to an unworkable theory and a failed commercial enterprise, causing both immediate and long-term distress in the settlement. The people suffered, yet still made the settlement work. Without question the small-ship hooker-men comprised a vital part of its struggle for survival.

THE NELSON EXAMINER, AND NEW ZEALAND CHRONICLE.

LIST OF VESSELS WHICH HAVE ARRIVED AT NELSON HAVEN FROM NOVEMBER 1, 1841, TO JULY 1, 1842, INCLUSIVE.

DATE	No.	NAME	TONS	MASTER	CARGO
1841:					
November	1	Arrow, brig	200	Geare	Stores.
	2	Whitby, barque	437	Lacey	Nelson Surveying Staff.
	3	Will Watch, ditto	251	Walker	Ditto.
	4	Eliza, schooner	11	Rolph	Ballast.
December	5	Kate, ditto	72	Webster	General.
	6	Eliza, ditto	11	Rolph	Pigs and Potatoes.
	7	Look-in, ditto	82	Cannon	General.
	8	Clydeside, barque	236	Mathieson	Ditto.
	9	Eliza, schooner	11	Scanlon	Blubber.
1842:					
January	10	Nymph, ditto	22	Bennett	Plank.
February	11	Fifeshire, barque	557	Arnold	Immigrants.
	12	Mana, schooner	13	Barker	Pigs and Potatoes.
	13	Pickwick, cutter	38	Williams	Immigrants and general.
	14	Gem, schooner	67	Pearce	Plank.
	15	Mary Anne, barque	600	Bolton	Immigrants.
	16	Lloyds, ditto	450	Greene	Immigrants.
	17	Sisters, brigantine	130	Clarke	General.
	18	Lord Auckland, barque	628	Jardine	Immigrants.
	19	Kate, schooner	62	Macfarlane	General.
	20	Eliza, ditto	11	Stenning	Ditto.
March	21	Cheerful, brigantine	129	Tulett	Ditto.
	22	Vanguard, ditto	61	Murray	Ditto.
	23	Abercrombie, schooner	146	Devlin	Ditto.
	24	Bolton, barque	541	Robinson	Immigrants and Stores.
	25	Brougham, ditto	227	Robertson	Passengers and Stores.
	26	Rory O'More, schooner	15	Sutton	General.
	27	Look-in, ditto	82	Cannon	Ditto.
	28	Ariel, ditto	146	Mulholland	Ditto.
	29	Nymph, ditto	22	Scanlon	Ditto.
	30	Gem, ditto	67	Pearce	Ditto.
	31	Hope, barque	600	M'Lachlan	Cattle.
April	32	Martha Ridgway, ship	621	Webb	Immigrants.
	33	Clifton, ditto	820	Cox	Ditto, Port Nicholson.
	34	Birman, barque	545	Cleland	Ditto ditto.

This newspaper record demonstrates the variety of registered trading vessels which supplemented the immigrant ships during the first months of settlement in Nelson. It omits small unregistered vessels including the many Maori craft which also traded into Nelson.

Courtesy National Library of New Zealand, Papers Past

3

Settlement by the Shore

WHATEVER FAIR STRAND on a foreign shore the preliminary survey party from England might have been led to expect, they looked about Blind Bay and were charmed – never mind that there were still thousands of flat acres needing to be found there. How they reconciled in their minds all the differences they would meet, and the distinct and quite disparate aims of landowners and labourer settlers we cannot know.

Edward and William sent their brother, Captain Arthur Wakefield to set up a colony somewhere in the northern region of the 'newly purchased' South Island. The expedition ships *Arrow*, *Will Watch* and *Whitby* initially anchored behind Adele Island, to explore Blind Bay's western shoreline. Arthur Wakefield reluctantly considered settling on the Kaiteriteri and Motueka side of the bay, which had been spoken of as a good harbour with much flat land behind, but inspection showed only limited river-flats. Local Maori were secretive about the haven further east known as te Wakatu, as they would have preferred the expedition to settle nearer their pa at Motueka. Wakefield sent off a Deal Boat eastward with an exploratory party consisting of Captain Frederick Moore, the surveyor Brown, with J. S. Cross as coxswain, McDonald a boatman and a Maori guide named Pito. They spent a night ashore near the Ruby Bay Bluffs and then followed the shoreline north-eastward to Mackay's Bluff, sailing outside the Waimea sands and the eight mile long Boulder bank oblivious to the tidal waterway it contained.

It was only by chance as they were returning cold and tired that they decided to land on the boulders. Moore jumped out, climbed the Boulder Bank and saw "a sheet of water considerable in extent and to all appearances a good harbour". Following the Boulder Bank south they entered through the "old entrance" by Arrow[28] Rock and they entered the unanticipated natural haven on 20 October 1841 as the first Europeans to do so in recorded history. Presumably Pito was already familiar with the location, for they spent that night at the Auckland Point camping place used by Maori on food-gathering visits, but unoccupied at this time. Moore later described how the woods were alive with birds and pigs, and the waters of the haven being in constant commotion with shoals of fishes. It was soon to have sea-borne traffic far busier than the previous occasional coming and going of the Maori[29] in their canoes.

---

28 Since renamed Fifeshire rock for reasons that will become obvious.
29 Ngati Kuia and Ngati Apa were settled here during Cook's and D'Urville's expeditions but were conquered in the 1820s by Taranaki iwi allied to Ngati Toa.

The news of their discovery on their return the following day was greeted with relief, and the three Company expedition ships managed to make their way safely through the rock-strewn entrance as soon as weather permitted. The hazards of the harbour approaches were immediately recognised as a priority to be dealt with before the first immigrant ships arrived, so Captain Arthur Wakefield in his position as Company-appointed resident agent in Nelson, saw to the erection of navigational shore leads, buoys in the channel, and a pile beacon at the south of the bulbous 'Haul-Ashore' end of the boulder bank. In addition a signal station and flagstaff on Britannia Heights were erected, overlooking the harbour entrance. From 13 December 1841, signals were erected to show the state of the tide – a red flag at the top of the staff for high tide and at half-mast for half tide. The harbour was not considered workable below half tide because of its depth limitations, and the sobering experience ten weeks later involving the loss of *Fifeshire* on her departure necessitated a re-evaluation of the impact of the currents on any navigation in and out of the inlet.

Navigation points quickly took on new names. To starboard as one entered, Arrow Rock's reefs stretched across to a rocky or 'iron-bound' shoreline, penetrated further in by small beaches at the Basin Reserve, Richardson Street and the indentation of Victoria Road. Mariners were then faced with cliffs having stony beaches at their feet, right up to Green Point. The view to one's port side was the continuous boulder bank.

Looking down from the elevated height of modern-day Princes Drive on a day when the water is sufficiently clear to see below the surface, it is easy to gain a very good impression of Arrow Rock, (or Fifeshire Rock as it soon became

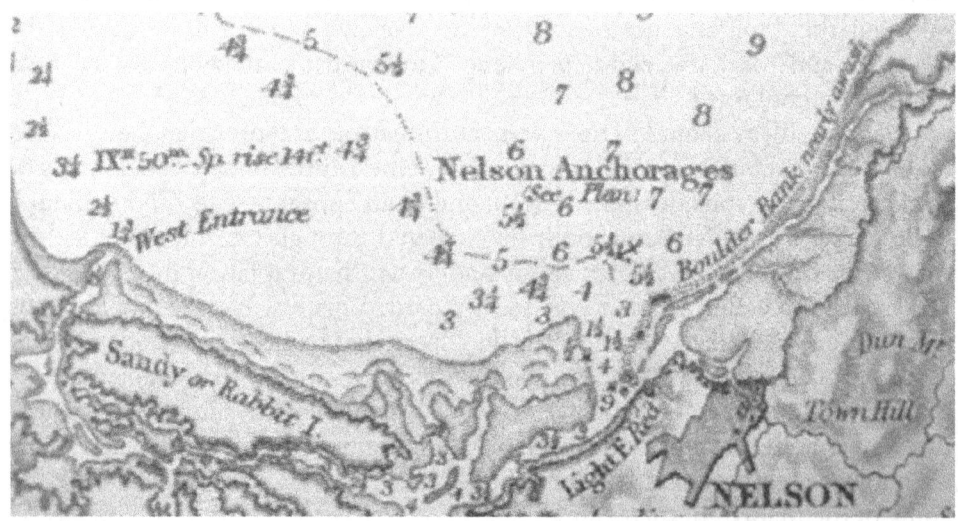

Extract from 1862 Admiralty chart #2616, showing the Waimea sands and Boulder Bank which enclosed Nelson Haven and the inshore mudflat channels at the south end of Blind Bay. Depths are in fathoms.
Alexander Turnbull Library Map collection 1830aj/1857-62/sheet-7Acc.1263

called) and the reefs (some of which have been removed) for the difficult entrance it was. Imagine the challenge of sailing an ungainly ship between the reefs and Haulashore Island.

The Maitai River flowed near the shoreline past Auckland Point (named later when the immigrant ship Lord Auckland discharged there). The channel swung more towards the north, and by the time it reached Green Point, the flow was dissipated in the tide. The Maitai, although tidal, proved to be convenient for lightering goods as far as Trafalgar Street. Well into the 20th century there was a landing on the river, just seaward of the Trafalgar Street bridge. I saw the scow *Pearl Kasper* unloading there in the mid-1940s. Below that were tied a nondescript collection of boats which grounded out between tides.

When the *Arrow*, *Will Watch* and *Whitby* had initially anchored behind Adele Island on 9 October 1841, Arthur Wakefield was on the verge of deciding he would have to settle on the Kaiteriteri and Motueka (Eastern) side of Blind Bay. That region had been spoken of as a good harbour with much flat land behind it; however he could see no significant flat land on this stretch of coast. Then Te Wakatu was discovered by an exploring party in one of the expedition's Deal boats, led by their Maori guide Pito. It is still argued who in the Deal boat saw it first. The haven was well known to Maori but they were secretive about it, as they would have preferred the expedition to settle nearer their pa at Motueka. The explorers first went ashore on the boulder bank, then sailed down to the tucked-away entrance and went on to spend the night at what is now Auckland Point, then a camp site used by Maori on food-gathering visits, but unoccupied at the time. Moore reported that the woods were alive with birds and pigs. Once he had seen the sheltered Te Wakatu harbour and been told that there was some flat land in the Waimea valley Captain Wakefield made his decision and Nelson had a location as well as a name. It was just as well, because there were shiploads of settlers not far behind!

Bitter-sweet early arrivals

With Nelson born in haste because migrant settlers were already on their way, we can picture in our imaginations, from the foredeck, these eager young men of the preliminary party, many in their twenties and some even in their teens, disembark with Captain Arthur Wakefield. It must have been a beautiful place then and a great relief to come ashore, first at the foot of what is now Richardson Street then at Auckland Point. This was the heart-warming reality of Nelson, and the men were excited by the prospect of new lives in a new land. With their arrival, the haven would never be the same. The first three Company ships were men-only, and during the three intervening months, between their designated tasks, those family men who had wives and children following on *Lloyds*, *Mary Ann* and *Fifeshire* found time to build temporary dwellings in the vicinity of Saltwater Creek.

Lloyds had been the first general immigrant ship to depart England, but *Fifeshire* was the first arrival, on 1st February. When *Mary Ann* followed in, a week later, the wait for *Lloyds* became tinged with anxiety. A close watch was kept on the bay, and tensions mounted. However the relief was short-lived when *Lloyds* dropped anchor in the Haven on 16th February. One look at the grim faces of most of the wives as they were ferried ashore was sufficient to freeze the gaiety of the occasion.

Sixty-five children had died on that voyage, the losses affecting three quarters of the 56 families which had embarked. Sixteen of the wives arrived with no surviving children to present to their waiting husbands. An outbreak of whooping cough was the principal reason, but it didn't take long for the finger-pointing to begin. The ship's surgeon, Dr Bush was viewed as negligent in his responsibilities, not least for allowing two cases of whooping cough aboard before departure. New Zealand Company directors had failed to carry out background checks on his competence, and one of his functions also had been to ensure distribution of adequate provisioning and medical supplies for the migrants in his care. This was another woeful failure in performance because of the Company's lack of care in choosing a suitable captain and surgeon. The ship was sent off in haste to evade official scrutiny which possibly would have revealed the skimping of food rations, particularly for the children, and the disastrous lack of calibre of those in charge. In defiance of Company rules the captain condoned liaisons between the defenceless women passengers and the crew and subsequently there was a gross failure in even basic care. Many families were bereaved on that voyage; some of the reconciliations between husbands and wives in Nelson's makeshift huts would have been sad, others bitter. Most ships more or less met the conditions drafted by the Company, which were up with the standards of the day, but the *Lloyds* was a notable exception. The Company issued a 'white-wash' report back in London, but the principled Arthur Wakefield, in charge of the Nelson settlement, would not allow a cover-up of this deplorable and sensational failure.

Food provisioning had been the principal responsibility of Company officials and the Captain, William Greene. The ship's water supplies had been taken direct from the polluted Thames River, presumably accounting for the dysentery aboard. It was also later proven that the quantities of food provisions recorded on the "Reeves List" (the list made by the Inspector for Shipping in England) and the actual ship's list of food shows that they did not have sufficient quantities of basic provision.[30] A further scandal that the captain and some of his crew had been sleeping with women passengers did little to placate the bitterness ensuing from this disembarkation. Captain Arthur Wakefield was also considered at fault for insisting that *Lloyds* would have no husbands aboard to help with family responsibilities.

Loss of infant lives were to be expected in the times, but certainly not to this extent. When my boatbuilding ancestor John Kidson arrived aboard *Bolton* four weeks later there had been eleven infant and child deaths aboard (plus twins,

---

30 Brierley B.F. *Sails of Suffering*, p27

shortly after being born aboard), but as a proportion of the 300 passengers aboard this was considered reasonable.

Captain Frederick Moore, and the loss of the barque *Fifeshire*

Frederick Moore was an earlier immigrant who had been employed as the pilot for Arthur Wakefield's Blind Bay exploration. He had the best of all reasons to be visiting from Port Nicholson – he was a young man in love. There was also an unconfirmed suggestion, raised by surveyor Frederick Tuckett in a newspaper controversy some years later, that Moore was spying out land for purchase. Moore was in Massacre Bay with the 67 ton schooner *Jewess* for ten days in June 1840 with Thomas Partridge, doing business for land buyer James Coutts Crawford, and in November of that year Moore took *Jewess* into West Wanganui to load coal to take back to Wellington. Whaler Dicky Barrett had taken a load of coal from the same place in 1836. The coal seam was at beach level, so extraction was a straightforward matter of breaking it loose and loading it aboard.

When he sailed, Moore left behind a young Maori beauty who had caught his eye and to whom he was betrothed in Maori fashion. In February 1841 he was back again and claimed Paru as his wife, although he observed the conventions of Victorian morality by not openly revealing the relationship. He was by no means alone in having a Maori wife and many of his better-known contemporaries also formed such relationships although others were simply exploitative. Moore and Paru lived as husband and wife for eight years but then he returned to England for a time and came back with a European bride. Then history loses sight of Paru.

In both its violence and its unpredictability, the sea did Frederick Moore no favours in the following two years. His first command, *Jewess*, was cast up on Waikanae Beach by a furious northwest gale in April 1841 and became a total loss. It was after this discouraging episode that he served the New Zealand Company's Nelson expedition as pilot. A few months later an even more serious disaster for his seafaring career occurred, on 27 February 1842, when he stood in for the Nelson pilot, James Cross who was ill on the day that the master of the first immigrant ship *Fifeshire* was keen leave Nelson for England. Human error played a big part in the ensuing debacle. The ship started too late on the ebbing tide without a commanding breeze, and Moore did not let an anchor go when the wind failed him. These were not good decisions, especially for a pilot. The ship was swept aground on Arrow Rock ledge, in the narrows of the entrance, and broke her back as the tide dropped. Moore too was left high and dry, his seafaring future in tatters, and serious questions were raised about the viability of the port. Subsequently the pilots learned to bring ships in and take them out near the top of the tide flow, avoiding the ebb, and this difficult entrance was used right up until 1906.

It was the *Fifeshire* episode that made Moore a farmer for the next eight years. He bought one of the *Fifeshire*'s boats, had it raised by a strake and decked it in, naming his new vessel *Mary Ann*. After a short and unsuccessful stint as a storekeeper in a town that was crowded with stores and their often-unsuitable goods, he settled with Paru at Motueka where they were offered Maori land. Sometimes he sailed *Mary Ann* to Nelson with produce and to collect supplies, and thus he became one of the bay's first small ship skippers, although *Mary Ann* served in both private and commercial functions. Ships' boats like *Mary Ann* were solidly and professionally built with large, clinker hulls. They were attractively shaped and, if sympathetically converted by a knowing hand, they made tidy little ships.[31] It is understood that several other small vessels were built using timbers salvaged from *Fifeshire* during subsequent years. The records of these have been lost in the annals of time, however it is believed that the 44 ft schooner *Emergency* was largely constructed from the recycled remnants.[32]

The settlement grows

Through 1842 that first wave of immigrant ships swept progressively into Blind Bay and there was an air of hopeful expectation and novelty in the finding of new homes for their passengers. The people came and Nelson turned on its welcoming face to charm them. Practical difficulties could wait. Nelson is still full of appeal but that quality experienced then, and throughout the first century of settlement, is harder to find now. For so many mornings the haven was still and quiet, in contrast to today's noise of traffic and waterfront industry which cuts us off from nature's stillness. Then the sea lapped the roadside (and later a sea wall), all the way to Saltwater Creek by Washington Valley. William Pratt gave a picture of it late in 1842 when he was anchored outside the Boulder Bank awaiting the tide.

"Next morning, just at break of day, I was startled by hearing the crowing of a cock on shore; it was so unexpected as, so far, no houses had been seen, the township not being visible from where the vessel lay at anchor. Anchored in that calm bay, in the quiet of the early morn, with no perceptible movement of the ship, and no sound save the gentle lapping of the water at the side, as with the strong ebb-tide it rippled and gurgled by the ship, it seemed as if the peace of Heaven had suddenly fallen around and upon us ..."[33]

As a young man I was in a rowing team, as a sport, on Nelson harbour during the summer months of the late 1940s. We were on the water training by 6am, and most often we shared its calm for a few minutes with one or other of the Wellington-Nelson ferries *Matangi* and *Arahura* coming in, to berth. It was magical.

A new market place

Once they were ashore in the Nelson settlement, just as in Wellington, a number of immigrant capitalists and landholders set up the panoply of trade in the belief that Maori and immigrant workers would flock to buy the goods brought with

---

31 Many years later I helped my brother Allen convert a similar boat for Captain Des Cross.
32 See chapter 11
33 Platt, P3

*This sketch of the foreshore opposite the Haul-ashore end of the boulder bank, about two years after the colonists arrived, shows a small group of significant buildings at the foot of the track known as Stafford Walk (now Richardson Street) which was the steep sole landward route into the town via a swampy valley. The Company store in the background was erected early to cater for the goods unloaded by ships anchored in the deep Bolton Hole south of the entrance. An undecked schooner, probably Moore's **Mary Ann**, is sailing outwards while a raft of logs is laboriously towed from Edward Baigent's pioneer Waimea operation towards Green Point, presumably for house construction and possibly ship-building.*

Longueville (attrib), Bett Loan Collection AC 804, Nelson Provincial Museum

them on the ships and other goods that were later imported. Their stock was not always suitable because they had been misled by the Company as to conditions in the colony.

They also brought in livestock, sometimes as speculation. Captain England, for example, imported a flock of sheep for sale. There was a dearth of agricultural implements which the whalers filled by selling their own second-hand tools to would-be farmers. At one time there was a shortage of crockery, which was met in at least one case with pioneering ingenuity when a chamber pot became a substitute kitchen utensil.

The first Nelson issue of *The Nelson Examiner* and *New Zealand Chronicle* appeared on 12 March 1842, demonstrating a detailed planning and foresight that had not been applied by Company officials to the more basic requirements of the settlement. With the advent of modern internet, interested readers can find this readily available in its entirety at the touch of a finger![34] The snippets published overleaf reveal a home-grown attempt to create a fresh, more egalitarian community (note the minutes of a Benefit Club, proposed aboard *Mary Ann* during her voyage, as well as a Temperance Society already making its voice

---

34 *Nelson Examiner* and *New Zealand Chronicle*, 12 March 1842

heard.) We can see the stamp of authority from Company officials and the new police, and the first indication that theft and prohibited tree-felling has already occurred. The pressing need for commerce and transport of essentials is already apparent, and may well be stirring the interests of boatmen amongst the settlers – the future Hooker owner/skippers.

The first issue also contained an essay-length editorial, extolling the principles of settlement outside the yoke of central government. As this newspaper was established by Charles Elliot with money loaned by the New Zealand Company, (like Wellington's *New Zealand Gazette*) it was viewed as a mouthpiece of the Company, opposing interference from the British Colonial officials in Auckland.

To scan the style and tone of the subsequent several years of advertisements and articles is almost to talk with the settlers as though there were not one and a half intervening centuries. After the first town acres were made available, some sites were immediately offered for resale or rent. Many sought quick fortunes by asking highly inflated prices for land that had not yet seen the sweat of their brows. Land ownership was quickly reflected in newspaper notices of prosecution for trespass or for cutting wood on privately-owned land. The Company had sent people off with unreal expectations which led to this preoccupation with the minutiae of property preservation within bare weeks of settlement. Most were still living in temporary whares and shacks, although there were one or two more substantial prefabricated buildings. Some of the newcomers readily rose to the challenge of scrub, fern and swamp, although it would take time for them to establish themselves. Others were overwhelmed by the reality of what they had come to. Hopes that Nelson would speedily have farm produce for export had not been backed by the necessary planning, so the practical realisation of agricultural production was too slow. A customs office could be set up, a newspaper could be provided, but when it came to self-sufficiency Wakefield's theories could not turn the plough. The newcomers had to contend with untested and unproven terrain, land that had first to be understood before they could deal with its idiosyncrasies. The town was dependent on food imports from around the coast as well as from overseas, and the port was kept busy with the stream of immigrant ships and smaller traders calling. Sea transport was the only communication with the settlements across Blind Bay, and after its early start boatbuilding activity slowed right down.

Poverty and general depression started in the latter part of 1842, although it was obscured by a false prosperity as the capitalists, confined to town without land, spent the cash they had intended for property development. Already the settlement was paying for the Company's eagerness to sell land regardless of the consequences, and its desire to enhance land values through occupation and development. But the tide still flowed and ebbed, the sun still shone, and people had as much independence and freedom as anyone could claim with an often-empty belly. Then it was that neighbour helped neighbour, and some of the capitalists went beyond any call of duty to help, too. A real Nelson was slowly

The Nelson Examiner,

AND NEW ZEALAND CHRONICLE.

Vol. I.]   NELSON HAVEN, MARCH 12, 1842.   [No. 1.

NOTICE is hereby given that Tenders in writing will be received at the office of Mr. Poynter, Nelson Haven, for Floating the Barque *Fifeshire*, now lying on the rocks off the Arrow Rock, at the mouth of the harbour. The said vessel to be brought into the harbour, and moored at any part that may be directed by the Agent on board. No tenders will be received after the 21st instant.

For further particulars apply to Captain Arnold, on board; or to Mr. POYNTER, Nelson Haven.
March 8.

Police Office, Nelson Haven, March 9, 1842.

TENDERS will be received for the BUILDING of a GAOL and COURT HOUSE, according to a plan to be obtained at this office.

By command of his Excellency the Governor,
H. AUGUSTUS THOMPSON,
Police Magistrate.

Police Office, Nelson Haven, March 9, 1842.

NOTICE is hereby given that any person erecting any Building or Place of Abode on any Public Reserve, or on any ground laid out for any Public Road, will be liable to be ejected without notice.

By order of his Excellency the Governor,
H. AUGUSTUS THOMPSON.

NEW ZEALAND TEMPERANCE ASSOCIATION.

THE Committee of the above beg to inform the public that a Society has been formed in Nelson in connection with the New British and Foreign Temperance Society; and that they will be happy to receive the names of those individuals who may be disposed to unite with them.

The books are kept by Mr. A. SAUNDERS, who will feel much pleasure in giving any information as to the nature, objects, and prospects of the Society.

FIVE POUNDS REWARD.

WHEREAS upwards of three thousand feet of boards and other timber have been recently stolen from the beach, near my residence; I therefore offer the above reward to any person giving such information of the above felony as will lead to the conviction of the offenders.
FRED. GEORGE MOORE.
Nelson Haven, March 8.

FOR PORT NICHOLSON DIRECT.

THE fast-sailing Schooner *Vanguard* will start for the above port positively on Monday the 14th instant. For freight or passage apply to Captain Murray, on board; or to WAITT and Co.
Nelson Haven, March 10, 1842.

PUBLIC SALE.

THE remaining CARGO of the Schooner *Cheerful* will be Sold, at Auckland Point, on TUESDAY next, at Two o'clock. P. GRAHAM,
March 12. Licensed Auctioneer.

PUBLIC AUCTION,

On SATURDAY, March 20, at One o'clock.

AN excellent assortment of superior CARPENTERS' TOOLS, and other suitable articles for early colonists.

AT a Meeting of Emigrants on board the *Mary Anne*, bound to New Zealand, held on Monday, January 10, 1842, for the purpose of considering and deciding upon the expediency of establishing in the settlement of Nelson a BENEFIT CLUB, or Friendly Association,

WILLIAM CURLING YOUNG, Esq., in the Chair;

The following Resolutions were proposed and carried:—

1. Moved by Mr. G. SAUNDERS; seconded by Mr. R. BODDINGTON:

That, inasmuch as it is desirable at all times to provide for the casualties and contingencies of the future out of the abundance or sufficiency of the present, as the habit of self-reliance is destroyed when men are accustomed to look for assistance, in time of need, either from individual charity or public provision; and as it appears to be especially the interest of persons belonging to the industrious classes, in case of their being disabled for work by age, sickness, infirmity, or accident, or in the event of death, to secure for their families a maintenance out of a fund which they themselves have contributed to raise; this meeting is of opinion that the formation of a Society in the Colony of Nelson, founded on the principles of mutual aid and friendly combination, and having for its object the support of its members when at any time unable to follow their usual employment, and of their families in the event of their own death, would be a measure of public importance and utility.

NOTICE is hereby given that no Timber is to be cut on the land about to be distributed to purchasers from the New Zealand Company.
ARTHUR WAKEFIELD,
Nelson, March 9. Agent for Nelson.

THE NELSON EXAMINER.

NELSON HAVEN, MARCH 12, 1842.

Journals become more necessary as men become more equal, and individualism more to be feared. It would be to underrate their importance to suppose that they serve only to secure liberty: they maintain civilisation.
DE TOCQUEVILLE.
Of Democracy in America, vol. 4, p. 290.

Various motives have impelled men, in different times, to plant colonies and settlements. The too great crowding of people—the tyranny of rulers—the troubles of adverse times—the ardour of adventure, thirst of wealth, impatience of inaction, or passion for renown, have been the chief motives which have led to the formation of settlements. Of these, by far the most powerful and universal is the first. The superabundance of people has ever been the fruitful source of distress and discontent.

These extracts from the first edition of Nelson's newspaper, printed five weeks after first settlers arrived, reveal much of settlement life.

National Museum of New Zealand – Papers Past

forged. Joint difficulties united people and if in some cases the help conferred advantage on the helper it still served its purpose. The community that developed was nothing like the one envisaged back in England. Memories of those times still existed in some families a century later, as we learned in my primary school class in the year of 1940.

Earliest shipping

The arrivals of the preliminary New Zealand Company party and the immigrant ships that followed have already been covered. Add in the non-documented seamen who had deserted visiting ships, some of whom had been about since the first whalers and sealers arrived, and there was a pool of experience that was the nucleus of the Blind Bay sailors. There were other ships about the coast too. Whalers operating from shore stations had small ships to serve their needs, take product to shipping points and bring in supplies. Some of these whalers bordering Cook Strait were quick to respond to the opportunities they spotted in the new Nelson settlement. James Jackson built his schooner *Nelson Packet* on Te Awaiti beach in 1841. At the same time Jack Guard was building *New Zealander* at Kakapo Bay, and Captain Fergusson built *Ocean* at Ocean Bay in Port Underwood.

These early local seafarers all engaged in coastal trade as well as serving the whaling industry, but Jimmy Jackson in particular was attracted to the Nelson settlement, where he found a young wife among the immigrants, and spent the following year working out of the Haven.[35] His *Nelson Packet* was in and out at least half a dozen times and must be recognised as a hooker along with Frederick Moore's *Mary Ann* which was sailed in both a private and commercial use. Sounds whaler Captain Thoms was also around with his *Three Brothers*, not to be confused with a later vessel of the same name. Captain J M McLaren, a whaler of d'Urville Island and, after 1846, of Te Matea Bay in the Croisilles, had *Ocean Queen*, and Captain Elmslie of Queen Charlotte Sound also operated into Nelson in his un-named whaleboat.

The New Zealand Company chartered the barque *Brougham* under the command of F.A. Carrington, a surveyor and a member of the Plymouth Company which was formed in 1840 to buy land from the New Zealand Company. The Plymouth Company sent emigrants from England's West Country to form a settlement to be named New Plymouth, hopefully near Cook Strait, but they were forced to disperse from Wellington after that region proved (in spite of Company promises), to have insufficient available flat land. *Brougham* had actually been investigating Blind Bay as a potential location for new Plymouth in January 1841, with Dicky Barrett aboard as pilot. His barque anchored in Astrolabe Roads on the eastern shore, but Carrington was not impressed with its lack of flat land there, so had sailed on to the Taranaki region in the eastern North Island.

---

35 Dawber, Carol, *The Jacksons of Te Awaiti*, River Press, Picton, 2001, p57

From the time of earliest immigrant settlement Nelson Haven was alive with shipping activity. Captain Sheridan's small 13-ton schooner *Eliza* had the distinction of being the first trading vessel recorded by the colonists as visiting Nelson with a cargo of pigs and potatoes, arriving on 5 November 1841 – amazingly within a week of the very first ships of the preliminary party. Perhaps Captain Sheridan acted on intelligence picked up in Port Nicholson, or he may have simply been on a buying visit to the Maori settlement at Motueka. *Eliza* sailed for Wellington four days later taking despatches from Arthur Wakefield to his brother William.

Eliza gives us a picture of the remarkable range of these small vessels. She sailed into Nelson on 15 December from Coromandel Harbour (600 miles north, east of Auckland) and was back in Nelson on 3 January (under Captain Scantling) from Wanganui in the lower North Island. On 29 January she arrived with West Wanganui coal (Westhaven on the South Island West Coast), as well as two tons of whale blubber which the crew 'tried out', or rendered into oil, on the beach. Three weeks later she was back again (under Captain Stenning) with general cargo from Port Nicholson, on 23 February. One cargo *Eliza* discharged later that year was received with less enthusiasm by a few settlers who intended a similar commercial enterprise in the near future: "Messrs Orr and Wright brought back the necessary supplies to open Nelson's first grog shop, by Saltwater Creek Crossing."[36] The settlement was still barely four months old!

It is remarkable how efficiently Nelson's new bureaucracy sprung into existence. Within three months the newly appointed port officials had set up an immediate revenue-raising system along with the requisite stocks of forms. Nelson's first registered ship, recorded on 28 April 1842 as a 38-ton vessel by the newly established Nelson Customs Office, was *Pickwick*, a 39ft cutter brought from Tasmania by her owner James Williams. It was not unusual for small ships to cross the Tasman and even to come from further afield – some shipwrights sailed in their own vessels from Nova Scotia to settle in Auckland and build ships there. In 1842 *Pickwick* came into Nelson five times with immigrants, timber and general cargo. Her master was William Stiles but by 1844 she was owned by Jack Guard of Port Underwood.

But perhaps the new bureaucracy was not as efficient as it seemed. *Pickwick* was number one on the Nelson registry but there is no record of a number two, and that may even have been a clerical error. The third ship, *Erin* registered in December 1842 as a 30ft schooner of 12-tons, can be considered a forerunner to the 'true' hooker that we shall get to know in the next chapter. Unfortunately *Erin* was wrecked east of Cape Palliser, on 22 April 1844. She had been sold in January, on the death of her part-owner Captain Ralph, to Henry Brown of Wellington, a butcher who was also her master[37]. *Pickwick* was driven ashore in a southwest gale off Cape Palliser on 29 June 1845. Her two crewmen were drowned and she

---

36 The Nelson Examiner and New Zealand Chronicle, 1 July 1842
37 *Shipwrecks* page 25.

was plundered. It was not a friendly coast.

In addition to the regular immigrant vessels discharging their determined and optimistic pioneers to a new life after months of privation at sea, there were smaller inter-colonial and coastal traders. Most of these were still large vessels in relation to the hookers. First in was the 72-ton schooner *Kate* (Captain Webster) bringing general cargo in December 1841. Others brought cattle, maize, shingles and potatoes, timber and spirits, sheep, pigs, goats and, of course, people. Nearly 7,500 tons of shipping entered Nelson in that first year of formal settlement.

The 22-ton *Nymph* was our sort of little ship. Under one or other of her two captains, Bennett and Barker, she was in with a load of sawn planks from Coromandel in January, followed with passengers and stores in March. Then in April she brought a cargo from Massacre Bay (Golden Bay) comprising limestone, probably extracted from Tata Island, and coal from Motupipi. She did four more trips that year, carrying mainly goats, pigs and potatoes. Captains Barker and Swinie ran *Mana*, a 13-ton small schooner which carried pigs and potatoes in February, flour in May, oil in June, spirits in July and general cargo in November.

It takes little imagination to trace the seasonal needs of the settlers from these cargoes. *Rory O'More* and Guard's *New Zealander* made a trip or two but in 1843 the *Rory O'More* sank when lightering manganese ore out to the *Tryphena* at the unlikely location of D'Urville Island's Catherine Bay.

The little 10-ton Wanganui cutter *Katherine Johnston* (probably around 35ft in length) started trading in and out of Nelson in July under Captain Taylor with 'general cargo'. This vague term often referred to pigs and potatoes in the first years, but might also include such various goods as axes (by the box), pipes (by the case), tobacco (by the cask), leather (by the bale), clocks (by the case), salt & sugar (by the ton), tea (by the chest), soap (by the box), and blankets (by the bale) – plus the inevitable quantities of ale, rum and wine by the cask!

Nearly all of these traders were operated from outside Nelson. Generally their cargoes were from Wellington or Blind Bay, but some trade was conducted along the coastline up to Taranaki and beyond. It was about due north and a relatively short hop to Mana Island and Porirua Harbour, Kapiti Island, Foxton on the Manawatu River, and beyond that to Wanganui, Patea, New Plymouth. It was not unusual to ply cargoes further north up the North Island west coast to Kawhia, Raglan and beyond. Coastal small ships worked the difficult east coast of the North Island too, with the pigs and potatoes that were staple diet for the settlers.

4

The First Locally-built Hooker

WITH SETTLERS NOW LANDED, and immediately experiencing conditions that were so different from their expectations, it seems unbelievable that Company officials in the colony would nevertheless continue to put in place the more transparently absurd aspects of the Wakefield scheme. It ignored not only the culture and occupation rights of Maori as first occupants, but also the coexistence of other pockets of settlers. Nevertheless, they went doggedly ahead, exacerbating problems they were attempting solve to their own advantage. William Fox, who was soon to become Nelson's resident Company agent[38] was so naively enthusiastic about the settlement scheme that he wrote before he left England: *'The Wakefield system is one of those discoveries which is so simple that its truths must be apparent to the meanest apprehension'*[39]. Except that it didn't work!

When the Company's preliminary expedition ships *Will Watch*, *Arrow* and *Whitby* first arrived in Blind Bay's western shores, near Adele Island, Captain Arthur Wakefield's key brief was to seek out good agricultural land. They had anchored in one of Dumont D'Urville's favourite spots, a protected anchorage with coves, beaches and streams, backed with lush bush and resounding bird song. Almost immediately the two surveyors, Frederick Tuckett and Samuel Stephens, were strenuously at work ashore, exploring the dense bush behind Astrolabe Roadstead[40] and immediately encountering mountainous terrain instead of the flat land others had hastily declared was there.

From a seaman's viewpoint, like our forthcoming hooker captains, it was fortunate that Arthur Wakefield was a naval officer, unlike his capitalist brother. Nelson Haven wouldn't have been so well buoyed, beaconed, and flag-staffed, of course, and the shoreline exploration may well have been less thorough. (One wonders what would have been the course of events had he been a country squire with a farmer's eye.)

The ships' boats and the Company's Deal boats provided easy exploration both to the north and south, and their crews were able to penetrate quite far inland in places along the southern shores of Blind Bay, like the Moutere inlet with its tidal waters and river. Their eventual discovery of Nelson Haven and the marginal flat land of Te Wakatu in the south-east must have been a huge relief,

---

38 Later *Sir* William, and a future premier of New Zealand, soon to succeed Arthur Wakefield as resident agent.
39 Requoted in *Temple* page 192. The late David Lange's biography showed his observation of the economic naivety of some politicians in his times, it continues to expect a miracle from formulaic economic dogma.
40 'Roadstead', a place where vessels may shelter, and ride at anchor some distance from the shore.

with less demanding toil for the surveyors for a while. However much of the subsequent exploration and survey in the region, taken up again six months later in May 1842, included difficult winter work in swamp and forest, bringing sickness in its wake for those engaged on it.

An astonishing discovery

When Frederick Tuckett, the company's able but dour chief surveyor, was sent North-west across Blind Bay in the schooner *Rory O'More* in March 1842, to find land in Massacre Bay, he found an astonishing sight. Two small ships were under construction in a Maori kainga (village) on the Aorere river-mouth, where Collingwood stands today. It must have been be akin to climbing a mountain and finding a restaurant at the summit! These unexpected vessels were being built by three pakeha men with a couple of Maori helpers. They were sailors and traders who had been about the area well before the New Zealand Company venture.

A similar unexpected discovery had occurred in Port Nicholson a couple of years earlier when the Brig *Tory*, with Colonel William Wakefield aboard, first entered on 30 September 1839. He had found an eight-ton little ship being built by Joe Robinson who was living among the Maori at Waiwhetu (later Hutt Valley), and even forging his own nails.[41] A year later the Company's Wellington-based newspaper *New Zealand Gazette* reported the launching of the first locally-built boat, a 15-ton schooner owned by William Wright, but Robinson's vessel seems to have preceded it. Up to this point New Zealand had seen two distinct waves of settlers, first Maori who had been living by their own skills for a thousand-odd years, and in recent decades the independent Europeans, like the whalers in the Cook Strait area and the west coast sealers. In the north-west corner of the South Island alone – land touted as 'empty' by the New Zealand Company, Tuckett counted a significant Maori population in Westhaven and Massacre Bay.

Australian-based capitalists had already been surprisingly busy with spurious land purchases from local Maori. For a mere £150, J.T. Goodsir had nominally acquired 15,000 acres at Pakawau, while J.C. Crawford had supposedly bought 250,000 acres scattered over the Massacre Bay and 'West Wanganui' (Westhaven) district for £301, and W. Cowper had bought another 8,000 acres. None of these purchases stood up to later scrutiny. Even earlier, in 1832, Captain John Blenkinsop had purchased "the whole of Marlborough's 'Wyroa Plains'" for the price of a "one Eighteen pounder piece of Cannon"[42] – a deal which was subsequently spiked. Whalers and sealers like Dicky Barrett, Joseph Thoms, Jimmy Jackson and Jack Guard were plying their ships around the area, and *Jewess* was already active too.

It is worth noting that the most common currency for these early land transactions had tended to be guns and gunpowder, with the value recorded as an equivalent. But there had been a subsequent cost in human life, with thousands

---

41 McGill page 116.
42 Washbourne, H.F. *Reminiscences of Early Days*, R.Lucas and Son 1933

of Maori lives lost in the inter-tribal Musket Wars of the 1820s and 1830s. There would also be a significant connection between the weapons distributed by Colonel William Wakefield as part of his 1839 land purchase, and his brother's subsequent death at the hands of those same recipients. Among the blankets ... and various consumer goods in payment, for the Nelson and Wellington districts, were 200 muskets, 24 single and double-barrelled guns, 81 kegs of gunpowder and so on distributed amongst Rangatira of the Ngati Toa and their recently victorious Taranaki allies. In due course they would be used against the Pakeha as well, as we shall see.

However Tuckett's unexpected discovery of a modest shipyard in the location which became Collingwood, had nothing to do with muskets. There on the Aorere riverside, using logs delivered by the river in flood, and coal for his forge from a seam nearby, Captain Joseph Ralph with co-builder Ezra Blowers[43] and probably another named Anderson, was building the 12 ton 30 foot clinker schooner *Erin*, and another supposedly larger ship which, however, has defied identification. Worthy of note is that *Erin* even had a figurehead of a woman. Tuckett had stumbled upon the district's first true hooker.

Tuckett's attention soon turned to potential survey work on the Aorere valley flats, where uncultivated rush and toe toe grass grew "like a great field of corn ready for cutting".[44] Groups of rata trees stood on knolls as if they had been planted there. With the exception of the pakihi terraces, the surrounding country was heavily bushed and resounded with bird song. Tui were as numerous as sparrows are now, and plump kereru hung and flopped in the branches, ignoring the activity below except for an inquisitive eye. The smaller birds near to hand were unafraid until events made them wary. The sand bar where Collingwood is now was swampy with tufts of rushes, stunted flax and pools. There were sand hills at the channel end of the bar, since eroded away but originally known as 'Warping Point' because of the ropes used to manoeuvre ships around it.

Erin's maiden voyage to Nelson retraced

The following is as accurate a reconstruction[45] as can be projected after so much time, of what was entailed in getting *Erin* to sea. The 30 foot vessel was launched by December 1842, with a good chance her seams would be more-or-less tight, or soon 'take up' as every builder expected. The need for regular pumping was taken for granted with most wooden boats.

What an exciting occasion it must have been, these logs from the river and beach given form by the thought, effort and skill of the builders and now about to take the water. It makes a nice image, *Erin* riding down the stocks to slide in gracefully, but the launching was likely to have been more prosaic. She would have been moved down at low tide or lowered from her chocks and the tide-

---

43 The spelling of their names on the documents although *Allan* reported other spellings too.
44 Washbourne H.P. pg 38
45 Howard Williams (the last Blind Bay trader under sail alone) endorsed this portrayal.

water would have risen around her. There would have been much splashing about and, as soon as she floated, she would have been boarded with some care because she was unballasted. There would have been an excited babble of accents and dialects from all corners of Britain blending with the comfortable vowels of the Maori and the harsher accents of the Yankee co-builder.

It is a very special moment when a new boat or ship is launched into her own environment and floats free of the bottom. A lilt and lift, a chuckle of water; suddenly she becomes palpably alive. A sailing boat of equivalent size nowadays has a fixed, weighted keel for stability as well as some internal ballast, including an engine, but the hookers were essentially cargo ships and owed their stability, like Captain Cook's *Endeavour*, to their hull shapes and load carrying capacities. There are identifiable piles of ballast stones, taken out to put a cargo aboard, still to be found at many of the small ports they used.

The two masts would next be dropped in, using sheerlegs – two poles lashed together as a bipod with a tackle at the apex. Because *Erin* was a schooner her taller mast was aft, and both were stayed with rope using deadeyes and lanyards which required regular tightening. It would be another two decades before wire rope would become an option for shrouds and stays (although since the late 1820s three-foot lengths of rod linked by eyes had been used on some ships). We can assume that *Erin*, like most soon-to-be-built hookers, was decked straight through with low bulwarks, a low small cabin aft and a hold forward. An equivalent boat nowadays will have a cockpit that puts the helmsman lower and the tiller at an easy height. *Erin's* tiller may have been pivoted to sit horizontal or at an angle suited to helming whilst standing on the aft deck, unlike later and larger hookers which were wheel-steered. The layout provided easier working areas on the deck, during cargo operations. *Erin* would almost certainly be rigged with long booms and gaffs, with a gaff sail broader to its height than what is customary nowadays; and both throat and peak halyards to raise and set it.

Now that *Erin* is afloat and at least partially ballasted with local beach-rounded rocks, she will be readily manoeuvrable by poling, rowing with her own sweeps, or towing with a pulling boat. On all our hookers and early ships the lack of ports with wharves, a pulling boat or dinghy was a necessity. (Watch for the pulling boats in old maritime photographs and you will see some whose elegance puts modern boats to shame.) Even large vessels were moved by kedging, pulling alternately on anchors run out by the dinghy. *Erin* will move easily in the shallow depths within the estuary with the long pole she carries to push against the sand bottom or towing with a pulling boat. But as the sea-breeze kicks in, windage from her spars and rigging makes poling or rowing too difficult. It will be time to raise her sails and test her merits.

Erin will now be taken on one or more trial sails, testing the gear and learning something of her handling characteristics, especially how responsive she was. This is a critical test-point of the success or otherwise of the design: the balance of her sails so that she is not heavy on the helm, and especially making sure that she will 'come about' – tacking through the wind and not get caught 'in

*This early photograph of **Supply**, one of Nelson's earliest hookers and launched in 1846 about three years after **Erin**, demonstrates the low-aspect gaff rig likely found on **Erin**, (although **Erin** was rigged as a schooner with a shorter foremast and foresail boom). The photograph hints at **Supply** being possibly of clinker construction.*
Copy Collection C35-44, Nelson Provincial Museum

stays', nor want to fall away when sailing a 'lee helm'. She will need adjusting to provide a slight 'weather helm' so that she will round up into the wind if the tiller is released; a lee helm could cause her to fall away towards a disastrous gybe. We shall see in later chapters far too many vessels getting into difficulties through being unresponsive in handling. The hookers' remarkably long bowsprits indicates a need to carry sails well for'ard to balance any tendency to extreme weather helm. A first-hand report from one who sailed in Galway Bay hookers confirmed that in a wind they are hard on the helm.

Finally, the time must arrive when the skipper says "*We'll take her to Motupipi tomorrow*". To imagine that voyage is to take a step back in time. It is a shining morning as we slip aboard unobserved, along with Captain Ralph, described as a passenger when *Erin* arrived in Nelson on 10th December 1842 under Captain Sheridan. We shall assume co-builder Ezra Blowers, Anderson and the Maori helpers are aboard too, at least to Motupipi.

Massacre Bay has very few good small boat anchorages, with only its river estuaries as harbours and the small Tata Islands in the eastern corner offering limited shelter. We may have to get around Separation Point and tuck into

Totaranui if there is a westerly blow and we should want shelter. Our skipper takes these things into account, but it is just a short hop across the bay and into the Motupipi estuary, so, as soon as the tide allows, we leave, to swing around Wapping Point under headsail. We'll take advantage of the slight flow of the Aorere River against the tide, and pick up the southerly air down the valley, *Erin* lifts gently as we leave the estuary for the bay. The start of any voyage is special, and this is the maiden voyage.

The crewmen have taken gaskets off to free the sails, and seen to sheets and halyards, all shipshape and 'Blind Bay fashion'. With *Erin* lying somewhere near head to wind, up goes the main, as wrinkle-free as is likely for a hand-cut sail that was sewn in a hut or out-of-doors. Next, up with the foresail, which also has a gaff, and later the two headsails. The skipper glances aloft and wonders if one day he may even set tops'ls up there to fill in the triangles between the gaffs and mastheads. Quickly he pays her off, and with the light wind tending more to the west, relaxes a little, listening like us to the chuckle of the water along her clinker topsides, and enjoying the view of a succession of bush-backed beaches and

This detail from an 1843 Heaphy sketch near Massacre Bay's Tata Islands shows a schooner coming in to anchor, which could be **Erin** *(but possibly one of the other schooners also about in that year –* **Nelson Packet**, **New Zealander**, **Rory O'More** *or* **Carbon**). *Note the Maori activity on the beach with two waka being readied for launching.*
B-043-005, Alexander Turnbull Library

headlands with the rather sombre mountain range behind, as we head south of east to Motupipi. Anyone seeing her from shore would be even more open-mouthed than we would be today.

The air is thick with discussion of *Erin*'s performance and qualities, and the Old Man wants a sheet tweaked here, a halyard peaked up there. (We find ourselves automatically calling our captain 'the Old Man'; it reflects an accolade, even when bestowed aboard our little ships where informality is the rule). Much of the conversation aboard Erin is self-congratulatory, and deservedly so, for we will soon read her description in the Examiner 10 December 1842, as a "very well-built craft ... her joint owners and builders have every reason to be proud of her, and of their own energy and perseverance"[46].

Massacre Bay – aka Coal Bay – later Golden Bay

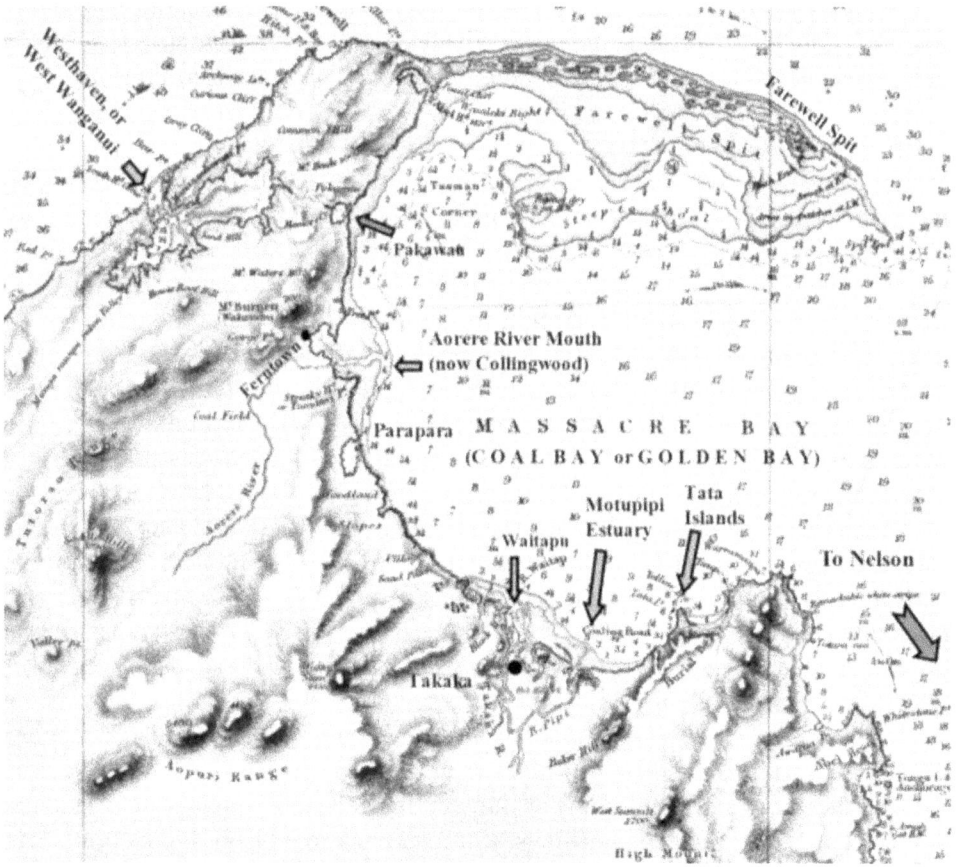

Motupipi estuary lies in the south-eastern corner of Coal Bay (as Massacre Bay is becoming commonly called now by members of the Coal and Limestone Association who have commenced operations here). A first cargo awaits *Erin*

---

46 *Examiner* 10 Dec 1842

here, and we are going to drop off the ballast (these stones may still be there) and load 15 tons of coal. She will certainly ride lower in the water across Blind Bay with this weight aboard. If *Erin* were mine, I would be anguished at putting this black stuff into my new ship, but it will clean up. The Motupipi folk are planning to use lighters to ferry their coal out to larger ships unable to enter the tidal estuary port, but *Erin* will manage.

As silent observers, we admire the skill and quiet efficiency of Captain Sheridan and crew in handling her over the slight bar and up the bends in the Motupipi channel, without the roaring and blustering that might be expected from a less experienced Old Man. He brings her right up to where the coal is being dug, just around the corner of the tidal headland, where she must lie as the tide recedes.

Is she to be loaded using wheelbarrows run up a 10 inch plank? The histories are silent about such details (I always puzzled, for example, how people managed toilet affairs in the freezing Arctic or Antarctic until a friend who went south could finally tell me – Quickly! The same applied to the hookers.) There were no special toilet arrangements and it was probably a matter of hanging on to the leeward shrouds.

Cabins and cooking

We now must wait for the tide. If Separation Point doesn't play a weather trick on us, we are only 12 or so hours away from Nelson with our load of Motupipi coal. Nelson Haven is less than 40 miles (60 kilometres) away by sea, but December weather can see us becalmed, or bring winds which may add days of sheltering to the voyage. We are to spend the night in the estuary, and being the odd persons out, guess where we'll be sleeping? Wrapped in a sail on the deck if we are lucky, rather than in the claustrophobic wee cabin right over the stern. Its four bunks will be like shelves, in head-bump range of the deck or the bunk above, with mattresses of the traditional 'donkey's breakfast'; palliasses of straw, grass or whatever was available, with pillows of the same stuffing inside a flour bag. We won't be sheltering in the galley, for the simple reason that there isn't one!

Erin's papers describe her as having a 'square stern' – most likely a transom with a rudder hung off it like a ship's boat) It probably didn't take her long to accumulate the distinctive cabin smells that Henry Washbourn[47] described as an aroma "in which cheese, coffee and onions predominated, and the combined smell was not easily forgotten." By my observation there could also be the permeating, mouldy smell engendered by wet clothes and bedding, and dampness in a wooden hull prone to leaking. Nevertheless, there was likely to be a rule of cleanliness.

In the morning a lime-burner Samuel Bartlett and a man called Dodson come aboard from the coal workings, to travel back to Nelson. Let us hope *Erin* has a favourable wind, or we may be rowing and in for blisters. But if Captain Sheridan expects the breeze to drop, he knows that the eastern coastline of Blind Bay offers a number of good anchorages. We could spend a night in Torrent Bay or Astrolabe although that is unlikely with a full crew aboard.

---

47 *Washbourn* page 48.

A Successful arrival
Fortunately we have made a good passage across Blind Bay despite being heavy laden, and Captain Sheridan lines up on the welcoming lead-marks to make our entrance on the incoming tide. We harden our sheets as we round the pile beacon to port, just off the end of the Haul-Ashore end of the Boulder Bank, and gaze at the hulk *Fifeshire*, stripped of her rig, still lying at a forlorn angle on Arrow Rock as we sail past. Once a proud ship, she has now become nothing but a resource. (The Nelson boatbuilders must have thought "tis an ill wind that blows nobody any good", benefitting from her spars, sails, rigging, fittings and timbers.) To starboard we see Captain Wakefield's house there, and the track leading over the hill and down Washington Valley to Saltwater Creek and the town. We beat up the harbour, hailed by a number of seafarers as we go, as *Erin* is a welcome newcomer.

Erin will discharge at Mr Otterson's Auckland Point jetty, off the Maitai River channel, anchoring for an hour or so while the tide continues to make, as we are relatively deep drafted with this load of coal aboard. We will likely need to resort to poling or towing at the last, in the comparatively shallow water there.

And so, in such a fashion, the coal is delivered. Well, someone will be shovelling it into a basket to lift it out, but we no doubt have important business elsewhere and much more to see, so bustle off along the jetty. Our first hooker trip is done, but our voyage to understand the men of the hookers, and those who used the little ships and where they sailed, moves on.

Nelson Haven is not empty, even in this first year of the settlement's existence. The records show that during 1842 there had been 132 recorded arrivals (some calling several times), including a stream of immigrant ships, traders from New Zealand and Australian ports carrying livestock (pigs, cattle, goats), potatoes, flour and general stores, timber, limestone, coal and oil. In addition there was an often unrecorded flow of more local marine traffic – the un-named whale boats and Maori canoes which moved about the bays and Sounds.

It has been a most satisfying maiden voyage. No wonder John Masefield wrote "I must go down to the sea again, to the lonely sea and the sky." We learned his poem "Sea Fever" in my class at Auckland Point School, well-peppered with the sons and daughters of seafarers like my own family. A sailing boat has its sounds; the slap of water, a range of notes from wind in the rigging, and the flap of sails, while the hull may talk a little in creaks and groans, and all this changing with wind strength, from a sigh to tumultuousness. Do you hear it?

Reflections on the experience
Different technology has supplanted these low-aspect gaff rigs but they are powerful, safe and relatively simple. Hands-on experience has proved they are surprisingly fast especially with sheets eased, and are less likely to lose a mast than the tall, modern rigs whose principal advantage is sailing closer to the wind. With tops'ls, flying jib, jib and stays'l set in a bit of a breeze, even a staid hooker would provide stimulating sailing. And they used to carry a lot of sail!

Some of the later literature offers first-hand descriptions of sailing aboard

New Zealand's gaff-rigged scows, developed in the late 1800s. Unfortunately there are few first-hand accounts written by those who sailed the hookers – they seemed to have taken it for granted, and it is likely that even if their time was not taken up with more pressing tasks, few of these men were sufficiently literate to provide the details we now would love to read.

I have often sailed on the 46ft gaff-rigged Herreshoff ketch *New Zealand Maid*, and particularly remember an overnight race in windy conditions from Napier to Long Point on Mahia Peninsula and back. Seasickness prostrated most of the casual crew so, with the skipper busy navigating, I spent hours on the helm, happy to be there or I too might have succumbed. We drove her hard on a broad reach, confident enough in the gear to carry full sail, and the *Maid* (as she is commonly called) loved it – although not all the crew did! It was windy, wet and wonderful slicing through the seas until we turned for the hard beat back. Then it was all tossing discomfort, and a modern rig beat us to the finish line. But it was sustained exhilaration while we sailed downwind.

Although not an actual hooker, **New Zealand Maid**'s *rig was modelled on vessels like the Westrupp-skippered* **Elizabeth**, *and* **Camellia**, *and she has spent much time sailing out of Nelson too. I helped in her construction. The power of a gaff ketch is obvious in this photo of her romping on a broad reach in Tasmania's D'Entrecasteaux Channel.*
Courtesy John Brown

5

A Struggling Colony

ONCE *ERIN* HAS BEEN UNLOADED and well-scrubbed free of coal-dust, one can imagine her proud new owner-builder, Captain Ralph and his crew coming ashore from Otterson's jetty at Auckland Point in search of a likely grog-shop where they can celebrate their successful maiden voyage as well as make enquiries for a likely cargo. The group are led by Captain Sheridan who had officially skippered *Erin* into Nelson. Sheridan had captained his little schooner *Eliza* into the Haven in its very earliest days of settlement activity – barely a week after the Company ships had 'discovered' the harbour. (How he had learned of this development so quickly we can most likely attribute to Maori grapevine). Doubtless he will keep up a valuable commentary as the small party of Massacre Bay boatbuilders step ashore.

Auckland Point, Haven Road, C1843. For a time Nelson's commerce centred on this spot. Maori commerce is clearly evident from the number of trading waka here. The Company's little crane, seen loading a small boat at the point, is a good reference point to Heaphy's earlier sketch. Here the tide is in, but at low tide the Maitai River channel and extensive mudflats would be seen outside the shore, where people waded out into the fresh Maitai outflow to 'fill the billy'.
Mabel Annesley, after Barnicoat, Bett Loan Collection AC450, Nelson Provincial Museum

It is less than a year since this shoreline has begun to be developed, but already this key landing place at Auckland Point has a cluster of merchants' stores and the other facilities close at hand to the jetty. Three Maori waka are drawn up on the beach, one with a low sailing rig, and there are a scattering of Deal boats and small ships boats anchored close off. A red-bearded labourer who has joined them tells how he and three friends from the preliminary party had purchased the whaler from the *Whitby*'s captain before she sailed over a year ago, a few weeks after he had arrived. The other anchored whaler had been bought from the captain of the *Hope* when she was in port during March.

A familiar scent captures their attention, overlying all the dank smells of a muddy shoreline – the pungent, resinous odour of stockholm tar, pitch, shavings and freshly-worked wood. Their red-bearded new friend points towards a rough hut by the tideway (which he calls a 'whare'[48]) explaining that his good mate George Edwards is being helped by by an educated fellow named William Pratt to build a couple of hookers there after already building a good-sized dinghy. Resisting the temptation to wander closer for a chat, the men gaze curiously towards Green Point to their west, where a number of small cottages are scattered along the foot of the hill. Many are on or near Russell Street, already a place where boatmen and seamen live among the general settlers. These port area land lots were among the first popular choices among the Company's 'Town Acres'; the first choices were in the port area and had been quickly subdivided (at a profit of course) after their purchase. Their new acquaintance explains that inshore from a small bay is a steep track, locally called Russell Street, across the ridge to the

*This sketch, depicting a year after **Erin**'s first arrival, shows Nelson from above Saltwater Bridge. The prominent building by the bridge is the 'grogshop' where Captain Ralph and his crew are sure to have visited, The one to the right is probably where George Edwards began boatbuilding with William Pratt as his assistant. Maori canoes show customary use. In the background beyond the Maitai River is 'The Wood'. The first Nelson-built hooker,* **Moonraker**, *was wheeled down from near there and launched into Saltwater Creek in February 1844.*

Mabel Annesley, after Barnicoat, Bett Collection AC 448, Nelson Provincial Museum

---

48 Maori built their 'whare' huts out of basic materials, particularly raupo (bullrush) stems and leaves.

less popular swampy town acres in Washington Valley. That valley also provides a short-cut into town from ships which would lie on anchor out in the deeper part of the Haven, and is a route used by sailors walking up another hillside track known as Stafford Walk[49].

But that is not the direction Captain Ralph has in mind. He is eager to step out to the left along the busy main track to town along the shoreline towards the bridge across Saltwater Creek, past the whares that had been erected a year ago for the families of the preliminary party. The group quickens their pace as they spy the grog shop on the bend by the bridge. Beyond this two-month old bridge is a well-worn track known as Bridge Street with its first shops already constructed, but no-one in the party takes notice. They can already hear a rumble of voices from within the ale-house. It is a long time since they have enjoyed the taste of a good ale and the company of like-minded seafarers and pakeha settlers.

While they sip their ales and listen to the gossip and grizzles of the grog-shop regulars we have time to reflect on what these men have just observed during their brief walk from the jetty to the pub. The passable track along Haven Road had recently been constructed by the otherwise unemployed labourers who commenced it in September 1842. However anything that we nowadays call infrastructure was not much in evidence. There were no funds available for water supplies, sewerage or drainage, although open drains were dug along Trafalgar Street, and for the rest of the century Nelson was to be plagued by typhoid, dysentery, diphtheria, scarlet fever and other such diseases. Nor was there any mechanism of local government outside the questionable authority of the New Zealand Company. In hindsight there was a cavalier attitude towards public health and local government issues, and there were deficiencies which will doubtless be being voiced already in the grog-shop.

The officers of the Company, and especially William Wakefield in Wellington, had been thumbing their noses at the British government while, at the same time, complaining to it when things did not please them. At the same time, (from its headquarters in Auckland, two weeks away by ship to the north) New Zealand's colonial government had no funds for provincial government, and its authority was represented in Nelson by only a magistrate and the customs office. It was one thing to set up a whole new community, as the New Zealand Company did, quite another to see it through the necessities and the niceties of interaction between private enterprise and colonial government. In many ways Nelson and other settlements really were making a raw beginning, and in so doing encountered much which had not been thought about in London.

The waterfront was undoubtedly the focus for much of the life of Nelson during the first year of settlement. Boat-building and ship-building had already started near to Saltwater Bridge, while along the foreshore by the Haven Road track individuals had commenced erecting various jetties and walls from which to discharge the cargoes brought ashore by lighters from the immigrant ships

---

49 Now Richardson Street

anchored out beyond Green Point. Already construction had commenced or was being planned on some privately owned bond stores and a Company wharf at Green Point, and the unscrupulous immigration agent Johann Beit's wharf further around at the freshly developing Wakefield Quay. In the absence of an authority to co-ordinate or finance better structures, the waterfront would continue developing in this ad hoc way for years, while shipping would continue uninhibited.

Rumblings of Discontent

For the *Erin* crew, having spent the past year living amongst Maori in Massacre Bay, the conversations within the Salt Water Creek grog shop must have been rather disconcerting. It was just as well that the grog was cheap, as there were tales of poverty and hunger in the colony. The most recent five immigrant ships had arrived to the shocking news that there would be virtually no work for the labourers who had shipped out with their families on the understanding that there would be a guaranteed two year contract.

The finger of blame was not generally being directed at the New Zealand Company's resident local agent, Captain Arthur Wakefield, who was being seen to be doing his best to confront the downward spiralling set of circumstances as best as he could. It was the Company officials back in England, comfortably blinkered on their padded boardroom seats, who were primarily seen as being obdurate. But there was little to portend the impending violent deaths that Arthur Wakefield and several well-known Company men were shortly to meet, and the upheaval it would bring to the fledgling settlement.

Inside the noisy grog-shop, Captain Ralph and his crew listened in concern to the tale of how the town had run out of flour, forcing the settlers to resort to eating potatoes – many brought in by waka from the Maori kainga[50] in the district – as their staple instead of bread. Arthur Wakefield had chartered the barque *Brougham* to make the roaring forties passage to Valparaiso in Chile to purchase flour, but his funds were rapidly dwindling, and there would certainly be no repeat if food stocks ran out again. The settlement would simply have to become self-sufficient.

Undoubtedly Captains Sheridan and Ralph, in their turn, were being questioned about their own broader knowledge of the coasts and hinterland of the region. Imaginations will have been stirred at the potential of building and operating similar small hookers to their little schooners, *Eliza* and *Erin*.

There had already been snippets of encouraging information fed to the community after the surveyor expeditions to the west (Motueka and Riwaka valleys) and northwest (the recent Massacre Bay expedition of September 1842). However every man in the grogshop was painfully aware that the Company had not yet secured anywhere near the acreage of arable land that had been promised in its literature. The most recent news was the hoped-for breakthrough; news

---

50 Unfortified small Maori settlements

that might be able to bring productivity, prosperity and work to the struggling community. Hopes were now pinned on those same 'Wyroa Plains' that Blenkinscop had supposedly 'bought' for an eighteen pounder cannon ten years earlier – the vast freshly explored Wairau Valley to the east.

The desperate pressure for land

In order to understand the avoidable train of tragic events which were to unfold during the coming months, it is necessary to re-visit the basic principles and promises at the core of this colony's foundation. Nelson was supposed to be a compact settlement embodying all the 'best' of English class and culture, with its landed gentry and a goodly supply of workers, but it was not working.

As we have noted, during the first year, exploration parties had penetrated some distances inland and around the coast. They would never find anything to match the promise held out by Wakefield of an advantageous, compact settlement, and the arable land they did find satisfied just a quarter of the overall requirements of the scheme. Nelson was already suffering all the ills that had assailed the earlier

It seems preposterous that Colonel William Wakefield could have laid claim to such a huge portion of New Zealand, delineating the Provinces of North and South Durham from the diagonal line in the north to the horizontal line at the foot of this map titled **The New Zealand Land Company's Possessions** *(see top left). The labels have been superimposed on Cook's 1779 chart by Captain E M Chaffers of the Tory in 1839. There would be lasting consequences from this arrogant assertion.*

Bett collection 314836, Nelson Provincial Museum

Wellington settlement but this compulsion to find land continued to drive the immigrants. As a result the planned Nelson settlement, and consequently the hookers that serviced it, would eventually become a carelessly flung patchwork garment draped along the coasts from Massacre Bay almost to Kaikoura, with many patches unsold and many others unoccupied by their investor owners.

Absurdities and hollow assurances

I would say with some certainty that if *you* contemplated buying and farming in the isolation that 12,000 miles from home represented in 1841, you would take due diligence regarding land quality, and feasibility. Otherwise we would be buying a pig in a poke. In 1841 those assurances lay in the Company prospectus, in Edward Gibbon Wakefield's book, pamphlets, other writings and utterances. Those who knew better, put their own gain before others' pain and claimed that a better society would follow from ever-expanding settlement. *'Britain without its bad features'* was postulated to the wealthy potential investors, ignoring the fact that what the class system embedded in his scheme *was* one of Britain's worst features for the great majority of the deprived population, and was not sustainable in the colony long-term, any more than it had been in Britain.

Probably the oddest part of the scheme was a lottery conducted in London in 1841, before the first emigrant ships sailed, to determine the order of choosing the sections once they were properly surveyed and the buyers had arrived in Nelson. There was no 'first come, first served', as the lottery was introduced to lure speculators when it became apparent there was not sufficient investment in the new settlement. The lottery ensured that those on the spot could not control the location or quality of their land ahead of absentee investors and the actual event was an animated social occasion, a matter of drawing numbers from the lottery barrels. Each piece of scrip covered an allocation of land that was in fact three blocks of an acre, 50 acres and 150 acres respectively, representing a town acre, a country block and a farm block. It was an appallingly short-sighted system.

Alfred Saunders, a capitalist immigrant of the Fifeshire cohort, wrote, *"We came into possession of our town acres, but the number of my choice for a section was 954 out of 1,100, so that I had to take one far from the business part of town, and with no timber growing on it."*[51] In reality, the success or failure of the few capitalist investors actually on the spot would dictate the success or failure of the settlement as a whole, but in fact the last purchaser, whether resident or absentee, had as good a chance of prime sites as the first in order to encourage ongoing sales. It was a raffle with prizes for all and an equal chance for late investors to win especially attractive pieces of land. Having people labouring away in the settlement could only enhance everyone's land values, but as only about 40 percent of the scrip had sold and a great part of that was to non-emigrating speculators, the situation was ludicrous. A further draw was needed for the 60 percent of unsold scrip held up in the London lottery barrel, and a later emigrant purchaser would

---

51 Saunders, Alfred: Tales of a Pioneer, L M Isitt, 1927, p37

buy in London, come to Nelson with their scrip numbers and find the corresponding pieces of land they had been attached to, good, bad or indifferent. Those migrants would have been better advised to come to Nelson and exercise their own judgement in buying from what was on the market, but the Company had to have ongoing sales from the lottery barrel to keep the cash rolling in.

For the New Zealand Company and for Edward Gibbon Wakefield himself, the Nelson colony was their Waterloo. Wellington scrip had all sold within a month, but that wasn't so much a colonising market as a speculative one with over half the sales to absentee landowners, many of them Wakefield's friends and relatives. When the organisers thought to repeat the process at a higher land price for Nelson, they badly misjudged because the market was already saturated, but Company officials were not prepared to admit the failure of their scheme.

First Clashes with Maori

Two significant events led to clashes between Maori and Pakeha. The first was when Cook Strait Maori, at the entreaty of various people including missionary Samuel Ironside, turned over to white justice a white man who had violated a whaler's Maori wife then killed her and her infant at Cloudy Bay. The murderer was tried in Wellington and released without conviction, on a weak technicality. The colonists did not appreciate that Maori could also read their often intemperate and ill-considered newspaper articles and so knew what was going on in Pakeha minds. This perceived 'failure' as perceived by the land-hungry colonists was to be followed by another confrontation closer to Nelson – a kangaroo court in Massacre Bay.

No doubt the *Erin* crew would have already known of this stand-off over a Company land 'purchase' that had occurred at the Motupipi coal seam whilst they were still building their little hooker at Aorere, 12 miles further north-west.

Captain Arthur Wakefield had sailed to Massacre Bay in the 75-ton schooner *Elizabeth* in September 1842 with an odd mix of followers, including the young newspaper editor George Richardson. There was a perceived urgency about striking a land deal, for fear that if Maori recognised the economic value of the coal and other deposits they would inflate their asking price. He and the other company officers expected to cement their land acquisitions by following the well-trodden path, distributing what Ruth Allan described as 'the usual gifts of guns and gewgaws'[52] to resident Maori despite the **1840 Land Proclamation** that had been issued by the British Colonial Office in Auckland, banning such dealing until earlier purchases had been investigated. There was considerable doubt whether William Wakefield's original land purchase (made in Wellington's Port Nicholson) had included Massacre Bay.

The party met with Maori leaders at Taupo Pa and in the Takaka River valley, then went on to the Aorere aboard Jimmy Jackson's schooner *Nelson Packet*, distributing goods which were happily accepted by local Maori although both

---

52 Allan p222

parties knew that Land Commissioner William Spain would decide whether or not the Massacre Bay land purchases were legal. (Indeed, Spain later excluded most of Massacre Bay from the deal.)

Six months earlier *Nymph* had brought coal and limestone from Motupipi, creating heightened interest in Massacre Bay resources, and this encouraged a group of labourer immigrants to raise among themselves the small capital needed to start mining. The *Examiner* patronisingly called them "that class that provide the community with the important element of labour" and hoped they would be content to market their coal at "the lowest remunerative price[53].

The mining party left Nelson almost as soon as the 'deal' was struck, sailing on 8 October 1842 aboard the *Nelson Packet*, bound for Motupipi. They headed to the clear shore margin where the Maori pa and settlement straggled up the ridge on the east side of the river which forms the western margin of the peninsula-like higher ground. The more distant eastern side of the peninsula faces mudflats, and an outer sandbank to the north encloses it. (Nowadays the golf links is out in the easterly direction where the first settlement was established.) The locality would lift any resource developer's heart, then or now.

These miners were equipped to mine Motupipi coal, burn limestone and cut timber, with Company storekeeper J Howard acting as their agent, and it appears that they planned to use *Erin* regularly to bring coal to Nelson and other ports. Coal was in demand everywhere and Howard soon returned from Motupipi on *Nelson Packet* with the first shipment of coal and limestone. To their frustration, at this point point the activities were held up due to a stand-off with local Maori, who had quickly come to realise the value of the coal and limestone that was being taken from their land under their noses. Not unreasonably, they demanded a share in the trade but they were refused. Their response was to sabotage the equipment, in protest.

The confrontation that followed had ramifications which totally passed by the officials, immured as they were in the conviction that they were dealing with an inferior race which needed to be shown who was boss. Magistrate Thompson and Captain Wakefield, himself a justice of the peace, took J S Tytler and a team of 25 special constables armed with old muskets, cutlasses and a singular lack of judicial impartiality, climbed into a boat and went off on an illegal jaunt to teach the Maori a lesson.

The Motupipi chief Puakawa (also known as Ekawa) was spokesman for his people in that area. However his influence was limited, as he was effectively a vassal of the Ngatitoa warlord Te Rauparaha, having been subjugated by Te Rauparaha's allies during the recent intertribal Musket Wars in the region. Although he fulminated against Wakefield's advances into his territory, he was not in a strong position to push the issue. Thompson's party misunderstood the politics behind his apparent backing down. They swiftly set up an English court on the river bank a couple of miles up the Takaka River and put Ekawa on trial

---

[53] *Nelson Examiner* 8th October 1842

for malicious destruction of a lime kiln and casks of lime. After a forced arrest he was brought before the seated magistrates and had the galling experience of being lectured by an arrogant young English magistrate who was entirely ignorant of and unsympathetic to Maori mores. Ekawa was fined in cash a total of one pound, including costs. Payment in kind (potatoes perhaps) was unacceptable to the bench, but Ekawa's wife managed to find the sovereign.

This ill-prepared, arrogant group of Englishmen was lucky to have such an outcome, but "*More serious in the end was the 'ridiculous elation' of Thompson at the success of measures that he deemed just; for it led to his unwarrantable, ill-planned and worse executed interference with the natives at Wairau.*"[54] Crowing reports in the *Examiner* infuriated Maori and brought resentment far beyond the Cook Strait region, and while the way was now clear for regular shipments of Motupipi coal and burnt lime to Nelson and other ports there was a price yet to be paid, a rent woven into the fabric of settlement that would show itself in time. The newcomers had created a demand for their skills, and Blind Bay shipping took another step forwards. Race relations took a step backwards, and the stage was set for a far more appalling encounter elsewhere.

Celebrations, while clouds gather

Meanwhile in Nelson, the men off *Erin* were doubtless making the most of their return to a semblance of 'civilisation' after their months spent in relative isolation in Massacre Bay. They would have heard many conflicting accounts of settlement events, and observed that here in Nelson at the end of 1842, anything seen as positive was good news. The most significant ray of hope on a gloomy horizon was the report that Cotterell the surveyor, had discovered a viable 'Tophouse' route to those much-anticipated fertile plains of the Wairau Valley. Seizing control of these plains would be the solution to the dearth of 150-acre blocks to meet the London demand. Land acquisition was by now illegal under the terms of the Land Proclamation of January 1840, but Company officials were keen to forgo the niceties of title and get on with it. They and the magistrates and justices were confident that they had taught the Maori a lesson in Golden Bay and, having established settler authority, could freely move into the Wairau.

And so, by the New Year's celebrations for 1843, mixed moods prevailed. Those who were of a mind, and could afford to, no doubt imbibed and celebrated during this customary festival although there was a strong street corner temperance movement brought ashore from Alfred Saunders' shipboard enthusiasm on the immigrant ship *Fifeshire*. (Although he was only 21 years old Saunders became the movement's leading light, proselytising at meetings that added colour to the town and no doubt entertained the inebriated.) However, the unavoidable and depressing fact, which had to be faced by drunk and sober settlers alike, was that the Company was running down financially. The directors in England were issuing instructions for staff and labour retrenchment, while at

---

54 Chief surveyor, Frederick Tuckett, quoted in Allan, p227

the same time casting around for people to blame for the Company's self-induced woes.

The anniversary of the arrival of the first immigrant ship, *Fifeshire*, was another opportunity for celebration; too good to pass by even though she was merely a hulk on the rocks. An anniversary committee of gentlemen was formed, planning a celebration, involving settlers from both classes. After just a year Nelson's settlers existed in a contrasting range of situations; crouching for shelter in a tent or under a bush, coping within the four walls of a hut with or without basic food, or living in well-appointed homes with servants in attendance. As always, money was good insulation although the nuances of upper English society had suffered in the move to New Zealand and there were now, according to Nelson lawyer Alfred Fell, only two social classes.

In one of the key events, Nelson showed its maritime origins by holding a regatta, demonstrating that there were sufficient boats about to make it a worthwhile event. The first day of February 1843 dawned wet and blustery, but still three boats contested a whaleboat-rowing race, won by Gully's *Henrietta*. Next was a canoe race, then a sailing race around the island with five starters, including Frederick Moore's *Mary Ann*, but in the rough conditions only the Company pilot James Cross finished in his Deal Boat *Pilot*. There were other events and functions including a free tea, no doubt popular with the hungry

*James Cross won the first (1843) Nelson Anniversary sailing regatta in his Deal boat, seen here trailing behind an undecked schooner, likely to be Frederick Moore's lengthened ship's boat **Mary Ann**. The records mention five starters, so it is likely that the artist (it is attributed to Heaphy) has used a little artistic licence in this otherwise wonderfully detailed painting.*

Nelson Provincial Museum, Marsden Collection: NPM2009.144.14

unemployed, and a precedent was set for Anniversary Day regattas to be held for many years. Little did they know that this event would prove to be the last opportunity for celebration for some time.

Sales by Auction.

THE PILOT BOAT.

CONNELL & RIDINGS

Are instructed to Sell by Auction, at their Mart, Queen Street, THIS DAY, at 2 o'clock precisely, unless previously disposed of by private sale,

MR. CROSS'S WELL-KNOWN BOAT "PILOT,"

With Masts and Sails Complete, 2 Anchors, 2 Cables, 10 fathoms Chain Cable, 1 ton Iron Ballast, &c.

This fine Boat was built at Deal, under inspection, for the Pilot Service; measures 28 feet in length, her draught of water from 8 to 24 inches, and when used as a Cargo Boat her regular load is 77 sacks of Flour.

Feb. 19, 1850.

The DEAL BOATS were the New Zealand Company's workboats, remaining in the colony after the chartered ships departed taking their ships-boats with them. They were 28ft clinker un-decked load-carriers, designed as multi-use luggers capable of beach-launchings and built at Deal (opposite the Downs Roadstead and Goodwin Sands in east Kent). In Nelson they were put to use in a variety of functions, including lightering cargoes, towing timber rafts and transporting personnel including surveyors around the coastline. One became the Nelson Pilot boat, operated by James Cross for the first years of the Nelson colony.

Note from the advertisement that the draft increases by sixteen inches from a mere eight inches unladen with a full cargo.

Whaleboats similar to this rare photograph of the Nelson Pilot Boat (seen under tow with George Williams at the helm) were used, along with Deal Boats, to carry survey equipment from Nelson to the Wairau River via the Sounds and Cloudy Bay. She has a mast and sail aboard for a run home if the wind allows and the rowing thwarts are braced to the hull with 'natural bends' for strength. In August 1883 W Morrison, C Johansen, W Reader and R Thomas were lost when the pilot boat capsized in a dawn gale returning from **SS Wanaka**. *It was in open boats like these that a number of survivors of the Wairau confrontation were brought back to Nelson in the winter of 1843.*

Courtesy Rob Williams

NOTE: When I was old enough to be useful and accompany my father in the Nelson pilot boat in the late 1930s, I often saw men transferred from launch to ship or ship to launch, sometimes in bad weather, like the episode that John Kidson experienced from the heaving deck of the Government Brig Victoria in the following chapter. Even in a launch with a motor there was a fine skill in catching the right surge on the peak so that both vessels seemed stationary for that brief instant, which allowed a measured step on or off the Jacobs ladder hanging from the ship's side. ("Trim the dish!" was my father's admonition to keep us balanced on an even keel.) My father would allow the pilot to go only when he judged it timely and safe. I was fascinated by the seagoing protocol; my father was answerable to the harbourmaster-pilot yet aboard the launch he was master, and I saw him insist the pilot wait until cleared to go safely.

6

The Winter of Discontent

THE MAN AT THE HELM of the faltering Nelson colony, Captain Arthur Wakefield, was between a rock and a hard place, and the settlement's defining moment was now at hand. The winter of 1843 was shaping up to be rough in Cook Strait, but things were soon to get much rougher and, like a storm hundreds of miles off, other waves would break on this distant shore. The storm's genesis was in England where the hot air of opportunistic economic jargon was meeting counter-currents of cold reality.

One eddy within that hot air was the Company's arrogant attitude to prior Maori occupation. Maori were not being portrayed as the warriors, farmers, poets and orators which they actually were. In the new Wellington colony just across Cook's Strait, the Resident Agent William Wakefield had echoed his brother's assertion that Maori longed for Europeans to come and civilise them and would gladly give away their lands in return. Even after the tragic events which were to unfold during the coming winter it was reported that "… *the native race was physically, organically, intellectually and morally far inferior to the European, incapable of refinement by education*"[55]. Magistrate Thompson was sure he had demonstrated this at Motupipi and even the intelligent and energetic Frederick Weld said, "… *the arrogance of some chiefs needed a sound thrashing as a cure.*"[56]

The cold hard realities within the colony were a complex mix. Most obvious was the fact that the Company funds allocated to Nelson had nearly dried up. Then were the widely different demands of two distinct pressure groups busily lobbying Captain Arthur Wakefield in his Nelson 'office'. At one end of the spectrum were the growing numbers of labourers who had arrived to find their employment guarantees had come to nothing, and they had no redress. They were now vociferously seeking compensation from the nearly empty coffers.

Meanwhile the more powerful moneyed class of landholder settlers had closed ranks and formed a lobby-group which became known as the *Supper Party*. Despite being smaller in number, they were substantially larger in influence, given the privileges of their class. Their frustration at the absurdities of the lottery allocation system had now reached boiling point. Only 4% of the 200 allotments that had been reserved for sale to colonials had been sold, and the London Company directors had instructed Captain Wakefield to put them into another random lottery drawn in Wellington. Not unreasonably, the Supper Party landholders thought they should have first rights over any non-resident

---

55 *The Nelson Examiner*, 6 July 1844
56 Burns, p280

speculators, and in April 1943, 44 resident landowners protested in writing to the Company about the gross preponderance of landless labourers in the settlement and the disadvantageous system of speculator land sales. Magistrate Thompson was the first to sign the petition, an indication of the powerful influence of this group.

Sensibly, Captain Wakefield saw an opportunity to appease both of his settler lobby groups by defying the London instructions. So instead he decided to sell them at auction, reserving some for subdivision and subsequent sale to labourers. Even with this compromise, sales were disappointingly slow.

With the festering backdrop of all these problems, including the Company's negative relationship with Maori who already occupied the land on the Wairau Plain that Cotterell had 'discovered' and Tuckett confirmed, Captain Wakefield now perceived an urgent need for definitive action. Back in London the Company didn't want to know.

Blundering into the Wairau

The Wairau beckoned, but Captain Arthur Wakefield seriously under-estimated the adamance of Ngati Toa leaders that these fertile plains had nothing to do with the Whakatu land of Blind Bay that they had sold to Colonel William Wakefield in 1840. The two paramount leaders, Te Rauparaha and Te Rangihaeata had even recently crossed Cook Strait to visit the Nelson Company officials and press home the correctness of their position. It is astounding that such a significant visit was totally ignored by the Nelson newspaper at the time[57]. Such was the power that the Company wielded over the colony's media that the *Nelson Examiner* simply continued to publish the viewpoint that Maori were being unreasonable.

Adding to the uncertainties, three Land Claims Commissioners had been appointed by the British Colonial Office in London during the previous year, to clarify the validity of a plethora of conflicting supposed land purchases throughout New Zealand during the previous decade. One critical figure was the lawyer William Spain, who was especially charged with investigating the New Zealand Company claims. Te Rauparaha waited with confidence for Commissioner Spain's likely judgement that purchases by William Wakefield had not included the Wairau.

In England the Company persisted in arguing the strength of its land title and, despite the fact that the Treaty of Waitangi formally recognised Maori property rights and citizenship leaving no doubt that the chiefs were in the right, Company chairman Joseph Somes wrote to Lord Stanley on 24 January 1843 ridiculing this ground-breaking Treaty "... *as but a praiseworthy device for amusing and pacifying savages*"[58].

The perception of Maori as simple savages, not uncommon among frustrated colonists, could not have been more naïve. Throughout New Zealand, Maori

---

57 Judge Broad commented in his history of Nelson that it was 'somewhat remarkable' that the chiefs' visits were not reported in the *Examiner*.
58 Burns, p247

were rapidly seizing any opportunity to become literate, and to adapt technology for commercial use. Ngatitoa leaders were well aware of what was being written in Company newspapers, and what legal redress they were due from Commissioner Spain's Land ownership ruling.

The Ngati Toa iwi were fiercely loyal to their leadership. Te Rauparaha was an intelligent strategist, while Te Rangihaeata had a reputation for ferociousness. Armed with an arsenal of muskets, they had fought their way south from Kawhia during the previous two decades, gathering a confederation of allied tribes along the way. Once established on the near-impregnable Kapiti Island, they and their bands of warriors including the Ngati Tama, Ngati Awa and Ngati Rarua had decimated and subjugated the Rangitane peoples of the Wairau and Marlborough Sounds as well as the Ngati Kuia nearer Nelson.

Against this backdrop of conflicting pressures, barely eighteen months after arriving in Nelson Haven and with the overland Tophouse route to Wairau confirmed, Captain Arthur Wakefield wasted no time in sending surveyors to examine the district. Shortly afterwards, and without any land sale agreements, contracts were let for the cutting of survey lines. Despite strong Maori objections, three survey parties left Nelson in late May by sea for the Wairau.

Open boat passages to the Wairau River

Whalers handled daunting weather in their relatively slight whaleboats as a matter of course, just as the Company colonists earned a seagoing reputation in their Deal boats. After Cotterell and his party discovered the way in to the Wairau valley via Tophouse in November 1842, they had worked their way overland to Cloudy Bay and subsequently returned to Nelson by whaleboat chartered from a Cloudy Bay shore whaling station. The Deal boats, and possibly the *Enterprise*, took up the task of conveying the surveying staff to the Wairau.

There was a matter-of-fact acceptance of such extended coastal trips in open pulling and sailing boats, which commonly used the waters of Cook Strait and Blind Bay, the Sounds, French Pass and d'Urville Island. It called for seamanship of a high order to handle the boats in often marginal and sometimes extreme conditions and to know when, where, and how to take shelter. The expression 'a freak wave', common when small boats get into difficulties today, would have cut little ice then. Wind against tide produced forces well known to men of experience and they watched for the unexpected. When circumstances demanded, they operated in conditions where the men would be cold, wet and hard-put to keep anything dry or indeed to stay afloat at times. When they got to calmer waters they would either have to get ashore and make shelter or rest in the open boat.

The first voyages to the Wairau were undertaken in May, at the start of winter. John Kidson, (my boatman ancestor), said; "*I left Nelson in the New Zealand Company's boat on the 27th of May, to go to the Wairau with Mr Tuckett, the chief surveyor, and was eight days on our passage.*"[59] In the course of their work on

---

59 *The Nelson Examiner*, Wairau Supplement, 24 December 1843

the Wairau plains they were obstructed by militant local Maori, who pulled out their pegs and burned their temporary Raupo huts, forcing them to abandon their task and return to Nelson. John Kidson's Deal boat was nearly back in Nelson when it was hailed from the deck of the brig *Victoria* off the Boulder Bank, sailing northward: *"We had a fine run, but met the Government brig off Wakapuaka, and were ordered alongside of her. We now learned that a warrant had been issued against the two chiefs, and Mr Thompson, the police magistrate, and a number of constables, were going to take them. We were ordered to accompany them [taking the boat under tow], which I did very unwillingly, as I wanted to see my wife and children ...*

"When we got to the Straits, it blew pretty stiff. Our crew was ordered into the boat, and told to make the best of our way to Cloudy Bay, and there wait until we heard from the brig. We made the Sound that night, and Cloudy Bay the following day, the wind blowing very heavy all the time. Some whalers informed us that the brig was at the mouth of the Wairau, for which we then started, and at night (Friday) got up the river as far as the grove of pine trees, where we found our party ...

"Captain Wakefield appeared very glad to see us; we were told he had been afraid that we were lost."

They would have been cast off in the Strait because their boat was being towed by the government brig *Victoria* and was in danger of swamping or impeding her. 'Ordered into the boat' meant jumping in rough seas from a heaving deck into the Deal boat, which was probably already half swamped, and the boat's crew would be in a risky situation. They had to get steerage way on the boat before she was overwhelmed, and then watch the brig draw away in a welter of waves leaving them to cope with the storm as best they could.

War party

For the unwitting John Kidson, having his Deal boat turned back – when so close to home – was the beginning of a shocking ordeal. The posse he had been ordered to assist at the Wairau was both ill-conceived and ill-prepared. Spurred by anti-Maori sentiments published in the Nelson newspaper[61] exhorting *"a salutary mission to end native outrages"* and reminding readers of the successfully quelled *"little outbreak at Massacre Bay"*, the plan was to arrest Te Rauparaha and Te Rangihaeata, teaching them a lesson similar to the recent arrest and conviction dealt to Puakawa at Motupipi. These two Ngati Toa chiefs were the pair who had very recently been responsible for evicting the surveyors and burning their temporary shelters (taking care to protect their personal property and provisions to avoid accusations of theft), so the charge would be arson. It conveniently ignored the fact that all materials for these raupo huts, as Te Rauparaha pointed out, had been made from Maori materials on Maori land.

There were 49 men in the posse, led by Chief Constable Henry Thompson along with Captain Arthur Wakefield and Justice England. The ill-armed force was supplemented by several hapless constables and about twenty unwilling and

---

61 *Examiner*, June 1843

inexperienced men coerced from a road gang, under threat of losing their employment. Some had their own fowling pieces, others were equipped with "defective muskets and rusty cutlasses, which had been purchased by a Nelson merchant for a mere song"[62]. They were augmented by the three Company survey parties and a number of gentlemen 'along for a lark'.

Most of the ill-fated party were between their mid-20s and 40s, beyond the age of impetuosity, and many were married with children. As well as the militants in the settlement there were those with misgivings because warnings had come from missionary Samuel Ironside and others who had intimate knowledge of the dangerously determined Maori resistance that the magistrate and Company were pitting themselves against. The labourers in particular felt ill-used. They owed no loyalty to the Company that had cheated them, certainly not their lives.

Some of the Nelson capitalist settlers also had misgivings about Arthur Wakefield's judgement. Alfred Saunders later wrote: "*I had been asked to join the ill-fated expedition, and had, without a moment's hesitation, absolutely refused to do so. I had two very strong reasons for this refusal. Firstly, although I knew Captain Wakefield to be a man possessed of exceptionally large physical courage, I had not entire confidence in his justice or discretion as the leader of such an expedition; and I had less in that of the terribly excitable police magistrate who accompanied him; and, secondly, I thought it was reckless folly to imagine that exceptionally brave and intelligent men, as the Maoris [sic] were admitted to be, would be overawed by a vastly inferior force, armed with weapons that were well-known to be defective.*"[63]

Saunders had hit the nail on the head. The Ngati Toa warriors were battle-hardened men immune to qualms about loss of human life after decades of inter-tribal warfare. Few, if any, of the settler posse had ever fired a musket in anger.

For whatsoever a man soweth, that shall he also reap

On his arrival at the mouth of the Wairau River in the Company Deal Boat, John Kidson was ordered to assist *Victoria*'s boats in ferrying the posse up the Wairau River to spend the night at the Big Bush (now Grovetown). The next day on 17 June 1843, almost mid-winter, the entire party marched up the surveyors' track alongside the Tuamarina tributary. Death marched with them.

They were to confront two of New Zealand's foremost warrior chiefs, backed by over a hundred of their trained and armed warriors along with a hapu of women and children, defending their own land. Predictably, the meeting went horribly wrong. Instead of acknowledging the mana of the chiefs, they faced off on either side of the stream while Chief Constable Thompson crossed on a makeshift canoe-bridge and made two unsuccessful attempts to place handcuffs on Te Rauparaha – an extreme insult to this high chief's mana, and a violation of his personal tapu. Then someone in that jittery and inexperienced Nelson posse fired a shot.

---

62 Saunders p47
63 Saunders *p46*

In the deadly fusillade which followed, Te Rangihaeata's wife Te Ronga (a daughter of Te Rauparaha), was killed along with three others, and more were wounded. Eyewitness reports differ but it is clear that the warriors retaliated swiftly, and thirteen settlers were shot or fatally wounded. Captain Wakefield and some of his party retreated up the hill where he told them to surrender. This group of nine prisoners, including himself and Henry Thompson, were subsequently executed where they stood, their deaths ensured through his ignorance of Maori codes of warfare. The remaining twenty-seven fled.

In his subsequent assessment of the incident, Alfred Saunders assigned political groupings to party members: *"Then the call came to surrender, Richard Painter shouted not to keep in a heap for the Maoris to shoot at, but to climb the hill ... it soon divided the leaderless men into surrendering **Royalists** and retreating protesting **Independents** – every man of the former to die without resistance, the latter to make a desperate, but generally successful struggle for life ..."*[64]

Standing on that hillside, the final realisation for the settlers facing execution must have been bitter. They were not dying for their beliefs, but for the misguided beliefs of others who had put them in that situation. Nor did death defer to English distinctions of class. Predictably, and in accord with Maori protocol in such affairs (and despite initial reservations from Te Rauparaha), the choice was Rangihaeata's and he summarily split their skulls open with his *mere* as 'utu' for the loss of his wife. He had his own beliefs and principles, had the newcomers bothered to find them out.

John Kidson, was one of the so-called 'independents', having been drawn into this affray purely through his position as a boatman, He must have been in a state of horrified shock, later recounting that he had *"... told Mr Thompson and Captain Wakefield that I thought the Maories would massacre all they caught, and begged them to make their escape. I also told them I would not surrender as long as I could run ... I was pursued ..."*[65] He was one of the 27 settlers who escaped, including the surveyors Tuckett and Barnicoat.

The aftermath

Frederick Maning in his first-hand account of living with pre-colonial Maori, describes how in traditional battles, the fastest running warrior would be sent to overtake the retreating vanquished warriors, crippling them with a single blow, to be slaughtered by the follow-up runner[66]. Fortunately for the fleeing settlers, Te Rangihaeata's demands for 'utu' had been sated; however their flight to safety at Cloudy Bay must have been a fraught experience, constantly fearful of further violence.

John Kidson's escape route took him to the Mission station in Port Underwood, where he and four others sought safety under the wing of the

---

64 Saunders p49
65 *Examiner 24 December 1843*
66 Maning, Frederick, p188, Old New Zealand, Creighton and Scales, 1863

influential Samuel Ironside. Others took different routes, some making it safely aboard the Government brig and thence to Wellington, and the remainder fleeing to one of the Cloudy Bay whaling stations, to be taken back to Nelson aboard open whaleboats. For Kidson, being obliged to return to the scene of the confrontation with Ironside to bury the dead must have been an awful experience, but at least may have allayed fears that his life was still in danger. From there, he and his four companions made the difficult decision to return to Nelson overland via the new route up the Wairau valley and through Tophouse. Their journey took eleven days and they were sustained on their way by only 21 pounds of biscuit and eight pounds of pork. Ill-equipped and ill-fed in that bad winter weather, they were found nearly starving by a search party a day's journey from Nelson.

This crude fence marked the 1843 gravesite where John Kidson helped Rev Samuel Ironside lay to rest the 22 Nelson settlers killed at Tuamarina in the confrontation over possession of the fertile Wairau Plains.
Watercolour by Charles Emilius Gold, Ref A-329-014 Alexander Turnbull Library

The burial site and the monument on the hill is worthy of a reflective visit. You can see the small area which contained the conflict, and its proximity to the river and Cloudy Bay. You can look out, too, at the area that was to be hooker territory in just a few more years. The monument at Tuamarina preserves the niceties of class even in death, awarding more space and detail to the 'gentlemen' with a double column of names of the men of lower stature. Ellen Petrie, wife of the young Hon Henry Petrie and daughter-in-law of a New Zealand Company director, was in Wellington at the time and she noted in her diary that "... *there*

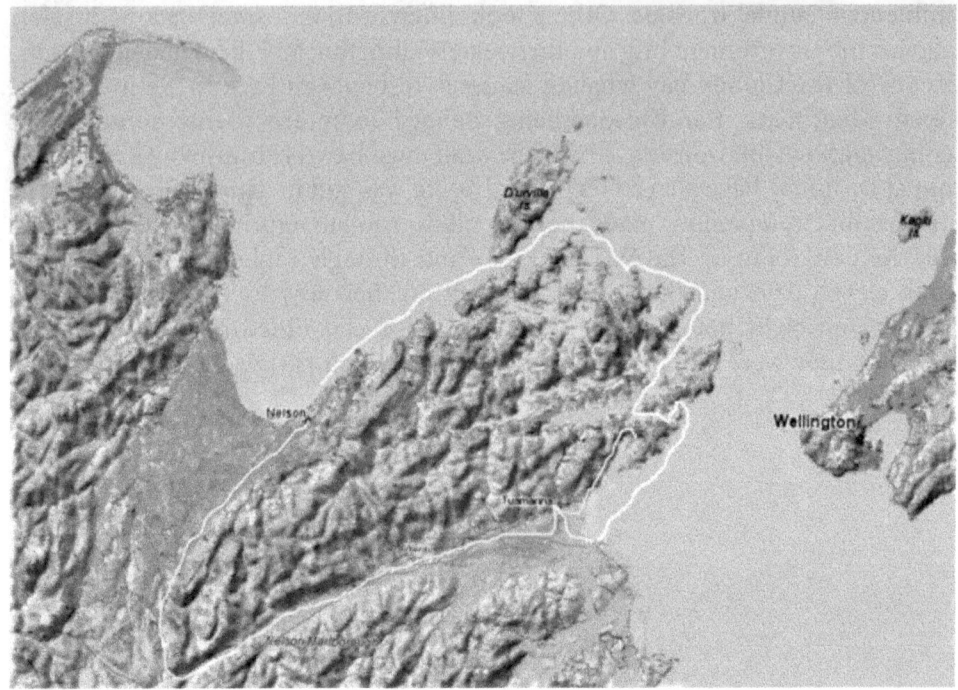

John Kidson was unwittingly drawn into the terrifying events of the Wairau confrontation, by virtue of his position aboard the Company Deal Boat. This map traces the likely track of his three week ordeal, by open boat and overland trek with little food.

were 19 killed unfortunately all the gentlemen of the party"[67]. The gentlemen had chosen to be there; the other men had no choice and the landholding surveyors in the party occupied a shadow zone between the two.

My personal connection remains too. My mother Ruby Westrupp, (née Ward), was born at the beginning of the 20th century and grew up in the Brook Street home of her grandparents John and Amelia Ward. Amelia was John Kidson's daughter and was four years old at the time of the Wairau incident, which affected her father for the rest of his life and was still spoken of in my mother's household. In such manner are past and present connected across multiple generations.

A badly shaken settlement

Nelson was appalled and fearful. The garrison on Church Hill was fortified against attack and some people even left the settlement, but the *Examiner* newspaper and supporters were as extravagant in self-justification as earlier they were partisan in advocacy for the land purchases. They blamed everyone, especially those who escaped, although not a single judicial body could find Thompson's action lawful. Even the most vehement must have realised it was also most foolhardy. Te Rangihaeata's response was deplored and the aftermath of the incident

---

67   Ell, Sarah (ed), p86 *The Lives of Pioneer Women in New Zealand*, Bush Press, 1993

included plenty of sabre-rattling from those who had not been there on that hill at Tuamarina.

Some finger-pointing was directed at Governor Hobson too, for his refusal two years earlier to allow the Nelson settlement to be located at Port Cooper (now Christchurch) with the vast Canterbury plains as a hinterland to be carved up. Wakefield's biographer's Philip Temple commented that "… *the land problem and the circumstances that led to the disaster at the Wairau can be sheeted directly to Hobson's obstinacy and William Wakefield's procrastination … There would have been no Wairau if Hobson had allowed Nelson to be established on the Port Cooper plains. There would have been no Wairau if William Wakefield had not deliberately obstructed the settlements of the Spain Land Commission.*"[68] In fairness to Hobson though, he was appointed Governor to look after Maori interests, too late to forestall William Wakefield's hasty initial purchase as soon as the Tory had arrived in Port Nicholson. Thus the seeds of disaster were already sown.

Besides, Governor Hobson had died of a stroke, aged only 39, nine months before this confrontation, and his humanist-aligned replacement Robert Fitzroy (captain of Darwin's *Beagle* voyage) was on his way from England to replace him. Fitzroy arrived in Wellington eight months after the event, to meet with Te Rauparaha at Porirua and listen to Missionary Ironside's balanced account of the incident. Ironside was delighted with the outcome : "*His Excellency represented to him [Te Rauparaha] the evil of his conduct etc, but has acted wisely in looking over this offence in as much as they were not the first to blame.*"[69]

The Deal boat that Kidson sailed aboard was a sister-ship to this lugger pictured at the lifeboat slipway in Kent, where she originated. Note the extraordinarily long boomkin used for sheeting the lug mizzen. James Cross also owned one which he used as the Nelson pilot boat until 1850, when he was called upon to take up pilot duties in Auckland.
Kentish Gazette 20-021876 Dover-Kent archives

---

68 *The Nelson Mail*, 8 August 2003
69 Letters of Samuel Ironside, 27 Feb 1844

Not unexpectedly the *New Zealand Gazette* raged against his "one-sided" judgement as "… *blackening the memories of the Wairau Massacre and palliating the guilt of the murderers … that they may with impunity annoy, plunder and harass the settlers …*"[70]

Such is the swing of the pendulum of public perception over generations of debate, that the affray which in my childhood was talked of as *The Wairau Massacre*, has in recent years been re-labelled the *Wairau Incident*, in acknowledgement that there were two sides to this unfortunate episode. For John Kidson however, the horror remained thoughout his remaining years.

This inscription was written into the bible given to Samuel Ironside by William Young (NZ Company Agent) in recognition for his insistence on making haste to the scene to ensure that the victims had a Christian burial. He had visited both chiefs immediately to let them know his intentions, later writing that Te Rangihaeata had said : "Better leave them to the wild pigs. But you can go if you like."

For John Kidson and his companions, the experience must have been shattering.

Samuel Ironside in NZ, p159

The homely appearance seen in this simple sketch of Ironside's mission house must have been a welcome sight for the horror-stricken survivors in Kidson's party.

Samuel Ironside in New Zealand, p 156

---

70 *NZ Gazette*, 28 Sept 1844

7

The Colony Mis-Stays

A STATE OF PARALYSED SHOCK descended on Nelson after the Wairau debacle. The land shortage, that the Wairau land-grab was expected to remedy, was a continuing issue so now the capitalists delayed further activity until they could see which way the wind blew. It was an uncomfortable time. A few more sensible landowners and the surveyors braved the animosity of the *Examiner's* drumbeaters to point out the facts. The workers were ambivalent – they owed the Company little, and saw their now-dead companions, who had been co-opted into the Wairau party, as unwilling sacrifices. This depressed state deepened the effects of the Company's misdirection.

The term 'missing stays' is a common one in the sailing terminology of this book, especially when ships were lost, and is a perfect analogy for Nelson by its third year of settlement. A sailing vessel beating its way up-wind progresses in a zigzag manner by turning into the wind or *tacking*. First the wind is on one side of the sails, with the helm over to turn her head into it, then a new course is set at about 90 degrees to the last so the wind is on the other side. The ship needs to be actively sailed around and there's more boatmanship involved than just pushing the helm over. When a ship floated high, with little cargo or ballast, it became crankier and made more leeway. To get through the *eye of the wind* required careful sail handling at just the right time or the ship would fall away again on the same tack, in which case it had *missed stays*.

Heavy winds and seas added to the problem. If she drifted astern, stalled head to wind and didn't want to come out of it, she was *in irons*, a term probably derived from the chains or fetters of convicts and miscreants. The helm would be useless until she regained sufficient momentum, either going ahead or drifting astern, for the moving water to act as a force on the rudder. Some hookers were more prone than others to such behaviour.

What to do? The vessel is out of control and needs sea room. You may 'wear ship' by circling the bow down-wind and gybing the sails over, if it can be done in a controlled fashion as the wind passes from one side to the other astern, but this raises its own problems of loss of control and potential damage. Some hookers were troublesome to go through a tack (or *go about*) even in good weather and for this sort of handling, especially when undermanned, any skipper would feel the strain of working a difficult ship in a tight corner. The experience would be alarming, especially when heavy weather, wind and seas prevented him getting his ship up into the wind at all or caused her to fall off again on to the same tack.

On some occasions, a 'handy ship' might be deliberately manoevred into irons; handy because in such a situation it would be necessary to get control of

Camellia *can be seen here in danger of missing stays as she prepares to tack just outside the pilot station slipway in a very light nor-westerly seabreeze. Captain Henry Young is attempting to push the stern around by backing the mizzen, while his crew is on the foredeck preparing to haul the staysail to leeward to assist the bow around as soon as she comes head to wind.*
Tyree collection 10x8-0486-G, Alexander Turnbull Library

her again quickly by setting or maybe backing either a headsail or mizzen to swing her head into the necessary direction and so pick up the wind again. It was a manoevre that might be used to exploit the strong tidal flow in the Nelson entrance, but was definitely unwise to attempt on an ebbing tide. The wreck of *Fifeshire* was a long-present reminder of the hazards when reefs and rock awaited.

I have a vivid personal boyhood memory of the horror of missing stays, a hundred years after Nelson was settled. I found myself daring Nelson Haven in a fierce northerly. My vessel was an ungainly borrowed eight-footer modelled on a P-class (oversized, bulkier and considerably less handy than my mate Gordon Nalder's seven-foot P-class). We had picked a sheltered way up wind in the lee of the wharf when a group of watersiders we knew challenged us to leave the relatively manageable water and race out around a harbour buoy in the wild brunt of it. To avoid capsizing I had to spill a lot of wind from the sail which, with the steep and broken water constantly striking my ungainly Topa left me short of angle and momentum to get about. I made several attempts and was mis-stayed before I managed to edge about with just enough way on to avoid capsizing. Missing stays was alarming but to rise to the challenge from our spectators on the wharf, we did the leg out to the buoy again.

A settlement in danger of capsize

Missed stays was an ideal metaphor for Nelson in 1843. The settlement had lacked a cautious helmsman and a small group of people had grabbed at the tiller to give it a good shove and change direction regardless of which way the wind was blowing. The Nelson establishment had naively thought brute force could prevail at Wairau, and had not read the signs accurately.

After the settlement's leader Captain Arthur Wakefield was killed at Tuamarina, the Company surveyor Frederick Tuckett succeeded him for a short time until William Fox became the New Zealand Company's Nelson agent on 15 September 1843. Tuckett had sensible ideas for settling the workers on land, but the Company rejected them, and he faced uncontrolled insubordination from an element in the settlement intent on causing trouble. He was pleased to withdraw from what became an impossible situation.

The immigrant ship *St Pauli* with her German passengers arrived in Nelson the day after the Wairau incident. The immigration agent who accompanied them, Johann Beit, had ruthlessly exploited and cheated them from when they first boarded their ship. After ongoing difficulties when he refused to meet his obligations to the new immigrants the New Zealand Company allowed them to occupy a few flood-prone accommodation sections at Upper Moutere in return for work on the roads. After a period of trials and a relocation to Sarau, the German immigrants became respected and valued members of the community.

Exodus across the Tasman

When the Company had repudiated its work contracts, 50 of the British artisans abandoned Nelson by chartering a ship and going to Tasmania. Now 60 of the Germans left for South Australia. Such an exodus did not suit the capitalist settlers, some of whom could not or would not employ labourers at that time, but still wanted them to be available when they would eventually receive their 150-acre rural blocks.

By October 1843, the overall Nelson area had an immigrant population of just over 3,000 men, women and children. About 900 were working men: over a third were agricultural labourers, there were about 270 artisans of various sorts and 80-odd farmers, and the rest were in commerce and professions. The workers lacked assets, employment and finally even the minimal wage paid out for roadwork. Men who had tasted the freedom of a new beginning would no longer accept exploitation and carried their protests further than some landowners found comfortable, expressing their dissatisfaction in various ways until many landowners, feeling their positions threatened, petitioned Auckland for the governor to send troops to put the men in their place. On the other hand there were landowners who discerned no risk. They too had been ill used by the dupes of the Company, and sympathised with the dissatisfied labourers.

The boatbuilder William Pratt, who was obliged to work as a labourer due to the depressed shipwright trade during these difficult months, wrote of his experiences in a road gang whose appointed overseer was the land-speculator (and former music teacher) Philip Valle. Valle was a dandy who was seriously miscast as a manager of rebellious men. He made his rather comical first appearance in a pair of long boots and an eyeglass. "... *the first symptom of insubordination was by one of the men coolly surveying him in true theatrical fashion through a piece of flax, twisted up in the form of an eye-glass, and as this marked attention was not fully appreciated, but on the contrary provoked some threatening language, a number of men immediately began to display great activity in tying flax together to form a rope ...*"[71]

The upshot was that Mr Valle beat a hasty retreat and finished up in a six-foot ditch of very dirty water, to the amusement of his gang. "*He was very quickly extricated, however, and after being tenderly tilted, to empty the water from his long boots, was permitted to quietly retire, with very dampened spirits from his moist reception.*"

Road gangs like this one working near the Basin (on Rocks Road) involved hard manual labour with picks, shovels and barrows. Small workboats and punts (like the well-known **Sudden Jerk** *pictured here) like these were an important part of the operation.*
Tyree Collection G-235 10x8, Alexander Turnbull Library, Wgtn

Valle was not only a salaried Company officer but had by a very curious 'coincidence' been able to purchase three adjacent sections at Waimea West which he immediately offered for sale or rent, having no intention of farming them. He soon returned to London where he claimed, and got, compensation from the Company for the land he had abandoned. By this stage Edward Wakefield was very chary of adverse publicity.

---

71 Pratt, p61

Appeals to the Governor

It was ironical that the government in Auckland, which had been ignored and even derided by Company officials until now, was called upon to meet Company and settler demands. When William Fox succeeded Tuckett as Company agent in Nelson, he was so alarmed at the unrest among disgruntled and disillusioned labourer immigrants that he resorted to a heavy-handed stance, requesting Governor FitzRoy in Auckland for troops. Fitzroy, a humanitarian official new to the job with more serious problems in the north to deal with, had little sympathy, sending a small military contingent too late (no doubt deliberately) in February 1844. By this time the Company had effectively failed and further protest by Fox was useless.

Fox's frustrations with government officials continued to mount for a host of reasons, not least that land commissioner William Spain was proving painstakingly slow in his deliberations. Spain did not get to Nelson until August 1844 to hold the land court, which even then did not investigate the Wairau at all. In fact there was tacit avoidance of the Wairau and for the following four years the hiatus was a burning frustration for Nelson settlers waiting for their rural land. Commissioner Spain did not uphold the Company's purchase and Nelson still didn't have its 150-acre blocks. The option of consolidating in Nelson by redistributing the unused land to the few resident landowners did not suit the Company.

At this point Nelson settlement had been reshaped forever. There were many adjustments to make, but the immigrants had no option other than to make it work. After all they were not just 'capitalists' and 'labourers' but an eclectic mix of professions and trades, of attitudes and abilities. Artisan John Perry Robinson stood out for his level-headedness and leadership, later becoming the provincial superintendent, but 50 years later his constructive part in the settlement was still ignored by some sectors.

People who were prepared to 'make a go of it' were getting about their business, as in its small way the story of *Moonraker*'s unusual launching shows.

The building of *Moonraker*

Ambrose and Elizabeth Ricketts had arrived aboard the *Bolton* and were now settled in Nelson, where their first child was born. Ambrose was a wheelwright who took up boatbuilding early, and may have put in some sea-time too. Ambrose and his family were closely connected with the whole hooker era and one of the more positive events of the early 1840s was the building and launching, in February 1844, of *Moonraker*. She sounds more the style of a ship's boat, being clinker built, as were *Erin* and Jimmy Jackson's *Nelson Packet* among others. Moonraker was built by Ambrose Ricketts and Henry Parnell at an unlikely location significantly inshore from the waterfront. She was a modest sized new hooker – an 11-ton, 29ft cutter with a square stern, later changed to ketch rig with a running bowsprit. William Jennings, a baker who was a *Mary Ann* immigrant, was a part owner. Merchants, storekeepers and other businessmen often invested in shipping and such interests helped to fund the industry.

The story behind this little ship's name is delightfully tied up with the Ricketts' family history, coming from Wiltshire with a well-established reputation as smugglers who had successfully tricked the excise men. Their booty was hidden in a pond and on an occasion when the excise men came upon them there with rakes at night, they pretended to simple-mindedness in trying to rake the moon's full reflection from the pond. The excise men thought them foolish and went off laughing and the name 'moon rakers' stuck. It was a kindly choice of name for a new boat in a new land, when the family roots were still in the old country.

Saltwater Creek had already seen other boats launched into it, in 1842 and 1843, but *Moonraker*'s launching was an innovation for the place and time. "A cutter, of about 15 tons, built at the end of Nile Street East, was wheeled down to the Haven Road bridge on Wednesday last, and there launched."[72]

Ambrose, as a wheelwright, would have found such a solution practical but it is tantalising not to have details. He lived at 'Little Sydney' towards the Maitai River and built his hooker adjacent to there at what is now Nile Street East, and her timbers probably came from 'The Wood' over the Maitai. *Moonraker* would have traversed Bridge Street to reach Saltwater Creek near the town end of Haven Road. The bridge, under which both dinghies and canoes could pass when there was sufficient tide, was adjacent to the hotel. The portion of Haven Road over on the town side is a short diagonal stroll to lower Bridge Street, and originally was a causeway on the margin with the sea. There would have been a number of suitable launching places on the sloping bank near the bridge.

In more recent years I had occasion to stop in traffic at the Saltwater bridge roundabout, and assist an elderly driver who had stalled, while traffic steadily backed up out of sight towards Bridge Street. In best pointsman style I stopped the incoming cars to clear the flummoxed driver's way up Halifax Street. Somewhere there, Moonraker rolled by on her wooden wheels all those years ago. Wouldn't my traffic have stared had we seen that 29ft cutter, with a bunch of cheerful and animated men and children and perhaps a horse or bullock team pulling her along? I hope we would all have stopped and cheered her and her builders.

Hooker-building in the earliest years

Despite the social and economic constraints of the first couple of years, by 1843 while *Moonraker* was being built in Nile Street there were at least three other hookers under construction on the waterfront along the Saltwater Creek and Auckland Point end of Haven Road. One was the nine-ton cutter *Enterprise*, a very early Blind Bay hooker which Cotterell advertised for a voyage to the Wairau. Another two vessels were built by George Edwards, a 45-year-old shipwright immigrant who paid his way on the *Indus* in 1842. The *Hydrus*, an 11-

---

72 The *Nelson Examiner*, 24 Feb 1844, p408. *Moonraker* has leapt to 15 tons here, but newspaper shipping reports were often inaccurate.

ton kahikatea lugger, was built on the waterfront by shipwright Thomas Freeman who arrived on the *London* in 1842.

There is a tale to *Hydrus*. She was built for W Claringbold, who came out on the *Will Watch* as one of the Deal boatmen and became assistant pilot at Nelson. *Hydrus* worked out of Nelson for a time and her cargoes included lime produced at a small works at Enner Glynn. It was probably loaded at what is now the end of Quarantine or Parkers Road, for use on those Waimea farms that could be approached by water. Because of the Company land debacle there were not more than half a dozen farms in the Waimea in the year or more after the settlement was founded. Claringbold eventually sold *Hydrus* but then instead of handing her over, skipped port and sailed her up the east coast of the North Island to Auckland where the law caught up with him. He was put behind bars but, according to the Examiner, was acquitted of felony some months later.[73] As for *Hydrus*, her kahikatea planking was not a durable timber despite its ease of working, and her life expectancy would not have been great.

Thomas Freeman became one of Nelson's major boatbuilders, continuing his work at Auckland Point into the 1850s. George Edwards was another such builder, and after completing his first two vessels in 1843 he next built a boat suitable for trading across the bay "for a Mr H, a young man, a fellow passenger in the *Indus*".[74] This was probably Alfred Hill, 28, a joiner who paid his own way steerage, but the name of the vessel remains one of those annoying loose ends of history. Surveyor Samuel Stephens, who worked in the Riwaka and Motueka areas in the first half of 1842, mentions several such vessels in his notes, although other details are lost in the absence of formal records. Meanwhile the new 33 ft 12 ton schooner *Carbon* also raised eyebrows when she sailed in to Nelson from Motupipi in Massacre Bay to be registered in December 1843.

We owe much to William Pratt, who recorded some of Nelson's early boatbuilding history. As a young man he came out with the Edwards family in the expectation of marrying the eldest daughter but was jilted by a certain Mr Hill, who married her and took her back to England where he died at an early age. Meanwhile Pratt became a successful businessman in Christchurch, and left us his valuable written record of early Nelson life.[75] It is rather a pity that photography had not yet come of age during these early colonial decades, for one could imagine him busily snapping images of these vessels had he lived a few decades later.

Expanding into the Waimea

In the early 1840s, the tidal river-scoured coastline directly south of Nelson haven was almost unrecognisable compared with modern times. There was navigable water all the way from Nelson town to the inland Waimea River, so from Wakapuaka to the Waimea (as well as from Blind Bay's villages to Massacre

---

73 The *Nelson Examiner*, 29 November 1845, 4 April 1846
74 Pratt P 18
75 Pratt W T: Incidents and reminiscences of thirty-four years in New Zealand, 1877

Bay) it really was a maritime colony. If tidal water depths allowed and there were cargoes to be delivered or collected then one or other of the available vessels, from pulling and sailing boats to paddle steamers, would provide the service because it was much easier to go by sea and river than to travel the land route. A few vessels, like *Hydrus*, were Waimea-based. The whole extended harbour area was known as 'the port', or the Waimea Roadstead, and use of its waterways was taken for granted. It takes a conscious effort today to imagine the difficulty of traversing swamps or deeply rutted tracks using bullock wagons with their narrow ironclad wheels, hence the preference for water transport where there was water access.

Even house frames were floated down the harbour in the tide, as when Magistrate Thompson's house was built above the beach end of Rocks Road about September 1842. Rowing and towing in a tideway is much easier in theory than in practice, except by using the tide flow. Edward Baigent is credited with rafting timber down the Wairoa and Waimea rivers to be collected on the estuary, and sawn timber was certainly taken through the Waimea River as waterborne cargo. So was gravel from various banks and beaches including the gravel banks at the east end of Tahuna Beach, but adjacent landowners objected and finally stopped the practice which they perceived as a threat to their own land.

The ferry to Cotterell's Landing

There was land access up Waimea Road and up and over the Annesbrook saddle to Richmond but it was still easier to get there by taking Cotterell and Burtt's ferry boat up the Waimea River's eastern outlet to Cotterell's Landing, thus avoiding the swamp. John Cotterell was one of the original capitalists who proposed and planned the Nelson settlement. He must have been a man of energy, and quick to seize an opportunity. With H W Burtt he leased the steep land opposite Saltwater Bridge and they had it excavated to make space for a store. They also ran their ferry service for a short time, carrying passengers and goods to the Waimea in a locally-built boat, with a lugsail and four oars, which went to Richmond twice a week. Cotterell had another store at the Waimea River and ran a delivery service there.

Cotterell was a company surveyor with his finger in multiple pies. Before he was killed at the Wairau, Cotterell had also advertised the services of the cutter *Enterprise* and it is a reasonable assumption that he owned her: "FOR CLOUDY BAY and WELLINGTON – The cutter ENTERPRISE will leave for the WAIROO on the 28th of this month, calling at Wellington on her return. For freight or passage apply to J.S.Cotterell, Haven Road."[76] He clearly had a vested interest in seeing the 'Wairoo' (Wairau) opened for settlement and had taken a leading role in the consequent disaster there, formally laying the charges against Te Rauparaha and Te Rangihaeata, partly at the behest of the magistrates. When the attempt to arrest them went wrong he was one of the first to be killed.

---

76 The *Nelson Examiner*, 18 March 1843

The Waimea Bank

For vessels working into the Waimea estuary south of the haven, the navigable channels were vastly different from modern times. In the 1840s the Waimea River flowed where people now enjoy themselves on Tahuna Beach and in the vicinity of the Modellers' Pond. With a channel initially twenty feet deep, the Waimea was navigable for ships during the first three decades of settlement. They turned west by south off Arrow Rock to sail the gravel shoreline that is now Rocks Road and the cliffs, then parallel to the dunes of Beach Road and across what is now the motor camp. The waterway passed Parker's Cove, then known as The Black Stump, which was an important shipping point and much larger than now. It continued up to Quarantine Road, declared a quarantine reserve in 1854, shallowing all the while. Beyond Monaco it continued through sandbanks and islands from its land channel at the Waimea end of the bay, yet by 1881 the Tahuna end had silted up so that the channel was dry at spring tides.

Ships from Australia regularly sailed up to discharge livestock at The Black Stump and the stock was driven from there to the quarantine grounds. Smaller vessels found their way both to the foot of Richmond and into the mouth of the Waimea River itself further to the west. This whole waterway, invisible nowadays, became host to smaller craft serving the Waimea plains right around to the Moutere. The further end was served by going outside Rabbit Island and in the western entrance. As nearly all the land between Nelson and Richmond was swampy, sea travel was the preferred choice beyond the Annesbrook rise. Looking west from Whakatu Drive you can see the expanse of water that, with less silt and a stronger river channel, provided a very handy sea route. On a high tide it is readily imaginable, and the shoal drafted hookers like the early *Hydrus* were the right vessels to work the margins.

This Barnicoat sketch looking northward from Annesbrook Rise in Waimea East was probably drawn at the time he drew the map on page 84. It shows the beginnings of arable farming in the area. The Boulder bank can be seen in the far distance beyond the Waimea mudflats.

Bett Collection 314875, Nelson Heritage Museum

Desperate early farming in the hinterland

Even before he was killed at Wairau, Captain Arthur Wakefield saw a need to ignore his brother's directives and grant some of the most desperately poor unemployed labouring families their own small acreages for subsistence cottier farming. In 1843 a significant number of working class families were sent to the Waimea Plains, Moutere and Riwaka under a cottier farming arrangement which obliged them to spend some of their time on road building work and some on their land blocks. The road work ran out all too soon but the artisans and labourers who remained were persistent people and they struggled on, finally succeeding in carving out new lives just as the seafarers did.

Squatting on unoccupied land was commonplace and was even encouraged by Captain Wakefield before he was killed, to the chagrin of capitalists who objected, expecting (from what they had been led to believe in England) that the people should rent land from them instead. At one point a number of workmen and families were put on small plots in Poorman's Valley (now Marsden Valley) where they nearly starved, out of sight and out of mind. But the workers were straining under such containment, desperate to find a better future than the bleak one to which the Company had consigned them. The capitalists, too, were becoming increasingly disillusioned. It was a sour settlement.

Various non-farming enterprises were set up. Beer was brewed, timber and flax were milled (the latter not very satisfactorily) and William Gardner advertised flax whale lines, log lines and twine at his Nelson Rope Works. There were brickworks and lime quarries, even a small coalmine at Enner Glynn. Coal and firewood were important fuels in those pre-petroleum days. Merchants and land dealers added to the commerce and, to facilitate it, a slowly increasing of boats and little ships plied the coast and inlets fetching and carrying. Because of the failure of the settlement to achieve its original goals people were forced to reach out in a bid to find a way forward. That took various forms and of course for one group of artisans it involved shipbuilding and transporting cargo.

Tackling the rural acres

For the early settlers hoping to establish tidy English-style farms, the prospect of breaking in Nelson's land must have been daunting. The natural water flow on this land of relatively high rainfall was quick run-off from elevated places, often ponding to swamps which were interspersed with fern, scrub and bush. Apart from 150 acres of 'wood' across the Maitai River, Nelson's ground cover was predominantly fern and scrub with raupo, flax, toetoe and tutu. A significant proportion of totally unsuitable land had been surveyed and included in the allocated plots. To be an effective farming settlement Nelson really needed a concerted effort in a smaller area of the better quality land, commensurate with the number of resident proprietors.

The New Zealand Company bought the Nelson area for £980.15s worth of goods, including weapons later used against them. It was about the price of three scrip allotments and the Company expected to sell a thousand such allotments.

The surveyors were challenged to peg 221,100 acres of good farm land with more adjacent, and they found about 60,000 arable acres in the wider Waimea area. Some of this land left a lot to be desired in both quality and contour. It was bush, fern or swamp, coastal mudflat or dunes, clay hills and mountains.

There were still only between 50 and 60 resident land proprietors in Nelson in 1843, each holding on average less than two allotments, so between them they took up less than a quarter of the available land. The Company plan allowed Maori one 'tenth' of what had been their own land (actually one eleventh) so the chiefs could enjoy the advantages of European culture and their people could join the labourers in the new settlement. If these allocations were adhered to then there would have been more than enough reasonable land to select from, but the scheme hatched in London demanded that 1,100 lots be laid out, interspersing idle land with the large areas of undistributed land when reasonably they could have expected to get access to their land as they arrived in the settlement. More land had first to be found to satisfy the grand scheme.

The fruitfulness of the land was taken for granted. No thought was given to whether English farming methods, which worked on English land with characteristics known for many centuries, could be transferred to the rough fern, swamp, scrub and bush of New Zealand. It proved not to be that easy. The ploughs the settlers brought with them were too light and farm development was hard, slow work. There was much to be learned and, although there were exceptions, it was not until the spring season of 1843-44 that planting began in earnest.

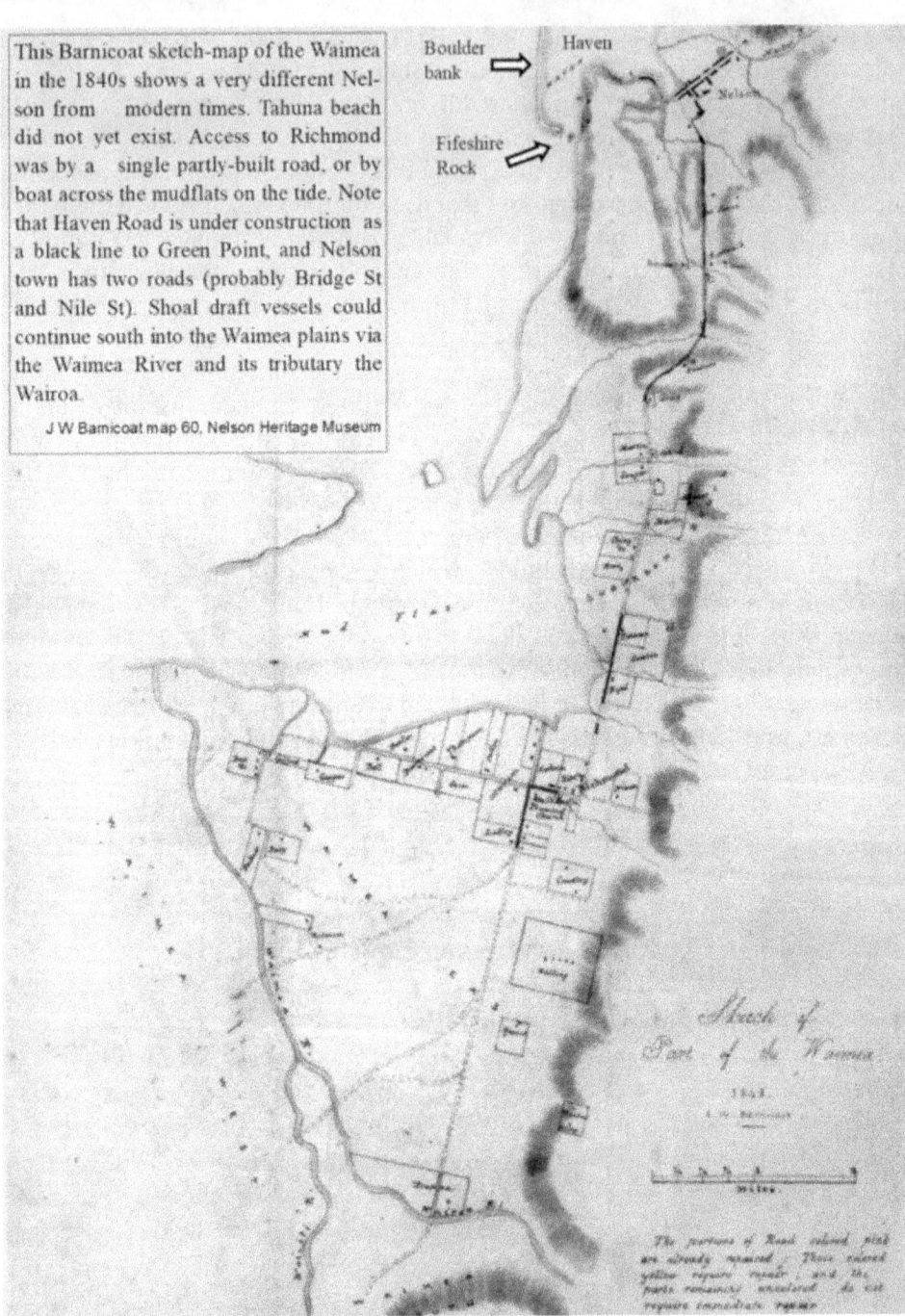

> This Barnicoat sketch-map of the Waimea in the 1840s shows a very different Nelson from modern times. Tahuna beach did not yet exist. Access to Richmond was by a single partly-built road, or by boat across the mudflats on the tide. Note that Haven Road is under construction as a black line to Green Point, and Nelson town has two roads (probably Bridge St and Nile St). Shoal draft vessels could continue south into the Waimea plains via the Waimea River and its tributary the Wairoa.
>
> J W Barnicoat map 60, Nelson Heritage Museum

John Wallis Barnicoat had carried out the first Waimea East survey between April and July 1842 with T J Thompson, after buying a whaleboat from the captain of the Hope, using it to avoid traversing the extensive swamp between Waimea East and Nelson. This map updates the subsequent developments.

JW Barnicoat Map 60, Nelson Provincial Museum

8

Nelson's Early Coastal Margins

DURING THE FIRST TWO HEADY YEARS of the rapidly expanding main town within Nelson Haven, the more adventurous settlers had already been looking westward across Blind Bay. Prior to the attempted take-over of the Wairau Plains, Company officials had been keen to survey whatever available arable land that could be located, in order to satisfy some of the pre-sold parcels, as the investor settlers trickled in.

For Nelson's early settlers, hugging the Blind Bay coastline was a relatively safe way to explore further west. From experience I know the appeal of safely sailing a small boat along this shoreline; different things to see, a sense of movement different from open water, a feeling of involvement with the land, and, sometimes, that special colour of water in all its variations. For those colonists there was the added excitement of potential land to explore and be developed.

In early years the only practical access was by sea, sailing and rowing, from Nelson to Bronte peninsula, in the western entrance past Mapua, around to Marahau, thence northwards along the fascinating coast of what is nowadays Abel Tasman National Park, and even around Separation Point to Motupipi. Here it was hooker territory for many years. Blind Bay simply had to have its small ships, at first from other places, but as Nelson grew it would have its own, initially very small, fleet.

In the exploring phase, parties penetrated some distances inland and around the coast. They would never find anything to match the prospectus; there never would be the advantages of compact settlement held out by Wakefield. Using the arable land located had satisfied barely a quarter of the overall scheme's requirement; the other three-quarters had yet to be found. Nelson was repeating all the ills that had assailed the Wellington settlement. But this company compulsion continued to drive them, and so the planned compact Nelson settlement (and therefore the hookers) finally ranged from Massacre Bay almost to Kaikoura, a carelessly flung patchwork garment draped along the coasts, many patches unsold, many unoccupied by their investor owners.

The concept of Nelson being a compact settlement embodying all the 'best' of English class and culture – with its landed gentry and a goodly supply of workers to serve them – was doomed from the start.

A New Social Order Ferments

Nelson did develop a special character, through the necessity of salvaging something from the company land shambles; a sturdy pattern of its own, struggling, but casting off many of the remnants of an impossible mould.

The company really subverted its own scheme through greed, and, decrying subsistence farming, finally left no other recourse; it was a matter of survival. Small farming was born. But there was class conflict as new ideas clashed with old, and advantage was the stake. Judge Broad, in his 1892 *A Jubilee History of Nelson*[77], characterised those few self-serving capitalists who did come to Nelson for a greater or shorter time:

"... *the resident original land purchasers formed themselves into a Society to watch over their own interest. When the New Zealand Company practically ceased to exist, this party, which was long known as the 'Nelson Supper Party', became the dominant power in the settlement. The Governor* [in Auckland] *made all appointments by their advice; they acquired the control of the only newspaper in the place; the land regulations were made to suit them; the runs were divided amongst them*[78]; *and the Nelson Special Jury was composed entirely of themselves and their friends.*"

Here were the very outcomes solicited by the company! The custodians of European intellectual culture, steeped in the belief 'that the right to occupy the land was an inherited privilege of a few'[79], also ruthlessly advancing their exclusive material self-interest, not making common cause with their fellow-emigrants, seen as beneath them. As they brought culture to Nelson, so they determinedly worked to sustain their dominance in, and the survival of, the pecking order system. But Nelson also embodied a strong spirit of survival and emancipation that burned in some of the workers. This was to become woven into Nelson's history, helping to give its individual shape, and thereby shaping the spheres of the various activities, including the hookers. Finally the lines would become blurred with time, and wealth would override inheritance as the social yardstick.

Absurdities and hollow assurances

I would say with some certainty that if you contemplated buying and farming in the isolation that 12,000 miles from home represented in 1841, you would take due diligence regarding land quality, and feasibility. Otherwise you would be buying a pig in a poke! However the sole assurances, which were swallowed by investors and settlers, were purely theoretical. These were declared in the company brochures, in Wakefield's earlier book, in his pamphlets, and various other writings and utterances. The more canny individuals (who knew better) put their own gain before others' pain, and acquiesced by their silence. Yet these people were, in a sense, only the window-dressing in a grandiose scheme for the great wealth that Edward Wakefield had claimed would follow from ever-expanding settlement. *Britain without its bad features* was postulated to the wealthy potential investors, ignoring the fact that what the class system embedded in his scheme *was* one of Britain's worst features for the great majority of the deprived population, and was not sustainable in the colony long-term, any more than it

---

77   Broad page 121. *Wright* gives a detailed New Zealand wide analysis in his chapter 4.
78   See also *Kennington*, chapters 3, 4, 8.
79   *Buick* page 393

had been in Britain.

Of all the absurdities, probably the oddest of all was a lottery conducted in London in 1841 before the first emigrant ships sailed[80], to distribute randomly the order of choosing the sections, once they were surveyed and buyers had actually arrived in Nelson. No first come first served here. The lottery had been introduced to lure speculative participation, when it was apparent there was not sufficient capitalist interest. It created near-disastrous outcomes for those investors who would actually settle on their randomly drawn lots, and was simply a jolly event, numbers-drawing from the lottery barrels, one for each area of land (1 acre, 50 acres, 150 acres), covered by each piece of scrip. The actual drawing event was an animated social occasion. It was also appallingly short-sighted.

Alfred Saunders, a capitalist immigrant on the *Fifeshire* wrote[81]: "We came into possession of our town acre, but the number of my choice for a section was 954 out of 1,100, so that I had to take one far from the business part of town, and with no timber growing on it." Being one of the very few capitalists actually on the spot gave no advantages, when in reality their success would be the settlement's success – or failure.

It intended instead that the last purchaser, resident or absentee, had as good a chance of prime sites as the first, thereby protecting ongoing sales – a raffle with prizes for all, and a chance of latecomers getting an especially attractive one from the allocated, but unsold, pool. The focus peculiarly was not on the reality at all, but to suit company and speculators. Having people labouring away in the settlement ensured absentees' land, and that unsold, could only appreciate in value as a consequence. It surely didn't help farmers. As only little over 40% of the scrip had sold, and a great part of that to non-emigrating speculators, the situation was ludicrous.

A further drawing was needed to tie choice to the 60% of unsold scrip held up in the London lottery barrel. A later emigrant purchaser would buy in London, come to Nelson with three predetermined choices, and find the corresponding pieces of land they had been attached to, good, bad or indifferent. Those migrants would have been better advised to come here, and then exercise judgement to buy from what was on the market, except that the company had to have ongoing new sales from the barrel to keep the cash rolling in. It showed no concern for the migrant investor-settlers.

For the company and Edward Wakefield, the Nelson colony was their Waterloo. Two years earlier, the Wellington colony's scrip had all been sold within a month. But it wasn't so much a colonising market as a speculative one; more than 50% of those sales were to absentees, and many involved were Wakefield's friends and relatives. When the organisers thought to repeat it at a higher land price for Nelson, they badly misjudged (or did not even address the question). The market was already saturated. In spite of Wellington having been through

---

80 Well detailed in *Allan*.
81 *Saunders* page 37

the same problems, the company would not budge. To do so would be admitting failure, and some hoped against hope there could yet be more rich pickings.

Frustrating early settlement in Motueka and Riwaka

About 15 miles to the north-west of Nelson Haven by sea lie the modest coastal river-flats of the Motueka and Riwaka Rivers. The Motueka River was navigable, and is said to have been twice as deep and half as wide before a major flood changed it, but there is little record of incoming vessels. When the New Zealand Company's advance party was exploring this area in 1841, Captain Lacey of the *Whitby* rowed a considerable distance up the river in his light gig, portaging "... *a succession of falls about two and three feet high until he reached one so steep that he did not attempt it.*[82]" From this description he had reached Pokorokoro, about fourteen miles up the river.

A plaque, 150 metres east of the actual site, marks the 1843 landing of the first settlers at what is now the foot of Staples Street just north of Motueka. This was the Manuka Bush road. There was a Maori settlement by the present Thorpe Street, and a landing area further on. Washbourn mentions seeing carvings and pieces of large canoes both here and at Doctor's Creek and the settlers quickly learned that the better places to land were those already in use by Maori, who named the harbour *Raumanuka*. Manuka Bush had a loading bank and mooring posts, which were to be used from 1842 until 1856. The whole of central Motueka

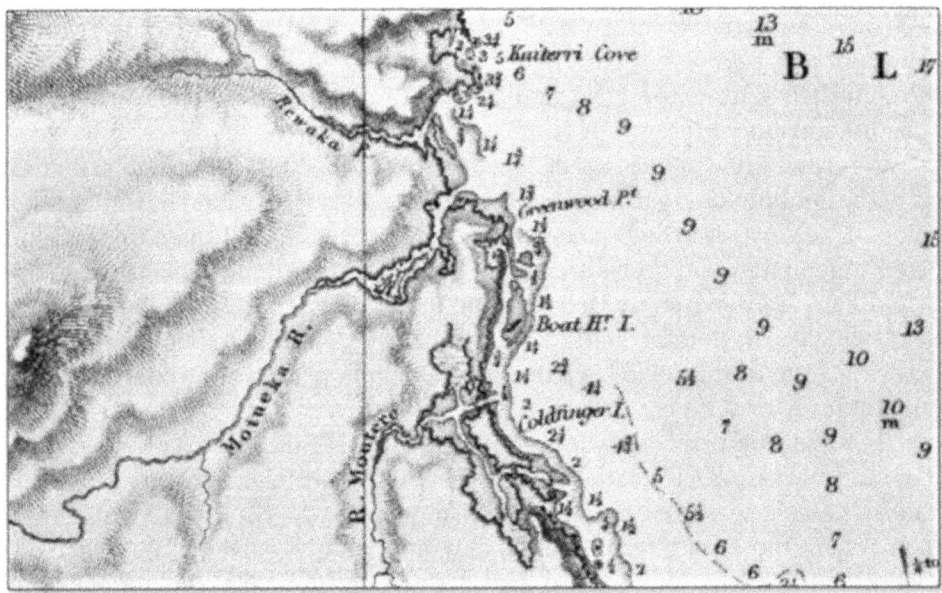

The topography evident in this extract from an early chart shows how little viable land was available in the vicinity of the Moutere, Motueka and Riwaka Rivers, and how tidal the estuaries were.

---

82 Brereton, C B, *Vanguard of the South*, A H & A W Reed, 1952, p213

was covered by a lush lowland podocarp forest known as Te Maatu (the Big Wood), which was of huge cultural value to Maori for its variety of resources.

Motueka village itself was literally cut out from the bush. Residents would first clear a house site and then extend their open area and the timber they cut was invaluable both for building and exporting to earn much needed cash. Outside the bush some of the land was farmable but the rest was either swampy or, towards the coast, divided by stony and sandy banks with lagoons between. The anchorage outside Doctor's Creek enabled larger ships to lie off and be loaded if they were too big to be beached on the tide.

Where there are people there are basic requirements beyond what can be produced on the land. At the very beginning, surveyor Stephens noted that Captain Moore's *Mary Ann* brought in window frames, and the settlers themselves would not have come empty-handed. They required tools, farming and household articles and some foodstuffs, even when their land became productive. Surpluses were shipped to Nelson, possibly in *Mary Ann*, although many settlers were quick to get their own boats.

The Greenwood[83] family were among the first investor colonists to be allotted parcels of this freshly surveyed land, arriving aboard *Phoebe* on 29th March 1843, a year after the initial settlement of Nelson. To their chagrin they found that the Nelson *town acre*, allocated by scrip, was a swamp, that would be useless until such time as the whole area would be drained. There was plenty of good town land lying idle nearby, but (like Alfred Saunders), being actually in Nelson was no advantage to them. Their *accommodation section* was well away, in Motueka, to where Dr Greenwood and his older sons moved in August 1843, the rest of the family living meantime in a rented Nelson cottage. There were still no 150 acre lots available for survey, despite having been part of their purchase agreement.

"*The (50-acre) section on one side of me belongs to an absentee proprietor, a Mr Grubb, Surgeon of Halifax, Yorkshire, who had given no powers to his agent here to lease or to sell. He has bought it as an investment, in fact, to become valuable through the exertions and at the expense of the actual colonists, myself, for instance, who has run a track 8 feet wide through his section and another ditch between the two in order to drain my own. Had the land been unsold I should have had a valuable neighbour and should have been spared two-thirds the expense. On the other side of me sections 250 and 251 are still in the wheel at London, undisposed of and may perhaps continue so for ten years to come, so that my friends thought themselves happy in getting a section half a mile off, though there are not more than five or six purchasers of land in this district.*"

A hungry settlement

The failure of the Company was soon to bite as deeply in Motueka and the surrounding areas as it did elsewhere. Sandy Gibson, an expedition man, told

---

83 Neale, June E.: *The Greenwoods, a pioneer family of New Zealand*.

Harry Washbourn that when the Company ceased to employ him and others like him their wages were only 9 lbs of potatoes a day. "*Motueka was very much in the position of that island of which it was said that the inhabitants made a precarious living by taking in each other's washing, as they were all producing the same thing, and there was no outside market.*[84]"

The Nelson settlement had been in this position also in 1842, running out of flour and substituting potatoes for bread. The Company's resident officers in Nelson had confronted the harsh realities and dealt with them as best they could, (chartering the barque *Brougham* to fetch flour from Chile although the London officials refused to provide funds for this to be repeated). This resilience and flexibility was to be the key to survival in the new colony.

This 1852 painting of Maori river-waka being paddled near the Motueka River mouth is attributed to the artist John Pearce (1808–1882). Mount Arthur can be seen in the background.
Ref E-455-f-081-1 Alexander Turnbull Library

Nearby in Riwaka

In 1842, when the Company survey party sailed to Riwaka in Jimmy Jackson's *Nelson Packet*, some wives came too, thus effectively commencing settlement at the Atua, on the coastal northern end of the plain and swamp of Riwaka. Other boats then brought supplies, and a pattern of servicing by little ships and boats was set that would last for years. The company Deal boat, Murphy's boat, Lewis' boat, Wilson's boat, and *'a small boat towed over for the survey party's use'*, all get mentioned in surveyor Stephens' reports, as does an injured man taken to Nelson by, most likely, Captain Moore's *Mary Ann*. Conditions have changed, but the

---

84 Washbourn p44

coast still buzzes with boats of those visiting the adjacent national park, and the people serving them.

Other small vessels were quickly built to fulfil needs at Riwaka as soon as surveying commenced. There is no record of their design, but one can safely assume that these were punts or similar work boats, built to carry men and their gear. The early survey stakes were pitsawn, as indeed was the wood for the boat construction. Canoes were also used.

*The punt **Sudden Jerk**, pictured here in Nelson Haven, is a typical example of a basic work-boat of the era. Vessels like these could be towed or propelled by poling and even by crude sail as shown.*
Copy collection C2877, Nelson Provincial Museum

The first survey depot was adjacent to the pa occupied by Maori, near the first rising coastal land to the north at the Riwaka River. There was soon a jetty on the beach there, where the Atua Stream joined the main channel of the river. It was said hookers could lie in nine or 10 feet of water. It served for over a decade, but other places were used as well. The Riwaka River could be traversed above that point, which made the waterway useful.

Coastal edges change with time from natural forces - flood, tide, wind, storm – as well as from man's intervention. Sands shift, channels fill and others are eroded, whilst the plant cover loses to the water in one place, and reasserts itself somewhere else. We need to enter further into the landscape as it was, to understand the pattern of settling the area. H P Washbourn noted it in 1933[85], so

---

85 Washbourn p 46

the cumulative time now will be over twice the 70 years he mentioned:

"The Riwaka of today is very different from the Riwaka of 70 odd years ago ... The centre then was a large raupo[86] swamp, with a ring of solid ground around it, and whatever settlement there was was round the edge of the swamp." So wrote Harry Washbourn. The Motueka river's course, he surmised, had flowed at one time along the foot of the western hills, then changed eastward to form a bank around the southern and eastern sides too, all at one time constituting the river's estuary mouth. *"On the other side the Riwaka River did the same thing, enclosing a large space which later became the swamp."*

It must have been daunting for the early Riwaka and Motueka settlers to be confronted by acres of Raupo swamp to be developed. The Greenwoods later went on to process flax for export while developing viable pasture land.

This swamp, with its dense 10 feet high raupo, was fed water from Little Sydney Stream and other streams coming off the hills. An 1851 map shows the swamp stretched back to those hills west of Riwaka where Swamp Road lies on a north/south axis, paralleled by Lodders Lane two kilometres to the east. The roads are within the old swamp area but close to the edges, which shows it was of considerable extent. Settlers later found drained swamps to be some of the most productive land. Riwaka was then, and still is, a most fruitful area, but only after manful drainage work. It took years, and it was second generation Drummond sons who did the final Factory and Swamp Roads ditches, work that had daunted others before them.

The serrated seaward margin offered small boat landing places, and the creeks allowed penetration inland. It is not obvious now, but it was tidal almost to the present Riwaka Hotel. Nowadays you will encounter hops growing or sheep grazing where once the tide came in, and drainage has diverted water that

---

86 Raupo is a bullrush.

ponded or flowed in creeks, changing the whole distribution pattern.

These days, hookers would be hard-pressed to get far up the creeks, whereas yesteryear the tidal waterways were the common access.

Ferrers Creek

In modern times if you drive towards Riwaka off the Motueka River bridge, after a few hundred metres you can turn on to Lodders Lane on the right. Unseen but nevertheless there, beyond it to your left as you drive down is a small waterway, Ferrers Creek, ending at the tidal estuary. In earliest days it was a popular fishing and swimming place. You cross the creek as you turn left (with the old Riwaka wharf straight ahead). On the far side of Green Tree point, the stream was a berthing and loading place for small ships, virtually at the back doors of the houses. Wheat was taken up another creek to the Riwaka flour mill. All the produce from the rich farmland around, that was not consumed locally, passed over the Riwaka wharves.

Ferrers Creek had little ships loading from the banks. It must have been a lovely sight to observe a hooker, maybe just its masts above the raupo, being poled quietly along one of these waterways, to unload and pick up a cargo, not necessarily a cargo of produce. Livestock was shifted, and there could be flax-dressing plants and saw mills to be relocated, possibly along with some household items. People too of course, for the hookers were almost like snail-paced taxis, even picking up the sick or injured for carrying to where attention was available.

Enter into this scene for a moment in your imagination, to see people getting aboard, perhaps using a plank from the stream bank, the boat dipping a little because they were quite small, and then being poled down between close banks to a channel through the marshy estuary. Then further, out to the blue water where the sails were hoisted. There is that changeover when one has to get an offing with an onshore sea breeze, but scarcely any way on the ship to start. If she is a bit of a beast, as some of them were, and wants to hang up 'in stays' or fall away, then even that could be exciting with the mud close by. It is easy to imagine the muttered imprecations and *'put some more into it with that pole or we'll be on the mud!'* from the skipper.

Vessels would later be seen loading near the present highway on Little Sydney Stream, which passes under the road, just a few hundred metres west past the tennis court, on the right-hand bend. That stretch was known as the Stony Road, because the stones and spoil from the ditches dug either side were thrown into the middle to build it up. Absentee landowners got a free ride on all this, because the people on the spot had to drain their land to use it. A hooker loading there at top of tide was commonplace, but if any vessel bottomed as her load was topped, a team of horses working nearby would hastily be co-opted to haul her along into deeper water. It was a hooker hazard to be caught by the tide, and at worst it could be a long wait for spring tides to get out of some of these corners.

Early Seafarers in Riwaka

There were several local families with seafaring involvement: Askews, Holyoakes, McNabbs, Woolfs and identities of later years Ted Reed, Manuel Smith, Patties, Wildmans, Williamses and no doubt others. The Green Tree Point land is the centre for a key family in the present-day equivalent to the hookers, the tour boats in Abel Tasman National Park operated by Wilsons.

Camaraderie amongst shipmates on the emigrant ship *Indus* subsequently played into the Riwaka grouping, in both cottier farming, where William Askew was a natural and accepted leader, and in boatbuilding and seafaring. George Edwards, an *Indus* passenger, went to Riwaka in 1843 '*to build a boat for some young men residing there*[87]' and whilst we cannot positively identify the people or the boat, its size or other features, we surmise both it and the very first he built at Haven Road were either dinghies, or slightly larger sailing vessels, inasmuch as larger vessels than that tended to attract better descriptions.

Within a few years, two young men from Riwaka, Thomas Askew and Henry Fowler (who would have been about 17 years of age in 1843), were seafarers, operating hookers[88]. Thomas became a captain, owner of several ships, and a merchant. Henry, with a life of promise opening to him as a mariner, illustrated only too well that there was another side to seafaring pioneering, as we shall find in following some of his voyaging.

Pratt mentions boatbuilder Edwards having been to Tahiti. He must have been there earlier. Another example, Richard Holyoake, 30, a carpenter on the passenger list, is mentioned as having worked on a whaler on the New Zealand coast, and thus knowing the area[89]. It seems obvious when one thinks about it, that some of the young men who had adventured as seamen and whalers then returned to England, could want to come back, and might take this opportunity to do so. Was Edwards one?

But, as a writer of the times would have said, we first have a sad duty to perform for poor George Edwards. He was the driving force in an 1845 foursome partnership, to build in Riwaka a vessel of between 30 and 40 tons and sail her to Tahiti with a load of potatoes, to sell them, and the vessel. Laying the keel for this has been mentioned in chapter one. Constructed over a period of about a year, it would allow them also (as Pratt said) '*to pursue their cultivations simultaneously*'. William Pratt (ex *Indus*, too) was one of the partners, and he intended to help with the construction, which probably took place on Little Sydney Creek. It would have carried more water then. One of these cultivations upon land on which they squatted was where:

"*The road from the valley turned at a right angle at this spot to the plains, the bush being in the angle of the two roads* (whence they had procured the rimu stem for their ship) *and enclosed by the ditch dug to form the roads* (Goodalls corner) ...

---

87 *Pratt*, page 66.
88 Detail is lacking.
89 Neale (*Pioneer Passengers*) p 107.

In clearing the land, instead of burning the brushwood where it lay, as usual in such cases, we carried it to the margin of the clearing, and with it formed a temporary fence on the other two sides. As the planting of this small patch was soon finished, and there was some good flax-land close by, I began clearing a piece of it by firing it in several places ...". We are back to the Stony Road.

Edwards, working alongside Pratt, thought the fire a hazard, and so Pratt extinguished it. However, it remained underground in the dry conditions, to emerge about a fortnight later in several different places. In fighting one of these, Edwards must have fallen in a hollow. He dislocated his neck and died[90]. The venture fell through. It is a safe surmise that one of the partners who '*shortly after went to Nelson, and made arrangements for one to be built of about ten tons, and with which he traded between Nelson and Wellington for several years very successfully*' was Henry Fowler, and one who '*apprenticed himself to a Nelson shipwright for two years*', with a view to completing the earlier project for himself, was likely to be Thomas Askew. The Askews were noted as boatbuilders about this time, and Thomas will be a future example of the fluidity of the class barriers under the onslaught of wealth.

There was an ongoing activity in small boats then, as now, and a good number of those with maritime experience would at least build a dinghy, certainly a skill through the 19th century. We can mention a couple, illustrative of the boats that didn't get recorded, except that they had one or another mishap. The *Mary* was a small vessel built by the Askew brothers at Riwaka, about 1844, to take wood to Nelson. Thomas was master and George the crew. She capsized four miles outside the harbour while en route from Nelson to Riwaka, and George was drowned[91]. This shallowing end of the bay is an unpleasant place with short, sharp seas in a bit of a wind, unless standing a fair distance off. Another from Riwaka was Richard Holyoake's small boat sailing to Nelson, wrecked on the Waimea Sands 16 August 1848. These were not horse-and-buggy days with so few roads, so any vessel whether dinghy, punt, ship's boat, whaleboat, or even canoe would have value as communication, people transport, and load-carrying. Virtually every material object had to be imported and exported via the water.

John Stuart Mill's Involvement

The land where Pratt once squatted (and poor George Edwards met his death) has a curious additional history which I stumbled upon when researching the 1843 survey map of Riwaka. To my amazement I found the name of the famous English economist John Stuart Mill emblazoned across that particular large section labelled number 51. Clearly he was an absentee speculator who had no intention of ever settling in Riwaka. His substantial block of land simply lay idle, roads dug around it by resident landowners developing their own lots without any contribution from its owner. A demonstration, if one were needed, of just

---

90 *Pratt* pp 116 to 121.
91 Allan: *Port* p123. NB. Miss J Askew of Riwaka has confirmed that it was George (not John).

how bizarre the company scheme was.

Undeveloped it remained for well over a decade, until Mill finally had to face the consequences of gambling with land. When John Fowler (the father of Henry the seafarer) bought it in 1855, via Mill's attorney, Alfred Fell of Nelson, he paid 175 pounds for the 68 acres "*being accommodation section No 51 bounded on the North, South and East by a Public Road and on the West by Sections Nos 50 and 56*", with William Pratt witnessing John Fowler's signature. (These accommodation sections, nominally 50 acres, were generally increased in size in the wheeling and dealing when the company was winding up.) Attributing only its nominal 50 acre cost to it, 75 pounds, and compounding the interest on it, and a bit for expenses, it did not return J S Mill much more than 5% over the 14 years he held it. So much for the expected rewards of speculation!

And as an interpolation to the story, but pertinent at this point, the last of the 150 acre lots in Marlborough sold in the 1880s, and brought their owners only ten shillings per acre. This also serves as a reminder of the small pool of capitalist investors who ventured cash for the Nelson settlement. Bearing in mind that less than half of the scrip had sold, and some of that to holders of more than one allotment, the coincidence is not quite so remarkable. But it *was* remarkable to the author, to find these characters already in the story, connected in this way.

To complete the story, in 1857 John Fowler's son James opened the forerunner to the present Riwaka Hotel on the land. It was called The Travellers Rest, and his bush licence required him to offer two bedrooms and one sitting room, as well as operate a ferry boat over the Riwaka River.

It seems appropriate to read John Stuart Mill, the leading English economist of the 1840s, eating a little humble pie on the subject. As a personal friend of the Wakefields, an employee of the wealthy East India Company living in the heart of commercial London, as an absentee Riwaka land speculator, he must have been doing some serious cogitation before confessing in his *Dissertations and Discussions* volume 1 (1859): "*When society requires to be rebuilt, there is no use in attempting to rebuild it on the old plan.*"

Map Opposite:

The Riwaka river-flats were surveyed prior to the tragic Wairau incident, with the surveyors and first settlers setting up a base at the mouth of the Atua stream in the lower right corner after persuading resident Maori to move out of their 'new pah'. The properties were principally 50 acre 'accommodation sections', although John Stuart Mill's **Lot 51** *was larger, seen here bounded by 'the Stony Road' on its right. Many of these sections remained vacant for years, belonging to absentee English speculators.*

Map prepared by H.N. Murray, courtesy Lynette Wilson

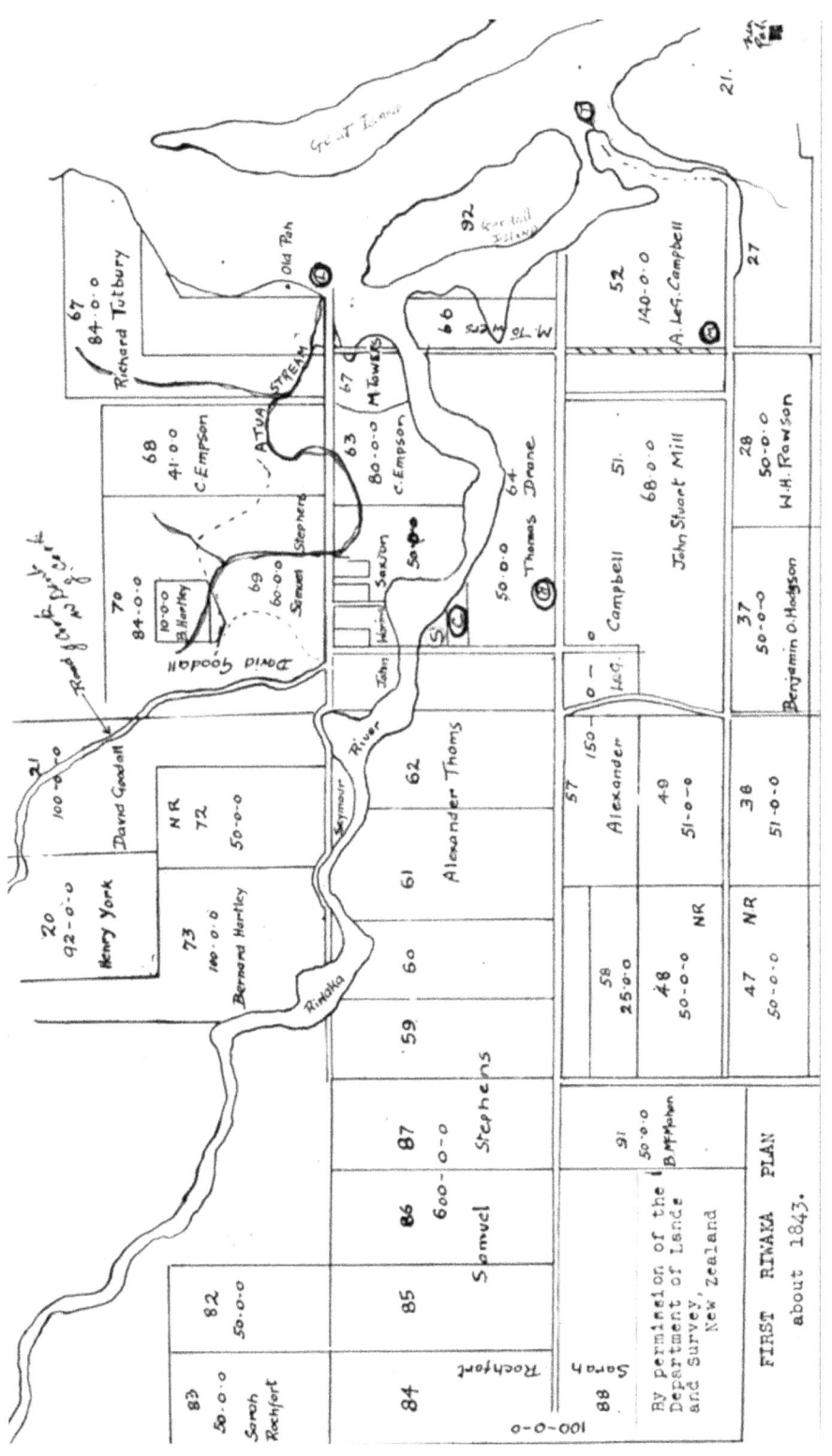

*Loading struggling sheep aboard the medium-draft hookers was an energetic affair. Wharf facilities were often nothing more than a sloping beach, and each animal was caught, tied and loaded into the ship's boat which was then rowed out to the larger vessel. This grainy photograph has captured the exercise in the very the late 1800s with the Ricketts brothers' hooker ketch **Pet** waiting patiently on anchor for her messy cargo.*
Copy Collection C11, Nelson Provincial Museum

9

Livestock Arrives by Sea

WITH THE LONG WAIT for the allocation of 150 acre blocks of land, the early 1840s favoured arable farming rather than pastoralism. Livestock in the form of milking cows and small cattle herds would be the more likely choice to be bringing into the Nelson wider colony. These beasts arrived by sea aboard ship and were, more often than not, uncomfortably transported about Blind Bay as deck cargo aboard smaller vessels including the newly launched local hookers.

Before long though, sheep would make their dominance felt, being easier to transport and with the seasonal financial incentive of wool to be marketed. Merino sheep first came to New Zealand with Captain Cook in 1773 but did not survive and merino from Australia were re-established in New Zealand on Mana Island where James Wright farmed in 1834. Merinos were the oldest established and most numerous sheep breed in the world. North Africa or perhaps Spain was their original home and, unsurprisingly, they do not thrive on lowlands, especially in high rainfall areas.

In 1842 there were already three flocks of sheep in the Nelson region, and there was growing interest in the potential viability of the wool industry once more land was opened up. This was to happen within the next five years due to the combined factors of Maori leasehold land becoming available further to the east (Marlborough was still part of Nelson Province), official depasturage licences and even simple squatting practices.

Seamanship and livestock

Coastal ships brought the first flocks and herds to Nelson, landing them at The Black Stump in the Waimea estuary. Initially the sheep came from Wellington and New Plymouth, then larger shipments came from Australia and these larger vessels would use the Waimea channel too. Some would even need to be fetched from across Cook Strait, with the demands of canny seamanship involved in this exercise. Later in 1843 Alfred Saunders had livestock held up on a ship in Port Nicholson, and he took the opportunity to get there and inspect them by taking despatches from Company agent Frederick Tuckett to William Wakefield. He and his crew left Nelson in a whaleboat, spending the first night at d'Urville Island, the second at Jackson's Bend and the third in Queen Charlotte Sound. Barney Miller was the helmsman. Somewhat reluctantly braving the major Cook Strait crossing, Saunders wrote: *"We were caught the next day in a north-west hurricane, which filled the boat with water, forcing us to bail for our lives. It was impossible to keep our course for Wellington, as we had to fly before the wind, which took us out of Cook Strait to where the cliffs of the North Island sheltered us somewhat from the violent nor'wester. We passed a miserable night, with, at one time, little hope of living till morning in such a sea; but, the wind moderating towards the evening of the next day, with very hard pulling we managed to get into Wellington Harbour."*[92] The hurricane force winds that he refers to would almost certainly have been the ten mile stretch between Cape Terawhiti and Sinclair Head, now locally known as 'the wind factory'! where strong north sector winds are commonly known to accelerated to storm-force by the v-shaped valleys, blasting out at double the speed recorded further out into the strait. With its strong currents and overfalls, the area is notorious, and even the modern cruising guide states that *"yachtsmen should reduce sail when entering this area ... and may find prayer of assistance."*!!

Surviving in an open boat like Saunders experienced takes both skill and courage, and such voyages depended on a pool of very experienced men who were well versed in small boat handling. I have twice been in very hard nor'westers in that same area and can imagine being in a clinker whaler pulling-boat (probably with a lugsail) caught in Cook Strait and running east in horrendous seas to beyond Palliser Bay. We have been in the same shelter in our hooker-sized ketch, which allowed us to get a meal before getting exposed to the weather again further up the coast. The next calm water would be Napier. These heightened survival skills and awareness of the elements, shared by men used to assessing and managing risks, helped stand men like Kidson in good stead during the disastrous events of 1843.

A hooker trip to the Wairau and Awatere

In 1846, when Marlborough was still part of Nelson, a small six-ton Wellington-owned hooker crossed Cook Strait to explore the waters and land that before long would buzz with Nelson-based activities and vessels. She was the cutter *Fidele*, owned by Wellington merchant John Wade. Accompanying him were Frederick Weld, an enterprising young Wairarapa pastoral farmer who later became a dominant political figure, and Tom Caverhill, a border Scotsman with a grand knowledge of sheep. Ill-thrift and heavy losses on the Wairarapa lowlands led Weld to follow his shepherd's advice and seek suitable land. Tom Caverhill had proved his skill and saved the sheep by taking them up on to high, dry ground, and now with a couple of crewmen they sailed for the Wairau to follow up a report of open grasslands on the north-eastern South Island.

It was probably John Workman who had told Weld about the open country across Cook Strait. John and his wife Rewhanga lived at Palliser Bay and he went with his Maori relatives each year to lakes Grassmere and Elterwater to catch ducks. Workman was a former whaler who served the Wairarapa by sea, rowing and sailing into Port Nicholson to a stream at the foot of Woodward Street (now off Lambton Quay). Often the wool bales he brought down were wet from their sea journey and would be taken to Scorching Bay to dry on the beach. The return journey would see his boat loaded with supplies to barely a foot of freeboard, and

---

92 Saunders p 39

then he would be off, under oars or sail, around Baring Head, into Palliser Bay and so up Lake Wairarapa.

Weld recorded a first-hand account of the *Fidele*'s trip to the South Island:

*September 23rd. Left Clifford's at 7pm to go on board the **Fidele** which has been engaged to sail this morning. After much delay found the boatmen at a public house and learned that the main sail was split and that they could not start. Spent most of the night in superintending the repairs and in ferreting the men out of all kinds of grog shops into which they bolted if left to themselves for a moment. At length Wade made them hurry a little by telling them that it was of importance that we should start before daylight as the constables were after them, a piece of information which evidently won their sympathies and which they most piously believed.*

September 24th. Got on board at 10am and after much delay weighed anchor and stood out of the harbour, we hardly reached Sinclair Head when the wind and sea increasing the Captain judged it prudent to shorten sail and bring up in Fitzroy Bay for the night. Our beds were composed of rubble stones laid in for ballast, the sea was rough and the little craft rolled heavily at anchor so we were heartily glad to get under way at seven in the morning.

September 25th. We stood across the Straits in a fair wind and by 3pm made Cape Campbell. As we followed down the coast we observed nothing but low grazing hills until about ten miles from Cape Campbell we came to the mouth of a little river which is marked by a conical peak and one or two hills white with limestone. A reef of rock here juts out into the sea from two very large white rocks called by the whalers 'Chancet' affording shelter from NW gales, we edged between two of the rocks of the reef and brought up just between them in comparatively smooth water. Mr Wade landed in the dingy to be able the better to judge the possibility of entering into a river basin which lay before us or even entering the mouth of the river. Having decided that this was easily to be effected he returned on board again and we again made sail – unfortunately however just as we were entering the river the dingy broke from the painter and we had to tack and before we recovered her we made so much leeway that the wind freshened into a gale, we were glad to cast anchor under the protection of a promintory of limestone rocks some two or three miles south of our intended port. Here we lay all night not a little doubtful as to whether our cable would hold.

September 26th. Our first care was to beat back to the little river, we entered the estuary where there was six to seven feet of water at low tide and then wishing to place the boat in a more completely land locked position we entered the river itself, no dock could be imagined more adapted for a small craft like ours. We instantly set to work and landed our goods and leaving our men to prepare our suppers took a stroll up country."[93]

---

93 *Journal of the Cape Campbell Expedition, September 1846*, in Kennington, A L , *The Awatere*, Marlborough County Council, P24

The party had arrived at the location of what was to become the famous Flaxbourne Run in the Awatere valley near Weld. They spent four days exploring until the wind moderated, working their way out of the river and setting sail at nightfall with the flood tide carrying them northward. They were becalmed all night off Cape Campbell but the next day the wind freshened and they were able to sail close-hauled across Cook Strait, entering Wellington Heads just on dusk.

To read such stories of those early hookers is to feel the wind in your hair as you cast an anxious eye at the horizon to windward if the breeze is increasing, and to leeward if there is a shoreline there not too far away. Irish judge John Philpot Curran said in 1790 that, "*The condition upon which God hath given liberty to man is eternal vigilance.*" For the seafarer, eternal vigilance is the price of safety, and if you are at sea and your skipper isn't squinting at the horizon now and again, watching the wind and waves and watching his ship, then there is every chance he isn't in his element.

The day-to-day concerns of coast hopping under sail are little changed, with the welcome security of a river anchorage well worth the anxieties of getting in

Gannet, *a hooker of the later era, once spent four days drifting in Cook Strait. She was brought to Nelson by Capt. Bob Goldie in the early 1900s and later lengthened by J.J. Ricketts at the gasworks wharf near Auckland Point, and converted to ketch rig.* **Gannet** *was wrecked on the beach at Ngaio Bay when a strong northerly came in while she was loading melons.*
Copy collection CC2289, Nelson Provincial Museum

through the rocks. But compared with the comfort of modern vessels, the open deck of a small hooker, was far more character-building. In those relatively primitive small ships, oilskins or well-worn worsted clothes were the only protection from the weather, while their only propulsion was the spread of sails above, and their only security the skill and judgement of companions. Charts ranged from primitive to non-existent, navigational aids were limited and there were no fixed lights along the coastline. Nights can be either very black or brilliant with stars and moon, and exact positions can still be hard to fix. There was a report years later that one Nelson hooker, the *Gannet*, drifted back and forwards with the tidal currents, in an extremely rare windless spell in Cook Strait, for four days.

Pasturage-rights

After his visit to the Awatere aboard *Fidele*, Frederick Weld and his business partner/cousin Charles Clifford lost no time in getting a lease of all the country they had seen, from the White Bluff down the east coast around Cape Campbell to Kekerengu, from the Ngati Toa chief Te Puaha. Then Clifford crossed to Australia and bought nearly 4,000 quality merino sheep. There were heavy losses in transport but the survivors were landed in Port Underwood and were driven around the coast to their new station.[94]

It was a journey of tribulations. The sheep were ferried across the Wairau River in whaleboats, but crossing the Clarence meant throwing each animal into the river and ensuring that it swam to the other side. The pastoral farming breakthrough in the Awatere had started, and some other sheep owners shifted their flocks into the Wairau too, but without authority. The work provided a welcome boost to the Cloudy Bay whaling community which provided boats, men and supplies.

When Marlborough finally separated off it became more like the place of colonial theory but it was a spread out version with vast sheep stations, established when land acquisition was reorganised by the landowners to suit their own ends, instead of 150-acre farms. Between 1844, when the New Zealand Company was first insolvent, and 1850 when it handed in its charter following a change of British government, it was bailed out twice and the financial burden finally came home to roost in the new colony.

The Company was still selling land and sending newcomers to New Zealand when it could, maintaining both its liquidity and its aloofness from the realities in the settlement. Francis Dillon Bell, who succeeded William Fox as Company agent, said, "In every case in which a rural land-order has been presented to me, the party concerned has declared that he was assured at New Zealand House he could have his land within a few miles from Nelson; whereas every selection of good land … has long ago been appropriated under the Re-selections."[95]

---

94 Kennington, Ch3
95 Allan, p386. Presumably the numbers in the lottery barrel had by now been attached to sections.

Those emigrating with limited capital were still being deceived, but the local agents allowed them to use their scrip to bid at auction for the surplus lands instead. It had to come to an end, and the key which finally freed up the land was an agreement to cancel the Company ownership of the unsold sections.

The new governor who succeeded Fitzroy, Captain George Grey, visited Nelson in March 1846 to meet a deputation of wealthy Nelson settlers who stressed to his sympathetic ear the urgency of getting the Wairau to resolve their rural land dilemma. Grey foresaw the future of wool production and supported the negotiations leading to the Wairau Purchase which was signed by Ngati Toa on 18 March 1847.[96]

By now the Nelson supper party and its adherents wanted much richer pickings. Depasturage licences were advertised by the Company from October 1848 and many opportunists, some absentee speculators and others lacking any background experience of pastoral farming, were allocated grazing rights at peppercorn rates to vast tracts of land which later became freehold in part or in full at 'give-away' prices. In the Awatere valley most of the runs were between 20,000 and 50,000 acres, a far cry from the 150-acre farm blocks first promised.

The labourers' attempts to get compensation for their broken contracts failed, but the opening up of the Wairau was of huge benefit to many Nelson landowners. The principal decisions allowed those who wished to retain their existing suburban allotments, usually because they had already developed them, to take first choice of the contiguous rural land now freed up. Seventeen landowners between them got 3,200 acres adjoining their Nelson suburban lands, an average of 190 per title instead of the nominal 150 acres.[97] Rural land was to be laid out in the Wairau, together with some suburban sections, in the original order of choices, and there were further conditions relating to arbitration and auctions. In practice the arbitrators, who had their own land interests, favoured the landowners over the Company.

Nelson was by now overrun with sheep and early in 1848 Nelson landowners started moving sheep into the Awatere and Wairau to stock the new runs. Many were looked after by managers and shepherds. They and their families endured the work, the isolation and the hazards but it was the names of the run-holders that were recorded in the histories. Surveying was in progress and in March 1848 the looked-for rural 150-acre blocks were finally laid out and allotted to the people who had bought and paid for them in England years before. Generally those in the Awatere were never used as farming blocks because it was not good farm country and 150 acres was scarcely an economic unit.

Once again there were the complications of absentee ownership, access to markets and unsuitable terrain, but change was coming to the Wairau, soon to become Marlborough, and great wealth would be produced there on the backs of those merino sheep.

---

96 Kennington, p20
97 McAloon, p4

An interesting postscript is that one of the last of the New Zealand Company's original 150-acre lots was re-sold in Marlborough in the 1880s and returned its owners only ten shillings an acre, which was the same as they had paid for it 40 years before.

In 1840 there were about a hundred European and Maori living at Port Underwood and adjacent areas.[98] Many Maori withdrew after the Wairau affair, and some former whalers moved inland with their families as the shore whaling stations around the bays diminished. The population did not increase appreciably, even with the new activities which were capital intensive rather than labour intensive as Nelson's agricultural practices were. Whaling itself still generated outward cargoes, and supplies came in regularly. Before long wool was also an important export and the active, rowdy settlement at the Wairau Bar, with its grog shop and behaviour that caused comment even in those boisterous times, became a shipping point and a social centre.

Waltzing Matilda

Squatters are part of Antipodean folklore, a squatter being one who got his right of pasturage from the government or other authority on easy terms. But in the case of the Wairau, the squatter culture was driven by dissatisfaction over the Company's failure to deliver promised land rather than by a desire to be pastoral pioneers. It was opportunism rather than intention in most cases, and some squatters had neither the ability nor the inclination to be sheep farmers themselves.

The wealthier settlers had been quick to realise that any unoccupied land could be utilised informally. Between 1844 and 1846 sheep numbers increased from 4,000 to 10,000 and they had doubled again by 1849.[99] From the end of 1845 Dillon and Stafford had an exclusive licence to graze their sheep in the upper Motueka valley on surveyed but not yet acquired sections for five pounds a year. George Duppa secured the same arrangement for the Wai-iti valley in 1846 and others moved flocks up the valley and over to the Wairau that year, clearly in knowledge and anticipation of the next step in land ownership and regulation. Morse and Dr Cooper had a flock at Tophouse which they drove through to the Wairau in November 1846, before the land was legally secured. Some flock owners did not even own land, which was a great annoyance to the Company.

What epics there must have been in the movements of flocks and herds, both by sea and through this wild, unsettled, unbridged and unroaded country. Coastal relocations by sea involved manhandling stock in and out of ships and whaleboats, while drovers followed the valley systems to Tophouse where their route comprised 24 miles of road, 18 miles of swampy valleys and 9 miles of dense birch forest. And that was just to the pass; there was more on the other side.[100]

---

98 Buick, T L, *Old Marlborough*, Capper Press, 1976, p226
99 McAloon, p41
100 *The Nelson Examiner,* 8 June 1852, reports such a journey in good detail.

On occasions when the stress of weather delays at sea made it imperative to get them ashore, some of the sheep were even landed at Nelson to be driven the long overland route to Canterbury. That journey was a droving marathon through Tophouse and the mountain valley systems of the Rainbow and the large sheep stations, across the rivers to where George Duppa established Culverden Station in 1852, and thence to the open country of Canterbury.

In 1850 Weld and Wilkinson walked back to Flaxbourne Station after a trip on the *Acheron* to Port Cooper (known in the 1840s as Port Victoria and later renamed Lyttelton after the chairman of the Canterbury Association in 1858). At the site of an unoccupied whaling station at Amuri Bluff, Weld and Wilkinson met up with two boatloads of Maori voyaging from Motueka to Port Victoria, and were hospitably received.[101] These and many other deeds of the pioneers have slipped into our collective background pretty much unrecorded, but whether on the coast, in the mountains or at sea they are the measure of people, both Maori and Pakeha, becoming one with this land of ours.

And the sea out there was the preferred highway. A slow build-up of locally-owned hookers and smaller boats served all the areas around Blind Bay, the southern shores of Cook Strait, and the Wairau. There would be radical change, and fortune hunting by those with the means, but nothing quite so tumultuous as that first decade from which Nelson was emerging.

*Loading livestock onto shoal-drafted hookers that could dry out on the gently sloping beaches was far easier than ferrying them out. In this later-era photograph a cattle-beast is being hoisted unceremoniously aboard at D'Urville Island, and can be seen swinging from the derrick just aft of the mainmast of the deck-scow **Pearl Kasper**.*
R Williams Collection

---

101 Sherrard, *Kaikoura, a History of the District*, Kaikoura County Council, 1966, p47

10

Onto a Steady Course

BY 1848, THE NELSON COLONY was no longer at risk of capsize, as the financial benefits of fresh commerce – particularly merino wool – began to be felt. The Company had lost its grip on the day-to-day running of the operation through local agents, after its temporary insolvency in 1844, and now acted principally as a land sales agency in London. The Provincial Government was beholden to the Governor and his Auckland officials.

When Her Majesty's steam vessel *Acheron*, surveying New Zealand waters from 1848 to 1851, was at Nelson in 1849 and recorded that *"Here all was smug civilisation: plenty of pubs offering 'entertainment for Man and Horse': a ruddy contented peasantry, something quite unknown then in Europe; cottages fat with flitches of bacon and sacks of corn …"*[102]

If the observation was accurate, this was a remarkable turnaround from the

HMS Acheron *must have made a stunning sight when she entered Nelson Haven in 1849 during Stokes' survey of Blind Bay (the first since Cook's) She was a Hermes Class wooden paddle-steamer built at the Sheerness dockyard in 1838.*
C-059-006, Alexander Turnbull Library

---

102 Natusch, Sheila, *The Cruise of the Acheron*, Whitcoulls. 1978, p134

state of the Nelson larders a few years earlier. At last there appeared to be a time of plenty and stability. New Zealand Company agent William Fox, on the suggestion of George Duppa, had abandoned the stated principles of the Company, helping the wealthier farmers to take up large sections and so employ labour and at the same time he offered the workers five-acre leaseholds, which they could buy if they actively cultivated them. This gave the labourers a first stake in the land and a chance to increase it over the years, and the landowners acquiesced because they were concerned the destitute workers might be desperate enough to steal their livestock and produce for food if they were not able to produce something for themselves. Nelson was no utopia, nor had generosity of spirit been especially evident when in October 1844 two sawyers at Motueka had been sentenced to ten years' transportation to Van Diemen's Land for killing a bullock. The harsh English 'justice' system was now applied in the New World where the law was still administered by property owners in their own interests. The sites of the penal colonies at both Norfolk Island and Port Arthur in Tasmania still open windows into the attitudes of the times, as does the report that Governor Arthur Phillip of New South Wales *unsuccessfully* requested, before he left with the first fleet, that recidivist convicts should be sent from his settlements to New Zealand to be eaten by the Maori![103]

In an interesting little sidelight on Nelson, historian Jim McAloon points out that towards the end of the first decade there were intensified arguments and tensions "...between those who advocated the rights of man and those who espoused the rights of property".[104] Michael King adds that "New Zealand was largely free of class consciousness."[105] Class, with its tradition of automatic authority, had failed the Wakefield scheme, and a significant unplanned outcome was that former labourers became landowners in Nelson far sooner than the expected 'master and servant' scheme could possibly have done.

Inadvertently, conservative Nelson found itself at the forefront of change, while just across the ranges the pastoralists of Marlborough had come to power through their landholdings.

The Crown Land Grant

Nelson immigrants had waited until 1848 for the government land commissioner William Spain to confirm a Crown land grant which finally set the boundaries of European settlement in the area. The southernmost line of land originally claimed by Colonel William Wakefield (after the 1840 Wellington 'purchase') was the 43rd parallel, somewhat south of Hokitika. Making the best of a bad job Commissioner Spain awarded the New Zealand Company a Blind Bay coastal area, from about Cable Bay to Riwaka, angling inland as a rough parallelogram extending approximately southwest into the Motueka valley below Mt Arthur. In

---

103 Barber, Laurie, *New Zealand, a Short History*, Century Hutchinson, 1989, pp37–38
104 McAloon, p62
105 King, *The Penguin History of New Zealand*, Penguin, 2003, p313

Massacre Bay the Company got a strip in the Aorere valley and a bit of coast and valley at Takaka. The intervening coastal strip, now mainly national park, was part of the Crown acquisitions of 1853–56 and was not available for purchase and settlement until after that.

Commissioner Spain's judgement ensured that the near-defunct New Zealand Company's scheme was securely embedded. Thus, despite of the failure of his venture, Edward Gibbon Wakefield's basic exhortation to 'possess yourselves of the soil and you are secure' had prevailed in many respects and it is only in more recent times that various injustices it created have started to be addressed.

Maori-owned hookers

Maori land occupants did not receive the fair deal that was originally promised, however their resourcefulness and ability to adapt to new technology helped to compensate as they adjusted to a new style of commerce. Initially they were easily able to improvise by modifying their larger waka to take sail, but very soon they were adopting the European-style vessels for their greater stability and load-carrying potential.

The Ngati Toa had already been quick to recognise the advantages of this more convenient form of transport for less benign purposes, with Te Rauparaha first chartering the brig *Elizabeth* for his devastating 1830 raid to Akaroa in the South Island, reportedly returning with barrels full of human flesh. When his niece's pakeha husband, the Porirua shore-whaler Joseph Thoms, built the 33 ton 45 ft schooner *Three Brothers* in Queen Charlotte Sound in 1842, it was a logical step for Te Rauparaha to use her to carry him and his armed warriors to the Wairau for that fateful encounter with the Nelson posse. In 1845 Thoms sold *Three Brothers* to three Ngati Toa Maori, David Puaha, Solomon Matakapi and Joseph Henia, her new master, who operated her as a hooker for the following two years.

Meanwhile at Nelson Haven's Auckland Point, ship-builder T G Freeman, launched a Maori-owned hooker in 1847. *Catherine* was a 10-ton, 32ft schooner built for a partnership of local Maori listed as Renata, Maka, Ruka and Pirimona, who were described in the registration document as 'naturalised citizens of Great Britain'. (She was initially registered in George William Schroder's name and it took until October 1854 for their names to be recorded.) Freeman next built the 12-ton, 32ft schooner *William and Horina* in 1848, also for a group of Maori owners, but her records are incomplete. Ruth Allan states that four hookers were built by Freeman in 1848 for Maori owners.[106] In 1851 *Tryphena*, 14 tons, was built for use in the North Island and another 14-ton schooner called *Mary* was built in 1853 for Hoeta, Paraone and Punupi Ohamaru. *Karorina* was also likely to have been Maori owned, being a 10 ton schooner first registered in Nelson in 1847, and skippered by Captain Mason.

---

106 Allan, Port Nelson, p12

Some Maori-owned small ships were built elsewhere in the district. One of these was *Erena*, a 12-ton clinker square-stern 35 ft schooner built at Motupipi by W Andrews. She was jointly owned by the Ngati Rarua chief Tamati Pirimona Marino in partnership with Samuel Strong. Tamati also was listed as the owner of another hooker named *Mio* which was wrecked at Astrolabe in 1856. *Lucinda* was a larger Motupipi-built 31 ton clinker square-stern schooner. She was built in 1847 by Lovell and Andrews for Hemi Kuka Matarua of Pakawau at the base of Farewell Spit, so will almost certainly have been designed to be beached while loading.

Many local Maori welcomed the settlers, even when they found their numbers overwhelming, They gave assistance, supplied food at critical times, and offered friendship, and some became active traders as well as growers of produce. In the earliest days of Nelson settlement Maori from the bays, d'Urville Island (Rangitoto) and the Sounds were regular callers, often with fish, livestock and produce. It was not uncommon to see up to a dozen canoes in the water or drawn up at Auckland Point[107], where resident Maori retained much of the land. Another landing area was under and through to the landward side of Saltwater Creek bridge. The transition from waka to the large, seaworthy hookers was prompt, with a number of Maori men already having crewed aboard the whalers' ships, gaining the necessary sail-handling skills. They were soon trading in this new style of vessel from the small ports on both sides of Cook Strait, carrying mainly flax and foodstuffs, especially pigs, potatoes and wheat in season, and timber. Maori farmers in this wider area later also supplied the Australian market during the gold rushes of the early 1850s, but this trade did not last.

The Wesleyan missionary Samuel Ironside had set up 16 outpost chapel mission-schools in 1842-43 throughout Cloudy Bay, the Sounds and Blind Bay (Whakatu and Motueka), led by 30 literate Maori preacher-teachers who taught an eager 600 'members'[108] the rudiments of reading, writing and even arithmetic with particular emphasis on the Bible. He writes of the eagerness of his flock to absorb the pakeha ciphering skills, marvelling at how quickly some were capable of mastering the pakeha-reo language, and claiming in 1842 that "over 100 could read the New Testament fluently in the mission class".[109] He periodically did the rounds of his circuit via canoe and also his own whaleboat, manned by Maori supporters, including the passage through the notorious French Pass.

By 1846 Maori farmers were transitioning to large tracts of arable grain production. According to Ironside[110] there were 1426 peaceable Maori living mainly in Wakapuaka, Motueka and Massacre Bay. The Motueka Maori sent 15,000 bushels of wheat to the Riwaka flourmill (situated close to the Riwaka School), and by 1850 they had 1,000 acres in wheat and 600 acres in other crops

---

107 See the Barnicoat sketch, ch 5
108 Letters of Samuel Ironside, 7th Jan 1843
109 Journal of Samuel Ironside, Nov 1842
110 Samuel Ironside in NZ p 206

such as maize and potatoes at Motueka. The mill was very slow (although it could operate considerably faster if grinding the proprietor's own product!) and it was occasionally even used by Maori from Aorere.[111]

One story relates how a visitor was squatting next to the huge revolving stone, intently watching the flour falling from the stones, when the two ends of his blanket were caught and the cogwheels forcibly drew him in. It was only the physical strength of the half-dozen bystanders who rushed to his aid, seizing the large driving wheel and stopping it revolving, that allowed the poor man to be extricated. Unfortunately the accident was too much for the cleverly constructed wooden cogs which were stripped off the wheel.

In 1849 Ironside[112] describes how the Maori ship-owners and traders *"were well aware of the effects of the imported grain on local prices and bargained accordingly. Formerly they had camped on the beach in half-open tents of sailcloth with bark on the floor: now they were provided with substantial hostelries when the ships they both owned and traded with put into port"*.

Hooker-building on the waterfront

With the increased opportunities from commerce, boatbuilding along Nelson's waterfront was accelerating. Samuel Strong, a 47-year-old immigrant described in the passenger list as a farmer and land purchaser, established a large boatbuilding yard at Auckland Point. Johann Beit's exploitation of the St Pauli passengers meant that the assistance they needed had to come from earlier settlers, and while Mrs Strong employed some of the German women in spinning wool her husband employed German immigrant Cordt Bensemann to help build a schooner from the timbers salvaged from the *Fifeshire* which had finally been removed from the rock at Nelson's entrance the previous year.[113] The schooner that fills the bill was the 26-ton, 44ft *Emergency*, registered as owned and built by Strong in 1847. She entered the coastal and Melbourne trade and is recorded as bringing livestock and merchandise across the Tasman that year. Earlier in 1847 Strong's yard completed the 15-ton, 33ft ketch *Supply*, also for himself. Once the Wairau territory was opened up she ran a regular service between Wairau, Wellington and Nelson, and she served the bays and West Coast for years under the well-known master Captain Walker. Seamen were always strong on humour and *Supply* seems to have attracted some. Surveyor Edward Jollie took passage from Nelson to Christchurch on "a small cutter called the *Supply* sometimes, but generally the *Roaring Gimblet*."[114] A gimlet is a drilling tool and undoubtedly the allusion is to her movement in a sea. Some vessels, particularly those which are beamy in proportion to their length, can have an unfortunate motion, twisting like a corkscrew in the water.

---

111 Pratt, p123
112 NZ Journal, 10 March 1849
113 Allan P329
114 E. Jollie, '*Reminiscences*', ref QMS-1071, Alexander Turnbull Library

Harry Washbourn wrote, "*In the late 50s early 60s Captain John Walker, cutter Supply was the principal trader to Collingwood and all things considered made very good trips.*"[115] He went on to say (erroneously) that *Supply* was built with considerable secrecy on Wakefield Quay near the junction with Victoria Road. When at last revealed at her launching, Washbourn said, there was a good deal of amusement as she had "*... the appearance of a fowl with its tail pulled out*". He described it (and the description has been picked up and repeated a number of times) as like the bow half of a good-sized boat that had been cut in the middle, and without any stern half. He said Captain Walker later had a stern put on her, which greatly improved her appearance, but there is no record of Walker owning her.

Some hookers had counter sterns, others were typical of lifeboat 'double-enders' and some had variations on a flat transom. We know *Supply* was built five years before the Washbourns arrived in New Zealand. However, she was altered from ketch to cutter rig in 1852, the year Harry Washbourn arrived as a lad. Possibly she was structurally altered at that time and there may have been a tonnage change from 15 to 16, although I have found no record of it. Perhaps Washbourn simply heard this description which must have appealed to him. *Supply* had an illustrious career in the coastal trade.

Life at the Haven

Nelson's central position made it an important shipping point for coastal movements and for ships coming across the Tasman Sea from Sydney, and by now Nelson people were well spread out around the bays and into the Wairau. Seafarers tend to widened interests through widened experience and contacts, although of course dogmatism existed there too. They were sociable men, often transacting their commercial business in the pubs and along the waterfront, and Nelson was a friendly place where most people had at least a nodding acquaintance with each other.

Haven Road was the hub from which hooker life radiated. A number of hooker photographs were taken there, in later decades, in the placid morning light before the sea breezes came in. At first Haven Road was a series of impromptu sea walls, jetties and breastwork wharves to berth at. Captain Nicholson had one wharf about eight feet wide, probably the one later used by the gasworks for unloading coal. It had a ramp down to the beach on the west side of it, out from what is now called Fountain Place. Later the Ricketts brothers would find it convenient to put hookers on one side or the other there at high tide, raising them on blocks to work on. *Gannet* was lengthened there, and *Argus* altered and sheathed with kauri, and one of the Ricketts' houses was straight across the road. Further along there was a slipway to a boatshed on piles to the west of the gasworks wharf, and there were other small structures and tidal wharves at Auckland Point and Green Point. By 1862, a tramway had been built alongside Haven Rd, shored up by a seawall which hookers were then able to lie alongside.

---

115 Washbourn, p48

John Westrupp's house is the small elevated one near the left of this early photograph of Haven Rd, taken in about 1862, over a decade after he moved to Nelson. He and the other seafarers who lived nearby will have benefited from the new seawall and tramline constructed during Nelson's second decade. Haven Road and the newly opened Dun tramway follows the foreshore towards Green Point on the right, as their hookers could now lie alongside the seawall which protected the tramway. Sailing ships and a steamer are at the Beit's and Company wharves, near the bond stores. The unpopular town acres of the Company lottery are clearly visible (eg; the triangular section at the base of Russell Street is section 40, lottery choice 90).

Copy Collection C294, Nelson Provincial Museum

This formed the end of a 13 mile line from the shortlived Dun Mountain copper mine, and became a useful additional piece of transport infrastructure for the budding port facilities.

Saltwater Creek Bridge and the causeway had allowed the commercial centre to move to Bridge Street, leaving warehouses, shipbuilding and houses on the flat at Auckland Point. Ships were built further around Haven Road at Green Point (the present wharf area) and along Wakefield Quay. Shipwrights and seafarers could be found living along Haven Road and adjacent, so there was the sea on one side and a distinct seafaring flavour on the other. The hookers tied up just across the road in the vicinity of Russell Street.

The 1849 census record shows my father's grandfather John Westrupp, a boatman, living with his wife Margaret and their first son John in an elevated cottage above Haven Road, part of section 51 and about three sites towards town from Russell Street. John and Margaret (née Parker, an immigrant on the *New Zealand* in 1842) remained there for many years and raised six sons who all followed in their father's wake as captains in the hooker years. Their daughter Sarah married a hooker captain who built the schooner *May* at Frenchman's Bay. With their cottage overlooking the activities of the little ships below, it was small wonder the Westrupps became part of that scene. Later the names of Haven Road and Russell Street residents would be like a roll call of hooker and steamer crews, along with the seafarer-boatbuilders like the next generation of the Ricketts family.

The New Zealand Company wharf and Beit's wharf at Green Point, each established in 1843 with a stone breastwork and jetty, had to suffice for years.

Even in 1855, the year when wharf builder William Akersten arrived, the outer piles of the customhouse wharf at Green Point were dry at low spring tide so the ships lay at anchor and their cargoes of people or goods had to be ferried ashore. It required a flat-bottomed lighter to shift goods to Morrison and Sclanders wharf at Auckland Point, even at high tide.[116] From the earliest days of settlement rowing boats had penetrated into river, creek and inlet, but the sea margins were still mudflat merging to swampy land. These edges were progressively reclaimed.

Hooker service

The build-up of Nelson-based shipping in 1847 coincided with the development of the Wairau. Earlier vessels were, in the main, short-lived or transient but with the opening up of the Wairau and Awatere pasture lands business began to flourish, although there was still not enough trade in Blind Bay to keep the vessels fully employed and they still worked to and from the North Island.

Much of the initial local trade had focused on Motueka's coastal edge which had a series of simple estuary landing-ports south of Riwaka. These were convenient for working the Company's *Deal* and survey boats as well as privately owned ships' boats like the ones bought from *Whitby* and *Hope*, the whaleboats and locally-built vessels. Frederick Moore's *Mary Ann* would have had a mooring place where she grounded out between tides in a sheltered estuary corner.

What distinguished the hookers was that they were vessels with holds, unlike the much later and differently-constructed scows which were deck loaded at first. Hookers were also able to 'take the hard' – like ships' boats they could be put aground to unload and reload, and they were built full in the bilges so they sat sufficiently upright to be worked between tides. Washbourn explained how they used the Doctor's Creek loading area in the 1850s:

"A vessel would anchor off Motueka, and the produce was lightered off to her as there was no wharf. It was rather a slow process .... The lighters were the 33ft **Elizabeth**, 15 tons, and the **Brothers**, 10 tons, and these had to be loaded sometimes in the water and sometimes lying on the ground, from bullock drays. The price of potatoes delivered on board was four pounds a ton, and this price was considered satisfactory. White pine boards and scantling were one pound per hundred feet."

Harry Washbourn records that several of the trading and passenger boats were converted ships' boats from 10 to 15 tons. The two hookers that Washbourn called lighters, *Elizabeth*[117] and *Brothers*, operated a service between Nelson and Motueka, where a flag was hoisted at the Manuka Bush as an indication of an imminent sailing.

Meanwhile at Beavertown (near Blenheim) on the Opawa River, the signalling practice was to light a bonfire on a knoll so everyone would know a hooker had arrived. At the Nelson entrance the flagstaff on Britannia Heights was used to signal ships in the offing; and later a separate one for coastal vessels which even

---

116 Broad, p182
117 *Elizabeth* was one of several vessels bearing this name in succeeding decades.

The ability to 'take the hard' and stay upright was an asset to beach-loading hookers, as can be seen in this later-era photo of **Argus**, *a 61 ft hooker built of steel in Melbourne circa 1856 and purchased by J.C.(Cocky) Burford in 1879 to carry coal. When this photo was taken, she had been sheathed in timber at the Ricketts yard, and converted from schooner to ketch. Few images exist of the mid C19 hookers, but generally the earliest clinker-built square-sterned hookers tended to be purely functional and less pleasing to the eye than most of the later vessels.*

Burford Collection 316759 Nelson Provincial Museum

indicated the rig of the vessel to help early identification. Visual signalling was the only way to announce arrivals and departures in those days.

At first there were few horses in the settlement and Riwaka folk would have to cross the Motueka River and travel along quite undeveloped routes on foot or in a bullock cart. Later there was a ferry across the river, then travellers would board a hooker for a trip of up to twelve hours, time spent sitting out on the open deck watching for the boom passing from one side to the other when she went about, and keeping out of the way of the crew. Although regular passengers developed handy skills and often helped work the ships it would not have been comfortable travel for most.

There is an often-repeated tale of a Nelson milliner who went to Motueka on the *Elizabeth* wearing a hooped crinoline gown. She was picked up by the boom when the ship went about, and deposited overboard but her unwieldy parachute of a skirt kept her afloat until the dinghy could be lowered to pick her up. That would have been a challenge in itself, with hoops to arrange and modesty to preserve. On such trips banged heads and lost hats were not infrequent.

To Riwaka to build

Ambrose Ricketts moved across the Bay to build the clinker schooner *Triumph*, 12-tons and 32ft, at Riwaka in 1848. She was built for Henry Fowler who was soon also listed as owner and master in 1849 of the 12-ton 31ft cutter *Catherine Ann*, built by Captain Salvator Cemino at Wellington in 1848. Such vessels had their social uses. William Pratt reports that Henry Fowler brought his schooner across the bay to pick up the widowed Mrs Edwards and her two daughters, along with Pratt himself and probably others, to attend a supper and dance in Nelson. Underlying this were developing romances between the young folk. It was daylight before the men returned to the schooner to snatch an hour or two's sleep, but Pratt decided to walk back to Motueka instead. He reached there by evening, intending to get back to Riwaka, but a swollen river held him up overnight.[118]

The other enterprising young seafarer from Riwaka was Thomas Askew, one of William Askew's five sons. Recorded as a co-owner of *Elizabeth* in 1848, Askew was mentioned two years later as master of the little 9-ton *William*. In the same year, 1850, the 29-ton 52ft topsail schooner *Mary* was built at Nelson by T G Freeman for the merchant Charles Empson.

In 1852 Askew had *Necromancer* built at Nelson, and he seems to have acquired the 78-ton brigantine *Return* in 1854. Then *Mary* was re-registered in 1856 with Thomas Askew as owner. It is possible he had merchant backing at this stage, as by 1859 he was established in Dundas House, Bridge Street, as a storekeeper and "Owner and agent of vessels running from Nelson to Massacre Bay, Wairau &c." Askew was master of the yacht *Waterwitch* at Nelson from 1863 and owner of *Gipsy* when she was lost on the Grey River bar that year. The old

---

118 Pratt p132

social class divisions were getting blurred, although in some parts of society they were staunchly maintained.

Hooker cargoes

The number of hookers slowly increased, and they began to trade further afield as Blind Bay still did not generate enough trade to utilise them all. But as many Wairau landowners were Nelson-based it was to Nelson as often as Wellington they turned for supplies and for on-shipping their wool clips. There was always some flax gathered and, surprisingly, Maori were the only producers of fibre in any quantity. Flax processing plants brought out to New Zealand proved unsuitable and none of those early machines could do as well as an adroit Maori woman with a mussel shell. It was much later that mechanical flax processing was developed to cope with the New Zealand material.

Nelson became the leading small farming area, producing a third of New Zealand's crops. Nelson beer was particularly popular in both Wellington and Auckland, and with flour it made up over 40 percent of the export value at the end of the 1840s.[119] As well as supplying the local market, produce and timber were shipped to the North Island, Canterbury and Otago. Later Nelson profited briefly from the 1851 gold rushes in Australia by shipping produce to Victoria. The inter-colonial ships carried oats, potatoes, barley, timber and vegetables, while local markets engaged the smaller ships in carrying wheat, fruit, hops, beer, bacon and butter.

Nelson's subsistence farmers were working their land at the lower end of the economic spectrum and it could take years for their work to pay off, in remarkable contrast to how quickly the trappings of civilisation and commerce were established in the settlement. Social life and trade were prominent even though there were stumps and shacks not far from the main streets, and the wealthy 'establishment' was cemented in place long before farming; that had required nearly a decade of hard work. Those building themselves hookers, who somehow had to supplement what their own labour could reap from the bush with bought necessities such as hardware and sailcloth, were in a similar position to the farmers and the outcome was that merchants often owned or held mortgages over the ships. This was not always in the best interests of captains and crews, as "In the absence of a statutory system of strict inspection for seaworthiness these vessels were, more often than not, equipped and manned with the barest minimum of expense."[120]

---

119 Broad p111
120 Sherrard p82

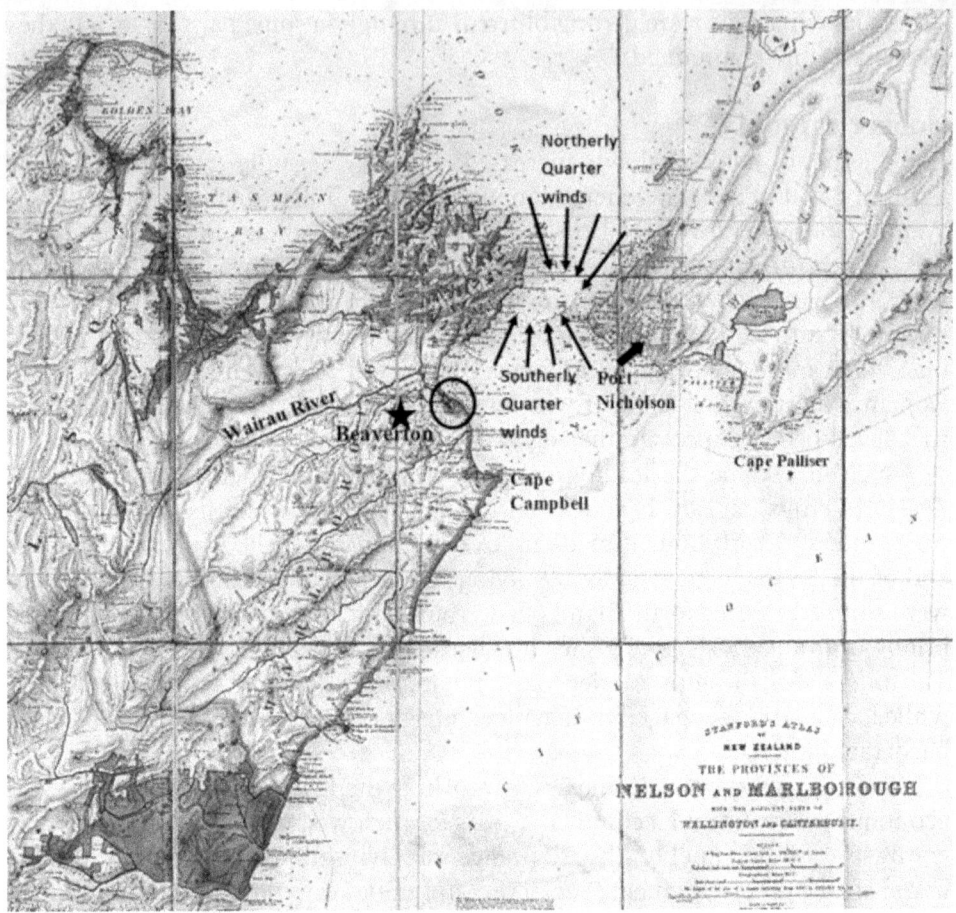

This extract from an 1864 Atlas shows how the (circled) bar entrance to the Wairau River lies in relation to Cook Strait and Port Nicholson (Wellington Harbour). Beaverton (later named Blenheim) was accessed via the Opawa River on the true-right after crossing the Wairau bar. Cape Palliser at the South-eastern corner of the North Island has a fearsome reputation, as does Cape Terawhiti at the South-western corner. The wind is funnelled through the narrow strait creating gales as a regular phenomenon.

From the Stanford's Atlas of New Zealand, courtesy National Library of New Zealand

11

Marlborough via Cook Strait

FROM THE EXPERIENCES ALREADY RELATED by John Kidson and Alfred Saunders, the potentially ferocious challenges of Cook's Strait were not to be taken lightly. Access to the freshly settled Wairau region (the name of Marlborough district until 1859 when it separated from Nelson province) was principally by sea, avoiding the arduous overland route across the Richmond and Bryant ranges.

The Wairau started producing as soon as the pastoralists gained access in the second half of the 1840s. Sheep spread through the plains, valleys and up the mountainsides of the grass country, growing wool as they moved. Some of the land was sparse and hard but, unlike agriculture, sheep farming developed the land quickly. Supplies were carried in, sheep were grazed on whatever vegetation was there, and wool became an immediate product to get to market. In earliest times wool was carted from the stations to Beavertown (now Blenheim) and loaded on board there. Hemp and tallow were other exports, while timber and supplies of various sorts were shipped up the river and sent back to the stations. As the farms developed, produce and grain were sent out to Australia for a short time while the gold boom lasted.

Vessels arriving at the Wairau Bar had a choice of two significant waterways which penetrate inland on the Wairau plain: the Wairau River and its tributary, the Opawa River. A natural boulder bank at the Wairau River mouth was protection behind which, in early years, the schooners *Triumph* and *Old Jack* discharged their cargoes into smaller boats capable of working the river shallows.

Both vessels were built for the Wairau trade, *Old Jack* at Cloudy Bay (Port Underwood) in 1847 and *Triumph* at Riwaka in 1848. *Old Jack* was named for her owner Jack Guard and was the first of two vessels of this name.[121] She was a nine-ton clincher ketch built at Guard's Port Underwood whaling station at Kakapo Bay. She is known to have sailed Cook Strait waters for about seven years but her fate is uncertain. For Hugh Fowler, who owned *Triumph*, her undoing came all too soon; in mid-June 1849 she had proceeded up the river to the Beaver Station with supplies on board for several of the sheep stations. A fresh in the river caused her to part her moorings and she was swept away and dashed to pieces. Beaver station ('The Beaver') gained its name from a Canadian who arrived in a flood on horseback to find his friends sheltering on the top bunk of a hut '*like beavers in a dam*'.

---

121 *Old Jack II* was a cutter built of kauri at Kakapo Bay in 1867. and was still fishing a century later. She had been reframed, re-engined and re-named, first Kyra (under Tim Daken of Port Underwood) and finally Marilyn when she worked out of Westport in 1967.

*Although this early photograph has been crudely labelled as Old Jack 1847, it is more likely that she is **Old Jack II**, built twenty years later and seen here sailing in Wellington Harbour. She is certainly typical of the hooker cutters of the era with her plumb bow and ample deck space for cargo.*
Westrupp Collection

    The small boats which carried loads to and from *Triumph* and *Old Jack* at the Wairau Bar during the 1840s were towed up the Opawa River to The Beaver by horses (trained to understand profanity, according to some listeners) using a towpath along the bank. The other settlement on the Wairau Plains was The Big Bush, later known as Grovetown. Developers competed to sell land and establish the leading town and The Beaver, which later became Blenheim, won the battle. This swampy site was not ideal, being prone to regular flooding. It had formerly been the site of a Maori settlement known as Waiharakeke (Flax-waters), and it was not until about 1880 that expensive flood-management measures allowed the town to expand without disruption.

    It was an unexpected major natural event that allowed river transport to abruptly become far more feasible in the Wairau. The 1848 Wellington earthquake changed the depth of water at the entrance to the Wairau River, as well as increasing the Opawa river depth by a metre. Now shoal draft hookers like *Triumph* could bypass the lighters and discharge cargoes some distance inland, Seven years later an even more severe earthquake in 1855 made it even more accessible. Medium draft hookers were now readily able to be towed all the way upstream to Blenheim via the Opawa and Taylor (Omaka) rivers, removing the need for the cumbersome trans-shipping of wool to Port Underwood in barges and boats. *Gipsy* was the first, closely followed by *Mary*, *Rapid* and Thomas Askew's *Necromancer*. *Gipsy* was a 17-ton, 44ft schooner built at Nelson in 1856 for J Smart and T Whitwell. She later played a pioneering role in the West Coast trade. Soon *Rapid*, a 15-ton schooner built by T G Freeman in 1849 for the merchant Charles Empson specifically for the Wairau wool trade, replaced the smaller *Triumph*. She was "*built with a spacious floor, almost like a barge, to allow the stowage of wool, and it is calculated that she will carry between sixty and seventy bales of wool, and yet draw only three feet of water.*"[122] There is no indication of what she was like under sail.

The long-suffering tow horses were provided by Sam Bowler, who farmed at Marshlands, in partnership with George Jackson (unrelated to the whaler Jimmy Jackson) who had settled at Robin Hood Bay. Bowler and Jackson also ran *Shepherdess*, *Seabird* and *Alert* in the coastal trade, and succeeded James Wynen at the Wairau Bar trading post.[123] The Bowler-Jackson partnership seemed to have been formed in the mid-1850s. *Shepherdess* was built in Sydney in 1842 and later registered in Wellington as a 46ft schooner of 38 tons, and she was in and out of Nelson from 1857. *Shepherdess* was a regular operator further south on Marlborough's rugged Kaikoura coast in the mid-1850s, necessitating a very close eye on the weather. A fire would guide her in to anchor offshore from the reef-strewn beach at dusk and the next day everyone would work furiously to beat a likely wind-shift. The wool clip was taken out to her by whaler or surfboat, and loading the wool bales into whaleboats required some men to stand in the surf virtually all day. In the latter stages they were fortified by brandy, "*as much grog as they could work well on and no more*".[124] It was surely a fine skill to judge the appropriate quantity.

A little later, the horse towing was superseded by a barge fitted with a portable steam engine and used as a tug to assist the hookers. It was named *Osprey* but was universally known as *Puffing Billy* and its comings and goings resounded over the plains letting people know there was activity on the river. Small steamers worked the rivers, too, notably the paddle steamer *Nelson* which maintained scheduled sailings to Nelson from 1864 although the paddle steamer *Tasmanian Maid* worked on the Wairau River in 1857. Over the years a regular service ran between Marlborough and Nelson (*Gipsy* and *Mary*) and Wellington (*Alert* and *Supply*). Within this period of activity, probably from 1872, *Dido*, *XXX*, *Falcon* and *Hope* also worked the Opawa.

Hookers would bring people and materials from Blind Bay. For a long time Marlborough lacked tradesmen. They would come from Nelson when they were

---

122 *The Nelson Examiner*, 12 January 1850
123 Dawber p81
124 Sherrard p194

needed: for example, when the cob house at Altimarlock station had to be replaced after the 1855 earthquake, Brown and Simpson came from Nelson to do the stonework, and Thomas Askew brought the timber by sea. That cargo was totara, milled near Collingwood and rafted ashore near the White Bluffs of Ruby Bay to be loaded.[125]

Although this later-era photograph is of a wool-loading operation on a different east coast rocky coast (Waipiro Bay,[126] circa 1908), the scene is likely very similar to the wool-bales being lightered onto a hooker like **Shepherdess** in the mid-19th century between Cape Campbell and Kaikoura.
PAColl-3047, Alexander Turnbull Library

Navigating the Opawa
The river's course changed in 1868 and floods eventually caused the route's abandonment, although some vessels continued to trade the Wairau and Opawa Rivers well into the 20th century. The auxiliary scow *Echo* used the Opawa River and berthed at Blenheim as late as 1965. I have been on both the Wairau and the Opawa rivers, racing on them in a rowing crew in the 1940s. That reach of the Wairau seems largely shingle now, as is the meandering way

---

125 I once had occasion to sit out a NW gale in my ketch *Matuku II* in the southern end of this very bay.
126 Kennington p66

*This crew shown in this highly stylised painting of **Shepherdess** in Cook Strait give an impression of a topsail schooner far larger than her registered 46 feet. This 'length between perpendiculars' was the internal measurements between rudderpost and stem, (like all hookers' registered lengths), so her length on deck will have exceeded 50 feet. It is unlikely she carried square topsails while working the Kaikoura coast due to their high windage.*
W M Forster painting, C-105-001 Alexander Turnbull Library

of rivers, and rowing on the short opening day Opawa course was suspended when we were on the water so the *Echo* could come past, under power, to her berth in Blenheim with a piece of greenery caught in the rigging.

Ron Perano later described the difficulties of navigating near the willows overhanging the banks: "*If she was loaded wrong she was very difficult to steer and she'd just bounce off one bank and then bounce off the next one. Big willow branches would get hooked up in the rigging ... She had quite a big bowsprit on her and she poked it behind a willow and snapped it off.*"[127]

While Marlborough had interests in common with the Nelson settlement their two seaward approaches offered distinctively different personalities. Blind Bay had its hazards including the westerly gales which, with reasonable prudence and some luck, were surmountable, although there were losses. But once the hookers entered Cook Strait, that stretch of water acting as a wind funnel between the two land masses, it was sea-keeping ability that was tested as options for shelter were strictly limited depending on the wind direction.

Although *Echo* was fitted with an engine, unlike the 19th century hookers, she had the same wild Cook Strait weather to contend with during her regular Wellington-Blenheim run. One of my 'ancient mariner' friends, the late Ken Sellars, was engineer aboard *Echo* when she ran from Wellington to Blenheim via the Wairau Bar, and described the strategies used for the trip: "*Departing Wellington for Blenheim, while approaching Wellington Heads we would put the canvas on her and shortly afterwards poke our nose into Cook Strait. The prevailing winds are, as you know, from the north, with a bit of westerly content at times. The*

---
127 *The Seaport News*, 2008

Echo still had her bowsprit when this photograph was taken of her and the local steamer **SS Wairau** at Blenheim wharf a hundred years ago. The Opawa River is placid compared with its early flood-prone days, and the willows have taken over the banks. With her centreboard raised for the shallow waterway, **Echo** had virtually no lateral resistance and was very difficult to steer, often hitting the banks and willow branches while underway.
S.C. Smith Collection G45783 ½ Alexander Turnbull Library

This 1872 photograph shows a well established town behind the Blenheim river-wharves. Despite the 1868 floods, the Opawa River was still sufficiently navigable for large shoal-draft vessels like the two shown here: the paddle steamer **SS Lyttelton** and the 66ft local hooker **Falcon** (a shoal-draft Tasmanian ketch).
William Collie photo, F-54285 ½ PA7-07-10, Alexander Turnbull Library

strength and direction of this wind would determine our course, and the centreboards were also lowered at this time. The end result was that the wind was generally just for'ard of being abeam on the starboard side. These conditions would usually take us down into Cloudy Bay, and our approach to the Wairau Bar. The canvas was taken in, and we approached the bar with some trepidation, as well we might, as on two occasions while I was on the Echo, we crossed the bar on a different date to the one on which we commenced the crossing.

"*The conditions were not good. The river itself had a great many bends on its journey to the mouth. These bends were difficult to navigate, especially at night ... there were plenty of obstacles to contend with, like crashing into the willows along one section. This was particularly bad during the early spring, and the ship would cross the bar, knee deep in debris and looking like a floating Christmas tree. If, through delays, we missed the tide at the bar, we would tie up at Cantwells, just before the beginnings of the mudflats inside the mouth.*"

Losses on land and in Cook Strait

The land could be as hard a taskmaster as the sea at times. George Kemp, who managed the Starborough run for R K Newcome, was coming back from the supply point at the Wairau River mouth one day when he was thrown from his dray on rough ground. The large, iron-tyred wheel crushed his bent leg both above and below the knee. There was no medical help closer than Nelson, therefore effectively none at all, and he died several days later on 5 July 1850, aged 41. He was the first European to die in the area since the Wairau incident.

In February the following year the Reverend T D Nicholson, a pioneer minister traversing the lonely miles to be of service to others, found Mrs Kemp dying of childbirth complications and there was no care available for her either. The next day George's remains were disinterred and reburied in a cemetery site, and the day after that came the melancholy task of burying his wife alongside him.[128] Some of their seven orphaned children found work in the area while the younger ones were taken to Nelson for fostering – such is the stuff of parents' nightmares. Similar tales can be found up and down the land, and around the coasts.

My personal experiences sailing Cook Strait waters gave me a feeling of kinship with those pioneer settlers, whalers and traders – it is considerably more challenging down there on the water among the waves than it appears from the deck of an inter-island ferry. In one particularly bad spell of January weather we waited in the Queen Charlotte Sound, watching for a window in the northwesters so we could sail our 36ft ketch back to Napier. The weather report gave us that window, but shortly after we sailed out into Cook Strait the forecast was updated to warn of a hard southerly front. Not being a strong crew for sustained bad weather time at sea, we planned our passage-making according to weather, distance and anchorages or shelter, including using Wellington's Port Nicholson

---

128 Kennington, p101

as a 'bolt-hole' - just as the hookers would have done – as the key to this particular passage was to weather Cape Palliser in reasonable conditions, and then run up the East Coast.

From 130 years earlier, the following account from William Pratt gives a first hand experience of exactly this situation during his 1849 trip with Henry Fowler on *Catherine Ann* from Nelson to Port Cooper[129]. The conditions will sound familiar to some who have spent sea time in Cook Strait, but the parameters were vastly different. A hooker had no engine and no external ballast, nothing for self-righting except internal ballast (often stones in the bilge) as well as cargo that could shift in extreme conditions. Fixed rigging was only rope, hopefully there was a compass but at best there was probably no more than a sketch for a chart. There were no lighthouses – Pencarrow lighthouse, the first on the coasts, was not erected until 1859. Nor was there the prospect of going to windward in heavy weather, a capacity that we did have to a limited extent in our marconi-rigged ketch *Matuku II*. It is well worth reading Pratt's detailed account of his passage aboard the cutter *Catherine Ann* with her gaff mainsail and two headsails, one on a long (possibly retractable) bowsprit, and with her topsides leaking quite badly when she heeled, probably because the planking had shrunk:

"We had a fair wind through the straits and were off the Kaikouras when we caught it thick and strong from the sou'west. After battling with it all night and making no headway, and there being no signs of its moderating, and the cutter leaking a great deal in her top sides as she lay over while close hauled, Fowler decided to run back to Wellington while he could ensure daylight to make the heads. The cutter was a capital sea-boat, and I had every confidence in the skill and judgement of Fowler who kept unwearied charge of the helm. Our small craft seemed no bigger than one of the numerous sea-birds screeching around us, in contrast with the mighty sea that was running, and is invariably found across the entrance to the straits between Capes Campbell and Palliser, after a twelve hours' gale from the southward; but we careered along in gallant style, topping the swell as buoyantly as the gulls, and made very pleasant weather of it. We were just sufficiently laden to make her staunch and firm under the canvas carried, which was a storm jib, staysail, and single reef in the mainsail, and I should have enjoyed it much if her head had been pointing south instead of north.

"As Fowler's coasting experience had hitherto been limited to the straits north of Wellington, this was the first occasion of his approaching the heads from the south; and knowing the number of fatal wrecks that had occurred through Palliser Bay being mistaken for Wellington Harbour, he was very anxious for the thick mist to lift that hung over the land, before running too far in. When a good sight of the hills was at last obtained, he found in his anxiety to give the fatal bay a wide berth, that he had kept her away too much and had overrun the entrance. It then became a question whether he should bring the cutter up in the wind, and beat back, or run her through the straits and round Cape Terawhiti to Porirua, where there was good anchorage

---

129 Later renamed Lyttelton

under Mana Island.

"The fact of the cutter leaking a good deal when close-hauled, and thereby damaging the cargo, decided him in favour of the latter course, though this he said had its drawback; as the tide being about half ebb and with the southerly wind, and the sea there was, he knew we should have to encounter a frightful tide-rip off Terawhiti. With the wind and sea right aft we were not long in finding his opinion verified. In the terrific uproar, and commotion of hissing, seething water in which we soon found ourselves, our tiny craft appeared to me no more than a cork in the Norwegian Maelstrom, and we seemed nearly as impotent to control her movements; anon, we were almost buried in the trough of the sea, with an almost perpendicular wall of green water on either side, so much higher than the mast that the mainsail flapped against the topping lifts, and the boom, relieved of all strain, would have been jerked inboard if Fowler had not taken the precaution some time before, of having a guy attached to it from for'ard; then instead of being swallowed up, as seemed inevitable, the gulf would widen and rolling beneath us would as suddenly elevate us to its crest, when a few brief moments in the gale just sufficed to give the requisite momentum to barely preserve steerage way when becalmed in the trough of the boiling sea.

"At last, we had the supreme satisfaction of rounding the cape and gradually edging into smooth water. I felt immensely relieved at what I could not help thinking was a providential escape, but this was my first experience. Fowler said he had often been caught in it before, only not so close to the cape as on this occasion."[130]

In our own nearly parallel situation 130 years later, choosing Port Nicholson as our bolt-hole aboard *Matuku II*, we kept good watch and saw the approaching southerly from mid-strait – a wall of dark and forbidding clouds near Cape Campbell, much earlier than predicted and at twice the strength. I was able to confirm good bearings for Wellington before the storm bore down upon us and visibility was lost in the tumult of rain, wind and wave. We were almost knocked flat with the initial onslaught despite being well reefed down, and prepared. You can be sure we watched anxiously for the lighthouse structures we were sweeping towards to emerge from the stormy gloom, then we would know we were on course for the boisterous entry to Wellington Harbour, tiller-steering over vicious tide-against-wind seas, then the slog up Evans Bay. There would have been no second chance in those conditions and the alternative, getting around Cape Palliser, was even less appealing. In terms of the experience, the thirteen decades that had passed since *Catherine Ann*'s similar close call might never have been, except that Henry Fowler was better positioned to head westward.

Early wrecks

Given that the odds were stacked against the scantily equipped early hookers with so few navigational aids, it is hardly surprising that there were heavy losses during those first few years when Nelson was finding its feet:

The 72 ton schooner *Kate* had the misfortune to strike rocks twice and was

---

130 Pratt, p183

wrecked near Cape Terawhiti on 10 July, 1842. Later that winter, the early 42ft Wellington to Nelson trading schooner *Rory O'More* was driven ashore in Palliser Bay, September 1842, barely a year after being launched at Great Barrier Island. *Enterprise*, the 9-ton Nelson cutter, beat about Cook Strait for several days in March 1844, before being driven ashore in Howland's Bay after seeking refuge in Queen Charlotte Sound. *Erin*, Nelson's earliest-built vessel (aboard which we imaginatively shared a voyage aboard in chapter 4), was wrecked east of Cape Palliser on 22nd April 1844. The schooner *James* was driven ashore in Palliser Bay in July, 1844.

Finetta, a smaller cutter registered in Nelson (February 1843) left Wellington in May 1845, ran into rough weather in Cook Strait, lost her mast and was driven ashore at Cape Campbell. The crew landed safely but two lives were lost aboard the 39ft cutter *Pickwick*, when she was wrecked off Cape Palliser in a SW gale in June 1845. A month later records show *Eliza* being wrecked in Palliser Bay in a heavy gale on 4th July, 1845. She was listed as a 35 ton ship, but is likely to be the 11 ton schooner-rigged hooker that was trading pigs and potatoes into Nelson to

It was not just the primitively equipped hookers that were vulnerable to shipwreck during the first two decades of the colony. One of Blind Bay's most famous shipwrecks was the Nelson-built brig **Delaware**, *driven onto rocks only 200 metres from the Delaware Bay shore in a nor'west gale on her maiden voyage, only 12 miles north of Nelson Haven's entrance in 1863. This painting demonstrates the horror of being caught on a lee shore with a vessel incapable of clawing to windward. The sole passenger and all but one of her crew were saved by the brave actions of four local Maori including the heroine, Huria Matenga, who became famous for her efforts in swimming through the breakers to help retrieve a lifeline.*

Painting 1/1-002018-G) Alexander Turnbull Library

immediately supply the preliminary party. Next on the roll-call of early shipwrecks was the little *Amelia*, a 9-ton schooner registered in Nelson, wrecked in Worser Bay just inside Wellington heads on 13th August 1846.

The loss of *Phoenix* was particularly tragic. Seven men were drowned when this 37-ton, 48ft schooner, built at Nelson in 1846 by her merchant owner Alexander Perry, was lost on her maiden voyage under Captain George Cooper between Stephens and d'Urville Islands in November 1846. Both crewmen were also drowned aboard *Matilda*, an eight-ton cutter, which was caught in a south-easterly on 5th July 1848 and driven ashore near Wellington Heads. The little cutter *Hero* was luckier when she was driven ashore south of Cape Campbell in November 1848 with all hands surviving.

The loss of seafaring lives continued, largely in the Straits waters beyond Blind Bay. The schooner *Petrel*, was caught in a hard northerly after leaving Wellington on 1st April 1849 going down with the loss of two lives while trying to reach the lee of Kapiti Island. *Emily*, a 15-ton schooner probably built in Nelson in 1847, was wrecked in Palliser Bay in a gale in June 1849, and seven were drowned. She had departed from Nelson for Otago with her owner and master B. Phillips at the helm. Another seven men died when the schooner *Comfort*, out of Wellington on 22nd August 1849, turned turtle and was found bottom up in Queen Charlotte Sound – a risk run by all internally ballasted hookers in beam seas. *Catherine Ann* was wrecked adjoining Port Gore, where she had run for shelter on 6th September 1849, but she was salvaged.

Carbon, our other Motupipi-built schooner, left Nelson in February 1848 to trade out of Wellington and was lost off Castlepoint with all hands in 1850. *Maria Josephine*, the 37ft sloop built at Port Nelson in 1849, was wrecked in Wellington Harbour in June 1851 when her rudder became unshipped in a severe southeaster.

The hooker *Fidele*, which took Weld south to the Awatere in 1846, was sold the following year to Kaikoura whaler Robert Fyffe. He and his Maori crewmate sailed for Wellington with a cargo of whale oil some time in April 1854 and soon afterwards *Fidele* was found cast up two miles south of Cape Campbell with Fyffe's body under the boat and his crewman's nearby. They were buried there, Pakeha and Maori side by side, but their graves are now lost. Fyffe House still stands at Kaikoura.

This is not the total sum of Cook Strait's earliest claims, but it does give us some insight into the perils facing the small ships that chanced its waters in those first few years when daring seemed to be the name of the game.

Surveying under steam-power

During the three years 1848 to 1851, a significant aid to navigation was carried out by the Royal Navy survey vessel *Acheron*, creating a detailed set of New Zealand coastal charts far superior to those of Cook, d'Urville and the NZ Company harbour surveys.

Acheron's accomplished navigator, Commander Richards, had already carried out some coastal surveying to North Cape in a small coaster supplied by the

Governor Sir George Grey. He knew from experience that neither the east nor west coast was kindly to the little ships. remarking in a letter to the Royal Navy Hydrographic Office in England that: "It is impossible to do anything on the west coast of these islands in the small coasters. Three or four are generally lost in the course of a year – and often all the crews, even in running the passages and watching the weather"[131]

Being a steam-powered auxiliary paddle-steamer, *Acheron* attracted a lot of interest, as already steam was becoming recognised as the future for shipping. She bunkered with coal for testing from Motupipi in Coal Bay[132] and found it burned well when mixed with a little Sydney coal. *Acheron* steamed around from Coal Bay to Nelson, where the crew observed four vessels, a timber scow and three small schooners in advanced states of building in the shipyards on the beach.

The East Coast route northwards

The Wairarapa coastline north to Hawke's Bay, Poverty Bay and East Cape tended to be worked more routinely by Wellington's hookers than Nelson's, but there was some overlap. Having personally sailed this coast several times in fair weather and foul aboard *New Zealand Maid* and *Matuku II*, I have experienced its extreme offshore northwesterlies and found the windgusts especially violent. There is a very strong funnelling effect from the Tararua and Ruahine ranges, particularly near Castlepoint, Cape Turnagain and Porangahau before rounding Cape Kidnappers for the first significant shelter in over 200 nautical miles. The return trip southwards sailing into Cook Strait is even more difficult, due to the frequency of NW head-gales through Palliser Bay and the possibility of a disastrous southerly buster between Cape Palliser and Baring Head.

The same conditions, with gusts and a short fetch pushing up short steep seas, can be met trying to sail from Hawke's Bay to Gisborne and even further north to East Cape and beyond. However we have also experienced near-idyllic sailing on this stretch of coast. with flying fish nearby, dolphins cavorting under the bow and a friendly crayfisherman tossing us some of his catch. The coast is free of the cool subantarctic currents this far north, and the water is subtly less brooding although less frequented by the albatross and petrels of the roaring forties. The seasons play a part in keeping the mariner from complacency too. In one El Nino year when we aimed for the Bay of Plenty one of its frequent gales turned us back at East Cape to shelter in Waipiro Bay where the occasional violent williwaws off the hills kept us from complacency.

The inevitable delays inherent in the early hookers trading on the east coast made timetables redundant. One notable misfortune befell a trusting East Coast trader who sent a cargo of pigs and maize to a Wellington agent for sale. After an inordinate wait for a remittance to come from the consignee, he was at last informed that the pigs had eaten all the maize en route, and then bolted into the

---

131 Natusch, p116
132 Massacre Bay was renamed Coal Bay before further renaming as *Golden Bay* after the discovery of gold.

bush! Instead of making a profit he had in fact incurred a heavy bill of charges.

Trading voyages were undertaken in the mid-1800s over greater distances than might seem feasible nowadays in such small capacity vessels. *Lively*, a 36ft cutter from Torbay in Western Australia, worked its way here and traded up the west coast of the North Island to Kawhia from 1844 to 1846. She was chartered in 1845 to take the first cargo to Auckland from Hooper and Renwick's brewery, opened in 1843 on the corner of Hardy and Tasman Streets, and she continued in the brewery trade. Nelson beer was an early and popular export that continued for well over a century until amalgamations spelled the demise of local breweries, a trend now happily reversed.

Mary Ann[133], a 38ft schooner built at Nelson by its owner W Mackenzie in 1846, traded to the east coast of the North Island before being wrecked at Tolaga Bay north of Gisborne in June 1847. She had put in to the bay for repairs in mid-winter, when days might be still or stormy, and while she was anchored in the river the mouth blocked up. Then a heavy freshet came down, forcing the bar out, and *Mary Ann* was driven ashore while attempting to sail her way out. She must have been salvaged as she is listed as having been wrecked again in November 1866 in Constant Bay on the west coast of the South Island.

Damage or loss became unavoidable at times when a vessel was adjacent to land, either with no wind or at the mercy of adverse winds and seas, hence the preference for sea room in a blow, although it is not quite such an imperative nowadays with mechanical horsepower available. We once also anchored *Matuku II* for a couple of really windy days in Tolaga Bay, tucked in on the south side after spending a night by the north side before the wind changed. We were sheltered from the direct southerly but there was a high swell coming in so we had set two well-spaced anchors as a precaution, and an eye on some transits on shore to see that they stayed lined up. If they parted, we would know that we were dragging. It was a bit tense, but with the comfort of an engine we were still in control, unlike those hooker skippers of earlier times when gear was often old or of dubious quality and everything had to be done under sail. Those seamen sailed on to their anchors and sailed off them again, and they had to get it right the first time because there were very few second choices or chances.

But the hookers were not just looking northwards for trading opportunities. With settlement spreading next to Otago and Canterbury, we are fortunate to have Pratt's first-hand accounts of his struggles to sail down the Kaikoura coast south of Cook Strait aboard the cutter *Catherine Ann*.

The East Coast route southwards

Hookers had come from afar when Nelson was founded, sniffing the opportunities. So when new settlements emerged further south a few years later their owners were quick to capitalise on the fresh trade potential. With the Otago Association founding Dunedin in 1848 and the Canterbury Association founding

---

133 A different hooker from the converted lifeboat operated by Moore from 1842.

Christchurch two years later, there were significant influxes of colonial settlers to the new towns and surrounding countrysides.

William Pratt was one enterprising man who looked south. We have already covered his account of one failed attempt to reach Port Cooper, and the following account reinforces the difficulties. In 1849, after gaining book-keeping experience in Wellington, Pratt planned to set up at Lyttelton in anticipation of the arrival of the Canterbury Association settlers. With the backing of his storekeeper acquaintance who would supply the stock, he prefabricated a combined store and house in Nelson and enlisted his hooker friend Henry Fowler's support to ship it to Lyttelton "... *on board the schooner of my friend who at this time was a regular trader between Wellington and Nelson.*" By now Henry Fowler's *Triumph* was committed to the Wairau trade and conveyed sheep and wool to Wellington, loading back to the Wairau with stores, but as we already know, Fowler also owned the 10-ton cutter *Catherine Ann*, built in Wellington. She was under charter to get a cargo of maize from Poverty Bay before she would be available for the passage to Lyttelton, but unfortunately it was the start of the bad winter weather and "... *owing to baffling winds, gales, loss of sails and various casualties, the cutter was absent upon this trip nearly two months; no uncommon occurrence with small craft trading on the East Coast in those days.*"[134]

How did the immigrant lad become the seafaring man, master of the skills needed to find his way about the still unlit and rough coasts? Henry Fowler, William Pratt and many others did so.

The exposed east coast had a bad reputation for sailing vessels, particularly because of its lee shore under strong winds from the easterly quarter; but Wellington drew her chief supplies of maize, pigs and potatoes from there and the small coasters had to go where the market was. Pratt expected to have finished framing the building by the time Fowler came back from his trip, but just before *Catherine Ann* sailed south from Poverty Bay in June 1849 poor Fowler received the bad news that his other hooker, *Triumph*, had been totally wrecked at the Wairau. Then, woe upon woe, four or five days later Fowler reappeared in Nelson on his own in the cutter's small dinghy, having rowed and sailed some 80 miles, to report the *Catherine Ann* a partial wreck in Port Gore. The dinghy was too small to carry two so he had left his crewman aboard to overlook cutter and cargo. The irony was that Fowler, having just lost his schooner, was being extra cautious and stood in to Port Gore for shelter when he otherwise would have pressed on in spite of rough conditions. If he had, he could have expected to reach Wellington Heads about midnight – he had experienced such weather before, and was confident about handling it. Prudence ill-treated him.

Anchoring seems a straightforward matter of dropping an anchor over the bow, but there are many things to be taken into account and *Catherine Ann's* misadventure was not an uncommon one. She was anchored in deep water and when the breeze dropped before daylight and a heavy swell began to roll in from

---

134 Pratt, p155

the southwest, an unmistakable sign that a wind would follow it, the crew buoyed their cable ready to slip it. They had about 30 fathoms of chain out in the deep water and that would have taken a considerable time to get in, leaving the vessel hard to control in the interim. As the swell increased, the cable had to be let out to the bitter end to minimise snubbing on the anchor but at last there was a breath of wind: *"... and presently all sail was got on the cutter, the cable slipped and they were speeding thankfully away on the starboard tack, and on the next board they would be able to lay right out. The breeze proved to be one of those fitful gusts that often precede a storm; before they could go about it fell dead calm, and having parted with their ground-tackle they were at the mercy of the heavy swell, which very soon hove them ashore on a rocky strand. A hole was soon knocked in her bows, and she filled and grounded, with the deck just awash."*[135]

Concerned that swelling of the barley could burst the cutter asunder they worked on, often under water, to get the cargo out to the point where they felt she was safe from that danger. When the weather moderated Fowler started his 80-mile voyage in the dinghy, reaching Nelson on the morning of the second day. With William Pratt's help he got back to *Catherine Ann* and called on shipwrights from Picton to assist.

"I had leisure to note that the carpenters had provided themselves with pit- saws, American felling axes, a small portable forge, a few bars of iron, and a bag of charcoal, besides several guns, and a couple of dogs for pig hunting; as in the execution of a job of this kind, upon a wild part of the coast, it was necessary to be prepared to improvise upon the spot everything that was required, from sawing the planking to forging a bolt; this also necessitated a certain versatility of resources and skill on the part of the operatives, that nothing but the exigencies of colonial life could develop."[136]

The anchor chain was recovered and they returned to Nelson but not before another encounter with the land in the darkest of nights, in spite of having a local Maori aboard as a pilot. Just before French Pass another lee shore was just avoided and the rudder and the forefoot were damaged. Safely back at the Haven there was work to be done on the ship before they finally loaded the cargo for Lyttelton, including Pratt's house framing (and I wonder where on earth they put it?). Then *Catherine Ann* sailed around the top of the Sounds and down the east coast to below Cape Campbell before she was blown back through Cook Strait to Porirua. in the storm described in the previous chapter.

Henry Fowler owned the rest of that cargo, comprising flour and bacon, and with the quantity of water coming aboard through the leaking topsides of the cutter he deemed it expedient to get into Porirua where they discharged and sold the cargo for a much-needed profit before returning to Nelson to caulk the vessel.

Henry had intended after this voyage to marry Mary Edwards, the second of the Edwards daughters, and if work was available for the cutter they would settle in Canterbury. The hold-ups made a change of plans appropriate. While the ship

---

135 Pratt p 160
136 Pratt p 172

was re-caulked in Nelson and a fresh cargo shipped, he and Mary were married and when *Catherine Ann* departed a few days later the skipper's wife was aboard. They had a good trip until they neared Lyttelton when they encountered a three-day southerly gale. They rode it out lying-to, the ship forereaching or moving ahead rather than just drifting in spite of the big seas. But during the night the wind died away and they found that a strong current had set them close inshore off what is now New Brighton Beach. They rigged the two sweeps they carried aboard and rowed for two hours, just besting the rip until a new current, probably the Waimakariri River, carried them further out so they could finally complete the voyage and berth at Lyttelton.

For Pratt it must have been the culmination of a frustrating saga, but these were all typical hazards for a ship under sail. There were problems with anchoring, dragging or broken ground tackle and lack of suitable back-up warps, and there were and still are the vagaries of wind and tides. This was seafaring in the 1840s and the final event was tragic for both Henry and his young bride Mary.

A tragic ending

Henry Fowler had come to New Zealand on 5 February 1843 as a fifteen-year-old lad, registered as an agricultural labourer like his father. Soon after arriving in Nelson he had moved to Riwaka before going to sea and quickly becoming master of his own two vessels. It was a huge upward step in prospects for an ill-educated working-class boy, typical of the opportunism available in the burgeoning economy of colonial New Zealand. However his new life lasted a mere seven years.

After eventually reaching the new Christchurch settlement in 1849 (following the tribulations already recounted), Henry found plenty of cargoes for the *Catherine Ann* at Lyttelton, bringing timber from the bays with an occasional trip to Sumner. But misfortune struck on an occasion when he was laid up with a fever. Another skipper aboard the cutter moored her too close to the jetty. An onshore gale came in with sudden violence so Henry, in spite of his wife's entreaties, left his sickbed to try to save the *Catherine Ann*. Someone managed to get aboard, but *"in easing the cable it was let run off the belaying bitts and in an instant almost the cutter was smashing among the piles and cross-timbers of the unfinished jetty. She was a complete wreck."*[137]

This was to be the final straw for the young, enterprising and adventurous Henry Fowler; *"An accession of fever supervened, and in three weeks after this stormy night he left a young widow to mourn his loss."* He died of pneumonia on 13 May 1850, and after the funeral Mary stayed with Nelson acquaintances at the port until she could get a passage back to England.

Ironically, as was often the case in those times, this event was not the end of *Catherine Ann*'s life afloat. She was eventually salvaged and worked for another six years in the waters around Banks Peninsula until being wrecked at Port Levy.

---

137 Pratt p 204

12

Nelson's Second Decade

BY THE EARLY 1850s New Zealand no longer had the appearance of a frontier town, although one did not need to go far out of town to find frontier dwellers. It had taken ten years for Nelson settlers to put their new stamp on the land, but that stamp was impressed deep. Nelson achieved its style from distinctly different inputs and, with the unlikely mix of residents now rubbing shoulders and carrying out their enterprises within the geographical restrictions that kept the settlement small, things were never going to be smooth. But Nelson was no longer a pioneer settlement based on hardship and improvisation. Great

Maid of Italy, *photographed here being quanted past Green point after the breeze has died, shows lines very typical of cutters of the mid-century golden era. She first arived in Blind Bay from Auckland waters in 1876.*
Tyree Collection G190 10x8, Alexander Turnbull Library

138 Hodder p 49

Britain had supplied a broad range of trained people, including artisans as well as labourers who brought with them knowledge, precedents and the will to implement them.

Resources like coal had been located and exploited; limestone made mortar for the bricks fired from local clay, timber was milled in quantity and some remarkably substantial and even ornate houses were built. Commerce flourished and, as Edwin Hodder remarked in 1862, "*In a young colony, greater improvements are made in a few years than there would be in an English county in a hundred.*"[138]

Nelson had an extra dimension in that culture and learning, the domain of the wealthy in England, grew like wildflowers outside the limiting constraints of old English gardens. Cultivated by liberal minds among the well-off settlers and by the enlightened men who had arrived as artisans, widespread education was developed at the same time as the professionals, merchants, seafarers and farmers carved their places. The provincial government instituted a free, secular and compulsory education system which has endured to this day.

It is a wry colonial twist that some of that education carried on English public-school traditions well into the next century. As a pupil in the 1930s, few if any of my cohort experienced the nannies, nurses and servants that 19th century literature made commonplace. We were taught about obscure English heroes, including those at sea, overlooking the heroism on our own doorstep. At Nelson College we sang along with the Harrow school song and the Eton boating song, (transposing 'jolly boating weather' to 'jolly *rugger* weather'), and generally transposed a lifestyle, tradition and a use of language which went unremarked at the time but which was peculiarly at odds with the colonial experience. This 'britishness' even played over into sport which, like warfare, was conducted on gentlemanly lines. Two of my Westrupp great-uncles, who joined the Wakatu Rowing Club for their leisure activity, were key members of the champion 'rowing fours' team. After they proved to be unbeatable, the 'gentlemen rowers' of the Nelson Rowing Club objected to their participation in the amateur sport, and insisted that they were reclassified as *professionals* because they were seafarers! Along with the other members of their team, they were then barred from competing against amateurs in any rowing club. Of course it is different these days, but those were the times and generally we accepted it. The past had a great hold and New Zealand, 12,000 miles away from England, took a long time to redefine itself. On the Nelson waterfront a boatbuilding and shipping centre was one of the first manifestations of a peculiarly New Zealand identity.

Hookers, thick and fast

Throughout the 1840s and 1850s many ships were built in Nelson and, with other coastal traders coming in, the bays were set to change. Smaller vessels included *Fairy*, with J Jackson as master, and *Flirt*, a 10-ton schooner built in Nelson for the coastal trade. Smaller still was a new whaleboat ordered from Freeman, the boatbuilder, for the harbour department. Pratt describes these vessels as "… *cockleshells … literally feeling their way into the harbours on the darkest nights, as there were no lighthouses or beacons in those days to guide the mariner; and the inter-communication between the settlements was so limited, that such small craft, with the occasional visit from an Australian trader, sufficed for its requirements.*"[139]

The little ships were between 30 and 40 feet long, each only the size of a moderate cruising yacht and nothing like as well appointed. Able to carry a limited amount of cargo they were only marginally profitable, so owners would skimp where they could.

Amelia, Atalanta, Flirt and *Fairy, Jackall, Jessie*; there is a poetry in the names that saves the list of their names from being tedious. And if you think of them as ships, hear the water splashing against their sides and see the men and women stepping aboard, then you bring life to the list. Dwell upon *City of Nelson* sailing to the Buller, or *Mermaid* upon the rocks. Although its shipping volume was still small, Nelson was by now a recognised boatbuilding centre producing not just its local traders, but ocean-going vessels like the 75-ton *Liberty*, which left for California in 1850, and the 32-ton *Sea Flower* which sailed, overcrowded, to the Melbourne diggings in 1852. *Comet*, a 92-ton schooner owned by merchant N Edwards, was built and registered in Nelson and traded between Nelson and Sydney. (She was re-registered in Sydney by 1859 and wrecked in Queensland three years later.) Along with the ill-fated brig *Delaware* already mentioned, these substantial larger vessels prove that ship-building in Nelson had come of age.

Imagine the delight we might have, if the technology of photography had been available in the mid nineteenth century. To see these vessels come to life as images on a page would open our imaginations far beyond the printed word.

Hooker survivors of the first decade

The early hookers that survived in the Blind Bay trade or ownership (some were based away) at the end of this first decade were distressingly few in number. Some were lost, others simply dropped out of record, transferred to other places and renamed, or perhaps succumbed to the ravages of time, hard use, poorly chosen timbers or the hazards of the sea. Many had short lives and as we have already seen, so did many of their crews.

Elizabeth survived from that first decade of settlement, so did *Catherine, Mary, Supply, Mary Ann, Necromancer* (registered in 1852), *Seabird* and *Rapid*.

Other vessels mentioned so far belong in the second decade when pastoral farming was expanding and wool, not only from Nelson's smaller flocks but also from the burgeoning pastoral industry of the Wairau and Awatere, became an important bulk export. It was a useful cargo for the hookers which took it from the Wairau to Wellington or Nelson for loading aboard larger vessels sailing to Europe. Some was also loaded out of Port Underwood. Without refrigeration there was no chance of beef or mutton exports yet, but 'boiling-down works' were established to extract tallow from sheep.

The population, and therefore the volume of trade, was still small. About

---

139 Pratt p 155

30,000 people migrated to the whole of New Zealand from 1840 to 1853, overwhelmingly from the UK, and at the beginning of 1850 there were 4,780 adults, both European and Maori, in the Nelson settlement. Nelson encompassed the top portion of the South Island, including Wairoa (Wairau), Waitohi (Picton), and Queen Charlotte Sound, and was the island's most populous province. It did not need a big hooker fleet to service it but it is worthy of remark that as the settlement spread wide around the coastline, the availability of shipping was particularly important to its development.

It would be inaccurate to picture the bay crowded with sails in 1850. By then ship movements had slowed right down; with only nine overseas ships and 48 coastal vessels entering Port Nelson in contrast to the 39 overseas and 86 coastal entries of 1842. Hookers would pick up simple cargoes such as firewood, hop poles and posts to carry to Nelson from places such as the Whangamoa and Croisilles once the resources adjacent to the settlement had been diminished. It was much changed five years later with regular traffic from within Blind Bay and a little further afield in Massacre Bay.

With the early discovery of coal, soon to be followed by an even more valuable commodity, hookers were soon rounding Separation Point with significant regularity.

Looking for a rainbow

When you see a rainbow, your back is to the sun. There is a rainbow to weave into this tapestry of the hookers, and it will have the elusive crock of gold at the end of it. One of the threads in the weft is a wry twist to Wakefield's injunction to *"possess yourselves of the soil and you are secure"*. The optimists always saw minerals and especially the metallic ores, recognised and utilised from the very first days, as the future wealth of the province and counterbalancing its limited amount of arable land.

Three young men hunting for goats amongst the hills behind Nelson in 1852 picked up copper ore, somewhere about Wooded Peak. They couldn't have known it then, but ten years later their find would spawn a short-lived industry, and, as a side benefit, a horse-drawn tram from the town to the port. Nelson had already been recognised as a potentially mineral-rich area, but this copper discovery prompted the formation of an English mining company. There was similar excitement in 1856 when a company was formed to work copper lodes found at the Croisilles. Those shares were taken up too, but neither company was a success.

Such company ventures tended to be heavy on promises, plant and infrastructure, light on results. This can still happen of course, but assessment of ore reserves is generally more rigorous these days. Prospectors are enthusiasts and in the 1850s mining companies often mined rich veins of enthusiasm. When the Dun Mountain venture was launched and the proprietors realised there were almost no copper reserves, they mined the adjacent chrome instead, to be used for dyeing cotton in Lancashire mills. That venture was also short-lived, but by then a 13½-mile railway had been built to transport the ore from mountain to the port. The line was opened on 3 February 1862 and pulled up ten years later, although the last mile of it lasted as a horse-drawn tramway along Haven Road until 1901 because the company was forbidden to use a steam locomotive in the town. The tram was a well-used amenity and a feature of the port but an irritant to some people because the rail tops and the road were at different levels for much of the way.

There were other positive spin-offs from the mining venture. The Dun Mountain Copper Mining Company laid out about £100,000, some of it spent in Nelson, although sales had returned only about a third of that. Nelson merchant Robert Levien bought the discarded Nelson assets for under £5,000 pounds and, more importantly, local labour and local businesses had been employed and paid by the company. The little ships (*Supply* from Collingwood, *Australian Maid* from Motupipi, *Oddfellow* and *Mary* from Mahakipawa in Pelorus Sound) brought in thousands of wooden railway sleepers for track formation. My own forebears John Kidson (who by now had a property in Brook Street), and his son-in-law John Ward of Glencoe Gardens next door, did contract work for the Dun Mountain company which gave them and others like them a welcome boost of ready cash. Such ventures were important to people finding their feet in times of economic restraint.

Put into perspective, in its second decade Nelson was a pretty little town, set in its impressive hills; it had shops and warehouses, churches and houses, although they were still interspersed with rough land. But in 1855 Nelson, in common with other New Zealand towns under a government short of funds, had its smelly shadow side, and there were no funds to address the shortcomings. There were open drains and cesspools, pigsties, dung-heaps, slaughterhouses "and other pestilential hot-beds without restriction"[140]. A dysentery outbreak killed ten people that year, and there was no water supply. Political change was in the offing.

Headway or sternway?
Two completely contrasting impulses had been finding vigorous expression in the upper South Island during the first decade. One was the desire of a select few to maintain a life of advantage and privilege by grabbing great chunks of country for themselves, while the other was the urge of ordinary men to make their way in a country accessible to all-comers. In terms of a class society based on land-holdings, the colony could be assessed as making sternway. However if we assess class division from the perspective of income and voting rights, one cannot deny that there was significant headway, relative to prospects back in Britain.

Nelson's first election for a Provincial Assembly (and for the first New Zealand Parliament) was held in 1853, once the **New Zealand Constitution Act** had been passed by the British Parliament a year earlier. For the wealthier reactionaries like Nelson's Supper Party, the enacted voting rights were overly liberal,

---

140 Broad p 119

compared with those back in Britain where the franchise was viewed as a 'privilege' that should be exercised by the educated few on behalf of the lower classes. In the new colony, it was extended to all 21 year old male British subjects who owned or leased property of a modest value. This certainly enfranchised many individuals who would not have any chance of voting rights before migrating.

The value of land required for eligibility varied. Freeholders needed to own property worth at least fifty pounds, while leaseholders needed to be paying at least ten pounds per year on land or a town house. Rural householders had a lower minimum rent requirement of only five pounds.

William Swainson, the Attorney General, claimed that it was *'the most liberal that has ever been granted to a British colony,'*[141] while one Canterbury politician stated that there was *'hardly any man who cannot get a vote in New Zealand'*, as long as he was *'not of the pauper or criminal classes.'*[142] But it is likely that many of the wealthier landowners would have shared the more forceful opinion of the Canterbury Station-owner Samuel Butler who ridiculed the idea that his farm labourers should have the vote, writing 'Their political knowledge is absolutely nil, and, were the colony to give them political power, it might as well give gunpowder to children'[143].

Certainly, the ability for colonial labourers to earn between forty and sixty pounds per year gave them a very real option to rise above the poverty of their male counterparts in Scotland where barely 12% could vote, or even England where a mere 20% were enfranchised. The contrast was outstanding, with 75% of colonial pakeha men entitled to the ballot.

Apart from the few Rangatira who had been granted town acres as part of the Company land purchase, almost all Maori were automatically disenfranchised, as despite having been bestowed the rights of British citizenship, almost all Maori land was in joint ownership within hapu or iwi tradition.

Where our hooker skippers and crews stood in the eligibility stakes is up to conjecture. It would be reasonable to assume that the town cottages that my Westrupp, Kidson and Ward forebears were residing in – whether rented or owned – would have sufficient value to place them onto the roll. Perhaps some hooker owner/skippers would have vested every available penny into their vessels, however with the healthy returns after a year or two of operation, their incomes would likely have exceeded that of the average labourer.

However in terms of the social advantage of significant land holdings, the colony made virtually no headway during its early decades. The Company had consciously imported reactionary wealthy settlers who were intent upon retaining or regaining old advantages, and it had also tapped the wealth of both immigrating capitalists and absentee investors. Except for Nelson small-scale farming, land continued to be held in very few hands so that even late in 1890 less than one per

---

141 William Swainson, *New Zealand and its colonization*. London: Smith, Elder & Co, 1859, p. 291
142 James FitzGerald, *The representation of New Zealand*. Christchurch: The Press, 1864, pp. 9, 21
143 Samuel Butler, *A first year in Canterbury settlement, with other early essays*, p. 129

cent of all landowners controlled 64 per cent of freehold land.[144] There were others on the land-wagon too. Even before Nelson was founded, Governor Hobson was under the influence of wealthy settlers concerned about protecting land they had already bought, and the subsequent governors appointed two extra land commissioners to assist William Spain.

The first wave of land acquisitions had been the dealings between Maori and Pakeha in the 1830s and 1840s and that process was still ongoing, but now came ideological conflict regarding English model of land held in a few hands and controlled by the privileged. This reactionary principle was stoutly defended by individuals in the Supper Party, but the voting power of the labouring majority undermined it.

Power politics came strongly into play in 1855 when the Nelson provincial superintendent, Edward Stafford resigned to become an elected member of New Zealand's colonial Parliament (rapidly rising to become Premier in 1856). To the frustration and disgust of the wealthy 'established order', their candidate for Nelson's replacement superintendent, David Munro was outvoted in favour of a more democratic candidate, John Robinson[145], a sawmiller, who was seen to represent the interests of the workers. From 1857 Robinson was supported by a new liberal newspaper, *The Colonist*, a rival to the landowner-dominated *Examiner* which ceased publication in 1874. The hooker seamen enjoyed these changes along with the rest of the working population.

As a reaction to this clear undermining of their political grasp on power, a

The grandiose Provincial Chambers looked rather out of place, viewed from the Maitai River offshoot known by Maori as 'the eel pond', later to become Queens gardens.
Copy Collection: C2771, Nelson Provincial Museum

---

144 King, p270
145 Robinson was subsequently drowned when visiting the fledgling town of Westport which was under his jurisdiction. The steamer Wallaby's lifeboat capsized trying to ferry him and others ashore.

group of powerful Nelson landowners who owned large holdings in the Wairau lobbied to split Nelson's eastern region into a separate province named Marlborough, where they assumed they would have the privileges they deserved.

Splitting away a smaller province in the late 1850s was a thorny legislative task for the fresh Stafford-led colonial parliament due to the small number of residents living within the proposed boundaries. These powerful run-holders successfully lobbied to allow them to be classified as voting residents of every region in which they owned land. As a former member of Nelson's gentry, Stafford succumbed to these personally familiar lobbyists, and in 1858 his Auckland based government passed the New Provinces Act, shaped specifically to Marlborough's needs. It stipulated 1,000 residents, although only 150 of them needed to be enfranchised. Despite this legislation, the proposed new province of Marlborough still did not contain enough people to comply, and it took a crafty boundary change (which brought the new province much closer to the town of Nelson) before it contained sufficient resident settlers to split Marlborough from Nelson in 1859.[146]

The few pastoralists in the new province of Marlborough were reluctant to release any of their predominantly leasehold land for subdivision and it was therefore questionable whether the province could survive independently. (Marlborough suffered internal political turmoil and had two superintendents at one time, each claiming the other was illegal.)

With the gentry doggedly clutching their large tracts, Nelson and indeed the whole of New Zealand was heading towards an economic crisis. *"By 1860 the great majority of the 80,000 colonists possessed insufficient land, and no alternative way of making a living seemed available to them ... Such was the state of New Zealand upon the eve of the gold rushes."*[147]

The instrument for change was beyond the power of the landed gentry to withhold. While their eyes were firmly upon the Wairau and Awatere, there was gold behind their backs in the wilder, rougher country. And for our hooker men, this was to become yet another boost to their rising fortunes, although for those who ventured further west, a potentially devastating temptation to tackle even more challenging waters.

Gold! Massacre Bay changes its name

Small wonder the locals in this part of the district had been quick to remove the stigma of its historic cultural clash from its name, and for a few years it became widely referred to as Coal Bay. This rather drab name was soon to be changed to one that lifted its profile enormously.

Gold was discovered by chance in Coal Bay, just as the copper ore had been in Nelson. Ned James and John Ellis found colour in a rocky creek in 1856, quickly leading to a gold rush which was to revitalise this northwestern corner of the province.

---

146 Buick, pp394-396
147 Salmon, J H M, *A History of Goldmining in New Zealand*, R E Owen, 1963, p22

Massacre Bay was originally named Murderer's Bay in 1642 by the explorer Abel Tasman, when four of his crew were killed after their dinghy was rammed by Ngati Tumatakokiri warriors who were possibly concerned for their precious kumara crops. This tribe was conquered and enslaved in the late C18 by Ngati Apa who were subsequently over-run by Te Rauparaha's allies, Ngati Rarua, Ngati Tama, and Te Atiawa.
Credited to Geo. T. Chapman, 1870

A lot had happened in the decade since *Erin* and *Carbon* began transporting coal from the Motupipi estuary, shortly followed by limestone and timber. By 1852 a newly discovered surface coal seam was being exploited at Pakawau near the base of Farewell Spit, and there were other sporadic mining ventures, most of which proved uneconomic. Mr J Watts kept a supply of Pakawau coal at his yards at Auckland Point and a couple of years later the blacksmiths gave the high price of coals from Pakawau as a reason for combining to fix a scale of charges. After this mine failed, there was an ongoing demand for coal in Nelson and further afield. Just which of the sources was available and when is by no means clear but some hookers continued carrying coal from Coal Bay to Nelson.

However the closing of the produce markets in Australia, following the end of Victoria's gold rushes, had brought a general downturn in the whole settlement and Coal Bay was ripe for new development.

During the early 1850s the Motupipi settlers focused their energies on developing the land, milling timber and working coal, instead of boatbuilding. Four settlers (Joseph Packard, Job Flowers, Alfred Wilson and Apiko) had attempted to drive twelve head of cattle from Riwaka to Motupipi in 1850 but the Takaka Hill defeated them so they dropped down to Sandy Bay and, after a week,

The only significant all-tide, all-weather anchorage in Massacre Bay was in the shelter of the Tata Islands, within striking distance of the Motupipi estuary, near the current breakwater harbour at Tarakohe. Hookers could wait here to catch the tide into various estuaries which later became important, especially once Collingwood and Takaka were established.
1843 Heaphy painting, B-043-005, Alexander Turnbull Library

procured a hooker from Nelson to complete their journey north while their wives and families were taken around to Motupipi in Lovell's whaleboat.

Elsewhere in the bay, new settlers had been trickling in. The Caldwell family landed with their possessions by the newly built shallow draughted 36ft schooner *Atalanta* in 1852, struggling at a subsistence level at Onekaka on land which was poor but attractively placed on the coast. The gold rush was soon to give the Caldwells a profitable, handy market for produce until they left in 1860 for Australia.

The Ellis, Roil and James families also came into the area in 1856, the latter two taking up a 150-acre section where they expected to grow wheat, oats, barley, peas and other crops. They first came over aboard *Supply* to check it out and later Captain Walker brought over cattle for them, landing the beasts at Puramahoi to be driven along the beach. *Supply* landed the families a little distance up the Aorere River. In the same year a partnership including John Perry Robinson (later to become the provincial superintendent) set up a sawmill at Motupipi.

Other new settlers were also to profit from the unprecedented boost from the gold rush. John Riley took up land on the estuary at what was later to become

Ferntown. William Gibbs was luckier after he bought 50 acres from Maori on the east side of the Aorere River mouth in 1855 (close to where our familiar hooker Erin had been built thirteen years earlier). This was unexpectedly to soon become valuable real estate as a consequence of the gold rush. He subdivided,sold allotments and set up business on his own account. The provincial government prepared a paper town on the terraces above Gibbstown but it was never developed, although the planner name of Collingwood was used for the tide-bound port which soon become the major gateway for all the district's needs.

In March 1857 a laborious horse track from Motueka to Takaka was finally opened, but the sea remained the main highway, with our trusty fleet of hookers plying its steady trade in people and cargoes.

The crock below the rainbow

The discovery of gold provided a new dimension for the whole Nelson province. Its first early rumblings were back in the hills up the Motueka Valley but it soon extended through Coal Bay (rapidly renamed as Golden Bay) then down the West Coast to the Buller River and beyond. Some of the sail-powered hookers played a valiant part in exploring, supporting the new ventures and then servicing places not accessible to steamships.

The Australian gold rushes had inspired Nelson merchants to offer a reward for the discovery of a payable goldfield, and storekeeper William Hough promoted organised prospecting. The Motueka gold finds started at Pig Valley, seven miles from Motueka, in May 1856. It was the beginning of winter, which tested the endurance of about 300 hopeful prospectors. Those first miners were men off the streets, clerks out of the stores, tradesmen and farm workers but later they were joined by experienced men from California or Australia, many of them university graduates and professional men.

Established merchants were quick to take advantage of the gains to be made, but, to use a modern expression, the gold rushes created a level playing field. It would be inconceivable in the old country for common folk to 'get their hands on the goodies' but in the depressed conditions of the 1860s the opportunity was surely welcome and the desire to speculate in land was less popular. However, this crock at rainbow's end yielded amply to only a few, moderately to some, and left the rest to ponder the meaning of the word. Some persevered at the Baton and Wangapeka, to the benefit of coastal shipping.

"The owners of boats plying between Nelson and Motueka congratulated themselves that the golden age had arrived, and having reaped a rich harvest by carrying passengers and goods to the diggings, soon had the opportunity of repeating the experiment upon those who had any money left to pay for their passage home; for these diggings were soon deserted, as the gold was obtained in such small quantities as to render the occupation unremunerative."[148]

The Nelson district's goldfields were never as rich as the West Coast fields

---

148 Broad p 119

proved to be but they gave a good yield to ship owners, while the storekeepers and tavern keepers always seemed to have the best of it. On the Aorere field as on many others, remoteness and rough, steep and fissured terrain made moving supplies a major problem but a good living could be made with hard work, and some had good luck to go with it. Reports from the Aorere began to lure miners in early 1857 and by April there were 500 men on the field, mostly Nelson locals. In May the number doubled. Promising strikes were made in the Takaka valley too and by November the fields had attracted miners from Victoria and also a number of Maori from outside the district who speedily became adept at winning the yellow metal that the Pakeha valued. Nelson, as the supply point, got a much-welcomed boost as did the hookers. It was a golden age, as Washbourn wrote:

"*Everyone was off to the diggings. Some arrived in boats of their own making, often a Maori canoe, but generally by one of the mosquito fleet of boats. The names of many of the local ones you will perhaps have heard of, such as the* Elizabeth, Nancy, Rapid, Atalanta, Mary Thompson, Necromancer *and the* Sisters *which sank at Totaranui through a stupid bullock putting his foot through the bottom of her ... I have counted nineteen craft of various sizes in the Collingwood harbour at the same time.*"[149]

Australian Maid, Catherine, Supply, Ann, Coquette, Three Brothers and *Mary Ann* were among of the small fleet of Nelson hookers which headed to Golden Bay laden with merchandise and diggers, returning with the gold of the successful ones and maybe with the luckless going home. They made the waters of Blind Bay active and colourful. In April 1857 *Harry* carried the first 20 diggers from Wellington. and Edwin Hodder reported sailing to the diggings in *Coquette*, her hold so full of miners and their gear that he slept on deck. One practice was to

In this rare photograph, the Bill Westrupp skippered hooker ketch **Lily** *is under full sail inside the Aorere estuary upstream of Collingwood towards Ferntown. However close inspection reveals her dinghy streaming to leeward, so she is presumably stuck in the mud! The Westrupps always enjoyed a joke, and Bill would have surely enjoyed seeing it here.*
Courtesy Rob Williams

---

149 Washbourn, p5

build a makeshift scaffolding in the diminutive holds of these craft to be used as bunks, which miners were only too happy to occupy if they were to get to the new fields. Such primitive arrangements even occurred aboard trans-Tasman vessels where some passengers, including women and children, simply slept in rows on the floors of the holds. Despite the discomfort and scant regulation, it was the start of the next major influx to the colony.

Collingwood district had a population of 1,500 by May 1857, and 2,000 in February the following year when it was proclaimed a Port of Entry. William Williams, one of the original New Zealand Company pioneers on the *Whitby* in 1841, was appointed deputy harbourmaster and pilot in Collingwood in October 1857 and held his appointment for 33 years before retiring. Thomas Askew, erstwhile hooker skipper now ship owner and merchant, moved in as a storekeeper, and was issued, along with a number of others, with a publican's bush licence. Stores and drinking places proliferated. One was run by James Lovell, the Motupipi pioneer who turned storekeeper, butcher and baker in Gibbstown. At the beginning of the gold rush he was also a banker and his doughty wife was several times a gold courier until regular gold shipments were established. She reportedly travelled to Nelson by hooker with the gold sewn into her hems. She wouldn't have wanted to fall overboard. The mosquito fleet regularly carried gold and the owner of *Ann* even advertised that she had a safe.

Gibbs later was to become laird of Totaranui, developing an estate the other

*These two cutters, **Planet** (lying alongside) and **Dauntless** (anchored) show the plumb bows, sweeping sheerlines and counter sterns typical of other cutters of the gold-rush era. Nelson wharves had expanded by the decade that this photograph was taken, but one can imagine **Supply** and **Three Brothers** discharging their cargoes and whistling for wind in the hope of a quick turnaround during the heady goldrush era.*
Tyree Studio Collection 182372, Nelson Provincial Museum

side of Separation Point where he increased his initial 1856 holding of 272 acres, built a very large and ornate homestead and lived on a well-developed farm in a grand style suitable to his position as Golden Bay member of the House of Representatives. He remained there, self-sufficient except for flour and sugar, until 1892.

From a shipping perspective, Totaranui was an important anchorage when conditions prevented passage around Separation Point. It had a little store which stocked basic necessities (including tobacco) and when telegraph became available in 1881 it became a communication point for messages to Nelson and elsewhere. Hooker people liked the sociability of it, whether they were delayed by westerlies on the Totaranui side of Separation Point or just bringing supplies or taking the surplus produce from the Gibbs farm. However, in common with the other settlements between Separation Point and Sandy Bay, nature did not repay the work that was done. The soil was impoverished and the farming marginal to subsistent; ultimately most of it was incorporated into the Abel Tasman National Park.

The mosquito fleet

Here is Blind Bay through the eyes of Edwin Hodder, who was in Nelson about 1857 when it was staging-port for gold rush traffic:

"From the shore, the harbour presents a very business-like appearance; two or three large vessels may generally be seen alongside the wharf, taking in and discharging cargo. The 'mosquito fleet' as it is called, is dancing over the waters, some leaving for the goldfields or neighbouring settlements, others just arrived with diggers bearing their precious produce, or returning to purchase tools and utensils to prosecute their arduous work ... and far out in Blind Bay – on the margin of which Nelson is situated – may be seen several schooners, or perhaps a large vessel or two, either going to or coming from Australia, between which continent and New Zealand a close intercourse is kept."[150]

Steam was on its way but this was still the golden age of the hookers. It coincided with the arrival of stately English ships, including the wool clippers, and they became familiar sights in Nelson waters for a time. The wool clippers belonged to the pastoral industry; the proliferation of the others to the new wealth in the country, gold, flowing in new channels. For the coastal fleet it was a simple matter of logistics; putting 2,000 extra people and their equipment into Golden Bay and then keeping the supplies rolling in as they were needed kept the little ships very busy indeed.

Any reader familiar with John Masefield's evocative poem 'Cargoes'[151] may well find poetry in the 1857 cargo manifests and masters of the little ships of Blind Bay and Golden Bay, as listed in the Shipping Intelligence columns[152]:

---

150 Hodder, p31
151 *"Quinquireme of Ninevah from Distant Ophir ..."*
152 *Nelson Examiner*, 1857

INWARDS 11 April:
: Cutter **Three Brothers**, 12 tons, (Westrupp), 26 ounces gold, Passengers 10.

: Schooner **Australian Maid**, 17 tons, (Davidson), 115 ounces gold, Passengers 5.

: Cutter **Supply**, 26 tons, (Walker), 5 ounces gold. Passengers 6.

OUTWARDS 11 April:
: Schooner **Necromancer**, 16 tons, (Hooper), 2 cases drapery, 2½ chests tea, 2 cases gin, 6 bags sugar, 1 ton flour, 6 sacks bread, 1 dozen tin dishes, 2 dozen buckets, 4 long toms, 1 dozen picks and spades, ½ ton hay. Passengers 18.

13 April:
: Schooner **Ann**, 15 tons, (Wright), 5 cases merchandise, 24 bags flour, 1 bag sugar, 35 bags potatoes, 2 bags onions, 2 casks apples, 1½ chests tea, 1 dozen buckets, 1 pair scales, 1 package diggers' tools, 1 coil rope, 1 barrel ale, 6 trusses hay, 8 packages merchandise. Passengers 10.

: Cutter **Three Brothers**, 12 tons, (Westrupp), baggage. Passengers 12.

: Schooner **Australian Maid**, 17 tons, (Davidson), 1 ton flour, 1½ chests tea, 4 bags sugar, 1 box candles, 1 box soap, 6 packages sundries. Passengers 4.

INWARDS: 17 April:
: Cutter **Three Brothers**, 12 tons, (Westrupp), 34½ ounces gold. Passengers 10.

: Schooner **Australian Maid**, 17 tons, (Davidson), 15 bushells wheat, 4 pigs, 18 ounces gold. Passengers 7.

: Schooner **Kate**, 7 tons, (M'Nabb), 3 ounces gold. Passengers 3.

: Cutter **Supply**, 26 tons, (Walker), 25 ounces gold. Passengers 6.

OUTWARDS: 18 April:
: Schooner **Pride of the Isles**, 28 tons, (Gilbertson), 10 cwt. hay, 10 empty kegs. Passengers 8.

: Schooner **Necromancer**, 16 tons, (Hooper), 2 casks beer. Passengers 10.

: Schooner **Australian Maid**, 17 tons, (Davidson), 2 casks beer, 2 long toms. Passengers 7.

22 April:
: Cutter **Three Brothers**, 12 tons, (Westrupp), 1 tent. Passengers 12.

: Cutter **Supply**, 26 tons, (Walker), 2 head cattle, 5 cwt. flour, 3 packages sundries. Passengers 6.

: Schooner **Catherine**, 11 tons, (Duncan), 1 ton potatoes, 1 ton flour, 2 cases sundries, 1 case apples, 1 case tools, 21 trusses hay. Passengers 7.

Reading through these simple lists, we can imagine the men clamouring to get aboard with their swags; gold pans, long toms for washing the gravels, boxes of candles (to be used sparingly) and soap (used sparingly too, perhaps to pick up the last of the washed gold). Old hands and new chums self-conscious in their new working gear were off to do a man's work and dream of rich rewards. The work would be brutally hard so the dreams were needed.

Meanwhile the sea waited, impartially, always reminding those who ventured to venture with care. Captain John Westrupp left Nelson one dark, wintry night in the cutter *Three Brothers* with two of his sons aboard. Halfway across the bay he trod on a rope which rolled under his feet, and he fell overboard. His oldest son John Edward (Jack)[153] was said to have been at sea from the age of ten and would still have been relatively young at the time of this incident. The boys, who had already bunked down, heard his cries for help and rushed up on deck to discover that their father's voice was coming from somewhere astern of the ship. One son jumped in the dinghy and went to the rescue while the other tried to keep the ship hove-to. Fully clothed in an oilskin coat and boots and not a good swimmer, John had no reserves left when after a hard struggle he was finally dragged into the dinghy and returned to the ship, freezing cold and a very lucky man. Events like these certainly forced pioneering children to become grown-up before their time.

*Although **Goldseeker** was not built until after the goldrushes, her name typifies the spirit of the era, and her hull and rig design is very similar to the cutters which regularly tacked out the Nelson Haven entrance past Fifeshire rock, with eager goldseekers aboard. Her yard topsail has seen better days but would have certainly been valued for the additional speed it enabled.*
Russ Ricketts photo, courtesy Carol Thompson

---

153 Jack Westrupp later became a respected shipowner and steamer captain in Wellington, dying in 1907.

This evocative photograph of a 'wharf-kid' near an un-named hooker at Albion wharf (circa 1870s) deserves scrutiny. With his schoolbag cast carelessly aside, his education may be of little importance to him, and like John Westrupp's sons he may also be soon to embark on a sea-going career. The ketch has its large hold uncovered and may have been recently discharging Adele Island granite blocks for the wharf's reconstruction. The tumblehome of its near-plumb transom is at variance with the counter-sterns more typical of the era.

N Baigent Collection: 316066, Nelson Provincial Museum

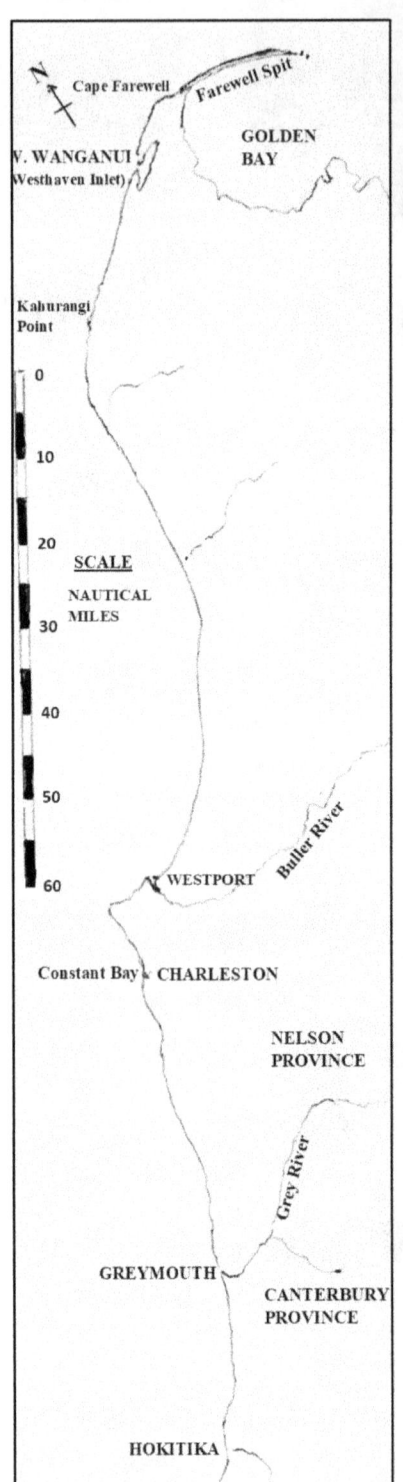

```
SHIPPING INTELLIGENCE.
PORT OF WESTPORT.
       HIGH WATER.
This Day ...   3.25 a.m.   3.50 p.m.
         ARRIVALS.
January 31—Bruce, from Hokitika and
Greymouth.
        DEPARTURES.
January 31—Bruce, for Hokitika.
Murray, for Nelson.
Dart, for Charleston.
```

A small paddle-steamer, possibly converted from a wooden sailing vessel, lies against Greymouth's Mawhera Quay, while the top sketch extract depicts shipping at Westport.

Details from J W Barnicoat sketches, drawn October 1867. Bett Collection 314771 and AC 715, Nelson Provincial Museum

13

The Wild West Coast

THE WEST COAST of New Zealand lies in the Roaring Forties – an onslaught of prevailing onshore westerly winds posing a severe challenge to any sailing vessels which were compromised in their ability to claw off a lee shore.

On his first voyage in 1770, Captain Cook described *"an inhospitable shore, unworthy of observation, except for its ridge of naked and barren rocks covered with snow. As far as the eye could reach, the prospect was wild, craggy, and desolate."* The permanent population of the West Coast was then only a few pockets of Ngai Tahu Maori who, after tending to their needs for shelter and food, traded in greenstone with other tribes. These original inhabitants survived on birds, seafood, potatoes and fern but the explorers and diggers who came in the 1850s and 1860s were dependent on having their food supplies brought in. The country is mountainous with a high rainfall, and back then it was bush-covered except for some open plains of sour pakihi soil and the snowy mountain tops. It was never easy to get around this kind of country, and the further hazard of steep rivers tumbling off the Southern Alps posed the ever-present risk of drowning.

This was the wild west which was to abruptly become a precarious destination for many Nelson-based hookers and larger vessels during the heady gold-rush era of the 1860s.

The decline of the Golden Bay rush

Although the Aorere Valley was the first recognised payable New Zealand goldfield, there were other discoveries. The mostly steep and wild country that was empty of settlers did not attract the attention of capitalist speculators until gold was discovered, and meanwhile the miners were out there shifting the boulders, shovelling the dirt, working in the water, washing out the gold.

The best yield on the Aorere field was in 1858 and the Golden Bay rush was over in a couple of years, although the field was worked for many years afterwards for about half that annual return. The number of miners decreased, but there were still enough for the beginnings of a much larger settlement as the men turned to other pursuits. Collingwood port became principally an outlet for timber, farm produce and coal for another hundred years. Some miners headed for the hopeful Buller field in 1862, while others were drawn away to join 6,000 others at Wakamarina's 'canvas town' when rich gold was discovered at the head of Pelorus Sound in early 1864. But this boom was also to collapse by 1866, leaving only a few miners still at work while others began trekking back to Nelson across the Maungatapu track, to ship out by steamer or find a passage by hooker, paddle-steamer or barque to the by now enormously rich West Coast goldfields.

Mackay's Soundings

In May 1860, James Mackay bought the entire West Coast south of the Grey River from Ngai Tahu on behalf of the Crown, paying £300 for what would literally prove to be a goldmine. The West Coast gold rushes were the end result of the activities of a few persistent individuals like MacKay. At the time, the upper West Coast was within Nelson province as far south as the Grey River while remainder was a part of Canterbury province.

Mackay had been fourteen when he arrived in Nelson in 1845, and became a fluent speaker of Maori during his boyhood among the Ngati Tama at Wakapuaka, In early adulthood he leased a run of 1,500 acres at Cape Farewell with about four miles of frontage on to Golden Bay, but his interests tended more to exploration, initially through the tablelands behind Golden Bay. When the Aorere gold rush started in 1857 he was away with two Maori companions about 50 miles inland up the Mawhera (Grey) River, following Brunner's and Heaphy's routes from West Wanganui (Westhaven). He took soundings of both the Buller and the Grey River bars from a canoe and found them to have good depths for shipping – contrary to Brunner's and Heaphy's assessments that they were generally unfit for vessels to enter. Mackay also sounded the Anaweka, Heaphy, Karamea, Little Wanganui, Ruatoki and Mokihinui rivers. These rivers and the open beaches along the coast were later used as landing places during the gold rush but they were never regarded as kindly to sailing vessels.

Mackay tried his hand at alluvial mining with the rest on the Aorere field, but decided it was not for him. However his fluency in Maori language led to his appointment in February 1858 as Assistant Native Secretary, to mediate in the frequent disputes on the goldfield, where about 30% of the prospectors were Maori. The following year he was given the task of negotiating the purchase of the West Coast and he travelled down with his cousin Alexander Mackay.

The Ngai Tahu chiefs refused to part with their land unless the greenstone-bearing area between the Grey and Hokitika rivers was reserved to them, but Mackay was not authorised to sanction such an extensive reserve and negotiations failed. The Mackays attempted to return to Nelson by way of the Maruia plain and Upper Buller, but weather and semi-starvation forced them back to the coast. At this point the more adventurous Nelson hookers became critical to the next phase.

The land purchase

The exhausted Mackay must have been elated to find the Nelson cutter *Supply* anchored in the south spit lagoon inside the Buller entrance.[154] She had been chartered by the Nelson Provincial surveyor John Rochfort to take provisions to MacKay at the Grey River entrance but bad weather had changed these plans. *Supply* sailed from Nelson for the West Coast on 30 August 1859 under Captain John Walker (with Captain Scott as mate and crewed by G Walker, F Millington,

---

154 Now the site of Westport

F Wilcox, and two Maori seamen).[155]

It was a brave move to tackle the Buller bar with its pronounced northward current and no leading marks. The only vessel known to have tackled the bar was Joseph Thoms' sealing schooner *Three Brothers*, fifteen years earlier, so *Supply* became the first[156] of a new generation of coastal traders to prove the viability of this harbour when Captain Walker and his crew unloaded the provisions near Packers Point.

MacKay was able to sail in her to Nelson, and then catch a larger vessel to Auckland for instructions from the new governor, Colonel Gore Brown, who was anxious to conclude a deal before local Maori became too aware of the real estate value of this district where they still held Treaty rights.

As a result, MacKay set off overland with a small party from Nelson in January 1860 with 400 gold sovereigns in his swag, walking to the Maori settlement at Mawhera[157] on the West Coast with considerable difficulty. Julius Haast also arrived on 2nd March 1860, after a rough overland trip from Christchurch. All reports of inland travel on the coast indicate that even a subsistence level of living off the land was difficult to achieve. The most animated living things were the sandflies and mosquitoes, which lived off the travellers instead.

Again right on cue a hooker arrived to meet Mackay. On 5th March 1860 the Nelson schooner *Gipsy*, under Captain Charles McCann, became the first sailing vessel to cross the Grey River bar. She was loaded with government supplies for both Mackay and Haast but had struck a rock off Separation Point and had to put back to Nelson for repairs, and then been delayed at the Buller by the weather.

After recovering from yet another rigorous journey, James Mackay reopened negotiations with local Maori. It is a measure of his forceful character that MacKay convinced the Ngai Tahu negotiators to accept a mere £300 instead of their original asking price of £5,000 for the seven and a half million acres involved. Furthermore although Ngai Tahu requested a reserve of 100,000 acres between the Kahutara and Conway rivers, Mackay signed away only 5,566 acres 'of the most useless and worthless description'[158], stating that if they wanted any more they would have to buy it back from the government. The deal was concluded on 21st May, with Mackay signing the purchase agreement on behalf of Queen Victoria, and with fourteen Ngai Tahu rangitira making their marks on the deed.

West Coast gold

Maori prospectors played an important role from the time chief Tarapuhi and his brother Tainui first reported gold at the Buller in 1858. As the Golden Bay

---

155 Faris, Irwin, *Charleston, its Rise and Decline*, Capper Press, 1980, p90
156 The larger schooner *Shepherdess* entered the Buller a fortnight later
157 Now Greymouth
158 It is worth noting that this included much of the current site of Greymouth. In 1997 an economic redress package of $170 million was paid to Ngai Tahu to compensate for unfair land purchases throughout the South Island.

yields fell, there was increased interest in this hitherto remote region from other prospectors.

The enterprising Collingwood storekeeper Reuben Waite advertised a public meeting in the summer of 1861 to start a joint enterprise to the West Coast. His friend Sanders Rogers chartered Captain Jacobsen's hooker *Jane*, and Waite persuaded sixteen Collingwood men to join them although most of the locals laughed at this undertaking, calling them madmen from Victoria. Arriving at the Buller, Waite exchanged some of the provisions he had in stock for gold from Maori prospectors and then undertook a hair-raising exploration voyage up and down the river in *Jane's* dinghy. He took four days to get up the river, spent two days waiting for flooding to subside and then claimed it took only a couple of hours to come down, including shooting the falls. Such were the weather and conditions underfoot on the first night out that Waite and his two companions stood back-to back under blankets in the bush all night, trying to shelter from the pouring rain.

Captain Jacobsen took Waite back to Nelson aboard *Jane* with his Maori gold. It was a hazardous voyage of 16 days of storms and a near-shipwreck but, undeterred by the hazards of the long sea miles between Nelson and the place which would become known as Westport, Waite returned immediately to the Buller with his wife.[159] He settled in enthusiastically as a storekeeper and part-time prospector, sponsoring other miners in the conviction that there was plenty of gold to be found. Rogers did not stay but *Jane* subsequently appeared on the coast from time to time. *Nautilus*, *Mary* and *Gipsy* were regulars by now, along with the others mentioned later in connection with Constant Bay.

Starvation was an ever-present spectre for the hardy prospectors around the Buller during next two years. The settlement at Westport was sustained by potatoes grown by local Maori and by livestock and supplies that Reuben Waite had shipped in aboard *Gipsy*. At one time she was six weeks or more overdue and was thought to have been lost, while the settlers were reduced to subsisting on eels and shellfish. Glowing reports from the southern town of Dunedin, of Otago gold in 1861–62 distracted attention from the declining Collingwood fields and the isolated Buller community.

Waite was no armchair merchant and walked the overland route from Buller to Nelson when the track was formed by the Nelson Provincial Council in 1860. He wryly commented that the river crossings were for washing off the accumulated mud. He doggedly persevered, and his patience was eventually rewarded, being in the forefront of the gradual build-up to the 1864 West Coast gold rush. He developed business interests as a merchant, hotel-keeper, ferry operator and shipping agent.

Meanwhile, after the fervour generated by Aorere gold, the early 1860s were a time of near-depression in Nelson, with various hookers tied up for long periods

---

159 The original Buller settlement was named Westport in 1863 when town sections were laid out and sold, but flooding and erosion made a change of site necessary.

awaiting cargoes. Small wonder that several were tempted to make paying passages around Farewell Spit and across the bar into Westhaven Inlet when gold was found south of West Wanganui, (as the inlet was initially named). Storekeepers who set up there from 1861, using the Anatori River as access for re-supply, engaged the Nelson hookers *Pearl*, *Sisters*, *Collingwood*, *Dauntless* and others for their hazardous bar-crossing into the Anatori river-mouth. Although details are lacking, some of those voyages must have been of heroic proportions, bringing in produce from Blind Bay and Golden Bay. Certainly the Motueka farms were to prosper from the new West Coast market, and some hookers were to relocate their base from Nelson to Westport, where much shorter passages could be planned around the barometer's weather indications.

The first major goldfield was discovered near the Buller Gorge at the Lyell in 1862, kicking off an exodus from Golden Bay. In this year more than one-third of the 10,460 ounces of gold produced in Nelson Province was found on these Buller fields[160] and the rush to Hokitika and the Grey followed in 1864–65. Thousands of men scattered in all directions looking for and often finding new gold deposits; thousands of ounces of gold were regularly brought to Nelson which benefited greatly, finding a ready market for its farming produce and work for its shipping fleet. For the hookers there was less of a bonanza, though, with steamers becoming a preferred option for transporting supplies, miners and all the camp followers around Farewell Spit and onwards south along the potential lee shore more safely and quickly.

Colonial life and prospecting carried many risks, but arguably the boldest and most daring of all colonists were the crews of the hookers and other little sailing ships who tackled the West Coast. Necessity drove them to pit themselves and their vessels, under sail alone, against the wild west coast of the South Island. They turned the windy corner south by west around Farewell Spit and tackled the prevailing onshore westerlies blowing from the Tasman Sea.

Once around the Spit their only sanctuaries were the bar-protected river entrances. Skippers and crews were driven by the need to earn their livelihoods and the incentives of profit to be made, although just how many profited is unclear. Sailors cannot have relished working the West Coast. It took audacity and it took a toll but they did it for a job because that was their calling. One can only hope that skippers and crews were paid wage bonuses out of the exorbitant sea freight costs charged for this route.

But it was not an even playing field for the vessels plying this new route. Steam had entered the fray.

Subsidised steamers

In the mid 1850s, the New Zealand Company released a sum of money earmarked for community development, which was then augmented by government loans to create a £7,000 grant for the novelty of a steamship service. The *Nelson Coast*

---

160 Salmon p 127

Steam Association was created to import a purpose-built paddle-steamer from London that would not yet have been viable on a purely commercial basis.

As a result, in 1857 the 108ft 53-ton shoal draft paddle steamer *PS Tasmanian Maid* arrived to a fanfare welcome in Nelson where she was subsidized by the Nelson Provincial Government by £1,000 per annum. She was the first of several subsidised steamers to operate out of Nelson in these early days of steam. In a calm sea, her 36 horsepower motor was reputed to enable her to sail at 10–11 knots and 8 knots in a head wind, and when it was reported that *PS Tasmanian Maid* steamed from Nelson to Motueka in an hour and from there to Collingwood within another six, it was obvious that the hookers' dependence on and susceptibility to wind and weather would work against them.

The technology of this early Nelson steamer was primitive, both in engine output and propulsion, and her coal consumption per nautical mile will have been high, as it was an era before efficiency improvements to multiple combustion marine engines. The motion aboard in a beam sea was awkward too, with first one paddle and then the other taking a grip on the water as the vessel rolled. Seven years earlier, paddle-steamers had been proven to have less bollard pull than screw- steamers when the *HMS Rattler* had beaten a paddle-steamer in a tug-of-war, and the British navy was already modernising its propulsion to propellors.

*Very few images of **PS Tasmanian Maid** exist, however she can be seen here in the lower right of this painting extract, during the two years she saw active service re-named as the gunboat **HMS Sandfly** between 1863 and 1865. Like all these inefficient little paddle-steamers, she carried a schooner rig as a back-up.*

C-030-013. Alexander Turnbull Library, Wellington, New Zealand

However paddles were still a preferred option for shoal draft vessels like the little 36-ton paddle steamer *PS Emu* which also came on the Nelson scene two years later. *PS Emu* drew under three feet of water and tackled Saltwater Creek as a 'go anywhere' publicity stunt. More effectively she ran excursions on the

Waimea River, but there was not enough work for both vessels and so *Emu* left for Auckland where there was a contract offering on the North Shore run. PS Emu was followed by the even smaller 19 ton round-sterned, carvel-built and schooner-rigged *PS Undine*, built in Nelson. Her steaming arrangements proved so defective that she was soon sent off in 1862 to Otago for sale.

During her five years working out of Nelson, *PS Tasmanian Maid* tackled the Wairau bar and any other shallow inlet where there was cargo or passengers, even landing sheep ashore at the Waimea estuary. Significantly for the West Coast shipping developments, she was the first steamship to cross the Buller Bar, entering Westport under Captain Whitwell on 29th January 1862 with a cargo of goods and 60 diggers, mainly from Otago, although the subsidy was withdrawn in this year and she subsequently became uneconomic to run, being fitted with two guns and temporarily converted to a river gunboat in 1863 during the Taranaki Land War.

In 1862 and 1864 the Nelson Provincial Council subsidised two larger replacement steamers that were purchased by Nathaniel Edwards & Co of Nelson (later known as the Anchor Shipping and Foundry Company): the 74ft paddle-steamer *PS Lyttelton*, and the larger 103 ton screw steamer *SS Wallabi* both of which were to make regular passages to the West Coast. Edwards and Co. soon also purchased two more paddle-steamers for the West Coast trade: the 125ft *PS Nelson* in 1866), and *PS Charles Edward* which was salvaged from her 1867 stranding on the Grey River bar. The paddle steamer *PS Moutua* was also subsidised in 1868 to link Nelson and Richmond via the Waimea estuary. Screw steamers were also brought in to serve the burgeoning West Coast trade, including

The attraction of early steel screw steamers can be seen in this painting of **SS Murray**, *seen here with steadying sails forging through a heavy sea which would have been most uncomfortable aboard a smaller slower hooker.*
W Forster painting, C-059-005. Alexander Turnbull Library

the 137ft *SS Sturt* (1863), the 136ft *Kennedy* (a twin screw steamer in 1865), and the 98ft *SS Murray* (1867).

Without question the unsubsidised hookers were being marginalised, especially for the West Coast trade. On 22 July 1864 the paddle-steamer *PS Nelson*, under Captain Leech, was the first steamship to cross the Grey River bar. She carried Reuben Waite, ready to set up storekeeping at the Grey, along with about 70 diggers who were his prospective customers. It is of interest that *PS Nelson* carried 27 tons of coal when she sailed back to Nelson. In contrast the next day the aging hooker *Mary* brought Isaac Blake, the new storekeeper whose name is still attached to Greymouth's Blakestown, along with more diggers. In December that same year both the *SS Nelson* and the *SS Wallabi* (Captain Whitwell) steamed over the Hokitika River bar and into the river within a day of each other. Reportedly the first of many steamships direct from Australia, *SS Beautiful Star* arrived at Hokitika on 21 February 1867. She stood off and was unloaded into tugs and boats.

Steamers were the key to the Coast's development. They were evolving into larger vessels with more efficient high-pressure engines. Their iron construction was immune to the early vessels' problem of timber shrinkage caused by heat from the engine, and was less vulnerable to the ever-present fire risk. But the West Coast development was on a scale that demanded steamships. Even to enter the rivers the larger sailing ships were dependent on the tug services of steam-powered vessels. It was inevitable that the hookers were relegated to underdogs on this difficult coastline, yet they too were still to be found despite the challenges.

The struggling hooker trade

Almost exactly a year after Thomas Askew's aging hooker *Mary* sailed into Greymouth with Blake and his gold-digging passengers, she was wrecked at Totaranui, breaking up quickly because her planking and timbers were "*in a very rotten condition*"[161]. *Mary* had sailed a month previously with a cargo of sawn timber for Hokitika, but was wind-bound and had to return to Nelson for repairs. Then she broke her main boom off Cape Farewell and sprang a leak which her defective pumps were unable to cope with so she came back to anchor at Totaranui, only to be caught in an easterly. Attempting to put to sea without the help of her mainsail she missed stays and went ashore. Her fate typifies the financial and safety risks taken by the owners, captains and crews of these little wooden engineless ships.

One of the most remarkable examples of the struggle entailed to work the West Coast under sail alone is the nineteen days taken by Waite's ketch *Constant* to deliver the remnants of her cargo between Westport and Charleston – a distance of only 15 miles, but involving a convoluted voyage of over 400 miles both north and south of her departure point. It is in stark contrast to a newspaper report which accompanied *Constant*'s sorry tale, of the iron steamer *SS Tararua* which

---

161 Ingram p95

> TO SHIPPERS OF GOODS TO CHARLESTON.
>
> THE Ketch CONSTANT will continue to trade regularly between Westport and Charleston.
> For freight, apply to
> E. SUISTED,
> Or, THOMAS ALLEN,
> Stanley Wharf.
>
> WESTPORT TIMES, 10 Dec 1868.

> The ketch Constant left Westport, for Charleston, on the 10th ultimo, and was knocking about at sea until the 29th before she was able to reach her destination, having been driven both north and south—round the Sandspit, and as far as Tonga Island, on the one hand, and below the Grey on the other. It was feared the ketch was lost; and her cargo, which was a large one, sustained some damage, and part of it had to be thrown overboard.
>
> NELSON EXAMINER AND NEW ZEALAND CHRONICLE, 9 Jul 1870.

reported a comfortable Tasman Sea crossing of less than five days from Melbourne to Greymouth and a subsequent single day passage onwards to Nelson in "a beautiful smooth sea[162]".

Misadventures

The West Coast certainly took a toll on shipping and people. Several explorers drowned in its rivers and lakes and a number of individuals were lost at sea. In September 1863, the schooner *Gipsy* (now owned by Thomas Askew) was wrecked north of the Grey River bar and surveyor Arthur Dodson nearly drowned. *Gipsy* was a veteran of many rough passages but she had ventured one time too many. The men on the little ships met with onshore winds, open beaches, poorly sheltered coves and changing river bars and they were often forced to stand off and wait for the weather to improve. The beaches, especially those at Greymouth and Hokitika, were littered with wrecks and among those kept busy were the undertakers burying the dead. In the twenty years between August 1859, when *Supply* crossed the Buller bar for the first time, and September 1879 when *Shepherdess* was the last ship lost at Constant Bay, 97 vessels were lost on the West Coast. Wrecks occurred at Cape Farewell (6), West Wanganui (5), Westport (3), Constant Bay (8), Grey River (18), Hokitika (39) and other parts of the West Coast (18).[163]

Disappearances too

Inevitably there were casualties lost at sea without trace too, although usually, being wooden vessels on a lee shore, there would be wreckage washed up along the coast. The West Coast was being worked by sailing vessels for at least six years before the Charleston gold rush, dating from the time of Waite's and McKay's activities in 1860.

The Australian-built 24-ton, 43ft schooner *Dove*, owned by Nelson merchant J H Levien, disappeared while sailing from Nelson to Hokitika late in 1865 with a crew of four and two passengers. *Dove* had been offering passage and freight to the Buller in 1862 but was lost before ships began to work Constant Bay.

---

162 *Examiner*, 9th July 1870
163 Ingram, C W N, *New Zealand Shipwrecks* (7th edition), Beckett Publishing, 1990, pp502–506

Also listed as lost for several years was *Amelia Francis*, a 23-ton, Tasmanian-built 42ft schooner with a beam of 12ft 3in and a hold depth of 6ft 1in. She was built at Launceston in Tasmania in 1854, and worked out of Nelson from May 1865. Hers was a tale that was only possible in an era devoid of efficient international communication link. When she disappeared between Nelson and Greymouth in July 1865 it was assumed she foundered. Years later it transpired that the master Captain Rhind, who had been mate on the notorious Bully Hayes' ship *Black Diamond*, made off with her, no doubt finding the northern seas more appealing than the West Coast. He sold her cargo in the islands and sailed *Amelia Francis* to California, where he sold the ship, too.

The Bonanza

During the West Coast gold rush era, nearly 300 tons[164] of gold was mined on the West Coast and Buller. It initially attracted the New Zealand prospectors, followed very closely by Australian miners and then those from much further afield. By 1866 Nelson merchant Robert Levien was bewailing "the overcrowded state of the various West Coast markets, by heavy shipments from Australia"[165]. Merchants like Thomas Askew from Nelson moved in and set up establishments in the coast towns of Westport, Greymouth or Hokitika.

Thousands of people poured onto the West Coast over a few short years; diggers, storekeepers, merchants, camp followers of all sorts and a smattering of officials. Many had the gold-fever that kept them moving on to new fields in the hope of the big strike and as fast as they had surged in they surged out but always some stayed and worked on, making at least a living and occasionally a fortune. Towns sprang up like mushrooms and some disappeared almost as quickly. Small sailing ships and steamers proliferated, keeping the people moving and ferrying the supplies that were essential for survival.

Merchants, ship owners and agents thrived. Thomas Cawthron, later a Nelson philanthropist, made most of his wealth as a shipping agent and coal merchant and among his other investments was able to buy 14,000 acres of freehold in the Upper Awatere Valley and owned it for more than thirty years without once setting foot on it.[166]

The *West Coast Times* in May 1866 estimated the population as between 25,000 and 30,000. By the end of the year it was estimated to stand at 50,000, and it was considered to have peaked the following year. This may have been an over-estimate. Salmon points out that the 1867 census gave the total West Coast population as 25,884, but "could not account for the nomadic mining population in remote areas."

Salmon also describes a delicate balance between social norms and legal niceties. The right to mine on freehold property was never established with

---

164 For perspective, NZ's total gold output from 1857 to 1904 was 693 tons, as detailed in 'Waratah', *Tales of the Golden West*, Capper Press, 1983, pp37–38.
165 Salmon, p1
166 Kennington, pp87–88

certainty in law, and goldfield law certainly followed the practical precept of co-operation (to a point) for the common good and to avoid friction. Title to the gold, a gift of nature, followed closely to the old lore of 'finders keepers' provided appropriate title to a claim had been observed. The goldfield wardens became lawmakers and peacekeepers on the goldfields.

Westhaven Inlet

In the newspapers of the time, references to West Wanganui repeatedly crop up. Derived from the Maori 'whanga (bay or harbour) and 'nui' large, it is little wonder that there were several other locations bearing this name about New Zealand, most notably the Wanganui settlement between Wellington and New Plymouth, Te Wanganui (Port Underwood) and the Little Wanganui River some 20 miles north-east of the Buller (a contradiction in size not grasped by the pakeha who named this!). Because of this confusion, the huge bar-harbour inlet at the extreme northern end of the West Coast has subsequently been renamed Westhaven.

For the southbound little ships which had rounded Farewell Spit into the teeth of a Kahurangi Sou'westerly[167], it offered the only shelter on this stretch of coast, and was huge enough to host a number of ships at any one time. However Westhaven Inlet has its challenges, and having myself been in and out over the bar just a few times it is not difficult to see them.

It is a curious fact that the coal seam adjacent to this inlet was known before colonial times. Perhaps some sealing gang had chanced upon it, or perhaps there was Maori knowledge of its properties. Frederick Moore first loaded coal from the inlet aboard *Jewess* in 1840, bound for the new settlement of Wellington, and in January 1842 *Eliza* brought a load of coal from the inlet before the first shipload of immigrants had even arrived. Once the more accessible Massacre Bay seams had been discovered, it appears that there was less interest in the more remote western coal source, but without an official port there, there is no record of vessels entering or departing.

Once sea traffic was rounding Farewell Spit more regularly in the 1860s, evidence crops up of continuing access to Westhaven coal, mostly from the resulting reported disasters.

In some cases their temptation to fill their holds with this dirty but compact cargo overcame their prudence. A half-full hold would likely be at the limit of a hooker's cargo tonnage, so it would have taken considerable willpower to halt the loading operation. (Even in modern times, reports of fishing vessels foundering due to overloading are not uncommon!) One recorded example, although not involving Westhaven coal, is of the Lyttelton hooker *Catherine*, which went down off the Canterbury coast when her planks gave way after being loaded with 21 tons of coal instead of her 15-ton capacity.

There are five wrecks officially recorded at Westhaven. Whether *Necromancer's*

---

167 The coastal topography between Cape Farewell and Kahurangi Point is notorious for deflecting and accelerating westerly quarter winds to generate head winds on a south-bound passage.

seagoing abilities were compromised when 'heavily laden with coal' from Westhaven was the cause of her demise is uncertain, however records state that she broke up after being beached on Farewell Spit in May 1869. The 15-ton shoal draft early Nelson schooner *Rapid* was another coal-laden hooker which foundered at Westhaven in 1867, presumably crossing the bar, while outward bound for Wanganui. A casualty of weather while on anchor inside the inlet was the big schooner *Heathcote* which dragged her anchor in a Sou'east gale in 1872 and stranded on South head where the breaking seas finished her off. Coal had its own dangers too, being a flammable cargo. Although nobody was aboard at the time, it was assumed that the fire which totally destroyed the cutter *Diana* in Westhaven Inlet on 15th October 1869 had very likely taken hold of coal in her hold from galley-fire embers while all of her crew were ashore digging for more.[168]

I have a personal experience of Westhaven inlet in more recent times, as well as a family one. In September 1891 Captain Robert Westrupp was master of the 62ft Tasmanian-built 'barge' ketch *Elizabeth* when she became a total loss on the south head of West Wanganui. She was shifting a flax dressing plant from Scrimgeour's Creek in Ferntown to this new location and the disaster was caused by the wind dropping when she was on the bar. Her crew landed safely and then stripped most of the gear off, but this elegant vessel was lost.

Seen here at low water on a calm day, the difficulties facing hooker skippers entering Westhaven Inlet under sail are obvious. The outlying bar was followed by sweeping currents through its sharply curving entrance, and then a potential loss of wind behind the southern promontory.
Photo Barbara Tucker

---

168 *Examiner* 23 Oct 1869

There is an adjacent cliff face where seamen over many years have carved their names. Although I did not find it myself, one of my uncles aboard a scow, and quite some time later two of my sons, have each separately found the name *Sam Westrupp* inscribed there and badly weathered. It may have been my grandfather or his nephew who signed the cliff, which serves as a reminder of regular traffic and my family connections with this now out-of-the-way place. My great-uncle Bill Westrupp also operated a steam launch on the inlet and my son Willy Westrupp operated a crayfishing boat from there for several years, even experiencing an engine failure on the bar once which forced him to anchor in breaking seas – just as the early mariners must have done when the wind failed them.

There is little now to show of the seagoing activities within this huge waterway. The rotting hulk of the scow *Kohi* lying alongside a rotting wharf provides the last relic of a bygone era.

The scow Kohi lies as a hulk at Westhaven inlet, 2019
Barbara Tucker photo

It seems almost unbelievable that so many small ships entered Constant Bay through this narrow rocky entrance under sail. This photograph was taken on a near-perfect calm day with light winds and a low swell.
Barbara Tucker photo

Inside the precarious entrance of Charleston's tiny harbour of Constant Bay, a schooner takes the mud while the crew of the pilot boat pose at the oars.
Courtesy West Coast NZ History (Contributor: Maye Dunn)

14

The Charleston Challenge

1866 WAS THE YEAR of the Charleston gold rush, and with it come tales of almost unbelievable risk for the little ships that serviced it. Constant Bay provides us with the best example of an extreme West Coast harbour entrance.

The descriptively named Cape Foulwind lies six miles west of Westport, providing a welcome lee from southerly quarter winds. Once clear of the cape, the coast swings south. Greymouth lies 44 nautical miles further south – an easy day's sail in the right conditions assuming that both bars are safe to cross. However it is not these towns that interest us here. A mere 9 miles south of the cape lie a pair of tiny keyhole shaped coastal indents in the rock-strewn coastline. The southern one of these little coves, Constant Bay, epitomised the wildness of the West Coast for small ships under sail.

We have already met Westport's enterprising Reuben Waite, who by 1866 had extended his business enterprises to run livestock on 6,000 acres of leasehold land known locally as 'Waite's Pakihi'[169]. Being a businessman, he was incensed that the provincial government would not let him buy the leased land to on-sell at a profit when gold was discovered in this area[170].

Reuben owned the hooker *Constant*, a medium-sized 14-ton Tasmanian ketch first registered at Hobart in 1862. When gold was discovered in the vicinity in 1866 she was the first to brave the challenging entrance to this cove, presumably with a load of hopeful goldminers and gear aboard, and the bay was named after her. The rapidly growing calico and canvas tent settlement behind this tiny harbour was immediately named 'Charlie's Town' (soon abbreviated to Charleston) in recognition of *Constant*'s plucky captain, Charles Bonner, who regularly braved stormy weather to bring *Constant* in with supplies when the people were near to starving.[171]

Constant Bay was a terrible hole to get in to, but it served both very rich adjacent goldfields when there was no practical alternative. Ships often had to wait outside, awaiting quieter seas for an opportunity to enter the precariously narrow entrance. In Charleston's heyday there was a port with a Signalman and a Signal Station, a town with a Police Camp and a Courthouse, a newspaper, three Churches (Anglican, Roman Catholic and Methodist), three banks (the Bank of New Zealand, the Bank of New South Wales, the Union Bank of Australia), two schools, a hospital, six lodges, (the Masonic, the Hibernian Australasian Benefit

---

169 Pakihi is the commonly used Maori name for swampy flats where kahikatea trees proliferate.
170 The Addison's Flat goldfield was discovered there about nine months after the Charleston field.
171 Journal of Nelson and Marlborough Historical Society, vol 2, no 4

Carved out of bush and pakihi swamp, the gold-mining town of Charleston grew remarkably quickly into a hive of commerce. The tidal nature of its harbour, and difficult entrance did not deter the little ships that frequented it.
Courtesy West Coast NZ History

Society, the Manchester Unity Order of Oddfellows, the Ancient Order of Foresters, the Independent order of Good Templars, the Loyal Orange Institution), forty or fifty hotels, the Casino de Venice, a Post Office, a cricket club, a rifle club, a football club, a race course (along the Nine Mile Beach), a town band, a fire brigade, unspecified brothels, and even some miners who lit their pipes with bank notes.

Vessels entering Constant Bay needed helmsmen with steady nerves, and crews handy with halliards and ground tackle. They needed to keep in the centre of a rocky sea-swept channel barely 18 metres wide and several boat-lengths long. When the Charleston people later sought status for their harbour as a port of entry, a provincial council member jibed that he had walked over the so-called harbour. It was worked by beaching the ships on the tide and unloading as the tide receded, a time-honoured hooker method, and it did silt up with accumulated tailings from the gold workings but it was always tidal and it was never a haven. It was open to the rollers sweeping in from the Tasman and offered little shelter in a gale. I have watched the entrance when all that was visible was a high-flung welter of foam with wild waves from the broken swells crashing through the narrow channel. It was a frightening sight, and in seafaring terms completely untenable.

In 1866 the provincial council arranged for signal stations to be erected at Charleston, along with other significant ports within its jurisdiction. A red flag at the masthead meant a ship could enter, blue meant wait for the tide and white indicated that the surf was too heavy and the entrance dangerous. From 1867 onwards some privately owned surfboats offered their services as lighters, to assist ship handling for a charge of ten shillings per ship's ton. They were also at times involved in courageous rescues and took their own losses. There was never any wharf; the only concession to facilities (in 1869) was a set of heavy ringbolts set into the rocks both sides of the cleft-like entrance, for lines to be attached to assist incoming vessels, with another ringbolt on a rock in the centre of the beach for securing ships' lines. It must always have been a precarious business.

It has been reported that the maximum number of vessels in Constant Bay's tiny harbour at one time was eight or nine, which seems almost impossible except that one should not be surprised at what hooker skippers accomplished. In the seven months to May 1867, upwards of 200 vessels had already traded into Constant Bay, and on 29th May 1867 the record shows six sailing vessels and the small steamer *Bruce* arriving during one single day.[172]

It is not hard to imagine the suspense aboard a cluster of hookers waiting out a westerly gale in the safety of Westport, in the hopes of a lighter northerly or offshore easterly to carry them and their perishable cargoes for the fifteen miles down to Constant Bay entrance, arriving near top of tide. On one such occasion after arrival outside the reef-strewn entrance, the surfboats towed in, one after the other, the ketch *Constant*, the cutter *Harry Bluff*[173] the schooner *Ann*, the cutter *Joseph Paul* and the ketch *Standard*, indicating that the cove had to be worked hard when conditions allowed.

None of the larger steamers, which worked into Greymouth, Westport and even Hokitika carrying the lion's share of the coastal trade, were able to venture in to Constant Bay so it was left to the small sailing vessels and a few of the smallest steamers (which often also served as tugs to larger vessels), to risk beaching below Charleston. The early small steamers recorded as entering Constant Bay were *Mullah*, *Kennedy*, *Waipara*, *Halcyon*, *Bruce*, *Despatch* and *Result*. The paddle-steamer *Result* later reappeared in Nelson as a ketch, her engine and paddlewheel transferred into her successor.

One early mishap involving the paddle steamer *PS Nelson* shortly after gold was discovered demonstrates that for the impatient gold prospectors, even travelling aboard vessels with engines was no guarantee of personal safety. Charleston was still commonly referred to as 'Waite's Pakihi' at this early stage, and *PS Nelson* was hove to off Constant Bay, disembarking the eager gold-diggers into a dinghy with their gear to be rowed through the difficult entrance. Then disaster struck, as reported later when the story reached the new Nelson newspaper:

"We are indebted to Mr O Wiesenhavern[174] *for the information, that on Sunday last, a boat, containing eight persons, that was proceeding from the steamer Nelson*

---

172 Faris, p 42
173 Probably the Maori-owned *Harry Bluff* out of Auckland.
174 Wiesenhavern was a tobacconist with establishments at Nelson and the West Coast towns, which he seems to have visited regularly, and also was holder of the Tophouse sheep run.

Four hookers lie safely aground in the shallow harbour as the tide ebbs, with one schooner leaving her mains'l set to ensure she settles to starboard in the light northerly breeze.
F-80471/2, Alexander Turnbull Library

to the shore, at the Pakihi, was swamped. It is uncertain if any of the men were saved, although it was reported that three of them were got out in an exhausted state. Mr Wiesenhavern had a narrow escape from drowning, in coming off from the shore to the steamer, by the same boat, which was much too small and fragile for the purpose. Previous to this, Mr Wiesenhavern was witness to two boat accidents, resulting in the death of three persons. It appears that the inlet through which boats have to pass is narrow, skirted by precipitous rocks, and that the passage by boats is most hazardous."[175]

Hookers from Nelson

It is worth noting how many of the Blind Bay hookers were trading into Charleston during the thirteen years that it was a viable harbour, over and above another two dozen vessels from other regions.

The smallest of these local little ships would have found the sea conditions off the upper West Coast challenging (especially striking the notoriously common Kahurangi Sou'westerly). Several were under 35ft registered length (around 10 tons) like the cutters *Supply*, *Ann* and *Kate*; the ketches *Mavis* and *Standard*, as well as the schooners *Elizabeth*, *Fairy*, and the little 7-ton *Kate*.

---

175 *Nelson Evening Mail*, 15 November 1866

In the next size range were several schooners of around 40-45ft registered length (about 15–20 tons). These included *Heathcote*, *Jane*, *Mary Ann*, *Gypsy*, *Rapid* and *Necromancer* (affectionately known as *Old Nick*).

The heavyweights of the local sailing feet working in and out of Charleston had a generous tonnage, and were registered at around 50ft in length or longer. The only ketches amongst them were both Tasmanian-built: the huge 62ft *Falcon* and the centreboard 'barge' *Pearl*, ideal to 'take the ground' for low tide loading. The remainder were all schooners: *Emerald Isle*, *Nautilus* and *Shepherdess*.

Cutter, Ketch or Schooner?

The sail configuration of this era is interesting. Naturally all were gaff rigged (marconi was a high aspect rig unheard of for many more decades). As noted in chapter 4, the low spread of sail has advantages when 'reaching' or 'running' with the wind from abeam or astern but makes pointing high into the wind rather compromised. It also is vulnerable to chafe in a seaway, but to lessen this nuisance, too much baggywrinkle on the shrouds increases windage and slows the vessel even more when beating to windward. The big topsail schooners like *Falcon* and *Shepherdess* had additional windage aloft from their two big yards (horizontal spars) and sails even when furled. On the West Coast of New Zealand's South Island with its prevailing onshore winds, the ability to claw off a lee shore was paramount for survival.

This leads us to the time-honoured debate between proponents of cutters, sloops, yawls, ketches and schooners. Sloops and yawls were essentially variations on the cutters of the times and were not a chosen rig of any working vessel. Generally a single-masted vessel – i.e. cutter – can be considered the handiest to windward, as it allows a higher mast and exposes a larger sail area directly to a head wind. This is presumably the reason for *Supply* being converted from ketch rig to cutter in 1852, five years after being launched.

The two masted rigs were considered more suitable for larger vessels, in order to avoid masts of excessive height, and to keep the individual sails from becoming too large to handle. Clearly the schooner was a preferred rig in New Zealand's earliest years, possibly more from the American than English fashion in rigs. However from a technical viewpoint, the ketch, with its foremast being the tallest, presents the largest area of canvas to a head wind, and therefore performs better when beating to windward. Certainly there was a trend away from schooner to ketch as the century progressed, especially as the Tasmanian ketches began to be purchased from across the Tasman and their superior performance noted.

As well as rig, the hull form had an important bearing on windward performance too. To work the tidal harbours, beaches and bars, shoal draft was a valued design option. However to beat to windward a vessel needs the lateral resistance of a deepish keel. Without this grip on the water, she will make too much leeway and slide sideways as much as forwards. The best compromise came from the centreboarders, common in the increasingly popular Tasmanian 'barge-ketches' and later to be adopted by the local scows. A few cumbersome bluff-bowed hookers like *Jane* will have found windward progress difficult because of their hull form. *Jane* was described as a 'galliot', and if this is accurate she will have had a rounded dutch-style barge appearance. With greater resistance in a head sea, even the sea-state will have made her progress slow (let alone her schooner rig). Ironically, she met her end not clawing out of Constant Bay, but inside Queen Charlotte Sound, unable to weather Kempe Point against a fresh Sou'easterly and heavy sea.

Without question, any captain working in and out of Charleston will have been vitally concerned with his vessel's windward ability.

Constant Bay, constant losses

The Tasman Sea spawned harsh conditions on this coast, and when the weather was bad the nearest safe haven was often many sea-tossed miles away with dangerous bars to be crossed. The ships stood off or, depending upon local knowledge, sought to tuck in to a semi-sheltered corner if wind direction and sea conditions made that feasible, but not all hookers had the ability to keep at sea in bad weather.

On 17 April 1867 the schooners *Iona* and *Cymraes* collided in Constant Bay. *Iona* was driven ashore badly damaged and considered a total wreck but later salvaged, while *Cymraes* survived only to be wrecked at the Grey River in November that same year. One of the features of these hookers was that their construction and finish was often so basic, virtually just the planked hull without linings or fittings, that salvage and restoration was feasible. The ready availability of timber and the skills of local handymen account for so many of them reappearing after being damaged.

On 26 August 1867 *Emerald Isle*, a 28-ton schooner which had been a regular trader into Nelson, foundered outside Constant Bay not long after clearing the entrance. She and her crew were lost and it was supposed that she was insufficiently ballasted and was struck by a squall. On 2 October 1869 the 11-ton cutter *Harry Bluff* was totally wrecked at the entrance, with the loss of two lives, after her master disregarded the signals of the harbourmaster.

On 27 December 1870 the 24-ton schooner *Betsy Douglas*, built in Otago in 1862 as a paddle-steamer, was lost after leaving Constant Bay and striking a rock off nearby Point Robertson, but her two crew were rescued by the pilot boat. On 11 June 1871, the *Brothers and Sister*, a 21-ton ketch, became a total loss inside Constant Bay because her mooring lines chafed on the rocks and broke in heavy seas, and on 14 May 1875 *Kate*, a small schooner in ballast, was badly damaged on the beach but sailed nevertheless, only to founder after leaving.

On 26 August 1876 *Flying Cloud*, a 46-ton schooner, was found on the nearby coast a capsized and shattered wreck with all hands lost. She had lacked the present-day advantage of a weighted external keel, and was underway to New York at the time. In June 1877, wreckage from the 31-ton, 52ft schooner *Kaikoura* also washed ashore near Constant Bay. She had been headed to Greymouth from Kaikoura and her master Captain Anderson and two crewmen were lost. On 16 September 1878 the 59ft schooner *Wild Wave*, with a cargo of grain and potatoes, broke her moorings in the heavy seas rolling into Constant Bay and

*The broken hull of the tops'l schooner **Shepherdess** lies on her beam ends at low tide after the storm which claimed her inside Constant Bay's exposed entrance. This once-proud schooner had survived many battles working exposed South Island coasts, so it is ironic that she was lost along with four lives while actually inside a harbour.*
Courtesy History House, Greymouth

was partially wrecked, but salvaged to survive for another year. The final straw for this hazardous little harbour came exactly a year later, on 16 September 1879, when the 30-ton schooner *Shepherdess*, the last of these vessels to enter Constant Bay, suffered the same fate. She broke her moorings with heavy rollers coming into the bay and was totally lost with her crew of three. The pilot, Charles Craddock, was also drowned during a rescue attempt, and the harbour was deemed unsafe for further use.

> **TELEGRAMS**
> [FROM OUR OWN CORRESPONDENT.]
> **CHARLESTON**
> September 15
> A man's leg, from the thigh down, was washed ashore at Constant Bay yesterday. It is supposed to be part of the man Craddock, drowned at the time the Shepherdess was entering.

The dangers facing harbour pilots like the unfortunate Charles Craddock are bought into tragic focus in this snippet from the Westport Times *of 16 September 1879. Craddock left a wife and three children to grieve.*

Sea rescues in these circumstances usually involved pilot boats for the first call. In those days these were pulling boats similar to whalers or surfboats, rowed by a crew with a coxswain helming. They were usually the only experienced and readily available resource when things went wrong. Later as a teenager I was involved a few times in less risky rescues when my father Sid was master of the Nelson pilot launches. Although he downplayed this aspect of his work, after his death we found among his personal things a small file of grateful letters from men whose lives were saved, quite frequently at considerable risk to the two men aboard the launch. One was my father, the other usually my uncle Albert Westrupp.

As well as the ships lost at Constant Bay, there were other incidents. *Flying Squirrel* and *Ada* had problems, and when *Fancy* tried to cross the bar in defiance of the signal and without surfboat assistance, she would have been lost had the shore staff not got lines aboard her and dragged her in stern-first. *Fairy* was in trouble on three occasions, *Flora McDonald*, *Ann*, and *Constant* were helped several times, as were *Mary Jane* and *Mavis*. The regular small paddle-steamer *Result*, one of only two or three calling regularly at Constant Bay, was damaged several times. The surfboats got into occasional trouble too, and there was one drowning.

But sometimes the gods smiled down. On 24 May 1868, the 32ft schooner *Fairy* received the signal to enter Constant Bay in spite of a very rough sea outside, with large combers breaking savagely across the bar. As she entered, a heavy sea carried away her rudder and she was thrown on the rocks. Then a big sea came thundering in, lifted her stern high in the air, picked her up and deposited her in comparatively smooth water where the surfboats managed to moor her. She was damaged, but able to be repaired.

Of the forty or so sailing vessels noted as coming into Constant Bay, often regularly, nineteen were on the casualties list, some more than once, and nine were lost. Were the gains worth the risk? A recital of losses in places like Charleston does not do justice to the skill and experience of the crews. Ships sailed under many different skippers and with many crew changes but on that coast it would be unusual if there was not a sea surge to contend with, on and on as the sea beyond seems to breathe. Add in the wind, because a ship under sail must have wind to have steerage, and the land is hostile territory for a relatively fragile ship.

In the case of *Ann*, damaged on the Constant Bay beach, the master put to sea because Constant Bay was no place to loiter. The ship sprang a leak and he knew that the only recourse was to run north for the Buller if she were to be saved. Her crew would be trying to stem the leak, pumping to keep her afloat, sailing as fast as they could without stressing her further. After hours of anxiety they managed to run her ashore through the surf at the Buller to avoid foundering and she spent three days on the beach before they were fortunate enough to get her off.

There were times when seamen headed boldly in through a rocky passage, having made a careful assessment or maybe simply having no alternative, only to be thrown off course by a rogue wave or a badly timed surge. Then would come the sickening crunch of wood on unforgiving rock, often in heavy rain, the seas coming aboard and the noise, the remorseless, impartial but unforgiving energy of it all. I have personal memories of wild pitch-black nights with seas like express trains, louder than the tumult, bearing down from some distance off to thump and flood over ship and helmsman with a deafening roar. When our little ship shakes herself and bounds on, those of us aboard thank the designer, builder, rigger and all those others whose skills put a stout-hearted vessel under us on such a rough, dirty night.

The last five years of Charleston's shipping trade were already in decline before the loss of *Shepherdess*, due to the 1874 completion of a viable overland route from Westport – the Addison's Flat road. Prior to this the tidal coastal route, which traversed Nine-mile Beach and included dangerous river crossings, was a severe restriction, although it didn't deter a group of hardy Shetland Islanders from Unst who beachcombed for gold on Nine-mile Beach in the 1870s. Once the road had been built, wagons began to compete with the little ships. The harbour was silting rapidly too with wash-out from the swampy hinterland. Only the rusty ringbolts remain as a reminder of the plucky seamen who once plied this unlikely little harbour.

The following official report has been made by Captain Beveridge, harbormaster at Pakihi, and has been courteously placed at our disposal by Mr Warden Kynnersley:—

"Captain Beveridge reports for the information of coasters trading on the West Coast of the Middle Island of New Zealand, that he has examined the coast line in and about Constant Bay, Fox's River, &c., and finds as follows:—

"That Constant Bay is a small cove, entering in from a bold rocky shore, 10 miles South of Cape Foulwind; Lat. 41° 56".

"The entrance is about 60 feet wide, and runs up about 150 yards, the whole beach from north and south entrance being no more than 300 yards.

"Vessels, on coming to the Bay, ought to be provided with good strong lines, anchors, chains, &c., for mooring purposes.

"In fine weather the bar is generally smooth; but if any way rough, no vessel ought to take the bar, the rocks being so precipitous on either side as to render it highly dangerous.

"Fox's River, 12 miles south of Constant Bay, is a small river running into the sea, close by the north side of a large bluff, which is situated in lat. 42° 4" on the Admiralty Chart; there are a few rocks stretching out from the bluff 600 yards; there is also a rock awash at high water about 200 yards north from the main body of of rocks on the south, the entrance to the river being on either side of this rock; the rocks bear S.S.E. from the bluff. A large rock and several smaller sunken rocks lie about 50 yards from the beach, and a quarter of a mile from the bluff.

"This river is navigable for vessels drawing at most five feet water.

"Woodpecker Bay is one and a half miles south of Fox's River; it is sheltered in moderate S.W. weather by a large rock stretching out from a high bluff; it is the best place for boats landing in the neighborhood, but the shore being so bold and rocky, it would be safest to get small craft into the river under proper signal guidance from the shore at Fox's.

Owners and masters of vessels visiting this port should take all necessary precautions to insure the safety of their vessels upon arrival. They who have once visited us it is needless to refer to, but any new arrivals should secure very strong lines for mooring their crafts inside, Constant Bay; indeed, the strain in adverse weather is so heavy that a good six inch line is none too strong. and since the arrivals have of late become very frequent, it is doubly necessary that measures of this kind should be taken to avoid accident. When freights are high and the risk great it very naturally happens that vessels of a very inferior character get into the trade, which, if they succeed in a couple of trips, more than earn their prime cost; it is not to be expected that these should be well found in expensive lines, but it is not the less necessary that they should be for the safety of more valuable vessels. At any time one or more of these second-rate vessels may part their lines and drive against others, doing considerable damage. There can be no reason, at any rate, that the Government should not furnish these necessary lines, and charge each vessel for the use of them. This is the only plan by which the damage which accrued to the Iona, Cymraes, and others may be avoided in future.

In crowded Constant Bay with its regular strong winds, damage caused by hookers with inadequate ground tackle dragging anchor onto well anchored vessels was a worry. The recommendation here to moor with six inch ropes is an indication of surge conditions in Constant Bay with a strong swell running.

Charleston Argus 24 Apr 1867
Advice published in Grey River Argus 4 Dec 1866

*The 49ft 22-ton ketch **Comet**, seen here lying against a stone jetty near the gas works, was built at Torrent Bay. She could reportedly carry 16,000 superfeet of timber, amounting to 37 tons dead weight.*
Collection 318495, Nelson Provincial Museum

*The large ketches like **Te Aroha** had their own derricks to load bundled timber into their holds. Here, Arnold Goodman stands on a bundle while another crew operates the winch. Jack Kidson stands to the right of the mast.*
Courtesy Rob Williams

15

Timber for the Taking

WHILE GOLD AND WOOL were the obvious money-spinners of the early decades in the wider Nelson region, a readily available commodity was obvious from the first days of the colony – an abundance of trees.

Land-clearing yielded timber as a by-product – a resource with many uses. The first immigrants must have taken one look at the forested slopes surrounding the settlement, and mentally converted them into building materials and firewood. Study the public notices in the first edition of the Nelson *Examiner* (see chapter 3) and it will become clear that this resource was jealously guarded by landowners and Company officials.

During the following decades, as the colonists spread out along the coastal margins and up the river valleys, the hookers were to play an important role in transporting wood, in its various forms, within the colony. Settlers were quick to recognise the qualities of available timber for the variety of specific uses. Most precious were the giant podocarps – known locally under the nickname of 'pines' because of their small seed-cones. Growing straight and tall, the Rimu (red pine), and Kahikatea (white pine) were the most valued for house-framing and cladding, followed by Matai (black pine), Totara and Miro. Totara became known for its ground-contact durability for use as house piles, fence-posts and sleepers. The abundant gnarled beech species were less valued as a building timber due to their lack of straightness and tendency to warp, but its bark was often harvested for use in the tanning trade.

The boatbuilders steadily became fussy about their selection of timbers. They were to learn the hard way which local timbers were sufficiently durable, as we have seen in chapter one, and they often sought out some of the minor species as their properties became better known. Without the wonderful Kauri and Pohutukawa species available to northern boatbuilders, there was much trial and error, with some recognising Tanekaha as a close species of the popular Tasmanian Celery top pine, and others selecting the Kaiwaka and Kaikawaka[176] (native cedars). Rata is closely related to Pohutukawa, and its strong curved roots and branches were used in a similar manner for grown knees and even naturally bent frames.

Agriculture had its own specific uses for timber too, not just fenceposts but even for the long thin poles (most likely Kanuka or Manuka) necessary for stringing up the burgeoning hop-growing industry in the Motueka and Riwaka

---

[176] Allen Westrupp valued the Kaikawaka sourced from d'Urville Island, as well as a species of beech known locally as Cherry Birch.

valleys. Cattle and sheep yards needed strong durable timber too.

Two names stand out as key entrepreneurs in Nelson's early timber trade – Edward Baigent and William Brownlee. Baigent was at work rafting felled logs down the Waimea River from the earliest years of settlement, well before Brownlee set up his operation within easy reach of the Pelorus Sounds waterways. For many of the larger hookers and inter-provincial sailing vessels these operations were to become a bread-and-butter trade.

The owners of Nelson's small ships were always on the lookout for a cargo of firewood, too. There was a symbiotic relationship between the hand-to-mouth coastal settlers and the struggling hooker captains regarding this readily available resource which was in constant demand within the town settlements. The 15-ton ketch *Jane* advertised as being capable of bringing ten cords of firewood from Croisilles harbour to Nelson, a load which equates to a volume of 320 cubic feet if it was carefully stacked, and a weight of between 12 and 15 tons depending on how seasoned it was. This would have been a significant load, stacked both below deck and on deck, with no safe footing for sail-handling. It would hardly be a load for a prudent hooker captain to bring in on a hard Blind Bay nor'westerly!

This grainy old later-era photo of the deck-loading ketch scow **Vindex** *with her massive cargo of firewood loaded at Anapa Bay in Croisilles, demonstrates the challenge of operating under sail with such a bulky commodity. How the crew were to access the main and headsail halliards is anybody's guess, and for stability she would be reliant on her beamy hull form to compensate for the high centre of gravity.*
Russ Ricketts Photo, courtesy Kerry Miller

The abolition of Provincial Government

Timber milling was particularly profitable during the 1860s and 1870s. Back-to-back were the demands for building materials for the goldrush towns, followed by the Vogel era of massive Central Government investment in public works. For operators like the 'Timber Kings' Baigent and Brownlee, the profits made during these decades were to sustain them through the lean years of the 1880s depression. In so doing, they were also able to benefit the hooker operators.

Julius Vogel had an impact on Nelson in political outcomes as well as financial. During 1870 to 1873 when he was Central Government[177] Treasurer he successfully borrowed £10 million for an ambitious regime of infrastructure development (roads and railways) and assisted immigration. For timber millers (and by association the hookers which would transport these across Cook Strait) the huge demand for railway sleepers was an instant boon.

During his three subsequent years as Premier, he set about destroying the power of Provincial Assemblies and consolidating centralised government control. This was achieved with the **Abolition of Provinces Act** of 1875, effectively ending the ongoing struggle for power between Nelson's gentry and the lower classes. This division had become somewhat blurred by the steady rise of an entrepreneurial middle class within the expanding colony; men who included the timber kings and little ship owners.

Baigent's Waimea operation

Edward Baigent was a sawmilling immigrant who arrived in Nelson with his wife and children during the first three months of settlement, bringing saws and basic equipment to continue his trade. It did not take long for him to locate the lowland forests of the Waimea river-plains which would be ideal for his purpose. He initially worked in a labouring gang, on contract to the New Zealand Company. This earned him sufficient money to set up a waterwheel on the banks of the Wai-iti River (near the fledgling village of Wakefield) which initially operated as a flour mill until he had sufficient money to convert it to a sawmill. In the meantime he rafted logs downstream and directly into the haven. It is evident from the painting in Chapter 3 that he was doing this as early as 1845.

River transport was the easiest method of transporting his flour and timber to Nelson until the inland track was consolidated. By 1850 he had eight employees and was also using bullock teams to help transport his logs which were used in the construction of the new cathedral in 1851. By 1869 his first timber yard in Collingwood Street was the crowning proof of his successful business venture.

Brownlee's Pelorus operation

Although Baigent's timber venture was not contingent on the ready availability of hookers, William Brownlee's success was vitally dependent on these little ships. He also was from a sawmilling background, originally migrating from Scotland

---

177 The NZ Capital had been moved closer, from Auckland to Wellington, in 1865.

The rather elegant 82ft, 77-ton Tasmanian-built centreboard ketch **Lizzie Taylor** *lies against the Brownlee mill's wharf at Blackball near Havelock, as a bundle of timber awaits on its trolley. Despite its windage upwind, the squaresail yard aloft is an item of rig which became more common in hookers in the later C19, (also seen on* **Matakana** *and* **Comet***) for downwind running with large square 'course'. All her sails have been left loosely furled which suggests a short-handed crew in a hurry to load between tides. A typical cargo from Blackball to Timaru in 1901 (where her timber merchant owner John Jackson lived) was 48,000 feet of sawn timber, with a return cargo of 120 tons flour for Wanganui. She retained her Tasmanian registration while under NZ ownership.*

Copy Collection C870, Nelson Provincial Museum

to Dunedin, and moving north with his wife and children as the Canvastown goldrush was unfolding. The family settled in the lower Pelorus Sound in 1864, living in tents while William secured cutting rights for 1,000 acres of prime coastal mixed podocarp forest in Mahakipawa, reputedly capitalising on the Canvastown building boom to make £7,000 in the first two years. From this point his ability to expand was easy, and he formed a consortium with other sawmillers. Their operation steadily milled through the best stands of accessible trees in Pelorus Sound's Mahakipawa Arm, Nydia Inlet, Kaiuma Bay, and Kaituna Valley, with 75 employees within two decades. William and his son John made the gamble of buying out the consortium's assets in 1881 as economic depression began to bite. The headquarters of Brownlee & Co. was the big steam-powered mill at Blackball near the settlement of Havelock at the headwaters of Pelorus Sound, although at the height of the operations there were three mills and an impressive series of tramlines.

The Brownlee wharf at Blackball was accessible to a significant fleet of sailing vessels, capable of navigating their way through the two mile tidal channel into deeper waters of the Sound. The tidal rise and fall here must have been a major concern for those hooker skippers, ranging up to 15 feet at spring tides, so timing for entry and departure will have been critical, especially heading out with a full load of timber on the last half hour before the ebb set in.

Across the Bay

By the 1860s, pockets of the forested slopes along the coastline on the eastern side of Blind Bay from Marahau to Totaranui were being milled by small operators, in some cases as a cheap source of boatbuilding timber, and in others as a saleable commodity to supplement their marginal farm-produce income. The breakthrough came when the Central Government acquired the coastal fringe in the 1850s. Some of it was sold to speculative buyers, like the 800 acres bought by Dr Ralph Richardson[178] who later became an MP, and some was bought or leased by people intending to occupy it, at least for a time. Several of these settlers were boat and shipbuilders, although others had broader ideas of how to make use of the resources.

From a sailor's perspective, this western side of Blind Bay offers more predictable weather conditions than the waters nearer Cook Strait. During strong westerly conditions across the rest of the South Island, the Arthur Ranges and local topography provide a lee with generally light winds close to this coastline. In settled summer conditions, the afternoon seabreeze is as predictable as a clock. Local settlers would plan their days around the tides (which have a range of up to 16 feet) and the barometer. Of the many reefs and rocks which sprinkle randomly along this stretch of coast, local knowledge soon ensured that these were seldom a danger. Nevertheless, drownings were not uncommon, especially as a result of dinghies being used in heavy conditions. Even short passages on

---

178 Richardson bought much of the coast from Torrent Bay to Awaroa including Tonga Island.

this coast experienced challenging weather on occasions. The ketch *Venture* once arrived in Awaroa from Motueka with twelve sheep which had drowned during the 18 mile passage.[179]

Marahau: the Sandy Bay boatbuilders

Within striking distance of Riwaka, Marahau was seriously constrained by the half-mile drying beach that extends beyond the Otuwhero inlet. It seems an unlikely location for boatbuilding but with good timber behind it, there was nothing to stop a beach-built shoal-draft vessel being manhauled towards the low-tide mark to be floated off on the tide during settled conditions. Tom Drummond had a stand of bush and a sawmill at Sandy Bay. He was a friend of Jack Ricketts who had learned boatbuilding further north at Awaroa (under the guidance of his father Ambrose). Jack had already built the straight-stemmed *Dauntless* in Riwaka in 1874, so it was not too far for him to make the move to Marahau, using Drummond's timber when he built the 49ft 21-ton ketch *Transit* there in 1885 (reportedly naming her for an eclipse of the sun on the day of her launching). He next built the smaller 10-ton *Anatuero* there between 1887–89 for

Jack Ricketts built the 49ft ketch **Transit** *on the beach at Marahau, out of timber from the Drummonds bush mill. That she was still at sea sixty years later is testament to her construction and durability.*
Courtesy Lynette Wilson

---

179 Dawber & Wilson, *Awaroa Legacy* p 191

Flowerday's attractive 52ft ketch **Wanderer** *was built on the beach at Torrent Bay and wrecked on a Timaru beach in 1873. She was an impressive example of the workmanship of settlers using timber harvested from the bush, remote from any recognised boatbuilding yard.*
Hocken Collections Box-071-002, Uare Taoka o Hākena, University of Otago (photographer unknown)

John Woolf, another friend of the Ricketts family, and Jack's son Russell was born there while the work was going on. The connection between these three families was strong, and John Woolf took over the sawmill when Tom Drummond died.

My own family connections with Marahau were through the hop-picking which developed in the Marahau hinterland as it was stripped of trees, doubtless using poles and posts harvested from the bush to hold up the vines. My father's family and many others of that early 20th century generation were hop-pickers, we Westrupps probably sailing across to Granny's family farm[180] at Sandy Bay in whichever vessel my grandfather Sam had at the time. That was our waterfront, still with strong overtones of the 19th century, and I have childhood memories of being carried across the mudflat on my father's back during one hop-picking season, and of much family camaraderie.

The Torrent Bay lease

Sailing north from Marahau, we pass through the relatively sheltered waters of Astrolabe Roadstead, partly protected by Adele Island and Fisherman's Island. However the short stretch of coast which follows is referred to by locals in small craft as 'the mad mile', flanked by the semi submerged Hapuka Reef, and stirred up by wind against current before rounding the treacherous reef off Pitt Head. The reward for this potentially wet ride is Torrent Bay. This now-popular location, with its relatively safe anchorage, golden sands and tidal inlet, was first leased by Francis William Flowerday who immigrated in 1855 as a baker and, being the son

---

180 The Woolf family hop farm connection was through my grandmother, Catherine Maria, who was John Woolf's daughter.

of a master mariner, was well educated for the times. He first settled and worked in Motueka where in 1860 he married locally born 17-year-old Ann Stanton when he had reached the respectable age of 29. By 1867 Flowerday was described as a mariner and was in a boatbuilding partnership with G T Blackmore. He leased 86 acres at Torrent Bay in 1870[181], thus becoming the first recorded settler in that bay, presumably utilising the timber there for the boatbuilding partners to build a pair of substantial but short-lived hookers. *Wanderer* was a 31 ton, 52ft schooner owned by Flowerday, which entered the coastal trade in 1871 to meet her end two years later with three other vessels driven ashore at Timaru during a north east gale with heavy seas. His second hooker, *Kestrel* was also a substantial sized ketch at 45ft and 20-ton. She was launched at Torrent Bay in 1872, with the intention of trading as far south as Lyttelton, but within a year she was wrecked at Port Underwood and her subsequent salvage must have been a considerable strain on Flowerday's finances, and when Blackmore withdrew due to illness in 1874 the lease was relinquished.

Andrew Devanny took over the lease briefly and then Flowerday resumed occupation until he moved to Frenchman's Bay in 1880. Burnard and Corless also leased land in Torrent Bay and Jack Ricketts lived there while he built *Comet* on the south shore of the lagoon in 1883. She was a handsome 49ft ketch with a yard aloft for running under squaresail, and became a well-known sight around Blind Bay for the next four decades (and then another two as an auxilliary cutter), attesting to the durability of her Torrent Bay timbers.

That was the end of permanent settlement until 1894 when the Tregidgas took up the lease and settled there. Richard Tregidga was a Cornishman who settled there with his wife Mary, daughter Emily and sons Billy and Sonny. They ran a small boat (possibly named *Petrel*) which Billy and Sonny would take to Nelson with a couple of cords of firewood to trade for supplies. The sailors of the time spoke fondly of Tregidga hospitality, and of being made welcome at their homestead, fed and helped with provisions if the stresses of weather or improvidence held them up. The Tregidgas became shipowners, taking over the cutter *Maid of Italy* which Billy commanded, while Sonny skippered the cutter *Turanga*. Later they owned the scows *Vindex* and *Pearl Kasper* and Sonny owned *Matakana* from 1903 to 1911.

Richard Tregidga and his family left Torrent Bay after six years and the lease was taken up by Henry Rainier who had a holiday home there. It was a precursor to a host of baches and it was not until 1907 that the bay had permanent residents again. Thomas Nalder, a son of early Motupipi settlers Charles and Mary Nalder, leased 640 acres and lived in the Rainier house with his wife Mary, their children, and his nephew Jimmy McCormack. The Nalders farmed the land and felled timber for posts and firewood. Their house continued as a feature of the 'anchorage' right through the 20th century.

---

181 Emily Host, p 125

Frenchman's Bay

Barely a mile north of Torrent Bay, tucked around past North Head and a scattering of reefs including Totara Rocks and Result Rock, is a short valley with an inlet that largely dries at low water. At its seaward end lies a beautiful beach especially eye-catching for its clear water. It is uncertain whether the name is derived from Dumont d'Urville's expedition or from some un-recorded French sailor. John Westrupp leased 50 acres there in mid-1870 when he was 48 years old.[182] He owned a house in Nelson, but as a seaman he spent much of his time aboard various boats including his own in Blind Bay. Four years earlier he had discovered a good oyster bed at Astrolabe Roadstead between Marahau and Torrent Bay, and because of the time he spent along this coastline he had probably noticed there was good boatbuilding timber handily growing within Frenchman's Bay. A century later after sailing south from Napier, we anchored our ketch *Matuku II* inside the 'L' shaped entrance on the rising tide and rowed to the beach where boats had been once built. It was idyllic, but not such a pleasant place to be in a fresh sea breeze.

*The 49ft ketch **Felicity** was built on the beach inside the entrance to Frenchman's Bay inlet in 1885 using timber hewn from the surrounding bush.*
Painting by Linda Cross, courtesy Rob Williams

The first little ship to be built in Frenchman's Bay was the 17-ton, 40ft fore-and-aft schooner *May*, built not by John but by his son-in law Bill Glover who had grown up near the Westrupps' house in Haven Road and married John's daughter Sarah in 1873. Bill obtained his Master Home Trade certificate the following year, and doubtless was thrilled to have the newly leased Frenchman Bay inlet and timber at his disposal to set himself up with a hooker of his own.

---

182 Emily Host, ch15. (The facts are recorded by Host but some details are inaccurate.)

Felicity is another excellent example of a large well-constructed beach-built hooker, seen here at Blackball and being careened off the Haven Rd seawall, where her shoal draft design demonstrates an ability to load at low tide. She later had a centreboard fitted under the ownership of Captain George Williams.

Left: Courtesy Rob Williams
Right:: S.H. Rawson photograph, Hocken Collections P2000-021/1-0277, Uare Taoka o Hākena, University of Otago

Records are incomplete, and it is not known whether other Westrupp hookers of that decade such as John's *Jubilee* or the 10-ton ketch *Standard*[183] were also built in Frenchman's Bay. The Westrupp lease was relinquished some time after 1876 and taken up later by Flowerday who moved the short distance north from Torrent Bay. The boatbuilding tradition continued there during the following decade. *Felicity*, a 49ft 27-ton ketch, was built there in 1885 by her owner H M (Gus) Burnard. It has been said that *Asa* was built there too, but conflicting accounts make that doubtful. Such are the confusions that lurk in the absence of definitive records.

Bark Bay

For the next mile north of Frenchman's, the prudent mariner needs a sharp lookout for the rocks and foul ground off Sandfly Bay. Bark Bay has an offshore

---

183 *Standard* was recorded entering Constant Bay in 1876 with Captain Westrupp (probably one of John's sons) as master.

reef as well as a scattering of rocks off South head. Once in the bay though, there is the reward of two sandy beaches and an extensive lagoon complete with a waterfall at its head. Bark Bay's leasehold land waited until the 1870s for permanent residents, although Timothy Huffam reported fishermen living in the rocks near the entrance and it had been used as a collection point for 'Birch' bark (hence its name). Sailors would want to stand in carefully because of the reefs, and because Bark Bay is open to weather from the east and is also tidal.

Timothy Huffam and his sons Blake, Fred, Richard and Gerard took up the 125 acre lease in 1870, soon after they arrived in New Zealand, and they stayed there for about fifteen years. Timothy was a widower already approaching 60 but determined to succeed in a pioneering lifestyle, and on arrival his sons ranged in age from 13 to 21 years. They settled enthusiastically into their new life, pit-sawing timber from local mamaku tree-ferns for their house, shooting pigeons, hunting pigs and herding goats for milk, cheese and meat. Lamp oil was obtained by boiling sharks' livers, crushing home-grown maize gave them their coffee and once they had their first boat they caught fish for themselves and for the Motueka market. They took their smoke-cured catch to Motueka or sent it if a hooker was about. Their preferred fish was barracouta, which were large and plentiful, but they caught all the common species including snapper. Extra income came from the firewood and Kanuka hop poles they cut from the surrounding bush, as well as fruit and other produce from their prolific garden and variety of fruit trees.

The Huffams had formerly lived in Cowes, Isle of Wight and the two older boys had been trained in small-craft boatbuilding by an uncle. They began to build small boats at Bark Bay, mainly dinghies for coasters and for Nelson folk as a source of ready cash. They soon built *Modest Boy*, an eight-ton half-decked cutter, and sailed her to Motueka, Riwaka and even Nelson with small cargoes.

The Huffams built their house, outbuildings and boats from timber harvested from the bush at Bark Bay and Awaroa.
Photo courtesy Newton Nalder collection

They also used *Modest Boy* to visit Awaroa and the other bays for boatbuilding timber, notably Rimu, which they rafted home. Bark Bay had another steady resource that had been garnered well before the Huffams' time, the 'birch bark' which had first been harvested there in the 1840s as a tanning agent for the Brook Street weaver Thomas Blick when he turned to leathermaking, naming the bay appropriately.

In spite of the isolation of these bays, the local settler families up and down led active social lives, travelling by walking tracks as well as by boats, and often rowed what now seem prodigious distances. A romance developed between Fred Huffam and the wealthy Mary Anne Gibbs of Totaranui and they later married in Motueka.

They were able to purchase the land freehold in 1890, but Bark Bay could not provide an ongoing life for the four young Huffam men so their father, now in his seventies, reluctantly agreed to move to Nelson where he died in 1893. In the early 1880s the boys undertook boatbuilding and carpentering in Nelson, and one of their projects was the Anglican Port Mission Hall which still stands after extensive renovation (and which I was required to attend as a child). Eventually Fred and Gerard moved to Motueka, selling the land in 1904, and their eldest brother married Jane Jacobsen from another seafaring family in Nelson. Huffam Stream and Huffam Rock (off Fisherman Island) are their main legacy of this era, as nothing now remains of their house except the flat granite slab they used as a table, and the ring-barked skeletons of the many introduced pines that they planted amongst the native trees.

Awaroa

It is a further five miles northwards past Tonga Island to the much larger tidal inlet of Awaroa, which has a rich history of settler occupation. The earliest recorded tree-feller was Ambrose Ricketts who had first ventured there in 1855 to seek out the best trees – probably Rimu – and gather them at Pound Gully before floating them out to a waiting hooker at high tide. Ambrose was one of a small group of settlers with interests in timber milling and boatbuilding, who settled on land within the inlet. The Ricketts family bought a substantial block, reputed to be 1,000 acres, there in 1861[184], probably prompted by the difficulty or cost of getting the right timber at Nelson. The first Awaroa baby, Charles Ricketts, was born at Awaroa on 30 May 1862, about the time that Fred Hadfield and William Lightband[185] leased another 2,000 acres (in partnership with a certain Mr Jackson) The Hadfield family bought another 1,000 acres there in 1863 and settled there that year[186].

---

184 Emily Host, in *The Enchanted Coast*, p102, says that Ambrose Ricketts bought one of the 80-acre blocks offered in 1855, but the Ricketts family papers show title, dated 18 April 1865, to 200 acres bordering the Great River and purchased for £95.
185 George William Lightband had a tannery in Brightwater and was likely to have been interested in the Birch bark obtainable from this leasehold.
186 Dawber and Wilson, *Awaroa Legacy* p35

Ambrose Ricketts' 13-year-old son Thomas died at Awaroa in February 1865 after a shooting accident and the family moved away soon afterwards. The records show the 10-ton cutter *Roving Bride*, with Ambrose Ricketts as owner and master, at Nelson from 1866[187]. She was reportedly built by Ambrose, either at Awaroa or Nelson, and there seems no record of her origins although she has been confused with both *Rover's Pride* and *Moonraker*. Ambrose regularly loaded cargoes of limestone from Tata Islands, and sometimes took *Roving Bride* to Awaroa.

Ambrose's son Jack Ricketts subsequently served a boatbuilding apprenticeship with a Mr Brown on the site of Lukins' lime kiln at Green Point in Nelson, and went on to become a recognised boatbuilder in a variety of locations around Blind Bay. He returned to Awaroa in 1875 to help Dan Gilbertson build the huge 71ft 60-ton schooner *Awaroa* there in 1875.

The Hadfield family continued to live in the inlet, building houses on both sides of the river as the extended family expanded. William, who was Fred Hadfield's son, built a number of small boats (including the 18ft workboat known affectionately as *The Old Tub*) which were necessary for the water-dependent lifestyle. William Hadfield has even been credited with building Nelson's first motorboat for the partners Moore and Healy, a 17ft launch powered by a single cylinder motorbike engine. By the turn of the century there was a substantial sawmill with a sizeable population and even a school. Fred Hadfield recorded the sale of 3,634 feet of 'white pine' (kahikatea) at 6 shillings and sixpence per hundred feet as well as 1,339 feet of Rimu.[188] *Transit*, *Oban* and even the steamer

Photographed from astern at Lukin's wharf, **Venture** *(grounded at left) shows her scow-like appearance. Other vessels in this busy scene are* **Matakana** *(inside)* **Pet**, **Transit** *and* **Gannet** *(outside) with* **Maid of Italy** *and* **Lily** *astern. The tall white chimney on the hillside was the Lukins' lime kiln. Limestone was laboriously winched up to this via a cableway after being unloaded at the wharf.*
Copy collection C596, Nelson Provincial Museum

---

187 Allan, *Port Nelson*, p120
188 Dawber and Wilson, p144

Wairoa were involved in transporting timber out of the inlet, and a wharf was built near the head. Some of the timber was taken further afield to Australia and Lyttelton by *Morning Light*, a schooner belonging to Kirk & Co. of Takaka.

The hooker which is even more closely associated with Awaroa than the larger Ricketts-built vessels was the *Venture*, built as a family project under William's direction, at the turn of the century. She was usually referred to as a scow, probably because of her scow stern and centreboard, however her

The design and construction of the 46ft centreboard ketch **Venture** *is evident from this photograph of her lying serenely inside Awaroa Inlet. Her curved sheerline and full bow (emphasised by the stealer planks shown tapering in her forward planking are more shapely than the hard lines of the Auckland-built scows, however she shows a distinct scow influence in her straight run of topsides and right-angled hard chine aft.*
Courtesy Lynette Williams

construction was somewhat different from the Auckland-built scows, with a curved bow planked in the style of the hookers.

Roy Hadfield was twelve years old when *Venture* was being built, and his later account[189] of the experience is one of the best available of the efforts required to scavenge materials for these beach-built hookers:

"I had many jaunts into the bush with Dad and brothers Fred and Darcy, hunting for crooks for frames and decking etc. There was timber from many of the bushes around Awaroa and Totaranui. The majority of the bends and knees came from rata roots from Totaranui, but there were deck beams 6"x6" squared from birch logs 14 feet long. All the masts and spars were obtained from the white pine bush in the swamp at Little River, all manpowered out of the bush and floated down the harbour at high tide."

At this point they ran out of money, so they scraped together five pounds to buy the derelict scow *Orakei* that was lying at Puponga in Golden Bay and jury-sail her back to Awaroa to resurrect. *"There was a lot of work to do before she was fit to trade again. Some of the sails were usable, all the rigging had to be relagged, but the worst trouble was that the keel was just about eaten out by worm. What a job to renew that. However we were very lucky to find a big rimu, which had fallen some years before. The sap wood had rotted off, only the heart left, just what we wanted. I don't remember the size of it, but it was about fifty feet long and 14 x 10 when we squared it up. However we got it fitted and a bit of planking repaired, new sheathing over the bottom and a paint up. We sailed it to Nelson, where it was sold to Jimmie Baird, for 300 pounds I believe."*

These vessels built away from the recognised boat yards are a reminder of the underlying network of friends, relatives and seafaring acquaintances that shaped the history of the hookers. Individual families were large but the number of families was comparatively small along this coast in the early days and often they were connected by marriage. Jack Ricketts' wife Eliza, born in 1866, was a Kidson. The Woolfs had five seafaring sons who all started their careers on Westrupp-run vessels and Sam Westrupp was married to Kate Woolf (my grandmother). It was a fine romance and she reputedly always knew when Sam's ship was in the offing, probably because she had a good eye for weather and passage times. Sonny Tregidga was married to my father's cousin, Ethel McNabb, through yet another connected line. Compete they did, and no doubt they squabbled too, but when push came to shove they would each put a shoulder to the wheel or a hand to the halliard. The coastal community had been this way ever since the 1840s, and the family names still endure.

Totaranui

For sailors and hooker captains, the northern end of the long sweeping bay at Totaranui provides the first good shelter from a northerly blow in Blind Bay after rounding Separation Point or even Farewell Spit, despite the inevitable groundswell discomfort. For this reason it features in various tales of the repair

---

189 *The Venture*, Journal of the Nelson and Marlborough Historical Societies, Volume 2, Issue 3, 1989

and recovery of small ships arriving to lick their wounds after aborted West Coast passages. It does not feature as a timber-producing or even boatbuilding location, but became a significant establishment on the coastline and stood in stark contrast to the cruder establishments of the pioneering families further south. William Gibbs' magnificent estate exuded wealth and graciousness. The 1865 Admiralty chart even noted "Gibbs' Station" as a landmark feature, with its avenue-style driveway leading from the landing stage to the two-storied gabled mansion surrounded by smooth lawns and flower beds, topped off by a fountain and goldfish pond. Gibbs was not from landed gentry, and was simply listed as a 'paper stainer'[190] when he brought his wife Betsey and seven children from England in steerage class via Lyttelton, but made his fortune after arrival from a small outlay when he purchased 50 acres from Aorere Maori in 1855 and profited hugely when it became the site of Collingwood during the goldrush nearby. This money was used to initially buy 272 acres of beach-fronted land at Totaranui in the following year for £122, followed by another 1,000 acres northwards including Separation Point and eastern Golden Bay, and a depasturage licence to graze an additional 6000 acres inland. The farm was well run by a number of staff, as well as his household. However the Gibbs family were not considered snobs, and their hospitality was legendary even among passing hooker crews.

The sheer volume of trade in and out of Golden Bay in the 1890s is apparent from this photograph of at least six large sailing vessels lying alongside Waitapu wharf near Takaka. As a port, Waitapu could only be entered at the top of tide via a shifting channel. The scow **Cambria** can be seen loading inside the black vessel at the left. Also recognisable are **Maid of Italy**, **Croydon Lass** and **Clio**. The wharf was located at the end of a lengthy reclaimed causeway, and serviced by a tramway.

Tyree Collection G-472-10x8 Alexander Turnbull Library

---

190 Wallpaper printing was in decline in by the mid 19th century, so he may have fallen on hard times.

The fact that his daughter Mary Ann Gibbs fell in love with and married the young pioneer Fred Huffam shows that social class was clearly not a barrier. William became a parliamentarian and later a magistrate until he retired and sold the farm to William Henry Pratt[191] in 1892. The Pratt family established a school and post office on the property and rented out holiday accommodation to supplement their farm income for thirty years. The substantial farmhouse that they built still stands.

The Golden Bay timber trade

Times had changed when the second wave of shipbuilding happened at Motupipi. Captain Henry Young's *Camellia*, built there by Norwegian Alf Wahlstrom in 1879, was the first of the new generation of hookers and she worked in Blind Bay until she was laid up and her registry closed in December 1909. *Camellia* was a 48ft 20-ton ketch, one of the larger ones built at Motupipi. She was a handsome vessel and Captain Young's sadness at the end of her days at sea and his own is easily understandable. It would be nice to trace an evolution of styles from the hookers of the 1840s to the ones built towards the end of the century. Some styles were very similar but both clipper ships and the Tasmanian barges probably influenced the design now seen in the *Camellia*, as did changes in measurement formulas.

In 1887 Wahlstrom launched from Motupipi the 64-ton, 75ft screw steamer *SS Waitapu*, built for J S Cross Junior. In the early 1890s Captain John Edward (Jack) Westrupp was her owner and master. *Waitapu* was lost in a fire on the Wellington Patent Slip in 1896 and Jack Westrupp then acquired the *SS Wairoa* which later passed into the hands of the Ricketts family. The old adage "If you can't beat 'em, join 'em" was applied by various hooker skippers and crews as sail gave way to steam. Captain Whitwell joined what became the Anchor Company, and Captain Walker of *Supply* and other sailing vessels became well known as master of the paddle steamer[192] *PS Lady Barkly*. After his time on the small ships (he owned *Three Brothers* by 1872) Jack Westrupp founded The Wellington and Havelock Steam Shipping Company with *SS Wairoa*, running about two trips per week to Wellington, Havelock, Motueka and Patea. (He was also a founder of The Patea Shipping Company with *SS Waitapu* and *SS Mana*.)

Golden Bay had not been standing still over these post gold boom years. Waitapu got a new wharf in 1875 and it was often crowded with vessels loading timber and farm produce. By then there were 200 families and four steam-powered sawmills in the district. Both Collingwood and Takaka were connected to Nelson by telegraph in 1881, although people had to visit the telegraph office to take advantage of the service. It all helped to integrate the districts as well as to serve commercial needs. Road communication slowly upgraded between 1885

---

191 Son of the adventurous early Nelson settler William Pratt whose adventures aboard *Catherine Ann* were related in chapter 11.
192 *Lady Barkly* was subsequently converted to a screw steamer.

and 1888, when the bridle track over the Takaka Hill was usable by horse and trap. But ships, and in many cases the hookers, were the only means of shifting bulk material and sea transport dominated well into the 20th century.

For the rapidly expanding timber trade in both Takaka and Collingwood it was the big schooners and ketches that were the main carriers. Names like *Owake Belle* (built at the Catlins River and registered in Dunedin in 1871), and *Huon Belle* (from Tasmania), *John Bell* (built in Sydney in 1885 and owned by Captain Kirk of Takaka), *Rock Lily, Clio, Clyde, Amelia Simms, Emma Simms, Joseph Simms* (these Simms vessels built in Sydney's northern waters) and *Morning Light* became familiar in both ports. They had their strandings and at times when entering or leaving Waitapu and Collingwood they were grateful for the assistance of steamers as tugs.

Collingwood had at various times a wharf outside and more than one wharf inside the estuary. There was one just around Wapping Point, a couple further up the true right bank of the Aorere River where the road enters Collingwood, and then several clustering around Ferntown on the other side of the river, one on the bank above the Ferntown Bridge and at least one on the Ferntown mudflat. These Ferntown wharfs also served the coalmine on that side of the unbridged Aorere River. The smaller ships could work Ferntown on the neap tides, grounding out between tides, and the *SS Lyttelton* advertised a service "every spring tides". The Aorere River entrance was also tidal.

Later a wharf was built at Onekaka to service the iron works and another was planned for Tukurua. As well as timber, flax and farm produce, cargoes included minerals like coal and iron ore. By 1875 the ketch *Emily* was taking out cargoes of hematite for paint manufacturers in Nelson and much later dolomite was shipped out from the wharf in Parapara Inlet. Further west the coalminers used a series of loading points ranging from a box on the mudflat in early days, filled from a dray between the tides, to the elevated loading system developed later at Puponga.

Cocky Burford's collier ketches *Argus* and *Elizabeth* served Ferntown from the 1880s and one sidelight into the economics of transport was that local coal cost more in Collingwood than in Nelson. In 1886 domestic coal was sent back to Collingwood on the *Lady Barkly* and at that point *Elizabeth* unloaded a cargo of Ferntown coal onto the Collingwood wharf at considerably less than the prevailing local price. A similar position arose in the 1900s when coal from the two local mines was all sent to Nelson. Land transport could not be developed until roads were formed and the many creeks and rivers were bridged.

Calyx was working Collingwood and the bays regularly in 1895, and two years later Frank Ricketts, late of *Transit*, bought the steamer *SS Wairoa* and competed with the several other vessels on the run, particularly *Lady Barkly*.

16

Shoal Draft Heavyweights

THERE IS A SOMEWHAT BLURRED DISTINCTION between the basic modest sized hookers of the early decades and the shapely more substantial small ships beyond the third decade of settlement. In many cases the older hooker owners had simply traded up, and were continuing to hook their larger cargoes in a similar fashion, but also there were wealthier owners in the game.

Many factors were coming into play – the deterioration of the original fleet through decay and hard use, the increasing quantities of potential cargoes, the development of more appropriate hull forms and the intrusion of maritime red tape into the fray. Fred Hadfield quickly ran foul of the authorities on his third trip into Nelson on his Awaroa-built ketch *Venture*, being slapped with a memorandum from Collector HM Customs: "*I hereby give you notice that your general transire[193] is revoked as from today, and also that the schooner 'Venture' is under detention at the Port of Nelson and must remain in port until a master has been appointed and until registration of the vessel has been completed. W.B. Montgomery, Acting Collector.*"[194] The gloss of being a new ship owner, after the hard work scavenging materials for her build, was now being quickly rubbed off by the additional expenses of paying registration fees, harbour dues and wages for a qualified captain.

The hookers were both helped and hindered by the increasing regulation of their industry. Concern for safety was a long time coming into marine law and it was not until 1876 that a load line had to be painted on British ships. Before then, overloading often cost the lives of ships and crew and the 'Plimsoll line' was named after the member of parliament who fought for it. In New Zealand the first Shipping and Seamen Act was passed in 1877. It provided for the establishment of the Marine Department and set up a system of certificates of competency for masters, mates and engineers who passed the requisite examinations and certificates of service to recognise those who had practical experience before 1871.

The size of ship on which each seaman had served his time and the nature of its trade was recorded on the certificate of service to qualify its scope. There was a load line requirement in the New Zealand act too, but vessels under 40 tons were exempted. A 'river limits' demarcation was introduced for some steamships, governing the ranging of the vessels and their skippers according to the certificate or ticket that was held. Steam ships were subject to survey or inspection, but

---

193 A customs document listing a vessel's cargo, to prove that it has come from a home port.
194 Dawber and Wilson, *Awaroa Legacy,* p156 (Note also that this ketch has been misrepresented as a schooner – a common error in many documents.)

sailing vessels were not, so some hookers continued going to sea ill-prepared. Nevertheless, first steps had been taken and not before time.

The next Shipping and Seamen Act, in 1903, tightened up certificate criteria and restricted limits and manning levels. Small ships were required to carry a certificated master and at least one able-bodied seaman or AB, a rating usually earned after three years of service as an ordinary seaman although there was variation between sail and steam experience. The limited certificates of service for masters became more restrictive compared with the experience and examination-based certificates of competency, so ships sometimes 'borrowed' a seaman with the appropriate qualification for particular voyages beyond their own tickets. Some regulations appeared a bit absurd, as regulations often do. For instance, Separation Point was a furthermost limit for some small ships out of Nelson, a restriction which contributed further to their declining role and denied Golden Bay part of the service it had enjoyed for a long time. Such regulation would have dramatically changed the fortunes of Constant Bay if it had been instated a few years earlier.

Ever since the 1840s, New Zealand ships had been obliged to be registered if they were over ten tons, while vessels under ten tons were licensed by the customs department to carry goods and passengers within a general locality. There were smaller and larger vessels which seem to have escaped both forms of registration. Length was not necessarily an indicator of a vessel's tonnage, because hookers with deeper holds would contain a greater volume, and therefore rate a greater tonnage, despite looking similar above the water line. The newer vessels entering the coastal trade tended to be larger.

At a later time, the Marine Department instituted a system of annual surveys, carried out by men with engineering training but often unaccustomed to wooden ships. Wooden ships were flexible; they 'worked', and surveyors often wanted them stiffened at great expense. New standards of crew accommodation were also imposed, and as a result of the cost implications, some hookers were laid up when another few years of service could have been squeezed out of them. There were also problems for skippers whose old 'certificates of servitude' qualified their areas of operation and tonnages; the particular anomaly was that a *deck* scow was measured at a much lower tonnage than the same sized *hold* scow, so a skipper could be certified competent for one but not the other.

Timber was hand-loaded and stowed a piece at a time until it was almost a solid block below, except for a bit of broken stowage in the bows. When this was completed, heavy wedges were driven under the four corners of the hatch covers to carry the weight of the deck cargo. About this time, customs used to issue a permit for each deck cargo load to keep it within bounds, but I remember my father calling us from our beds early one morning in the 1930s to see *Pearl Kasper* coming into the harbour. Her deck load was so high there was no hope of conning her from the ordinary wheel position except by relaying word to the helmsman and I was told this particular arrival was made at that early hour to avoid unwanted scrutiny by officialdom! The days of turning a blind eye were

Despite the loading regulations, some hooker captains pushed the limits, as seen here with Sonny Tregidga's deck load of hops aboard **Matakana**.
Courtesy Lynette Wilson

past, so her captain, Sonny Tregidga, regularly resorted to a little guile. When he was running *Matakana* years earlier, he had carried a cargo of baled hops from Riwaka by stacking them three high over the deck and cabin, and the mainsail had to be double-reefed to clear them.

One of the key factors influencing change among the Nelson hookers was the need to adapt away from the English and Galway style of hull design, with their slack bilges and long deep-forefooted keels, to designs which would cope better with tidal harbours and beach loading. They didn't have far to look, because just across the Tasman Sea on the same line of latitude, Tasmanian boatbuilders had a four-decade head-start on hull design for similar conditions.

The Tasmanian Ketches

Tasmania was endowed with excellent boatbuilding timbers; the super-durable Huon pine, the plentiful celery-top pine and the strong light King Billy pine were all ideal for planking, decking and superstructures. Their 'Tas Oak' Eucalypts (Blue gum, Stringybark and Swamp gum) were dense knot-free timbers widely used for keels, stems and deadwood timbers, and even for hull planking, (particularly below the waterline where they were less inclined to warp). Frames and knees were fashioned from selected grown crooks. 'Birdcaging' was commonly used during construction, leaving every second plank missing until any shrinkage had stopped, and treenail fastenings were common.

The key factor influencing the design evolution of the 'Tassie ketch' was the demand for coastal timber transportation. The early boatbuilders were looking for load-carrying barge forms capable of beaching, and for inspiration they turned to the Thames barges with their flat garboard sections and tight turn of the bilge. The early ones carried leeboards like the canal barges and Dutch botters, but before long they turned to centreboards which were easier for short-crewed handling despite the greater complexity of watertight construction.

As a result they were commonly referred to as 'barges', but I hesitate to refer to them with this inelegant term, as they were among the loveliest styles to be developed in the British Empire. Not only did they present a wonderful sweep of sheerline, but also they were noted for their large spread of sail; they commonly carried two headsails and, surmounting their gaff main and mizzen sails, a pair of huge jackyard topsails.

The 'barge' sectioned hull form had the advantage of being able to sail unballasted with their wide beam and nearly flat floors (they did have a rise of a few degrees in the middle sections) but despite their powerful 'initial stability' they were vulnerable when heeled beyond their 'angle of vanishing stability', and a sudden squall could upset them, loaded or unloaded, just as a number of New Zealand scows were lost. They suited New Zealand waters although unlike areas like the Hauraki Gulf which had protected waters, the Blind Bay hookers and others about the coasts could sail out and face extreme conditions.

The first to come to Blind Bay was *Huon Pine*, a 58ft 22-ton leeboard ketch built at Port Davy on Tasmania's Southwest coast in 1839, possibly with convict

The Tasmanian ketch **May Queen**, built in 1867 and viewed here 140 years later on a Hobart slipway, shows off her flattened underwater sections and rounded bilges. Her squared counter stern is typical of Tasmanian ketches built in an era before they evolved into the more elliptical style.
Barbara Tucker photo

*The Tasmanian ketch, **Good Intent** is shown here carrying aloft the distinctive jackyard tops'ls which were typical of these vessels. Her elegance flies in the face of the term 'timber barge' which was commonly used for these shoal-draft centreboarders. She was built by the Wilsons of Cygnet in 1877, a decade after they built **Huon Belle**, which was regularly seen loading timber in Golden Bay.*
Mercury Historical Collection, Tasmanian Archives: NS4023/1/148

labour. Her beam was only 14 feet, under a quarter of her length (later they were built beamier), and she had less than four foot of hold depth. *Huon Pine* was a fore-runner of these ketches. They had raked sterns, square across and changing to a concave curve tucking under to the keel, with the rudder hung on the deadwood and its stock coming up through the deck, but there was some diversity in appearance.

The raked stem of the Tasmanian barges terminated under the bowsprit in a beak, also called a billet or cutwater which gave the profile of a clipper bow. Some of the later vessels were built with a slight hollow or flair and a true clipper bow. The sterns evolved too, changing first to a counter stern but still 'square' across at deck level and then finally to round, semi-elliptical, elegant counter sterns like that of *Lizzie Taylor*.

A really handsome line of vessels had emerged, and many that were built to work the Australian coasts found their way to New Zealand, while deeper draught vessels continued to be built for the rougher waters of Bass Strait and further afield.

The 56-ton *Zephyr* was built in Hobart in 1851 and was about Nelson between 1859 and 1864, when she was wrecked at New Plymouth. *Huon Belle* was a 42-ton ketch built in Tasmania in 1864. She worked in the timber trade out of Collingwood and Waitapu from the 1880s, until about 1937 by which time she was a hulk and the register was closed.

The 33-ton, 49ft barge *Pearl* was also built in 1864 at Port Cygnet, Tasmania and came to Nelson for the Sounds and Bays trade in 1866. She was recorded as wrecked on Arrow Rock 22 May 1874, but must have survived to be finally wrecked at Long Point, Hawke Bay, 8 June 1879. She probably lent her name to Pearl Creek at the mouth of the Waimea River, from where the last of the Waimea sea exports of produce were loaded. The 58ft *Fawn* was built at North West Bay, wrecked there in 1876. Patea also claimed *Alert*, built at Peppermint Bay in 1856 and lost on 11 September 1875. A couple of larger schooners, the 63ft *Star of the Sea* (built at Port Davey, Tasmania in 1873) and the 68ft 50-ton *Croydon Lass* built on the Torquay River, Tasmania in 1877) were in and out of Blind Bay or Golden Bay until they were lost in 1882 and 1903 respectively. There were many others working in different ports throughout the region, especially in the timber trade, including *Elizabeth*, *Falcon* and *Lizzie Taylor*, mentioned elsewhere.

Australian-built schooners

In mainland Australia the hull designs remained more conventional, with moderate draft fixed keels which were better suited for the Tasman Sea and

Amelia Simms, *seen here at the old Motueka wharf in 1903, was one of the Australian-built inter-colonial topsail schooners which regularly shipped timber from the ports of the Nelson bays.*
Courtesy Lynette Wilson

*The big schooner **Morning Light** must have had a crack crew to be pictured sailing up the channel into Collingwood in 1897 with both square topsails still set. She was a regular visitor to the wharf just around the corner here, and when the town was nearly totally destroyed by fire on November 7th, 1904, her crew helped fight the blaze, and provided shelter aboard for women and children.*
Tyree Studio Collection 180480, Nelson Provincial Museum

exposed coastlines. A number of these big schooners, some with square tops'ls, found their way in and out of the Nelson bays trading scene, many working interprovincially with passengers and substantial cargoes. There are too many to list, but several crop up regularly in the records, some coming under local ownership for a stretch of their working lives.

Shepherdess and *Australian Maid* were among the smaller early Sydney-built schooners to work the local coastline. The three big Simms schooners (*Amelia Simms, Emma Simms* and *Joseph Simms*) were all built by Rock Davis at Blackwall, just north of Sydney, between 1895 and 1905. *John Bell* was another schooner from Sydney, built in Balmain. *Morning Light* was also identified as Australian-built. The Melbourne-built schooner *Argus* was a rather different hull design, built of iron with very full sections suitable as a water-carrier and later converted to a timber-sheathed ketch and adapted by James ('Cocky') Burford as a collier.

Scows from the north

The sailing traders which finally supplanted the smaller hookers were developed in the Hauraki Gulf and were basically huge rectangular punts with masts and crudely pointed bows. During the last decade of the century they were brought to the Nelson bays because of their versatility and greater capacity. They were rigged as either ketch or schooner, and built either as *hold* scows or *deck* scows. Ironically, despite being relatively few in number, their reputation and photographic records have survived in far more detail than most of their plentiful smaller hooker cousins.

In New Zealand's north, particularly the Hauraki Gulf near Auckland, shallow water backed by great stands of kauri trees had spawned this new style of ship to carry logs to the mills. These sailing scows derived from the punts of the Great Lakes and those on San Francisco Bay in North America, with similar construction but with angular bows terminating in a stem, unlike the American shovel bows. The name was originally derived from the dutch 'Schouw' which was a rectangular leeboard sailing vessel.

The first New Zealand-built one, in 1873, was named *Lake Erie*. She was almost rectangular, 60 feet by 17 feet by 3½ feet, and was expected to carry 80 tons. She was internally-braced, square-sectioned and flat-bottomed, with a great protruding barn door of a rudder, and rigged as a schooner. She was specifically a 'deck scow', as her closed-in deck left a void as buoyancy space below and she carried high deck-loads of logs.

Lake Erie had a centreboard, swung at one end and operated by a winding mechanism, but others started their working lives with leeboards similar to those on Thames barges. They were ungainly vessels but their retractable leeboards and rudders allowed them to load and sail in the shallows. They were first known as barges, probably as a transference of the Tasmanian name, and it was some years before the term scow was used. Prodigious amounts of kauri were consumed in their heavy construction, something that would not be possible today.

Their construction was particularly distinctive, with the structural planking of their flat bottoms running athwartships in a crude manner similar to many sharpies. This made the distinctive upwards curve of their wide square counters easy to construct, as can be seen from the remnants of *Kohi*'s aft planking ends in the photograph. These were overlaid with sacrificial fore and aft planking which was able to be replaced at intervals, as visible on the photograph of *Southern Isle*'s capsized belly. The scantlings were massive, with the squared chine timbers reaching 12x12 inches, and considerable internal bracing inside the deck scows. The bows transitioned abruptly from the rectangular topsides into a hard v-shape achieved with a combination of diagonal planks.

During the last two decades of the 20th century they evolved into larger and slightly more handsome ships, some even with a curved sheer line, and they had one, two or even three drop centreboards for keels. They still had their rectangular, square-bilged sections and flat bottoms but many evolved from deck-carrying to hold-carrying vessels.[195] Despite their stiffness under sail, the downside of the scow's keel-less square section was the potential to capsize in heavy weather when over-canvassed. They were as stable upside-down as when upright! This fate tragically befell the Picton-bound 92ft three-masted hold-scow *Southern Isle*

---

195 Clifford Hawkins, *Out of Auckland*, Pelorus Press, 1960, also 'Neath Swaying Spars' by P.A. Eaddy, and *Phantom Fleet* by Ted Ashby.

*Close scrutiny of **Kohi**'s decaying aft timbers reveal the straight athwartships planking which rises to meet the squared transom. The topsides also run straight towards the bow creating a rectangle in plan view, apart from the abrupt transition to a V bow. The boat-builders could use large planking and sheathing timbers without the need to steam bend.*
Barbara Tucker photo

*The capsized hull of the scow **Southern Isle** clearly shows the underwater shape of the box-like scows. The massive barn-door ridder has snapped its bottom pintle, and some of the sacrificial fore-and-aft bottom sheathing-planks are lifting. The shaft-logs are evidence that she was fitted with a pair of auxiliary engines.*
Courtesy Rob Williams

*Three-masted **Southern Isle**'s iconic 'scow bow' is obvious in this photo taken from above John Westrupp's Haven Road home, not long before her tragic capsize. Behind her is a mix of hooker ketches, scows and steamers. Alongside Lukins' wharf are the ketches **Comet** and the (dark hulled) **Result**. The ketch **Jane** and the larger scow **Pearl Kasper** lie on the main wharf with the raked masts of **SS Waimea** and **SS Waverley** (partially obscured) behind.*
Courtesy Rob Williams

in May 1916 when, despite being laden with coal from Puponga, she exceeded her angle of stability inside Farewell Spit in squally weather. A vessel of this size needed five men to work her, and all were missing presumed drowned when her upturned hull was spotted by the spit light-house keeper four days later. The co-owners[196], Captain Gibson and engineer A Foster employed two ABs – C Monteath and John Clifton as well as a cook. Despite the tragedy, the vessel was salvaged and eventually converted to become the grab dredge Te Wakatu.

The scows elbowed their way into Blind Bay at the turn of the century, and

---

196 These two men had wives who were sisters, from the Clunies-Ross family.

their reputations were built during the following decades, surviving well into my lifetime. The cargoes available within the region suited scows admirably. There was granite from the quarries at Adele Island, Torrent Bay and Tonga. Limestone and marble, bound for Wellington, was loaded straight off the beach at Marahau after being brought down from Kairuru[197] and across the Sandy Bay flats by tramway. Other beach-loaded cargoes included timber, produce, livestock, wool and even sand. In later years they transported bulk cargoes of Golden Bay cement and dolomite. Right up into the 1960s they worked throughout the district from Westhaven Inlet and Golden Bay, across Blind Bay to Croisilles or Elmslie Bay via French Pass, further around to the Sounds and Cloudy Bay and right up to Blenheim on the Opawa River.

For a hooker skipper the temptation to trade up, perhaps in a partnership, would have been similar to a small truck owner ditching his four ton Bedford for a Mack Truck. Most of the scows hooked for cargoes in the same manner as the earlier generations of hookers, but their loads were markedly bigger.

The first scow to arrive on the local scene in 1899 was the 17-year old 70ft deck scow *Orakei* which was bought by the Puponga Coal Company to bring timber and construction materials to their mine. She was soon laid up at Puponga, where the Hadfield family picked her up as a derelict for £5 and onsold her in 1910 for £300 after restoration[198]. She carried timber from Croisilles to Nelson for a further decade.

Next, arriving in 1903, were two hold-scows, both built by Darroch at Omaha, north of Auckland, and re-registered in Nelson – the 92ft *Southern Isle* to W O Caldwell, and the older 68ft *Oban* to A McNabb. Both scows had a number of owners, and serious mishaps. *Oban* suffered five strandings, three capsizes and a foundering (with the loss of four lives). It is interesting that the Marine Dept ordered her rig to be reduced three years after her arrival – clearly the high windage aloft was of more a concern in central New Zealand than it had been in the Hauraki Gulf. However her hull was clearly built of stout stuff, as she survived 23 years in Blind Bay waters before being returned to Auckland (renamed *Motiti*) and serving out a further two decades.

The deck scow *Pearl Kasper* arrived from Great Barrier Island with a full load of kauri, some time between 1910 and 1917. She had an engine from the unfortunate *Southern Isle* installed in 1917 by Sonny Tregidga who was her owner and master until April 1942 when his son Albert (Albie) took over. The deck-scow *Vindex* (1919) came next, worked by Bill Tregidga and co-owned by Charles Slade. *Vindex* lasted two decades before becoming a total loss at the mouth of the Hutt River in 1939.

The big 104ft schooner-rigged hold-scow *Echo* arrived on the scene in 1920, fifteen years after she was built in Auckland. She traded mostly on the Cook Strait run to Blenheim for 45 years, although she occasionally appeared in Nelson

---

197 Kairuru was the location of an early Takaka Hill quarry.
198 See chapter 15

*The centre of gravity aboard a loaded deck scow would have been a potential capsize factor, especially under sail, as is apparent from this photograph of **Pearl Kasper** laden with export fruit at Motueka harbour with her scuppers awash.*
Courtesy Rob Williams

during this period. She was one of a few scows in the region to carry a schooner rig (along with *Kohi* and *Talisman*), and lasted another fifty years on the hard as an ornament on the Picton waterfront. The 92ft deck-scow *Kohi*, skippered by Morrie Sawyers and Bob Goldie, worked the Cook Strait run alongside *Echo* until after World War II when she was salvaged, after sinking at Picton, to retire as a floating jetty at Westhaven Inlet.

Both *Pearl Kasper* and *Kohi* were used by the Public Works Department to install gun emplacements in the Marlborough Sounds in 1942, and at the end of that year *Kohi* was taken over by the Americans and made her way into the Pacific, along with *Echo* and a number of other scows and small coastal vessels, to support the troops fighting in the Pacific.

The Karamea Shipping Company owned *Vesper* up to September 1965, when a marine surveyor wanted her through-bolted as she had only been 'spiked' when she was built. She went to a Sounds owner and was used as a barge to bring timber to Havelock until competition and red tape defeated the operation, but she found a new lease of life as a mussel barge and was still working in the 1980s.

Later arrivals were the 95ft, 99 ton *Talisman* and the 72ft, 81 ton *The Portland*. Both were schooner-rigged hold-scows imported from the Hauraki Gulf during the 1930s and trading out of Nelson until the 1960s and 70s. It is interesting to note the large rated capacity of these vessels compared with similar length deck scows, such as the 73ft *Pearl Kasper*, at only 53 tons and the 81ft *Vindex* at only 44 tons.

Oban was skippered by my grandfather Sam Westrupp towards the end of the era of the smaller hookers and the end of his own seafaring days. Unfortunately I have few first-hand family reports of his time aboard *Oban*, but the late Howard Williams, a friend during my childhood, sailed with him as ship's boy and related to me his experiences during the last of the unpowered sailing days.

"The Oban had no engines fitted when I was in her, and three men, Skipper, AB and deck-boy-cook. One hot meal a day and all done on a linseed oil drum standing on deck."

Apparently that five-gallon drum was known as a 'bogie' and needed some water in the bottom to save burning the deck. The earliest hookers simply used a camp oven on its three little legs, with a fire in it and a couple of bars laid across for a frying pan to sit on.

"The drum had holes punched in it to let the air in, and a small wood fire started, then coal and sometimes coke for fuel. There were a couple of rods across near the top, and the cooking pot stood on the cross rods. Most times it was corned beef and veges all done together, never any sweets, and a billy boiled for tea after the meat and veges were done."

Howard also said that "If there was no wind the lifeboat [a pulling boat for two oarsmen, about 14 feet long] was put over the side and the AB and I had to row and tow the scow, whether loaded or light, and we managed most times to hold our own against the tide in the bay. Some of the scows used big sweeps and rowed the scow itself."

By the second half of the 20th century the surviving scows were regular sights entering and leaving Nelson under power with their bowsprits lopped off, perhaps reduced to one mast kept mainly for cargo handling. They had effectively become informal training ships for young men who wanted careers at sea, and many Nelson seafarers shipped aboard one or other of the local scows as boys. Enduring among the last of them was *Te Aroha*[199], whose long-serving master was Ken Wells, and *The Portland*, whose master Bill Ricketts also skippered *Te Aroha*. These were the last two cargo vessels to use the small Milnthorpe Wharf at Parapara, an inlet east of Collingwood which was one of the last of the out-of-the-way ports in the region. Commercial fishing boats also used the wharf to land fish for on-transport by truck. I was manager of Golden Bay Dolomite Ltd at the time and as the Marine Department required a nominated person to take responsibility I claimed, somewhat tongue in cheek, that I was harbourmaster of Milnthorpe.

After Bill Ricketts, *The Portland*'s masters included Bob Walling, Wally Greenem and Dave Potts. *The Portland*'s 'swansong' voyage from her final base in Otago to the sub-antarctic Auckland Islands, apparently taking about four weeks to get there and four days to come home.

Talisman was skippered sometimes by Alf Henry but in later years mainly by

---

199 The 86ft schooner *Te Aroha* was not a true scow, being round bilged rather like a Thames barge, but has often been included as a part of the later trading fleet of scows.

'Tiny' Drummond, and I once had a very short trip on her when Des Collins was standing in as master. She served her final days as a floating wharf at Nelson's inner yacht-basin, and was ultimately replaced by a large steel pontoon bearing her name.

Practical advantages of the scows

For a time the deeper drafted hookers were disadvantaged by conventions of ship measurement which gave an advantage to the deck-scows with their sealed off spaces called ballast tanks. These scows were required to have small crews but could load more cargo while drawing less water. *Oban* (68 feet by 17 feet by 4ft 4ins) is worth brief mention as a 'dog', until she was modified. She originally had a small auxiliary engine for working confined ports and rivers, so the collector of customs insisted she be registered as a steamship and have modifications made to her top hamper. This would have reduced her sail area and so impaired her sailing abilities and when further regulations forced her to carry an engineer, the solution was simple! Out came the engine.

Oban is an interesting case study of the advantages and disadvantages of the scow hull-form in the more challenging local weather conditions than the more benign subtropical waters of their northern origins. During the quarter century that she traded out of Nelson, she suffered a series of serious incidents. She first capsized inside Pelorus Sound in 1901 (when a crewman was drowned), capsized again two miles off Torrent Bay in 1904, and sank by the head when she was being towed by a tug at Wellington Heads in 1905. Three men were drowned in this last accident and the Marine Department stepped in as she was considered unsafe at sea, although safe enough for the extended river limits for which she was built. Her hull was altered, probably with work on the bulwarks as the regulations of the day required three foot bulwarks right around. Her masts were shortened and her rig reduced, allowing her to ply in restricted home waters for a trial period in 1907. She must have proven to be more stable, as two years later she was resurveyed and allowed in extended limits once more.

My grandfather Sam Westrupp skippered *Oban* from 6th January 1917 probably until the end of her time in Nelson in 1924. He had owned various of his own hookers (all of which were lost at the hands of other skippers), but for the greater period of his working life my grandfather ran other people's vessels. His last hooker *Result* was lost in Torrent Bay (15th December 1917) nearly a year after he had taken command of *Oban*, and with the loss of this 60ft ketch he lost an equity that he didn't (and probably couldn't) replace. The hookers were seldom lucrative sources of income.

Scows versus traditional hookers

Oban was a significant competitor when she came to Nelson about the turn of the century. She was larger than the hookers but drew less water, so she could get into the Waitapu and Motupipi river entrances earlier on the tide. Often by the time the tide was sufficiently high for a hooker to berth the cargo was already bespoken for by *Oban* and she would continue to lie alongside until she was filled, sometimes waiting for more timber to come down from the mill. Hookers waiting for cargo at the same wharf would often give up, resort instead to getting a fill of limestone from Tata Island or going home in ballast, although some hookers did have regular arrangements and the scow could not be everywhere.

Russ Ricketts, who crewed on *Transit*, recalled quarrying limestone on an occasion when *Oban* shouldered them out of a timber cargo out of Motupipi.

"[Limestone] was always an alternative cargo for the Blind Bay vessels. Ted Lukins would always take a load, although he was a bit tough to get any money out of. Beside owning the lime kiln, Mr Lukins also owned the wharves opposite and was agent for all the vessels in the Bay with the exception of the Argus, which was owned by Mr Burford who also had a wharf, wood and coal yard alongside Lukins'. However, back to the limestone. We pulled the Transit *on to a small flat beach on the little island of the Tatas and moored her. We broke out the crowbars, hammers and gads to quarry the stone. All vessels carried this gear as part of their equipment. We put aboard all the stone that was handy and small enough to handle.*

"We needed a considerable amount to complete the load. We went up on to the top of the cliff about 70 or 80 feet high and started to quarry some stone out. Hanging on the face was a great slab of rock which I reckon weighed about sixty to seventy tons. Harry Kidson got on top of this slab and was working some small pieces loose when suddenly down went the whole slab. Harry fell between the slab and the cliff face. Both his brother and I were standing well back from the edge, so kept clear, which was fortunate as I do not think any of us would have survived if we had also

This rather grainy photograph of the scow **Oban**, *going through a tack as she sails out the original Haven entrance, is one of the few family records remaining of my grandfather Sam Westrupp's seven years as her captain between 1917 and 1924.*
Westrupp Collection

been standing on the slab. When we saw Harry going down we realised he could be killed; his brother threw a flip backwards and fainted. When we began to realise what had happened there was Harry sitting in a fissure half-way down the cliff at the side of the landslide. These fissures are common in any limestone formation. As he was going down he fell into it where there were several large pieces of stone and the whole slip went past him which fortunately did not break until it crashed onto the beach below."

Tata Islands' limestone had been either a commissioned or a fall-back cargo for vessels without a load from Golden Bay to Nelson from as early as 1842. Limestone was good ballast and was always worth something in Nelson. These islands were a source of limestone for Lukins' kiln in Nelson and the Picton Lime and Cement Company, but removal of limestone from there was stopped under the Public Works Act in about 1908 after there were real concerns the Picton company would finally quarry right away the only safe harbour in Golden Bay.

*The scows often sought a wide variety of cargoes, like this deck-load of sand being hoisted aboard **Kohi** in wheelbarrows at low tide in Torrent Bay.*
Courtesy Lynette Wilson

17

Steamers Near and Far

WHILE THE HOOKERS WERE PLYING local waters, they were often dispersing cargoes which had arrived in Nelson via longer sea routes, both inter-provincial and inter-colonial. By the third decade of settlement, these routes were becoming dominated by steam-driven vessels, despite the ongoing presence of sailing ships.

By the time of the land-wars during the early 1860s, in Taranaki and the Waikato, the early paddle-steamers were asserting their usefulness. During the following two decades, local steamship companies were popping up wherever there was a perceived profit to be made. Three were based at Auckland's western harbour port of Onehunga: the *Waiuku Steam and Navigation Company*, the *Manukau Steam Ship Company* and the *Northern Steam Ship Company*[200] which traded south to New Plymouth. A little further south was the *Waikato Steam Navigation and Coal Company Ltd* which operated on the river. If we ignore the steam-ship operators of the Hauraki Gulf and north, there were other significant players further south too, such as Taranaki's *Patea Steam Navigation Company*, Wellington's *New Zealand Steam Navigation Company*, Dunedin's *Harbour Steam Company*, Christchurch's *Canterbury Steam*, and Napier's *Richardson and Co*. Each was able to survive competition by limiting their routes and cargoes within specific parameters.

Whilst most of the significant steamers were built of iron – a material far better suited to the heat generated by external combustion engines, some were composite, like Auckland's *SS Tam O'Shanter* planked in kauri in 1874 over iron frames fabricated at McIntyre's Clyde ironworks in Onehunga, and powered by a high pressure engine built by Auckland's Fraser and Tinne foundry. By the 1860s foundries were being set up around the country, such as Nelson's Anchor Foundry which was established as an adjunct to the fledgeling steam-ship operations based there. Some of the early iron paddlesteamers were imported in pieces and assembled in New Zealand, such as the stern-wheeler *PS Maori Chief* which was fabricated in Leith in 1864 and assembled in Onehunga in 1865.

The Nelson steamer scene

In Nelson, two men were key competitors in the drive to introduce steam to the bays. Edward Fearon established the subsidised *Nelson Coast Steam Navigation*

---

200 The *Jubilee Steam Ship Company* briefly competed with the *Northern Steam Ship Company* on behalf of the NZ Seamen's Union in 1887–88 on the Onehunga to Taranaki route in an attempt to improve working conditions.

Company[201] as early as 1855, purchasing *PS Tasmanian Maid*, and commencing work on the infrastructure that was necessary for vessels like this to operate. The first Motueka wharf – a ten foot wide T-shaped jetty, built at Doctors Creek in 1856 and extended in 1858, typified the developments which were to benefit the hookers as much as the expected small steamships. Fearon's ambitions were cut short when *Tasmanian Maid* was badly damaged on the Wairau bar in 1862 and a rival company seized the moment to pounce.

At forty years of age, Nathaniel Edwards was in his prime, with a steady income from his flax mill operations, and a realisation of greater profits to be made from the looming gold rushes. He had already been in a partnership with George Bennett for five years operating together as merchants and shipping agents in Nelson. In 1862 a fellow merchant John Symons joined the partnership, and it was decided to establish a local competitive steam-ship company, *Nathaniel Edwards and Co.*, beginning with the purchase of a 48-ton paddle steamer, *PS Lyttelton*. She was for sale in Wellington after an eighteen month maiden voyage from a Middlesex shipyard and now owned by an insurance company after being given up as lost! His rival Edward Fearon must have looked on with frustration as the repairs for *PS Tasmanian Maid* dragged on, partially funded by her subsequent charter to the government as a gunboat, while Edwards and Co. raked in huge profits shuttling *PS Lyttelton* back and forth to the West Coast

*The 48-ton **PS Lyttelton**, seen here loading wool at Blenheim circa 1863, was the first ship of the total 37 owned by the Edwards/Anchor company during eleven decades of operation in Nelson's local waters.*
Copy Collection: C2152, Nelson Provincial Museum

---

201 Amending the name to *Nelson and Marlborough Coast Steam Navigation Co.* when Marlborough broke away from Nelson province.

SS Wallabi was Nathaniel Edwards and Co's second ship, plying the West Coast run during the early goldrush days. The strength advantage of an iron ship is obvious from this photograph of her under later ownership, being pounded by surf on Greymouth's Cobden beach in 1881 before being successfully salvaged.
James Ring photo, courtesy West Coast NZ History

goldfields. The price of a berth for the voyage to Greymouth was a substantial £10 (a week's wages for a ship's engineer), with many desperate gold seekers paying £7 for standing room on deck. Business was so brisk that Edwards & Co. purchased the 103-ton *SS Wallabi* in 1864, and immediately began searching for an even larger vessel to share the West Coast route.

It did not take long to find one – the 149 ton twin-screwed *SS Kennedy* that had recently been built at the Pyrmont shipyard of the Australian Steam Navigation Company in Sydney. She was fast and reliable, capable of completing the run from Nelson to Greymouth in 36 hours often with her low schooner rig complementing her single boiler, carrying cargo as well as passengers. Painted the smart new company colours of salmon pink to the waterline, black topsides, white superstructure and a black-tipped funnel, she served the company, largely on the west coast run, for over five decades.

Other ships were to follow, such as the paddle steamers *PS Nelson* and *PS Charles Edward* already documented in chapter 13, creating a network of timetabled services throughout the region. In 1870 John Symons bought out his two partners and renamed the company the *Anchor Line of Steam Packets*, with its subsidiary the *Anchor Foundry*. After his death nine years later his widow sold the entire business assets including Albion wharf to a partnership dominated by Sclanders & Co. and John H. Cock & Co. who promptly renamed it the *Anchor Steam Shipping Company*. At the turn of the century a fresh partnership renamed the business as the *Anchor Shipping and Foundry Company*, duly recognising the valuable financial turnover of the ship-building and repair yard on the waterfront. By now there were regular timetabled runs radiating out of Nelson to the north, east and west, dominating the coastal passenger and mail runs, to and from Greymouth, Collingwood, Wanganui and Blenheim, as well as an overnight ferry service between Wellington and Nelson aboard *SS Tasman*, *SS Nikau* and *SS Kaitoa*. The cargo scraps about these ports were left for the cheaper hookers and scows to squabble over.

Despite the Anchor Company's dominance in local coastal shipping, its ships did not have a monopoly. Maverick ship-owner James Cross (Junior)[202] established his own small *Red Cross Line* comprising the steamers *PS Lady Barkly* (later converted to screw) and *SS Waitapu* which plied a very regular timetable between Nelson and Golden Bay. At the turn of the century the coal merchant James Burford owned the 178-ton *SS Tasman* which also was a regular Golden Bay coaster before the Anchor Line took her over in 1907.

John Edward (Jack) Westrupp also kept competition alive when he founded the *Wellington and Havelock Steam Shipping Company* with his *SS Wairoa* after losing *SS Waitapu* by fire while on the Wellington patent slipway, later also trading into Nelson and Patea with *SS Mana*. In turn, Frank Ricketts took over *SS Wairoa* in competition with *SS Lady Barkly* after the turn of the century.

The Red Cross Line's **PS Lady Barkly**, *photographed here at Collingwood during the 1870s, plied a regular timetabled run between Nelson and Golden Bay between 1867 and 1934. She was later converted to a screw steamer.*
Nelson Historical Society Collection: 326857, Nelson Provincial Museum

---

202 James Smith Cross Jnr was son of the original Nelson pilot and harbour-master James Smith Cross who had operated the Deal Boat in the earliest years of the colony.

Inter-provincial players

Although the Anchor Company plied routes between Nelson and its closest provincial neighbouring ports, there were longer New Zealand-wide routes linking the ports of northern provinces with those in the south.

The pioneering interprovincial steamers were expensive to run, but they set the benchmark for a reliable service linking Auckland's western harbour (Onehunga) with Dunedin, calling at several provinces including Nelson on the way. The paddle-steamer *PS Nelson* commenced this service in 1854, charging £7.10s for a cabin on passage to Nelson, £10.10s to Wellington and £15 for the entire voyage to Dunedin. Steerage class travel was cheaper, at £7 to Wellington for example. A year later she was succeeded by the 130ft 60-hp wooden steamer *Zingari*, with a more efficient oscillating engine, followed by *SS White Swan* in 1858.

The mail contract was clearly worth securing, as it presumably guaranteed a baseline income. By 1860 the contract was won by a bigger international player, the *Intercolonial Royal Mail Steam Packet Company*, which owned steam-ships operating between Britain, Australia and New Zealand via the Suez peninsula from the late 1850s. Their larger ship *SS Airedale* took over the inter-provincial mail contract in 1860 taking a route to Bluff via the west coast of both islands, while *SS Lord Ashley* and *SS Lord Worsley* took over the well-established run from Onehunga via Nelson and Wellington as far as Dunedin.

By the 1860s, the mail run was a vital communications link between central government and the provinces, even more so by 1865 when the Capital was relocated from Auckland to Wellington, and the gold rushes were bringing a big influx of prospective settlers into the country.

The next significant big player was the *New Zealand Steam Navigation Company*, established in Wellington in 1862, quickly securing the government contract for a subsidised monthly mail service between Auckland and Bluff. Within two years it had six steamers, each over 400 tons and capable of carrying passengers and mail. The regular route began in Auckland's western port of Onehunga, down the North Island's western coastline to New Plymouth, thence to Nelson, Picton, Wellington, Christchurch's Lyttelton, Dunedin's Port Chalmers and Invercargill's Bluff Harbour. The clockwork regularity of the timetable saw the mail ships departing each port at noon – a regularity which engendered a confidence not available from the more weather-dependent barques and brigs of its competitors. The company's schooner *Ladybird* would trans-ship passengers from Nelson to Greymouth and Hokitika in competition with the Nelson fleet.

Despite its promising beginnings, like its predecessors this company was hampered by the inefficient engines of its first-generation iron ships which included the 429 ton *SS Wellington*, and the 443 ton *SS Taranaki*. By 1873 its assets were bought out by the Christchurch-based *New Zealand Steam Shipping Company* which also absorbed the *Federal Steam Navigating Company*, operating coastal steamers such as *SS Waitara* and *SS Waimea*, but principally was focused on international trade, shipping farm exports including refrigerated cargoes to Great Britain.

MINUTES OF EVIDENCE

TAKEN BEFORE THE INTER-PROVINCIAL COMMUNICATION COMMITTEE.

EXAMINATION OF CAPTAIN MILTON.

WEDNESDAY. 28TH MAY, 1856.

1. *By the Chairman.*—You, as master of the "Zingari" steamer, have been on the coast of New Zealand for about eighteen months, and are acquainted with all the ports between Manukau and Otago?—Yes.

2. Would it be possible to maintain a fortnightly communication, with one steamer, between Manukau and Otago, calling at the intermediate ports of New Plymouth, Nelson, Wellington, and Lyttelton, both going and returning, provided that a detention of not more than twenty-four hours was allowed in any one port?—It would be possible to make two trips a month, calling at the ports mentioned, provided a detention of a few hours only took place in each port. The actual time of steaming would be only nine days, which would leave twenty-one days for detention in harbour.

3. From what you know of the coasting traffic of New Zealand, what size vessel would be best adapted for the trade; and what power should she possess to enable her to make, say twenty-two trips in the year, calculating that two trips would be lost in making repairs, &c.?—I think that a vessel of 350 tons register would be large enough, because she would not be required to carry cargo; she ought to be guaranteed to run eight knots an hour.

4. Would you object to state to the Committee what, in your opinion, should be the probable bonus which such a vessel should receive, to induce her to enter on such an undertaking?—I should think not less than £10,000 a year; but I think that an arrangement might be made by the owners to run a vessel, by guaranteeing a fixed interest on the capital advanced.

5. Do you believe a vessel of the character described could be procured from the Australian Colonies, which would be willing, on receiving the bonus you have named, to undertake the maintenance of such a communication?—No; I think not; I made enquiries when I was in the other Colonies, and there was not a single vessel that would answer the purpose.

6. Will you favour the Committee with an opinion as to the best mode of proceeding to obtain the services of such a vessel?—I should think by advertising, first in the Australian Colonies; and if not successful there, then in England.

7. Do you think a rapid communication between the ports mentioned could be maintained regularly by sailing vessels?—No; most decidedly not; I think there is no part of the world where it would be more difficult than on the coast of New Zealand.

8. *By the Colonial Secretary.*—What is at present the average stay of the "Zingari" in each port?—About three days in each port, with the exception of Taranaki.

9. What is the average speed of the "Zingari"?—I cannot say for certain; I think about six knots an hour in fine weather.

10. Do you not think that the speed might be increased?—By the substitution of a new boiler her speed could be increased to an average of six knots an hour in all weathers; but she would be obliged to go off the coast for about two months, for the purpose of making the necessary alterations. The owners of the "Zingari" would not be disposed to make this alteration unless there was a contract entered into for not less than two years.

11. Supposing the above mentioned alterations to be made at what rate per annum would the owners undertake a monthly trip to all the ports including Otago?—I think for about £6000 per annum, but I am not prepared to enter into any contract at present.

12. Supposing the Government to enter into the arrangement, when could the "Zingari" commence her trips?—About four or five months from the time of the arrangement being entered into.

13. *By Mr. Graham.*—Could you suggest any improvements for landing passengers and goods at any of the ports?—Vessels cannot get further up than the White Bluff in the Manukau. If a jetty of about 500 feet was made at the White Bluff, it would be very convenient for landing passengers and goods; at present there is a great want of some accommodation of that sort. In the event of not being able to procure the necessary accommodation, a landing place at Onehunga would be of great service.

14. Could you state the average number of passengers you carry?—I could not do so without going through all the agents' books; but I think about ten cabin and six steerage passengers would be about the average.

15. What would be the charges for the trip to Otago and back?—£30; £15 there and the same back again.

This frank and detailed interview with Captain Milton by a government committee gives a valuable insight into the evolving efficiency of mail correspondence around the entire country sixteen years after nationhood was established. Steam-powered vessels were clearly a key consideration.

Courtesy New Zealand National Library, Papers Past

The Southern Octopus

Dunedin entrepreneur James Mill became the pivotal figure in interprovincial shipping during the 1870s, creating a company which was to eclipse all competitors within a few decades. His shipping connections began during the 1860s, managing the Dunedin based *Harbour Steam Company* for the Otago land magnate Johnny Jones. When Jones died in 1869, Mill began casting around for a financial backer to establish his own company, while continuing to run *Harbour Steam*.

The breakthrough came in 1875, when the Scottish ship-builder Peter Denny became his business partner on the condition that all of the new company's ships would be built by Denny's Dunbarton shipyard. A new inter-provincial and inter-colonial giant was born, named the *Union Steamship Company Ltd*, and variously also referred to during the next century as the *Union Line*, *Union Company*, or even (by the competitors it steadily absorbed) the *Southern Octopus*!

As well as having such a significant backer, the Union Line was able to benefit from the huge technological advances with the succession of new ships it brought to New Zealand's coasts. Triple combustion engines were now becoming commonplace and with New Zealand's population growing steadily, so too was the demand for larger reliable affordable coastal ships.

Mills had big ambitions, initially eying the intercolonial run between Dunedin, Auckland and Sydney with the first two efficient Denny-built steamers, *SS Rotorua* and *SS Wakatipu* running a synchronised timetable, stopping at each significant port along the inter-provincial route, including Nelson, as well as the

*The Union Line's **SS Penguin** is visible here at the Nelson wharves behind a line of waiting Hansom cabs. She ran a regular overnight ferry service between Nelson and Wellington until her tragic sinking in 1909 with the loss of 72 after striking a submerged object in Cook Strait.*
Tyree Studio Collection 178493, Nelson Provincial Museum

Tasman Sea crossing. The fleet initially included older vessels such as the 750 ton 220ft *SS Penguin* which was later to run an overnight ferry between Nelson and Wellington. New vessels ranged from regular coasters such as the 400-odd ton *SS Ohau*, *SS Hawea* and *SS Taupo*, to the larger 1782 ton *SS Wairarapa* and 2003 ton *SS Waihora*, all built during the 1880s. A decade later came the large intercolonial vessels over 3000 tons being built by 1900 such as *SS Wairarapa* and *SS Warrimoo*.

One by one the octopus began pursuing its competitors, either absorbing them or buying a majority stakehold. Christchurch's *Canterbury Steam*, Napier's *Richardson and Co.*, Wellington's *Holm Line* and Nelson's *Anchor Line*[203] would all ultimately feel the squeeze of its tentacles. Australian shipping was not spared the competition either; the Union Company began undercutting or shadowing the Trans-Tasman routes of competitors like Hobart's T*asmanian Steam Navigation Company* and Melbourne's Huddart Parker Line[204]. At its peak the *Union Line* was the biggest in the Southern hemisphere.

The Union Company steamer **SS Maori**, seen departing Nelson during the 1880s, ran a regular service to the West Coast.
Tyree Studio, Nelson Historical Society Collection: 292049, Nelson Provincial Museum

---

203 The Union Line secretly acquired a 50% shareholding of the Anchor Line in 1908.
204 An agreement was reached with this line in 1895 to bypass competition.

While steam asserted itself nationally, however, despite the encroachment of timetabled steamship services, the hooker fleet was still able to prove competitive at a local level as the last two decades of the 19th century approached. For example the records show that in just over a three-year period to mid-1879 the old wharf at Motueka had 345 visits from the paddle steamer *Lady Barkly* (as well as various other steamer visits), but in the same period the cutter *Planet*, which shared a regular service with the steamer, called 360 times. Other hookers using the old wharf to bring in supplies and load out the wool, hops, potatoes and grain crops included *Three Brothers* (which called 12 times); *Prospect* (11 times); *Arthur Wakefield* (9); *Dauntless, Pearl* and *Standard* (5); *Maid of Italy* (3). *Cossett, Flirt, May, Modest Boy, Mary Ogilvie, Richard and Mary, Phoenix, Waihopi, Mermaid* each called twice, and there were visits by *Dart, Waitohi, Midge, Aurora* and *Uno*. It is understandable that from the bridge-deck of a steamer these busy little ships were looked upon as a 'mosquito fleet'.

The 178ft 733-ton iron barque **May Queen** *leaving Nelson at high tide under tow from a small steam coaster in 1883. (There was no Harbour tug until the following century) Her anchor is hanging un-catted, ready to drop if the cable parts. The catspaws and smoke hint at a possible seabreeze, which will be necessary for her to work her way north, well clear of the boulder bank until a true wind sets in. She made 16 voyages to New Zealand before being wrecked near Lyttelton in 1888.*

Tyree Studio Collection 182212, Nelson Provincial Museum

In 1875, the Union Co mail steamer **SS Taupo** achieved the interprovincial round trip from Auckland to Dunedin (via New Plymouth, Nelson, Wellington and Lyttelton) and back in a record 12 days. This Forster painting showing **SS Taupo** racing against the Government-owned **NZGSS Hinemoa** (between Lyttelton and Wellington in 1876) demonstrates the use of supplementary sail-power of the coastal steamers of the era.
Ref: C-059-004. Alexander Turnbull Library, Wellington, New Zealand. /records/23069459

It took three coastal steamers to tow the barque **Lutterworth** off the sand on the next tide after she grounded leaving the heavily silted haven entrance under sail in 1904. James Cross's **SS Lady Barkly** and Burford's **SS Tasman** were unable to shift her until the Anchor Co's 141 ton **SS Charles Edwards (Charlie)** added her greater bollard pulling power. By the turn of the century it was becoming increasingly apparent that a Port Authority needed forming to deal with the Haven's deteriorating southern entrance and the need for coordinated infrastructure.

Tyree Studio Collection: 180994, Nelson Provincial Museum

18

Changes along the Waterfront

DURING THE FIRST SIX DECADES from Nelson's earliest European settlement, there occurred many remarkable physical changes to both the natural and the built coastal landscape. On one hand were the multitude of alterations along the haven foreshore, and on the other hand the changing river channel of the Waimea delta, which in turn impacted on the Haven entrance and its shipping. These changes laid the foundation for further changes during the subsequent twelve decades to modern times, where reclamation has created a seascape unrecognisable to the early settlers.

Inside the Haven

For Nelson's mariners and waterfront dwellers, the Haven contained many key features which were to be progressively modified as commerce grew. Saltwater Creek modifications, the Haven Road seawall (with the proliferation of jetties and wharves between Auckland Point and Green Point and beyond to Wakefield Quay), and interference to the Boulder Bank's tenuous high-water small boat pass and difficult southern entrance; all were to transform the harbour's viability, while vessels continued to come and go throughout the 19th century.

At its innermost extreme, the early settlement first had to deal with Saltwater Creek. The track over Richardson Street and down Washington Valley met Haven Road at the crossing of this nuisance of a tidal creek which rose in Toi Toi Valley, drained a couple of swampy valley ends and reached a finger into Washington Valley. Saltwater Creek produced a sheet of water at high tide, making the ground boggy up to what is now Gloucester Street. It spilled out on to the tidal flats which included the areas now known as Anzac Park and Halifax Street. These flats extended along the foot of the town, which merged with the shore about where Wakatu Lane and New Street are. The creek in summer was barely an agile leap wide at low tide but it ran fifteen metres across at high tide when, for a small fee, a muscular Maori would offer his back to the traveller who wanted a dry passage across. Saltwater Creek was a natural town boundary at high tide when it was necessary to walk up as far as Parere Street to get around the tidal pond. By October 1842 the creek had been bridged and it connected Haven Road, as a curved causeway, with Bridge Street. It was inevitable that considerable energy would be spent during subsequent decades into taming this impediment through bridges and on-going reclamation. An initial attempt was to construct a one-way tide gate to keep the tidewater out, however its engineering must have been somewhat haphazard, as it also served to keep fresh water in, and on at least one wet-weather occasion the local houses upstream reported two feet of seawater over their floors as a result.

There has been much water under the bridge since those days. According to Captain Ted Reed, who always spun a good yarn, some time in the 1880s my great grandfather Captain John Westrupp who had retired from the sea but still harvested and sold cockles, found himself over the side of the road and into the mudflat at Saltwater Creek, wheelbarrow and all. Being in a 'happy' state of mind the old captain, with his hat cocked back and a grin all over his face, remarked to his helpers, "I think the blarney old ship must have miss-stayed". In modern times the tidal impediments of this part of the young town are difficult to comprehend, as they are now so far inland.

Moving westward from the town we have already glimpsed the changes along Haven Road in previous chapters, but certainly the jetties and seawall deserve mention. The first three jetties were constructed within two years of settlement – at least two of them being substantially stone structures. Within two decades there were two deep-water wharves (the Albion and Napier wharves), both in the vicinity of the current-day main wharf, with the Provincial government-owned Napier wharf extending 380 feet from the shore by 1859. Unfortunately, due to the poor durability of its cheap black birch piles, it was to be condemned and replaced after only fifteen years of use. Meanwhile other shorter jetties such as the customs wharf, Franzen's and the Bond Store's were situated slightly closer to town.

The seawall between Auckland Point and the port, built of granite blocks from Adele Island in 1879, extended the shoreline between road and mudflat, to

Two hookers lie careened on the mudflat beyond the Haven Road tramline in this photograph probably taken during the late 1850s. In the background is Franzen's wharf with two hookers aground alongside, in the location where Lukins' wharf was soon to be built.
Bett Collection 315010, Nelson Provincial Museum

*The railway and seawall, pictured here from behind John Westrupp's house at the turn of the century, marked the earliest reclamation efforts (necessary to allow a track which curved less abruptly). The hillside in the background has been extensively quarried for infill. Hookers could lie against the seawall at spring tides. At the Hadfield slipway are **Hera** in the background, and the Huffams' **Modest Boy** alongside.*

F N Jones Collection: C1829, Nelson Provincial Museum

cope with the new railway line which supplemented the older tram rails in 1880. Meanwhile the road had been steadily extended beyond Green Point to become Wakefield Quay, and by 1892 the seven-year project of building Rocks Road began, with the extensive use of convict labour and a total cost of £11,000 of taxpayer money. The project was to provide alternative access to Richmond Borough and Waimea County, and was made more possible by the assistance of nature when the Waimea River conveniently relocated its course from the location of present day Beach Road, further west to present-day Blind Channel in progressive scouring events between 1875 and 1882.

Tahuna and the Waimea Estuary

In modern times it is hard to imagine that during most of the nineteenth century, the western end of Tahunanui Beach was part of a huge semi-submerged sandbank known as the Waimea Bank, and that the suburbs of Tahunanui and Nayland were part of the Waimea river channel, and its surrounding mudflats or sand dunes.

With a channel initially twenty feet deep, the Waimea River was navigable for ships until the mid-1870s. They turned west by south off Fifeshire Rock to sail alongside the gravel shoreline that is now Rocks Road and the cliffs, then parallel to the dunes of Beach Road and across what is now the motor camp. The

Opposite page:

These two charts (Stokes' 1850 survey above the current navigation chart) provide an insight into the coastal changes (natural and man-made) affecting Nelson Haven.

Bett Collection M50 Nelson Provincial Museum, and courtesy LINZ NZ [Not for use in Navigation]

---

waterway passed Parker's Cove, then known as The Black Stump, which was an important shipping point and much larger than now. It continued up to Quarantine Road, declared a quarantine reserve in 1854, shallowing all the while. Beyond Monaco it continued through sandbanks and islands from its land channel at the Waimea end of the bay.

During northwest gales, ships were known to sail a mile inland to seek shelter in the lee of the Waimea bank, rather than stay out in Bolton Hole. Ships from Australia regularly sailed up the river channel to discharge livestock at The Black Stump and the stock was driven from there to the quarantine grounds. Smaller vessels found their way both to the foot of Richmond and into the mouth of the Waimea River itself further to the west. This whole waterway, invisible nowadays, became host to hookers and smaller craft serving the Waimea district right around to the Moutere. The western end was served by going outside Rabbit Island and in the Mapua entrance. As nearly all the land between Nelson and Richmond was swampy, sea travel was the preferred choice south of the Annesbrook Rise.

Ships visiting Port Nelson would sail across Blind Bay to approach the Haven entrance by Fifeshire Rock, leaving 'the flats' (as the Waimea Bank was called) to starboard. To their port stretched the Boulder Bank, not discernible as such but merely looking like the shoreline. There were buoys in the fairway and leads on shore to steer to, but approaching the shallow flats in a sailing ship still required a nice judgement of how far to stand on towards the guardian sands and when to turn to beat into the Haven without loss of control. Sea captains quickly learnt to use the local tides, particularly the slack water at the top of the tide, and sometimes used warps fixed on Haulashore Island.

For the first four decades the Waimea Bank at its closest point was dry at a distance of only 700 yards west by south from Fifeshire Rock, with deep water only in the middle 300 yards. Two very strong water-flows kept it clear. The flow from the Haven, helped by the Maitai River, scoured a channel to keep Fifeshire Rock and its reefs clear while the Waimea River, with its very extensive basin enclosed by the sands, swept in from the other side. This conjoined force kept a hole south of Haulashore up to 11 fathoms deep. It was called Bolton Hole, from the immigrant ship *Bolton* which first used it as an anchorage, and the wider area was the Bolton Roads. (In June 1842, *Eagle*, *Elenor* and *Clifford* were there, and none of the ships anchored in Nelson Haven.) The flow lost velocity as it spread, allowing sedimentation to form shoals around the seaward perimeter but there were still four fathoms over the bar at high tide, enough for the largest ships.

Nelson was effectively a bar harbour, although access was not as extreme as

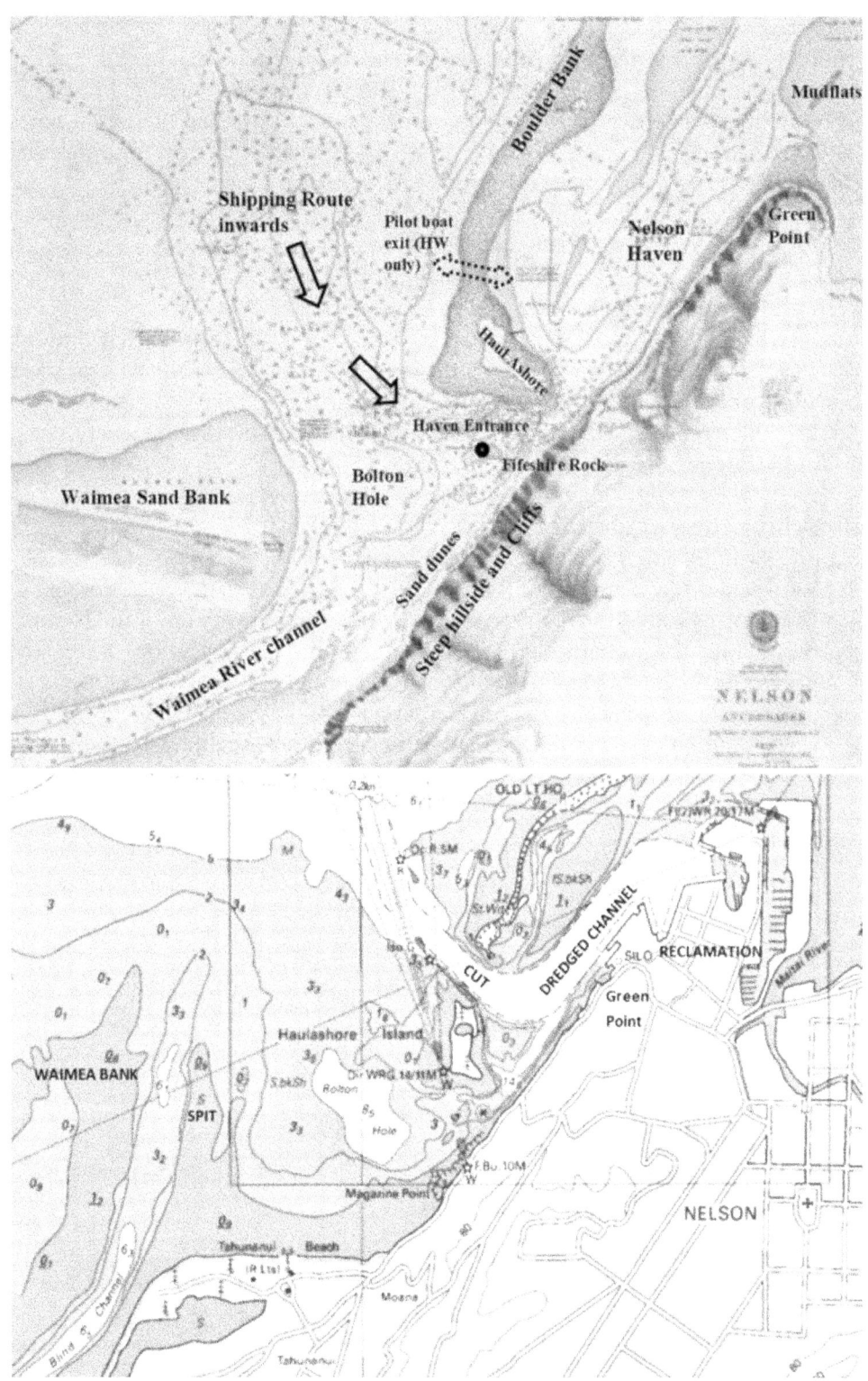

at the river bars. The 82-ton schooner *Look-In*, a regular caller at Nelson, got into difficulties in a southerly gale and dragged from her anchorage in the Waimea River to come ashore on the Waimea Bank. Six of the crew got ashore but had to stand in the water with waves dashing over them until they and their crewmates were rescued. *Look-In* was salvaged but the experience of her crew indicates that the bank was largely under water at high tide in bad weather.

In modern days, looking west from Whakatu Drive, you can see the expanse of water that, with less silt and a stronger river channel, provided a very handy sea route. On a high tide it is readily imaginable, and the hookers were the right vessels to work the margins.

A whale came ashore on Rabbit Island in 1861, one of a sporadic few through the 1850s and 1860s, and when it was spotted by people in Nelson several boats put out from the haven to claim it. In the ensuing race John Westrupp, in his hooker *Three Brothers*, dashed up the Waimea eastern entrance, reached it first and flagged it as his prize.

Breaching the Boulder Bank

Nature began playing tricks on the young settlement in 1875, when the Waimea River breached the Waimea Bank during a severe flood event. The subsequent scouring during the following seven years led to a total diversion of the channel westward, into the present-day Blind Channel, and the formation of a beach known as 'the Sands' (renamed in 1902 as the Tahuna Sands).

The implications of this major change of water flows soon were apparent at the Haven entrance, where the Sands were steadily encroaching on the shipping channel from the south. In 1884 the distance between the sand bank and

The rock shelf extending well beyond Fifeshire rock was a navigational hazard for vessels entering the Haven at the mercy of fickle winds. This grounded ketch (which I am confident is the Tasmanian 'barge' **Pearl**) *awaits the next high tide with her sails scandalised on 22nd May 1874, luckily surviving the incident.*
Copy Collection 2291, Nelson Provincial Museum

Blasting the 'old entrance', 7th April 1892, to deepen the rocky sea-bed. The caption reads 'Mine – 80 lbs gun cotton'. One wonders how many stunned fish may have been collected in the aftermath.
Brusewitz Collection 313923, Nelson Provincial Museum

Haulashore was 600 yards, but within a decade this had nearly halved. Meanwhile depths at the entrance were reducing, discouraging larger deep-drafted ships from visiting the port.

For the adaptable smaller hooker skippers, these developments were certainly a nuisance but not a major impediment. However local businessmen and officials were increasingly concerned that the port was steadily becoming inadequate for the region's commercial requirements. Ratepayers' money was allocated in 1892 for a three-year project involving dredging and blasting the channel near Fifeshire Rock to deepen the entrance – supplementing the blasting of the early 1850s when explosives had first been used to remove hazardous underwater rocks between Fifeshire Rock and Haulashore.

By 1899 the authorities were considering a total re-think. The waterflows out of the haven had been permanently impaired, and the port was fast becoming a true bar-harbour. A £58,000 plan was proposed, to cut a major new dredged entrance through the Boulder Bank just north of its Haulashore end. To manage this ambitious project, a Harbour Board Act was passed, with elections held in 1901 to create a body which would oversee the resurrection of the port's reputation. It is somewhat surprising that it had taken sixty years to create a harbour authority. Hitherto, without a harbour tugboat or formalised foreshore development, the ad hoc construction of navigation aids, wharves and seawalls had come under a variety of initiatives from both government and private enterprise.

It was five years before the ambitious 'New Entrance' cut was open for shipping. It was an impressive development, flanked by a pair of moles and dredged to 15 feet at low water. For the hooker skippers, the 'old entrance' was still available, but steadily silting to render it marginal except on the flood tide. It was inevitable to all mariners that the newly dredged cut and internal channel were to dominate the water flow in and out of the Haven for the coming century and beyond.

Dredging the 'Cut' was a four-year project. In this photograph the old entrance is clearly visible in the background left, between the hook of the newly created island of Haulashore and the pyramid-shaped Fifeshire Rock. The dredge **John Graham** can be seen at the extreme right, with a row of floats supporting the pipe which is sluicing the debris ashore to Haulashore.

Courtesy Kerry Miller

The Waterfront of my childhood days

Nelson was ninety years old by the time of my pre-school years. I have since witnessed the changes of a further ninety years. For the many older members of my extended family, hookers had been their livelihood and the changes during their lifetime were doubtless remarkable too.

I remember when the hookers were suddenly personalised for me. I was the youngest in my family and one of the younger of a wide array of cousins but, although I was mad keen on sailing, no one had bothered to tell me of the family's sailing skippers. Captain George Williams and his second wife, Emily Berry of Moetapu in the Pelorus Sound, had their home in Stepneyville up the gully behind the Nelson Yacht Club. George died in 1932 but we lived handy to his widow and spent time with the younger Williams boys Frank, Ivan and Jeff. I was in their house from time to time and was intrigued by a painted fire screen in the parlour depicting Blind Bay and a mosquito fleet of little sailing ships darting about up and down the canvas and quite meticulously detailed. I was intrigued enough to ask about the picture so Mrs Williams took me in and described the various vessels, familiar to her and later to me.

"That is your grandfather Sam's *Result*," she pointed out to my surprise. Until then I had never really imagined this white-haired grandfather of mine at sea, but the real surprise came with her next words. "Your grandmother painted it for my husband as a wedding present."

I did not meet all the hookers of course, but Granny Westrupp had painted

The 63ft Tasmanian ketch **Elizabeth**, *seen here lying against the Haven Road seawall, (not far from John Westrupp's cottage) was a common sight in the Haven discharging timber and coal from Collingwood and Waitapu between 1884 and 1891. Two of John Westrupp's sons (my great-uncles Jack and Robert) captained her during this period.*
Tyree Studio Collection 182263, Nelson Provincial Museum

The 60ft hooker ketch **Result** *lies alongside the seawall outside the railway line alongside Haven Road. My grandfather Captain Sam Westrupp owned her from 1908 to 1917 when she was struggling to compete with the larger shallower scows. He lived nearby across the road (nearer the foot of Russell Street). The sea wall continued to Auckland Point and across the creek. It is now buried by reclamation.*
F N Jones Collection C1829, Nelson Provincial Museum

My grandfather was one of these surviving Blind Bay sailor/skippers photographed here in their Sunday clothes during the early 1900s. From rear: Tim Tonkin, George Ramage, Sam Westrupp and Russ Ricketts. Between them they would have had many fascinating stories to tell.
Russ Ricketts photo, courtesy Kerry Miller

a vivid picture of the latter ones going about their business. It exercised my mind for years, how to depict this large area in a painting without primitively darting up and down the canvas. If I were nostalgic I expect it would be for the associations of that painting, and a grandmother I didn't really know because she died before I was four. She is only a misty figure to me, but she found time in her busy life to paint a gift for a friend. I learned later that it had been painted on sailcloth and so was unlikely to have survived, but perhaps it is still out there somewhere?

    I was one of the waterfront kids, and without knowing it at the time, reaped the benefits of our families' reputations. At around the turn of the century, the surnames of seafaring families living along the port from Russell Street to

Ricketts Bros shipping office and boatbuilding workshop on Haven Road by the lime kiln, about 1905. From left: Russell, George, Edward Ambrose, John James and Charles Alfred Ricketts. It was unchanged when I knew it – a place of boats and the fresh smell of worked wood and aromatic stockholm tar.
Copy Collection C2799, Nelson Provincial Museum

Richardson Street read like a roll-call of boatbuilders and hooker-men: Ricketts, Westrupp, Lukins, Smallbone, Gabrielsen, Grossi, Henry, Graham, McNabb, Thomson, Wildman, Horton, Kidson, Reeves, Woolf, Johnson, Doig, Scully, Winstanley, Morrison, Everett, Gilbertson, Fowler and Williams. Looking back or forward a generation there would be a change or two in the names, but almost all still had a direct maritime connection and the list for my own generation would include most of the same names.

As school-age boys, my brothers and I would sometimes stop by at the old Ricketts Brothers boat-builders workshop on Haven Road, (originally established by Frank Perry Ricketts in 1883). I remember kindly old Mr Charles Ricketts, on my first visit, asking my name and when I told him I was a Westrupp he said, "I know your grandfather!" and was satisfied. It has taken all these years to realise that my family heritage that I took for granted was in fact a waterfront 'open sesame'.

This shed had been their shipping office when they operated hookers and the larger *SS Wairoa*. There was a green-painted model of the scow *The Portland* in their workshop, and there was always a dinghy under construction accompanied by the unmistakable aroma of shaved wood, oakum and paint. Mr Ricketts would sometimes find us a piece of wood to turn on the foot-treadle wood lathe. Not surprisingly, my brother Allen grew up to become a well-respected boatbuilder with his own workshop which in turn attracted boat-lovers (as well as those who just wanted to gossip inanely without understanding that boatbuilders had little time to spare!) As youngsters we had an emerging understanding that Mr Ricketts was a busy man, with work which required both hands and a steady eye to shape another plank or timber into place in a complex form. Perhaps he recognised our passion for his craft.

As waterfront kids, we were accepted too, at the Anchor Shipping pattern-makers' shop and foundry, as well as at Johnson's boatshed (now a restaurant on piles over the water but then a boys' place with dinghies for hire and sometimes one being built). We could get an uncertain welcome if we encountered Ernie Johnson, the father, unless he wanted someone to hold the dolly while he riveted or help him on the water. He had the contract to collect explosives from the last trans-Tasman sailing ship, the topsail schooner *Huia*, which used to anchor outside the Boulder Bank when she had explosives on board. Although he didn't take me out to her there were two or three occasions when I helped transfer gelignite cases from his large clinker lighter to the magazine on the Boulder Bank.

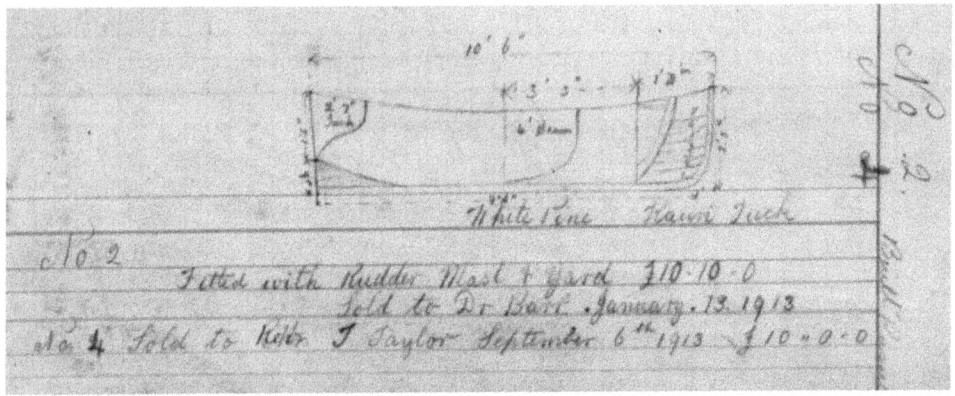

These simple plans accompany Russell Ricketts' quote for a new clinker dinghy to be built of white pine with a kauri tuck, rudder mast and yard in 1913, at a fee of £1 per foot. (The Rev Tommy Taylor seems to have got 10 shillings ecclesiastical discount.) This simple plan from Russ's daybook shows the tuck and sections at two stations plus profile, adequate to replicate the first one built and to read the shape. It would be set up and planked from stem to transom using just these two temporary moulds and fairing battens. Early hooker hulls were probably done the same way.
Russ Ricketts notebook,
Courtesy Kerry Miller

Percy Williams' son Rob, a waterfront distant-cousin of my own generation, used the same clinker-building methods as the Ricketts family's to build three clinker dinghies during the 1990s for his grandchildren, keeping the tradition alive.

The picturesque topsail schooner Huia was a regular visitor to Port Nelson during my childhood years, transporting gelignite to the Magazine building on the Boulder Bank. The signal flag 'Bravo' would fly at her masthead to warn of her dangerous cargo aboard.
PRG 1373/41/8, courtesy State Library of South Australia

My brothers and I had the additional family-based privilege of access to the pilot station, as our father skippered the Pilot boat. By those times the Leading Lights (beacons on which to line up entering harbour) had become electrified, but the barrel buoys in the harbour and the pile beacon in the entrance channel were still lit with kerosene lanterns. I remember the first time my father allowed me to row the dinghy around the buoys on my own to change the lanterns. It was a daily routine, wind, rain or shine. Those were the times when men could still pause for a moment to have a word for an enquiring boy, and there was something inclusive about it all. These were the last of the hooker people, and this was the waterfront ambience that Russ Ricketts and Percy Williams experienced at the turn of the century. Percy had a father at the pilot station then, and nothing much would have changed since the 1840s.

In the 1930s we would walk from our cottage, well above the boatsheds at the port, to Auckland Point School, with sea lapping at a seawall most of the way. We had a firm injunction from our parents not to go out on the mud, all too visible on our legs when we did so. Now that it has changed with reclamation, it is only the curves in Haven Road that give a hint of the old shoreline where the railway used to be and where the little ships berthed. In modern times a new wave of large dwellings has sprung up above Wakefield Quay, along Fifeshire Crescent, where we grew up alongside other seafarers' and fishermen's families in their cottages. In my childhood the milkman delivered milk to our doorsteps (ladled into our billies from his churn) with a horse and gig. That long-suffering horse would find it hard to squeeze among the clutter of parked cars on our still-narrow road these days.

The Mission Hall and Limeworks

The Port Nelson Mission Hall, (renamed in 1951 as St Matthew's Church Hall) was another part of my childhood, and its recent restoration completes a tangible link spanning fourteen decades. My personal memories stem back to the brief phase when my parents sent me and my brothers off to Sunday School at the hall, armed with a penny each to drop into the collection plate. (I well remember the doleful ditty, "Hear the pennies dropping, Listen while they fall, Every one for Jesus, He shall have them all ...") At the time, my brother Allen was desperate to have a boat of his own, and had set his eyes on a one-man tin canoe, constructed of corrugated iron in a style forbidden to us by our seafaring father. This wonderful little vessel belonged to Ron Nalder, (a son of Newton who lived further around Haven Road), who agreed to sell it on time-payments of twopence per week. It was depression times in the mid-1930s and we never had any spending pennies, so Allen decided that we should each tap the church collection plate to simulate the penny dropping, and pocket the coin instead. I recall nearly being unnerved until I realised that no one would hear my penny drop because there was green baize all over the plate, so I slipped it into my pocket it as instructed.

Alas, the scheme fell around our ears before the day was out. Allen proudly took delivery and carried the vessel away to secret storage under the sailing club shed on the waterfront, but our nemesis arrived and Allen was made to return the vessel. Our father showed neither then nor later the sailor's understanding of Allen's need. But we had imaginations and minds to feed, and being waterfront kids, the prospect of owning our own modest vessel continued through our childhood years.

The Mission Hall began its story when it was built for Bishop Suter by the Huffam Boys from Bark Bay in 1883, on land subdivided off the original one acre 'Town Lot' 37 owned by Lukins' Limeworks. James Lukins had been the first prospector at the Glengyle gold-diggings at Parapara in the late 1850s and presumably was one of the success stories at the claim, for when he came back to Nelson in 1860 he promptly purchased the ketch *Rapid* and the schooner *Dove*, commanding one of the vessels himself. Each hooker could carry up to 15 tons of firewood and limestone from Golden Bay which was wheelbarrowed over Haven Road and hauled up a steep tramway to be burned at his new Green Point Kiln. He quickly secured the contract to supply lime and sand to build the Nelson lighthouse in 1861, which set the business up to build a wharf next to Franzen's, and subsequently load sacks of lime bound for New Plymouth, Wanganui, Picton and elsewhere.

My childhood memories of Lukins involve a wheelbarrow as well as happier scenes at the wharf. Calcined lime made mortar, and slaked lime was used in agriculture. My father sent me on more than one occasion with a wheelbarrow to the cottage beside the Limeworks, where James' aging daughter Amelia[205] still lived. I was instructed to purchase calcined lime for my father, which he needed to make whitewash for the wall. My strict instructions were to bring it home dry! This I did, but it is a steep road up the hill to Fifeshire Crescent pushing a barrow.

The area was still bustling beyond my childhood days with a chandlery, store and sailmakers' building across the road into the 1940s. The store continued – run by Smallbone – but the wharves were soon demolished. Boatbuilding continued at the old Ricketts' location, passing to Doug Robb in 1941, then possibly to Hughie Wells (who had been working for Charlie Johnson at his boatshed over the water near the old Iron Duke/Rowing Club shed) and subsequently to Guard's Sea Services in 1957, with Jack Guard restoring the Guard family name to Nelson's maritime heritage.

Ninety years is a fair span of time. My mother's grandmother, Amelia Ward [nee Kidson] was three years old when she arrived with her parents John Kidson and his wife Amelia, aboard the barque *Bolton* in 1842. If she had lived as long as I have, she would have been ninety when I was a toddler. The changes she would have seen to Nelson's settlement and waterways during those nine decades would likely have been as remarkable as the changes I have observed during mine.

Hooker ketches **Argus** and **Old Jack II** lie on anchor inside the Haven, calmly reflecting on the decades of change during their years of service.
F N Jones Collection: 311056, Nelson Provincial Museum

---

205 James Lukin's daughter Amelia lived to 99 years of age, giving 50 years' service to the adjacent Mission Hall as a Sunday School teacher, secretary and supervisor.

The Nelson Evening Mail.

COLLISION IN THE HARBOUR.

ONE LIFE LOST.

Shortly before nine o'clock last evening news was brought to town that a collision between the s.s. Charles Edward and the cutter Phoenix had occurred in the harbour, and that Cockram Westrupp, the master of the latter, was drowned. The facts we have gathered regarding the accident show that the cutter Phoenix, which is owned by Mr T. Harley, left Motupipi on Monday evening last for Nelson with a cargo of coal, having on board the deceased and two other men, Frank Bailie and John Nalder, and arrived about six o'clock last evening off the lighthouse, the night being very dark and foggy. The pilot boat, which was outside the bank, on the lookout for the Grafton, hailed the cutter, and Westrupp answered. The cutter then drifted with the flood tide (two of the men on board using sweeps) towards the entrance. Those on board heard the whistle of the Charles Edward, which was leaving the wharf, and were on the lookout for her. Meanwhile the steamer had left the wharf and proceeded at half-speed down the harbour. Just as she was turning round the point of Haulashore Island Captain Whitwell, who was keeping well into the shore, saw the lights of the Phoenix, and put his engines hard astern. At this juncture the crew of the cutter brought her round and she was drifted by the tide broadside on to the bows of the steamer, which was at the time practically motionless. The lights of the Charles Edward had been seen for several minutes before the accident took place by the crew of the cutter and when abreast of the beacons, fearing a collision with the steamer which was only a chain or so away, they all shouted as loudly as possible, and they say that they then heard some one call out on the steamer "Back her hard, full speed astern." The tide, however, was running so strongly that the cutter could not get out of the steamer's way, and the collision took place, the Charles Edward's bow cutting into the cutter's hull. At that time Nalder was in the rigging of the cutter looking after the light, which was burning brightly. Bailie and Nalder scrambled on board the steamer, but Westrupp is supposed to have jumped overboard, and was seen from the steamer's deck beating his hands on the water, as he was carried by the strong tide up the harbour, and was heard to call out, when opposite the baths, in reply to some one who called out that a boat was coming, "Look smart, I am nearly done." After this nothing was heard or seen of the unfortunate man, although two boats, one from the steamer, and the pilot boat, continued to search for some time. After the collision the Charles Edward returned to the wharf, where she remained until this morning. The Phoenix has drifted with the tide and settled on the beach opposite Mr Guly's house, where she has been made fast. It has been stated that the steamer Grafton was following the cutter in, but we learn that this is incorrect, as she was anchored two miles away from six o'clock last evening until early this morning. When the Charles Edward left the wharf the fog had lifted, but directly after she had left it dropped again, and became thicker than ever. Under ordinary circumstances an enquiry would have been held to-day by the Collector of Customs, who, however, is, in the performance of his multifarious duties, holding Magistrate's and Warden's Courts in Golden Bay instead of being in charge of the Customs Department, where, as is proved in this case, he may at any moment be wanted.

Constable Phair and others left the Port this afternoon in a boat to search for the body of the unfortunate man Westrupp. The party will search the harbour as far as the water will permit them to go in the direction of Wakapuaka.

Phoenix, recently renamed **Ida** by her 29 year-old captain Cockram (Cocky) Westrupp, had been in the Westrupp family since the 1870s and was bringing in a full load of coal from Golden Bay when the steamer SS Charles Edward ran her down near Gilbertson's wharf inside Nelson Haven. Cocky was drowned, and the hooker was towed to the mudflats, too damaged to be salvaged.

Courtesy Lynette Wilson

19

A Perilous Occupation

HARDSHIP WAS A FACT OF LIFE for nineteenth century settlers and mariners. In order to raise a family, hard work and occasional risk-taking were taken for granted. There had been several periods of hardship leading up to the end of the century. Swaggers were common during the 1880s and some pioneer settlers, including the seafarers, finished their lives in poverty. Widows and women whose husbands were away also faced the difficulties of earning a living and for some of these folk, who had been vigorous young people when they first emigrated, Nelson's ill-equipped and crowded poorhouse was the only option. 'The Depot' was under the hospital's supervision and sustenance was served up with a heavy dose of moralising, especially if the inmates were lucky enough to get themselves an occasional ale or two. Those with families fared better but it was not until 1898 that New Zealand introduced the first old age pension, limited to the 'deserving poor' who were considered destitute through no fault of their own. A widow's pension followed a decade later and pensions as we know them came in only with the Labour government of the 1930s. These were the harsh realities, softened only where they were recognised by people of means who did something to assist.

For the hooker families of Blind Bay, risk was a factor in daily life. Hookers had low bulwarks and little freeboard when laden. Few seamen knew how to swim, and lifebelts or lifelines were not commonly used. Many of the hooker skippers struggled to make adequate profit to keep the hulls and rigging of their little ships adequately maintained.

By the late 1860s a number of hookers were ageing and needed to have money spent on them, but it wasn't available. Put aside the blue and green waters, the foam at the bow, the whistle of the wind and the crack of the canvas coming about – life was immediate for hooker skippers and their crews. Topsides leaked, and the leaks below waterline were likely to increase when maintenance was skimped. Where rainwater penetrated, the wood rotted in the dampness. It was called dry rot and salt water was seldom the culprit. Fittings pulled off and masts simply rotted at deck level, higher if there was something to trap water. Too few New Zealand trees yielded enduring timber, and too few owners yielded the cash for proper maintenance so instead of the crack of the canvas there were occasions when a more ominous crack signalled a broken boom or mast. A significant number of these losses were in the winter's bad weather.

Percy Williams, who was a hooker skipper of the final generation once commented about the battered sign on Lukins wharf which read, '*E H Lukins – Agent for Transit, Asa, Pet, Comet, Turau, Camellia, Felicity, Anatuero, Planet, Maid of Italy*'. He had been a waterfront boy a generation earlier than me, also with ready access to the Pilot Station. In his boyhood he spent hours at this wharf, looking down on hookers like *Matakana, Gannet, Result, Lily, Old Jack, Calyx,* and *Mavis* as well as the scows *Orakei* and *Venture* which also worked at this wharf. Percy observed that the condition of a vessel depended on the type of man who was master and the type of trade the vessel was employed in. "Some of the vessels were pretty parish rigged and little good whilst others were well found and kept," he said.

Westrupp successes and tragedies
The Westrupps were one of the prominent hooker families during the second phase of hooker shipping, and the tragedies which they experienced give an indication of the potentially perilous nature of their occupation. John and Margaret had six boys and a girl who survived to adulthood. The six sons and one son-in-law[206] all became hooker captains, and three were drowned in separate tragic episodes within Blind Bay waters at a relatively young age. A brief look at the family background helps build a picture of their place in the hey-day of the mosquito fleet.

John Westrupp had settled in Nelson during the first decade, marrying Margaret Parker and skippering a number of vessels including his own *Jubilee* and *Three Brothers*. Various of his sons gained their sea-legs from a young age (as the tale of John and Bill's father's near-drowning relates in chapter 12). The elder two brothers progressed up the ladder, gaining qualifications which could be endorsed according to their experience. For example Bill was satisfied becoming a qualified master of *a cargo sailing vessel up to 55 tons register trading between Nelson and places in Blind and Golden Bays and between Nelson, Croisilles, French Pass, and places in D'Urville Island*, happily sailing within these limits as owner/skipper of *Lily* until retirement. Jack was more ambitious, moving up from owning and skippering hookers to skippering and ultimately owning a pair of steamers, working Cook Strait waters. while George skippered a number of hookers including *Felicity*, and his son James (my father's cousin, known as Brimbo) eventually owned and captained *Maid of Italy*.

Sarah's husband Bill Glover was not so fortunate. He had built the 40ft schooner *May* at Frenchman's Bay in 1876, three years after they were married, and their second child was still an infant when tragedy struck on the morning of 8th May 1877. *May* had been in the Croisilles with her skipper Bill and one crewman, cutting hop poles and firewood, and was returning home loaded with a substantial deck-cargo. They were in a heavy northwester ten miles seaward of Pepin Island, and William Smith, on the helm, had called the skipper up from below to shorten sail. Bill successfully reefed the mainsail, but while attending to the foresail fell overboard. He was probably holding onto the fore-boom topping

---

206 John Edward (*Jack*), William (*Bill*), Sarah, George (*Kemo*), Robert (*Bob*), Cockram (*Cocky*) and Samuel (*Sam*, my grandfather). Sarah married William (*Bill*) Glover when she was 18 years old.

lift, which broke away. *May* miss-stayed when Bill Smith tried to put her about to rescue her skipper, so he had to wear ship to get her back to the lifebuoy he had thrown. He brought the vessel up into the wind and went up the mast to look for Bill Glover, to no avail, then sailed *May* down to the Waimea estuary and signalled the pilot boat for help.

For 21-year-old Sarah, with a baby and toddler this was heartbreaking. Bill still owed £171 to Burchard Franzen for *May*'s fit-out expenses, which he had been working hard to pay back, so it is unlikely she received much to sustain her young family when Franzen took over ownership. She remarried Alfred Stringer and settled in Wanganui two years later.

The next of John Westrupp's sons was George, who was a master with a full ticket, skippering a number of hookers, possibly including the 10-ton Burford ketch *Standard* which traded into Constant Bay[207]. However John's fifth son Cocky was only 29 years old when the steamer SS *Charles Edward* ran down his 11 ton cutter *Ida*[208] at night inside the harbour entrance on 11 March 1891. *Ida*, loaded with Puponga coal on her way in to discharge, was nearly cut in half and she went straight down. The other two crewmen on board survived and the enquiry found the steamer at fault, but that was small comfort to this second Westrupp generation who were shortly to lose yet another son to the sea.

John and Margaret's fourth son Robert (Bob) Westrupp, was 36 years old and probably making his living as a fisherman from necessity, with the downturn in hooker activities. He and his teenage crew Billy Reed (I knew him as a veteran repairing his nets at Nelson's old fisherman's wharf in the 1930s), were caught in that situation on 2 March 1893 in an 18-footer belonging to Antonio Wett, another of the old fishing hands. Bob and Billy were well out in the bay when the wind changed from a sou'westerly to a hard northerly. The boat was overwhelmed, swamped and rolled in the confused seas, and the two men struggled to stay with it until Bob didn't reappear. Billy, a powerful swimmer, struck out for shore and landed, completely exhausted, but Bob's body was never found. He left a widow and an eight-year-old daughter – yet another family grieving from the loss of seamen and fishermen in Blind Bay over the years.

The youngest Westrupp son was my grandfather Sam, who (luckily for me) lived to a relatively ripe age. Fifteen years younger than his oldest brother Jack, Sam followed the family footsteps to pass his Master Home trade examination and become a qualified hooker captain. He captained Burford's *Argus* for many years bringing Ferntown coal to Nelson (probably crossing paths with his brother Bill on *Lily* in Golden Bay at times), as well as the scow *Oban* and his own hooker *Result*. Even after retirement, Sam kept his Master's ticket valid, and was called upon from time to time to take vessels on routes where their regular skippers were insufficiently qualified. Being generally engined vessels, these were relatively straightforward for hooker-trained skippers like my grandfather to handle after a

---

207 Shipping notices only recorded surnames, so the Westrupp may have been John or any of his sons.
208 He had recently renamed her as *Ida* from *Phoenix*. She had been a Westrupp vessel since the 1870s.

lifetime of berthing and getting under-way under sail alone.

Sam had his own crop of sons too, including my father Sidney who was known on the waterfront as Dick (nicknamed after the Premier 'King Dick' Seddon). He was born into an era when hookers were no longer a career option, so instead he went to sea on various coasters including *Pearl Kasper*. Younger than his two brothers who enlisted in the military forces during World War I, he served as a sixteen-year-old deck-boy on the troopship HMNZT *Tofua* for two voyages to England. Other note-worthy stints also included passages to New Zealand's sub-Antarctic islands as an A.B. aboard SS *Hinemoa* resupplying the shipwreck depots.

When he became a family man, my father 'came ashore', securing the position as skipper of Nelson's pilot boat. This seafaring tradition is reflected now with his great-grandson serving aboard the Police Launch *Lady Elizabeth IV* in Wellington and Cook Strait waters.

Other tragedies

The number of drownings and losses in and about Blind Bay is far too great to record here. It is not difficult to imagine the apprehensive wives looking out the windows of their waterfront cottages as the clouds rolled in, wondering whether their husbands or sons had made it into a safe anchorage. My brother Allen had a habit of tapping his barometer every time he passed it, doubtless a habit handed down for generations since our father or grandfather first purchased one of these vital weather forecasting aids.

John Westrupp's daughter Sarah was only one of many widows left with a family to feed from uncertain means. Another of the Franzen-owned hookers, the 40-ton schooner *Richard and Mary*, was in the news five years after Bill Glover was lost. She sailed for Nelson from Greymouth on 27th May 1882 with three crewmen under the experienced Captain R Hamilton, but was never heard of again. Captain Hamilton left a widow with seven children. How she (and the widows of his crew) managed to sustain her young family during the ensuing months and years is not recorded, but it would be another fifty years before a social security net was established, so hopefully the community was able to support her in her loss, and that her elder children could step up to help put food on the table.

Some drownings were not caused by weather or poor gear failure. One distressing incident occurred in March 1867 aboard the Lukins-owned 41ft cutter *Midge*, which was on a cargo run between Nelson and Wanganui at the time. The sea was running very high when Captain Duncan and the mate, described as 'a Frenchman' which in those days was often a derogatory term for any foreigner, had a quarrel which led to blows. A scuffle developed and both men went over the side. A vessel under sail has limited options available and although the sole remaining crewman threw rope and oars they were soon out of sight in the rough conditions. The crewman then tried to launch the ship's boat, which immediately swamped, and the two men in the sea were never seen again. Her lone, unnamed crewman managed to sail her into Patea, and the newspaper report ended: "Captain Duncan leaves a wife in Wanganui to mourn his untimely end". The 'Frenchman' did not get a line.[209]

Amongst the tragedies were tales of heroism which lasted through the stories down several generations. Ethel McNabb[210] was still a girl when she accompanied her father Captain W F McNabb and her brother Albert in the dinghy rescue of three fishermen off the Riwaka bar. In an onshore gale their open boat had jibed and capsized and the anchor dropped out, thus anchoring her in the middle of the bar. Ethel's young brother Allan had also set off in a small dinghy, but his father sent him back because of the rough seas. After a hard row of nearly a mile Ethel was exhausted but two of the three fishermen, E Rowling Snr and W Owen, were saved. The third man in the capsized boat, A Goodman, was washed away and drowned. The McNabb men were presented by the community with medals, and Ethel was given an inscribed gold brooch to mark her heroism. I well remember her telling me of this when I was a boy, and showing me her brooch which she was actually wearing at the time.

THE GOLDEN BAY ARGUS
(FIAT JUSTITIA, RUAT CŒLUM.)

THURSDAY, JULY 25, 1907.

On Sunday morning last, during the heavy south-east gale which blew from Friday till Monday, Mr W. Westrupp's ketch Lily, was dismasted off Separation Point, while on the voyage from Nelson to Collingwood. After leaving Nelson on Sunday morning, the ketch, which was manned only by Capt. George Westrupp and a son of Capt. W. Westrupp, ran before the gale for four hours, and when off Separation Point, the stay-sail gear carried away and eventually took with it the foremast, the whole falling over the side. While the crew was attempting to save the wreckage, the ship broached-to, and for three hours the little vessel lay in the trough of the huge seas. Ultimately the gear had to be cut adrift, and after some trouble and by use of a steer oar put out forward the vessel was put again on the wind, and subsequently took the bar at Collingwood at five p.m. in foaming seas, with only her mizzen sail set away aft. and the plucky navigators reached port just at dark on Sunday night. The foremast was of kauri and the loss of this, with sails, rigging, and gear means a serious loss (estimated at £40) to the popular skipper of our little local trader. To those who witnessed the heavy seas and high winds which prevailed at the time, said to be the heaviest experienced here for fifteen years, it is a matter of wonder and congratulation that this vessel herself managed to reach port in safety.

Bill Westrupp's **Lily** *was one of the last Blind Bay hookers without an auxiliary engine, which puts the seamanship involved in this episode into perspective.*
Courtesy NZ National Library

---

209 *Nelson Evening Mail*, 8th April 1867
210 Ethel was to marry Sonny Tregidga, and was known in adulthood as Ethel Tregidga.

Less tragic outcomes

Misadventure at sea was all too common, and the outcome often depended on a mixture of seamanship, weather, tides and the condition of one's vessel. Many of the hookers were regarded as old and faithful friends. Some were handsome, and had a fascination that sailing vessels share. When, a generation later, we bought our cruising ketch *Matuku II* and sailed her back to Nelson from Napier, Dick Stringer, a waterfront engineer and long-time acquaintance, scrutinised her and remarked, "She'll look after you" (and certainly she did).

During the years preceding the first World War, a number of hookers and scows fitted auxiliary engines. By modern standards they were cumbersome and lacking in horsepower, but they took away the total dependence on wind and currents that the last generation of sail-dependent hooker-men lived by. When Bill Westrupp's engineless Lily was dismasted off Separation Point in a severe gale, it was his ability to use a forward steering oar to counteract the weather-helm of his surviving mizzen sail that enabled him and his crewman to successfully make port.

Four years later (in November 1911) Sonny Tregidga was also able to use his seaman's ingenuity to survive when he lost his cutter *Matakana* in the southern corner of Blind Bay. He and his crewman Allan McNabb had sailed from Nelson

Sonny Tregidga's cutter **Matakana** *was a typical hooker, significantly reliant on internal ballast for stability. When she was knocked down off the Moutere bluffs, she was unable to self-right, but although she was lost, her skipper and crew survived.*
Courtesy Rob Williams

for Puponga on the coal run at 3am in a favourable south-easterly. This changed to a westerly during the early morning when *Matakana* was about seven miles off Moutere bluffs, and as the weather thickened they encountered a number of wind changes. With a squall impending, they hastened to get the jib down and let go the topsail sheet but were laid right over before sail was reduced. With *Matakana* still on her side Sonny got the dinghy loose but she rolled keel-up, trapping him and the dinghy underneath. Allan, who had been up for'ard trying to attend to the jib, simply climbed from the shrouds out over the side to the keel. Sonny emerged and Allan managed to get him up on the hull where they perched, at the mercy of a raging sea, for the next hour and a half. Then suddenly the dinghy which had been trapped under *Matakana* bobbed out and they managed to catch it before it blew away.

Despite the dinghy's ribs being broken they were able to make adequate repairs by using its floorboards and a cut up waistcoat. For a makeshift hammer for the lining nails they used a six-inch marlinspike that was fortuitously in the dinghy. Then, using a floated-up cartridge box for a bailer and two floorboard battens for paddles, they kept the dinghy heeled to keep the damaged planking as far out of water as possible, and managed to make headway. Their makeshift equipment got them to Motueka, the nearest landfall, two and a half hours later. They were exhausted after bailing continuously with the cartridge box while they paddled and, just as they made the shore, the wind went around again to a hard offshore blow. Had it come in a bit earlier the wind change would probably have proved fatal.

Sonny's wife Ethel Tregidga was a strong-minded woman. After this near-tragedy she kept the six-inch spike they had used for the rest of her life as a reminder of the near-loss of her husband and younger brother.

Wind and tides

Russ Ricketts' rather more cheerful story of a missed opera performance highlights how much a hooker-man's life was at the mercy of wind and tide. Russ was crewing for Captain Gus Burnard on *Asa* loading sawn timber from Riwaka to take to Richmond via Blind Channel (as a supplement to their occasional trips to Tata Island for limestone). *Turanga* (captained by Sonny Tregidga) and *Maid of Italy* were in Riwaka loading timber at the same time, and the deckhands decided to work all day Sunday so their ships could get to Richmond, unload at Wharf Road (now Beach Road), and then get to Nelson. They wanted to attend Pollard's opera performance on the following Tuesday night.

Asa, *Maid of Italy* and *Turanga* got away for Richmond on the evening tide. On *Asa*, Russ stood the first watch, and woke the skipper about 2am with a cup of tea to take the next watch. They chatted before Russ turned in, but some hours later he awakened to a gentle bumping and could see Gus sound asleep on his bunk! Russ dived out of the hatch to find *Asa* touching on a sandbank. He unshipped the poles, at the same time yelling to Gus, and somehow between them they managed to get her bow around and off again.

Meanwhile in the distance they could see *Maid of Italy* and *Turanga* were making the Blind Channel. Fortunately the sea breeze came in and *Asa* made the channel too, but as she was a bit late on the tide she could not get far enough up the mudflats to discharge the timber which was destined for Wilkes' timber yard. The other two vessels were perhaps a mile further in and were making rafts of their loads, a procedure which seems to have been commonplace, so the men on *Asa* did the same, and floated them ashore across the shallowing channel. Russ relates how the nor'wester came in with the tide that night, and "*the other two got out because they were yacht-like and therefore able to beat to windward. The Asa – being something like a soapbox – could not make it. So we ran and anchored behind Grossi's Island. That was the end of the opera for me.*" For the record the other two deckhands, Tut Marshall and Jack Brunell, had turned in and gone to sleep when they reached Nelson so none of them saw the opera in spite of their Sunday work.

Fun and games aboard

Seafaring had its share of characters; some competent, some with great understanding of the natural world about them, and others who only pretended to both. Order in the form of cleanliness and tidiness were insisted upon on most vessels but things were pretty rumpty on others. That is how life was aboard – sailors were a mixed bunch. Ashore along the coast when the hookers were anchored, their crews appreciated the sociability of the settlers with an evening at cards or other entertainment, maybe a practical joke, a home-cooked supper and then back to the ship. The 30 or 40-foot length of a hooker doesn't leave much space to get away from it all, and dissension in the small crew could be unpleasant for everyone aboard. Like any group, seamen had their eccentricities.

The story was told of my uncle Albert who had a bunk above a rugged old Scandinavian who was an inveterate pipe smoker. Albert disliked the smell so one day he slipped the parings off his toenails into the pipe bowl. Lief came off watch, sat on his bunk and lit up as usual, seeming not to notice the stench.

"What's that you're smoking in your pipe?" Albert finally asked as the additional odour of burning toenails assailed his nostrils.

"Same old baccy, Albert," came the lugubrious reply. "Same old baccy."

Russ Ricketts told another humorous tale of a scrap between Alf Browett and Bingo Blick, (a crewman once known to have put the ship's clock forward to get himself to his bunk sooner). This time, aboard the hooker *Pet*, a surfeit of beer was to blame. *Pet* was on the hard at Lukins' wharf for repairs, as she had struck the beacon on Haulashore Island while drifting in with the flood tide, and sprung a bad leak. Alf was on the wharf arguing and finally leapt down after Bingo, who nimbly ran around the covered hatch. Alf took the direct route across, not knowing that the hatch boards were off and only the canvas cover was stretched across. The cover folded inwards and Alf fell through into four and more feet of water while Bingo hopped on to the wharf quick and lively, letting others help Alf out.

Russ's uncle Jimmy (actually Ambrose Edward but obscure nicknames flourished on the waterfront) had to go into the bush over the bay and find a

*The 49ft 21-ton ketch **Pet**, seen here at Franzen's wharf, was built as a schooner on Haulashore in 1888 and had many ownership changes during 19 years of hard use.*
Copy collection C2291, Nelson Provincial Museum

black birch tree to replace the beacon struck by *Pet*, and that satisfied the marine department.

Another story that became a legend involved the 50ft ketch *Felicity*. Her owner George Williams, committed to his pilot station job, was unable to go to Motueka and collect *Felicity* from where she had been lying idle so he detailed Tom Reeves to do a bit of an overhaul, sufficient to get her to Nelson. Tom went off with money and with oakum to caulk the badly opened-up topsides and with instructions to do any essential work, but Tom was rather lax about it all. He did rub some bar soap into the worst of the seams, then he bent on the sails, reeved the running rigging and set off, without crew, in a brisk south-westerly wind which was surely tempting fate. Once at sea there were various things that needed attention, including the pump which became crucial to the voyage, but Tom was quite unable to leave the wheel in the windy conditions. Heeling compounded the leaking of the topsides and *Felicity* settled further and further in the sea as she filled up.

Legend has it that George, on the lookout for his ship, spotted her out in the bay about a mile off the Nelson mole and realised she was in trouble. He rushed to the pilot station to enlist help but before it could be provided *Felicity* capsized and Tom appeared on top of the starboard side frantically waving his shirt. Captain Scully took out the steamer *SS Lily* and, with considerable difficulty and damage to *Felicity*, managed to bring the stricken vessel in and alongside the main wharf. George enlisted his brothers Harry and Jim and a small army of helpers and with much jocularity at Tom's expense, and much concern for George, she was got upright to be pumped and bailed free of water. She then spent months on blocks at the gasworks wharf where Jack and Charlie Ricketts, assisted by Bob

The 50ft ketch **Felicity** alongside the gasworks wharf undergoing repairs after foundering in Tasman Bay.
Courtesy Rob Williams

Goldie (another steamship, hooker, and scow skipper recently arrived in Nelson), repaired and re-rigged her. Hookers were often taken in on a spring tide, then jacked up to be clear of the water to work on, but at times this involved lying on one's back in the mud to do some of the work on the bottom.

Of course the whole episode cost George Williams a lot of money, but the punch line was that a friend of Tom's in Motueka had given him a side of bacon to take home. Tom, who was a stutterer, was loud in lament of its loss, as he had looked forward to telling his wife, "Mammy, I'm b-b-bringing home the b-bacon!" Another version of the story describes Tom emerging on the topsides clutching the precious haunch under his arm, exclaiming, "at least I've s-s-saved the b-b-bloody b-bacon!"

Hooker-men as fishermen

A significant part of hooker work was always seasonal, and it was necessary either to find or make work in the off-seasons or to go without earnings. When vessels could be laid up for quite long periods before work offered, many seafarers shipped out on larger ships.

There is some mention of Maori trading fish in the early days of European settlement, and fish was a valuable food in the starvation years, but fishing itself is barely mentioned in historical records. However when some of the hooker sailors started to record their experiences it became clear that a hooker captain with no cargo in sight was prepared to become a fisherman, and a fisherman with a cargo was happy to become a trader, so from very early times the 18ft to 28ft pulling and sailing boats were not only used as lighters moving cargo from ships anchored off or ferry boats for passengers but also for catching and selling fish. The boatmen worked both the Waimea roadstead, netting and line fishing, and Blind Bay itself. It was well into the 1900s before refrigeration was available ashore and until then the best that could be contrived were wet-wells, which only a few boats had, to hold live fish.

According to Ted Reed, both *Wave* and *Eclipse*, which must have been primarily fishing boats, had fish wells in the hold with one-inch holes through the bottom to allow water in to keep the catch alive, thus prolonging sea time and ensuring fresher fish. Ted's brothers Billy (called 'Plugger Bill') and Jack were ticketed masters as well as fishermen. Billy also ran firewood from the Croisilles on *Calyx* while Jack was on the coal run with *Argus* at some stage. George Westrupp was a fully ticketed hooker-man who captained a number of the traders, but he was also a fisherman, as was his brother Bill who apparently fished with his ketch Lily when no cargo offered. The Collingwood *Argus* even referred to his hooker as a fishing-boat in 1899 with this rather amusing newsclip:

"... *a prominent member of our local bodies (who ought to have known better) lost his way on the Aorere mudflat and did a heavy 'freeze' in the incoming tide near Ferntown ... [being saved by] the timely appearance and assistance of Mr W Westrupp's commodious fishing boat, the occupants of which fished up the whole concern (horse, sulky and inmates) ...*"

The Waimea estuary and Rabbit Island beach were favoured seine net fishing areas, used by Nelson fishermen to make a night-time or early morning catch that could be got back to Nelson by 8 or 9am for the fish hawkers. Seine netting was done in open 18-footers equipped with sail and oars, and in wintertime fishermen worked ten or more miles out into Blind Bay hand-lining for cod. The men had to be good readers of the weather, but a hard sou'wester would see them hugging the weather shoreline and calling on all their skills to get past the rips in Blind Channel, or coping with hard weather from the north which made the bottom end of the bay into a lee shore while making for the deteriorating 'old entrance' to the Haven.

In the lean times aboard the hookers, fish would be welcome, as would any other gleanings along the coast. There are tales of ducks shot 'by mistake' and goats hunted for the pot. Russ Ricketts said that three feet of sausages and a loaf of bread were the usual provisions taken aboard *Comet* in Nelson by his uncle for a Bays trip, so it seems most hooker and scow seamen kept an eye out for usable resources.

Oysters paid well in a time when 'oyster parlours' were in vogue. It was a busy seasonal fishery until a slime which was some form of algal bloom spoiled the various beds. John Westrupp is credited with discovering the oyster bed off Adele Island in 1866, and Sam Westrupp found a bed off Rangihaeata in Golden Bay soon after the Pratts discovered another off Totaranui in 1895. Billy Reed found good oysters off the Croisilles in 1890 but they were very deep and hard to fish.

Oyster dredging entailed dragging by hand, running out the dredge by dinghy and pulling it back to the ship or setting out a long rope, anchored at each end, and pulling the dinghy hand over hand along it with the dredge out astern. It was hard work, and whether a dredge was ever pulled by the vessel under sail I do not know. These early fishermen were a great mix of nationalities: Italian, Greek, French, Hungarian, Fijian, Portuguese, Austrian, and from all around the British Isles. Some whose names have survived were 'Rock Cod Tommy' Norton (who wore a bun hat), Joe Mallarmo, 'Briny Jim' Pawson, Antonio Boniarto, Tony Wett (a great humorist), Frank Perano, Sandy Sorcenelli, William 'Billy the Rat' Emms (a grand old man at odds with such a nickname), Thomas 'Old Sharkie' Ancell (a sailor off the square-rigger *Hermione*), Harry 'Father Wobutus' Anthony, 'Old Bogo' Symonds and 'Fiji Jack'. Then there was the Grossi family who lived off Monaco on Grossi's Island which has since been renamed (in the inscrutable way of officialdom). There were many cross-overs between fishermen and hooker men.

The Reeds

Certainly the Reed brothers, Billy and his younger brother Ted sailed with a foot in both camps – fisherman and hooker-man. The brothers' grandfather James Reed came to New Zealand on the whaling vessel *Cheviot* and settled at the Cloudy Bay shore whaling station. He married Ekaumoenga in 1835 and they lived for nine

William (Billy) Reed at work repairing his nets.

years on Sunday Island, now Raoul Island. The couple had ten children, including a son called William who became a seaman and settled at Washington Valley in Nelson where he married and raised a family of six. His four sons were William (Billy), John, Edward (Ted) and James.

Billy had been an 18-year old when his skipper Robert Westrupp drowned after their open fishing boat capsized. My memories of him are as a veteran fisherman, often seen repairing his nets at Nelson's old fisherman's wharf.

Ted Reed, born in 1880, was one of the seafarers who wrote about his experiences, giving us an insight into an era when hookers were still significant.

Ted left home when he was eleven and shipped as boy on the cutter *Anatuero* under Captain Charles 'Gabriel' Gabrielsen. At seventeen, Ted was Sonny Tregidga's mate on the 12-ton cutter *Turanga* and he later held a master's certificate of service under the 1903 act for '*a sailing vessel up to 15 tons register carrying cargo and fishing between Nelson and places in Tasman and Golden Bays*'. As mentioned earlier, these certificates of service dealt with the specifics of previous service. Ted was 23 years old when he was issued his master's certificate, and he captained *Anatuero* for several seasons oyster fishing. He next captained *Maid of Italy* and *Turanga* carrying firewood from the Croisilles to Nelson, and later ran *Asa* and *Lily* in the Bays trade.

He formed another link with my ancestry, remembering my great-grandfather Captain John Westrupp as an old man, while he himself was an elderly captain to me as a youngster. Such is the span of generations, and I feel fortunate to have been able to weave some of his fascinating yarns into the narrative of this book.

The cutters **Maid of Italy** *and* **Turanga**, *seen here at high tide alongside the Riwaka wharf, were two of the last working hookers in Blind Bay. They were owned by the Tregidga brothers, and variously crewed and skippered by Tregidgas, Reeds and Westrupps during the first two decades of the new century.*

Copy Collection C2285, Nelson Provincial Museum

20

The Last Hooker-men

THE LAST GENERATION of hooker-men served both aboard traditional hookers and the larger flat-bottomed scows. It was a transitional phase too, with auxiliary engines gradually becoming more commonplace aboard both types of sailing traders. There was no fanfare to see the hookers out of their era. They gradually faded from the scene, slowly decaying as the income they generated became insufficient to sustain their increasingly expensive maintenance.

As a child, born during the 1920s, I was fortunate to have known some of the seamen of this last generation, and to have heard their stories.

The Williams family

Percy Williams was one of the last generation of hooker captains, and I encountered him in his later life, with my father when I was a college boy. At the time he was a relieving mate on the ferry, resplendent in his brass-buttoned braided uniform and white cap. His grandfather, Welshman Charles Williams, had migrated to Auckland and married in Onehunga, Auckland's port for the western entrance of Manukau. Charles' son George Patrick Williams, who was born in 1864, settled in Nelson and took a seaman's job with Ricketts brothers on the ketch *Transit* before moving on to other hookers, and along with his brothers, becoming a well-respected hooker captain, passing on his skills to his sons. Percy was born in 1893. Tragedy struck when Charles' first wife died from complications after teeth extraction, but he re-married later at Moetapu in Pelorus Sound in 1909, and Howard Williams was born of the second marriage, later to also become a seafarer known to me, as were his four brothers and sister.

Captain George Williams

Captain George, as George Williams was known, was for a time a seaman on Anchor Company ships and came ashore for a while as one of the boat crew at the pilot station. In those days the pilot service maintained a crew for the pulling boat and these men lived in cottages across the road from the pilot station, just to the south of what is now called 'The Boathouse'. About 1901 Captain George bought the ketch *Felicity*, but when he sought to run her himself he found his own master's certificate of service was limited to 16 tons because he had done his time as master of the smaller *Goldseeker*. His newly acquired ketch *Felicity* was 24.9 tons so he was required to study and sit for a competency certificate for under 25 tons register, which he appropriately set about doing. In the meantime, George leased out *Felicity* to a slothful skipper whose lack of maintenance later was to prove costly.

Felicity, was a vessel built for beach-loading, and had her drawbacks, being a shallow and beamy vessel with nice lines aft but a very bluff bow. Percy Williams crewed aboard her, and made the interesting observation that her draft when empty was only three feet three inches for'ard, and four feet three inches aft. As a consequence she was difficult to stay or get about and made quite a bit of leeway close-hauled. But loaded, and drawing about six feet two inches aft, she was a splendid sailer. Captain George recognised this failing, and acting on his observations of the centreboard scows, arranged for the Ricketts Bros to fit a centreboard in *Felicity* in 1908. This was about ten feet long, off-centre (so the casing could be bolted to the side of keel and keelson), and extended into the hatchway by about four feet. It was claimed that it made her very easy to handle – even when light she made no leeway and could tack like a yacht. These points are inherent to good hooker handling and one wonders whether it was innate conservatism that had made the Nelson boat-builders discount the advantages of a centre case in the shoal-draft hookers.

After Captain George upgraded his Master's ticket, he took over as *Felicity*'s master with his son Percy as crew, trading between Nelson, the Sounds and the Bays. Their first job when Percy was aboard was to take the last working sawmill from Kenepuru Sound to the Croisilles, and later trips included shipping Puponga coal to Blenheim. George Williams eventually sold *Felicity* to Captain John Anderson in 1910, purchasing the ketch *Comet* in 1911 from Lyttelton where she was lying idle.

Despite being slightly smaller than *Felicity*, *Comet* could reportedly carry 37 tons deadweight or 16,000 superficial feet of timber. The 10-inch false keel that had been fitted for working around Banks Peninsula proved unsuitable for working Puponga coal, so George had it removed by Jack and Charlie Ricketts, and do the same centreboard installation as on *Felicity*. It proved equally successful. In 1920 *Comet* was altered to a cutter rig and had an auxiliary oil engine fitted.

Percy Williams spent four years on *Comet* serving under four masters: his father George and his uncles Henry, Jim and Joe Williams. The changing face of shipping later saw Percy move on to steamships after obtaining his home trade mate and his under 25-ton master's ticket, and eventually he earned his full ticket. *Comet* continued to carry Puponga coal to Nelson and, through French Pass, to Picton and Blenheim. She picked up timber from Nydia Bay and Havelock for Nelson, and when she left those waters is unclear. According to Ted Reed, Captain George's brother Frank Williams had charge of the ketch *Champion* and traded between Nelson and Onehunga and so did another brother – Jim Williams – later on.

Jim was also master of *Calyx*, trading between Nelson and the Croisilles, and Harry Williams captained the hooker *Mersey* in the same trade. Both ships

*Originally built at Torrent bay, the 49ft hooker **Comet** was nearly 30 years old when George Williams purchased her in 1911. During her six decades trading she was fitted with a centreboard, converted to cutter and fitted with an engine.*
Copy Collection C1829, Nelson Provincial Museum

seem to have been quietly laid up as work became scarce. Frank went farming in the Motueka area and Harry went into steam until he came ashore and worked as foreman for the Motueka Harbour Board. George came ashore after *Comet*. By then the Anchor Shipping Company had small colliers as well as general cargo steamers, and with more scows coming on the scene there was no longer a place for sailing hookers.

Percy went on to skipper the deck scow *Vindex*, and in his memoirs writes of a mind-numbing experience which arose through circumstances quite beyond his control. It was supposed to have been a straightforward voyage to Golden Bay with a cargo of absorbent bricks for the new furnace at the Iron Works:

"We had loaded 60 tons of firebricks in Port Nelson from the SS *Corinna*, and were instructed to take them to Onekaka, calling at Motueka first to collect covers to protect them. We arrived in Motueka on Saturday evening in heavy rain, only to be told that there were no covers to be had, so Sunday morning we sailed again for Onekaka in the continuing rain. The decks were almost awash amidships, the bricks having soaked up so much water, and the deeper the vessel became, the more water the bricks absorbed. When we arrived off Onekaka lagoon I went in with the dinghy to sound the channel and I discovered there was insufficient water, being neap tides, for Vindex to float over the bar so I went to Collingwood for three days to await improved tides. It rained most of this time, with the vessel getting gradually deeper all the time.

"I tried to get a carrier to lighten the cargo but no-one would take it on as I think the payment was doubtful so back we went to Onekaka with the water four inches over the deck amidships. There was a slight easterly when I cleared Collingwood and I have never felt a vessel so sluggish. She remained completely underwater except for the poop deck and the bow. I was very relieved when we finally made it across the bar and got some of the soaking bricks ashore."

Percy's son Robert (Rob) Williams served his time aboard coasters, and later became the harbourmaster at Motueka. His passion for traditional seamanship saw him building several clinker dinghies, as well as a 30ft brigantine as a retirement project.

Felicity's fate

As a beach-built hooker, *Felicity* had a good run, partly thanks to the money that Captain George Williams spent on her. However despite the centreboard that improved her tacking ability, it was the ferociousness of Cook Strait's head winds that proved her demise.

Within a few months of George Williams selling *Felicity* to Captain John Anderson she had just left Wellington in a nor'west gale for the Sounds to load timber. Carrying ten tons of cargo and with the ship's boat and an oil launch on deck, she turned back when the gale and confused seas outside the Heads were too much to contend with. It was a fateful decision. As she was beating back against the notorious Wellington Heads wind-funnel, the jib's tack-pennant carried away and she mis-stayed, going on the rocks near the Pencarrow Head low-level light-house. The boats washed away in the seas and *Felicity* slipped astern off the rock and sank. Fortunately the three crewmen managed to get a footing on the rocks, crouching there throughout the night until the lighthouse keeper saw them after dawn.

I can personally vouch for the ferocity of this patch of water. During the late 1970s I left Wellington one miserable, dark night in similar gale conditions, as part of a three-man crew to deliver a new, unrigged yacht under auxiliary power to Napier, 200 miles northward on the east coast. Being a traditional design with low freeboard, and with her bulwarks and coamings yet to be built, the sea was very close to me as I helmed in the growing dark. Once outside the Heads we turned for Cape Palliser, near beam on to the seas, and she was like a whale with water sweeping over the cockpit. Although it was self-draining it was overloaded and seldom emptied completely. Our skipper was busy watching his navigation; with all the city lights and the heavy sea spray it was tricky picking up beacons. After a soaking and exhausting time on the helm getting her out of Wellington past Pencarrow and on the way east towards Cape Palliser in the dark of night, I was relieved by slightly-built Colin, a newcomer still earning his sea legs, who later sailed around the world.

The skipper would have been keeping an eye on Colin but, as I entered the companionway hatch, I turned to watch in the dim light for a time to see that he was coping. There he was, secure in his safety harness but occasionally washed almost sideways by the seas coming aboard, perched for all the world like a drenched sparrow peering at the dim compass but managing. Satisfied, I went below to lie down on the bare cabin sole, tossed about, wet, and unsuccessfully seeking warmth close to the noisy engine, before succumbing to my seasickness. Experiences like these lend the fate of *Felicity* a more vivid reality.

The Tregidga family

Among the final roll call of hooker skippers, various members of the Tregidga family stand out too. A Cornish immigrant, Richard Gill (Dick) Tregidga appeared on the boating during the 1890s when he and his wife Mary were living in Torrent Bay. Captain Dick owned and skippered the 12-ton cutter *Turanga*, while his sons William (Billy) and Richard Gill Jnr (Sonny) cut their teeth sailing their little *Kestrel* (possibly *Petrel*) to Nelson selling firewood. These two brothers went on to own and skipper the hookers *Maid of Italy* (Billy's), and *Matakana* (Sonny's). During my childhood days they had moved up to scows, with Billy co-owning *Vindex*, and Sonny owning *Pearl Kasper* (later passing her on to his son Albert in 1942).

When I knew Sonny, as a near neighbour during my childhood years, he was stocky to the point of rotundity but still energetic and tough. He contracted me, a spindly boy, to wheelbarrow stones up Victoria Road for a garden wall he was building. I first had to gather the big ones he wanted from the foreshore, which ordinarily was not permitted, and lug them up the seawall. It says something for Sonny's influence on the waterfront scene, that the harbourmaster turned a blind eye to this indiscretion. That heavy, iron-wheeled wooden barrow was tough to push up the hill even empty; my productivity was not high enough and I was pleased to be superseded by a bigger boy with more brawn, from off *Pearl Kasper*.

Sonny incurred my mother's unspoken wrath one Christmas Eve. It was a custom for my father Sid (Dick) Westrupp to call on Sonny about Christmas time when *Pearl Kasper* was laid up for the holiday. It was a time to have a chinwag and a drink but, by an unfortunate set of circumstances, my father could only call before noon on Christmas Eve. He was a modest drinker anyway and had to breach his 'sun over the yardarm' rule that day. Later in the afternoon I was puzzled by the sudden illness that overwhelmed my father and by my mother's complete lack of sympathy for his obvious suffering, which meant he could not accompany us on a long-anticipated Christmas Eve in town. It was revealed to us some years later that Sonny had plied him too generously with whisky and milk that day, and my father reckoned the milk did not agree with him.

The fate of the last hookers

The generation of young men who went to sea after World War I could still experience life under sail, but the opportunities closed as hookers were lost or laid up through age or lack of work while the scows were gradually being motorised, their bowsprits lopped off and their rigs reduced, giving a degree of independence from wind and weather. *Echo*, *Pearl Kasper*, and *The Portland* continued trading as late as the 1960s principally as motorised wooden coasters.

Vesper lived on into the 1980s as a mussel barge in the Sounds. *Talisman* became a marina landing at Nelson, and *Kohi* became a fishermen's jetty at Westhaven.

However, of the surviving traditional hookers, only a handful had motors and screw propellers installed, so most became sadly unprofitable in their latter years. The work continued as hard as ever, hand-stowing timber and other cargoes, hoisting sails without the aid of winches, manoeuvring under sail or assisted by the ship's boat being rowed, depending on the vagaries of wind and tides.

Bill Westrupp's *Lily* was the last Blind Bay hooker working under sail alone. She had cargoes of case timber from Robertsons of Wainui for case-makers at Motueka. She loaded flax at Wainui too, and timber from other mills, but in 1924 Bill Westrupp reluctantly made the decision to run her up on the mud of the Aorere estuary below where he lived (and where the last of her still lies – her anchor was unearthed there in 2005).

During the first years of the new century the rest of the fleet had gradually left the wharfs. *Turanga* was wrecked in 1903, and *Pet* was wrecked in 1907. *Camellia* was laid up on the Nelson mudflats opposite the gasworks in 1909. *Planet* had the brief hope of a reprieve in 1909 when elderly Neil Swanson bought her with the ambitious (and unfulfilled) intention of refitting her while he lived aboard her on the hard at Haulashore Island. The following year saw *Felicity* wrecked and *Anatuero* laid up. Sam Westrupp's *Result* had a full load of coal aboard in December 1917 when she met her end on a rock in Torrent Bay (now named Result Rock) while skippered by Tom Reeves. *Gannet* came to grief igno-

*Some of the surviving hooker fleet (probably **Maid of Italy**, **Argus** and **Gannet**) dry their sails at the inner berth on the south side of Nelson wharf, in about 1910. The Anchor Company steamers **SS Koi** and **SS Kaitoa** are also visible.*
F N Jones Collection, Nelson Provincial Museum

miniously in 1918. Sonny Tregidga had already laid her up indefinitely when Billy Reed arranged to borrow her to load pie melons at low tide, on the beach at Ngaio Bay. She was pounded to pieces in a rising northerly before she could be sailed off (Russ Rickets spoke of a melon-gathering frenzy by locals all along the beach). *Transit* was laid up in 1920, followed by *Argus* on the Nelson mudflats (still visible from Queen Elizabeth Drive) in 1922. *Asa* and *Venture* became rotting hulks in Torrent Bay and Awaroa respectively.

Three hookers had engines fitted, and continued trading for a while. Brimbo Westrupp's *Maid of Italy* lasted until the late 1920s, to be laid up on the Nelson Mudflat near Trafalgar Park after 50 years of service. *Comet* survived until 1941, and *Old Jack II* was still working as a fishing boat out of Westport (renamed *Marilyn*) in the late 1960s after being re-rigged, re-framed and re-engined.

Given the low financial returns of the hooker trade, the pleasure yacht *Maritana* bucked the trend in 1915 when Russ Ricketts bought and converted her to become a motorised trader during World War I. She was licensed to carry passengers and cargo. She worked Mapua until the trade built up enough for the Anchor Company to take it over.

The 44ft **Maritana** was built as a low-freeboard yacht, but was registered to carry cargo and passengers in 1915.
Courtesy Rob Williams

Neta – following in the hooker tradition

A generation after most hookers had been laid up, Captain Johnnie Reeves was working his 36ft motor-sailer *Neta* around the Moutere estuary shifting cases of apples from estuary-edge packing sheds to Motueka for on-shipping. This resourceful old skipper had adapted with the times to find a niche which the steamers and surviving scows were unable to fulfil. With her shoal draft and adequate horsepower, Neta could work the tidal backwaters behind Rabbit Island, Jacket's Island and into the Riwaka estuary where there were still cargoes to be found – very much as present-day truck-owners now do.

Neta's crewman Howard Williams wrote to me about his own experiences aboard her. *"I was away on a trip with old John Reeves and we went to Sandy Bay to load 10 tons of potatoes, and every bag was handed aboard and put below. It was quite a job. They were brought to the vessel in drays. I think all the farmers in the area were there to help so as to beat the tide. There were two on the dray, two on deck and John and I in the hold stowing them. It took us almost 3 hours to load the 10 tons."*

Neta didn't have full headroom in the hold and Howard's simple account doesn't do full justice to the backbreaking work, much of it done in a stooped position. It was hard, but when she was afloat again and had made an offing there would have been respite and compensation in the relaxing chuckle of water, sunshine, sea birds and companionship on the voyage. For those few hours under-way her crew were kings. Neta endured. Jack Reeves rebuilt her in Motueka and she later went to Waikawa, then to Bluff for the Fiordland crayfishing. She was lost on a reef at Dusky Sound in 1974.

I had my experience of Neta as a boy when my brother Allen and I were co-opted by Captain Johnnie Reeves to assist him with a careening at Haulashore

Captain Johnny Reeves worked his shoal-draft ketch-rigged motor vessel **Neta** *as a trader through the shallow estuaries near Motueka and Riwaka until the 1930s.*
Hargreaves Collection: A43188285, Nelson Provincial Museum

Island. Allen had to row the dinghy from the boatshed on the port to the island, towing a couple of massive wooden blocks to sit *Neta* on when she was beached so that her bottom was accessible. Against the incoming spring tide this was a near-impossible task but he managed it. Captain Reeves was elderly and experienced enough to wear thigh waders while we had only bare legs, and we spent an interminable time in the water scraping the heavily encrusted bottom as the tide ebbed. Sea lice assaulted our legs and we made very sure we were never within 'volunteering' distance again. The Harbour Board's slipway was in operation by then, but habit dies hard, and facilities cost money which *Neta* probably was hard-put to come by.

Even though these smaller traders were now powered and no longer dependent on the wind, road services became more efficient and inevitably trucks took over the work.

Personal memories

Right up to the second half of the 20th century Nelson's Haven Road was still a haven for men who had spent a lifetime at sea, based in Blind Bay but ranging much further, and they still enjoyed a Sunday morning chat with one another on the waterfront.

As a child, many of my memories of the surviving hooker men in my family and neighbourhood linger as misty figures – older men, often with little to reveal the many seagoing challenges of their past livelihoods. Some like Sonny Tregidga and Percy Williams were still active as I grew older, and featured more significantly.

My uncle George Westrupp had retired in Wanganui, operating the time ball (at Durie Hill) as his brother-in-law had done before him. It was a fitting task for a mariner who had been surely reliant on time-pieces for tidal calculations to have served his final years on a device which allowed mariners to correct their chronometers, (as well as for the town's inhabitants to correct their household clocks). George did this task for twelve years and it was discontinued when he died in 1932. My grandfather Sam Westrupp retained his ticket after he retired, enabling him to occasionally take vessels where the current skipper's ticket was inadequate.

It is simply not possible to mention all the hooker sailors. Records are slight and inadequate, but these stories of the men and their vessels are representative of them all.

My memories are also of the decaying hulls scattered across the mudflats. I recall my older brother Allen taking me on a forbidden foray to visit the remains of *Maid of Italy* at low tide on the mudflat off Trafalgar Park. She was weathered and very decrepit, and I remember her counter stern, probably shaped with an adze on one side to take the planking, but left very much a tree surface on the other. I was also taken by her massive internal timbers and planking, which were very different from the more lightly-built launches with which I was more familiar. We were very young at the time and we endured our parents' wrath when our muddy legs gave us away.

Conclusion

In recent decades, historians have delved beneath the rose-tinted surface of the New Zealand Company's history and found out a great deal more than was available during my school days, about the triumphs and hardships of colonial immigrants. The hookers were very much a product of their times, and their heyday was quite brief, but vital. They were the necessary links and the prime movers of their time, stitching the settlement together to make possible what must have seemed at times impossible. Most of all they connected people with the sea. The story of Nelson is the story of seafarers, and of their womenfolk who were staunch participants in the pioneering lifestyle. They all came by sea.

The generations of old salts who ended their days by the sea front or up in Russell Street were the people in this story, and I have tried to give them their due according to Voltaire's dictum: *One owes respect to the living; but to the dead one owes nothing but the truth.*

Looking back on that time of Nelson's development, most of those who lived through it would acknowledge a satisfying life where much had been achieved in spite of the difficulties. Yet I doubt many would wish to relive the times. Respect and admiration for the hooker days, yes, and something to learn from them should we have a mind to – and a little nostalgia too.

Argus *gradually melted away on the Nelson mudflat. Her iron construction is discernible in deck beams and suggested by the fragment in the foreground, while her later sheathing in kauri shows at the stern.*

Hugh and G.K. Neill photograph, P1971-008/6-004, Hocken Collections Uare Taoka o Hākena, University of Otago

Te Aroha, *at Milnthorpe Wharf, Parapara when I visited as Manager there to check on her loading of bagged dolomite. Note how her spars are useful as derricks.*
Photo by Geoff Wood for author's collection

The Portland *also used her spars as derricks to load parcels of timber into her hold. This Westhaven Inlet wharf was fed by a tramline from the mill.*
Russ Ricketts photo, courtesy Kerry Miller

The Golden Bay poet and friend, the late Frank Soper, has graciously allowed me to finish with the evocative verses of his poem 'The Little Ships', the title poem in *The Little Ships, a Golden Bay anthology*.

The Little Ships

*I wish I'd seen the little ships
That used to pass this way
From Collingwood and Waitapu
Around to Tasman Bay*

*Their piles of ballast rock all lie
About the channel here.
And still above Waitapu wharf
The seagulls poise and veer;*

*And twice a day the tides come in
And twice run out to sea,
But never more the Morning Light
Or Maid of Italy;*

*And Huon Belle and Croydon Lass
Who flirted with the gales
And danced all night upon the waves
Have long since furled their sails.*

*So paint for me a picture of
The estuary at dawn,
With snow upon the mountain tops
And, on the water borne,*

*A little ship just moving out
Upon the morning tide
And listing from the valley wind
Along her starboard side.*

*And, as she dips into the swell,
I know that I shall see
The ghosts of all the little ships
Go sailing out to sea.*

FRANK SOPER

Matakana, *seen here romping downwind with her improvised squaresail, purveys the spirit of the hooker fleet which criss-crossed Blind Bay during six decades of early settlement.*
Courtesy Rob Williams

APPENDIX 1

Common 19th Century Rigs in Blind Bay Vessels

Several of the hookers changed their rigs during the course of their working lives. Newspaper reporters of the era added confusion to the matter through their apparent lack of knowledge of this subject. (Time and again we see cutters or ketches referred to as schooners, or vice versa, in their reports). This book draws from official registration records wherever possible for greatest accuracy.

Schooner:
Surprisingly common among the early smallish hookers (possibly due to the influence of American whalers), this rig has the tallest mast and mainsail closest to the stern. A smaller foresail on the shorter forward mast. Its windward performance was not great, but it sailed well with the wind on or abaft the beam, and its sails were small enough for easy handling.

Cutter:
The majority of 30ft to 36ft hookers soon transitioned to a simple low-aspect cutter rig with a single mast set about 30% aft of the stem, and with two headsails — a staysail set inboard and a jib set from the end of a fairly long bowsprit. Many carried a topmast capable of setting a gaff topsail above the mainsail in lighter airs. Its windward performance was considered superior to the schooner rig, and the cost of standing and running rigging was much less than a two-masted vessel.

Ketch:
For hookers over about 36ft, the ketch rig was often chosen in order to keep each sail to a manageable size for a two-man crew. With the taller mast forward of the smaller mizzen mast, the sail-power when beating to windward was better than the schooner, as the rig presented a taller surface in clear air. Gaff topsails were often set on a topmast in light to moderate conditions.

Topsail Schooner:
The larger trading vessels of the later C19 often carried this powerful down-wind rig. The pair of square topsails carried on three yards above the foremast created unhelpful windage when driving to windward, but were extraordinarily useful with wind on or abaft the beam. A topmast fidded above the main (aft) mast was capable of carrying a powerful gaff topsail.

Brig:
The smaller square-riggers of mid-century were often rigged with only two masts, both carrying a set of squaresails, and a spanker (mizzen sail) behind the aft mast. The early government coastal ships were often brigs.

Barque:
Large intercolonial square-riggers sailing in and out of New Zealand ports were generally three-masted barques, with the aft mast carrying a spanker and gaff topsail with no squaresails. The larger barques carried four masts.

APPENDIX 2

Conversion from Imperial to Metric

As the era discussed in this book was one which used imperial (British, not US) measurements, these have been retained despite being published in a principally metric era.

It is also important to note that a vessel's registered length was not the total length on deck, as it was measured on internal dimensions, generally from the inside of the stem to the forward side of the rudderpost (which would exclude any counter overhang). The registered tonnage was a complex formula relating to internal (cargo-carrying) volume, with little reflection of the vessel's displacement. Huge variations existed, depending on the whim of the surveyor, and in many cases the records provide a variety of widely differing tonnages for the same vessel. Note that, being a primarily maritime publication, the sea miles given in this book are all nautical miles. (There are 60 nm per degree of latitude.)

Accurate conversions are readily available online, but for the purposes of simplicity, the following tips should suffice:

LENGTHS

Note: 12 inches make a foot, and 3 feet make a yard.

Feet to metres	– divide by 3.2 (a foot is about 30cm)
Yards to metres	– treat as roughly similar as a rule of thumb (a yard is about 90cm)
Fathoms	– these are two yards or about 180cm
Cables	– technically a tenth of a nautical mile – often approximated as 200 yards
Inches to cm	– multiply by 2.5
Nautical miles to km	– multiply by 1.85 (nearly double)

WEIGHTS

Pounds to kilograms	– divide by 2.2
Tons to tonnes	– Treat these as roughly equal

VOLUME

Gallons to litres – multiply by 4.5

Pints to millilitres – multiply by 600

Note: *Two pints make a quart and eight pints make a gallon*

A cord of timber equates to 8 foot x 4 foot x 4 foot tightly stacked (3.6m²)

CURRENCY

Note: *This conversion is purely academic, as monetary value is best measured against cost of living and average wages (which varied immensely due to inflation over the decades). (In the 1860s a ship's engineer earned £10 per week.) The following simply translates the shift in terminology when New Zealand converted to decimal currency in 1967.*

An example can be seen in the Ricketts dinghy quote in chapter 18.

Pounds to dollars – divide by 2

Pennies to cents – roughly equivalent (10 cents replaced 12 pennies)

A sovereign was a coin with a value of a pound (£1)

A guinea had the value of a pound plus a shilling (21 shillings)

A ha'penny was half a penny, and a farthing was a quarter penny. (These were still commonly in use during my boyhood.)

A half-crown was two shillings and sixpence, written 2s 6d or 2/6

Ten bob was a common term for ten shillings

There were 12 pennies in a shilling and 20 shillings in a pound

These all may seem confusing to the modern reader but were perfectly understandable to my generation and even my children's.

APPENDIX 3

Relevant Maori Words

For overseas readers, the Maori words which crop up in this book will be unfamiliar, although most New Zealanders will be very used to seeing and hearing them.

The following loose translations may help readers who wish to dig a little deeper within the narrative.

Words relating to places:
Awa = river (eg Awaroa = long river, Awatere = fast river)
Maunga = mountain or significant high hill (eg Maungatapu = sacred mount)
Motu = island (often part of a name eg Rabbit Island: Moturoa = long island)
One = beach (pronounced *or-neh*) eg onekaka = beach of *kaka* (parrots)
Puke = hill (pronounced *pook-eh*) eg Pukehau = windy hill)
Wai = water (usually joined with an adjective (eg Waiiti = small waterway)
Whanga (or **wanga**) = harbour or sheltering bay (hence Wanganui = large harbour)

Words relating to people and culture
Hapu = a smallish subtribe within a tribe
Iwi = a larger tribal entity
Ngati = tribal grouping prefix (eg Ngati Toa = warrior people)
Ngai = southern dialect for Ngati (Ngai Tahu settled most land south of Nelson)
Rangatira = the elite members within Maori society
Pakeha = people of European descent (pale skinned)
Kainga = Maori unfortified settlement
Pa = fortified Maori defensive settlement
Whare = hut or small dwelling
Mere = a sophisticated stone weapon, used as a short sword or club.
Waka = canoe (waka taua = war canoe)

Note 1: **Te Rauparaha** and **Te Rangihaeata** were key Maori figures in 1830s/40s central New Zealand.

Note 2: **Wakatu** (the placename for Nelson Haven) has in recent times been also spelled as **Whakatu**. The five possible origins of these alternative names are discussed in detail in *theprow.org.nz*

*This pencil sketch of **Te Rauparaha** is one of several which show his distinctive moko (facial tattoo) and piercing gaze. It was drawn two years after the deadly encounter at Wairau, and his continued defiance shows on his face. Here he is posing in a cloak of feathers which immediately reveals his chiefly status.*

Sketched by Edward Abbott, 1845

APPENDIX 4

A Chronology of the Blind Bay Hookers

This appendix is a chronologically listed table of the majority of sailing coastal trade vessels that have been traced as serving Blind Bay and adjoining areas and which have Nelson connections. It excludes larger coastal vessels that did not work the small ports, except some which were well-known at Collingwood and Waitapu. Inevitably there were also vessels that were not recorded or whose records were lost. Vessels which appear in the text but were not 'hookers' in general usage of the term are not listed here.

Ruth Allan's *History of Port Nelson* (published 1954) has been a key reference, but that information has been extended by my subsequent research. I found original Nelson customs files of earliest registrations, licence and transfer documents at the Nelson Provincial Museum. Other government records have been lost, notably those destroyed in the Hope Gibbons building fire of 1953 (at which coincidentally I was a spectator). Information has been verified wherever possible (given the elapsed time and paucity of detail), and a number of errors have been encountered in secondary records and photographs. My comments are qualified accordingly.

Where available there are three figures after the vessel's tonnage. They are: **internal length** (from the inner part of the main stem to the fore part of the stern post); **breadth** (beam) and the **depth of the hold** (*not* the ship's *draught*). Precisely measured, they were intended both as a means of identification and for tonnage calculation. Tonnage in this case referred to internal volume, not of weight. Such measurement derived historically from the tuns of wine a medieval ship could carry, and indicates the cargo-carrying capacity of the vessels, *not* their *displacement*. Hence many large shallow draft vessels (with lesser hold depth) often had a similar registered tonnage to smaller vessels of deeper draught.

A significant number of vessels were clincher built (by my time the term had become 'clinker'). The very first, *Erin*, even had 'a woman figurehead', as recorded in the builders' and surveyor's certificates. This was certainly impressive for a vessel which began construction on a remote estuary before European colonisation in the Blind Bay area!

Some confusion may have occurred where more than one local vessel shared the same name (*Elizabeth* being a typical case), or where a vessel changed names (or rigs) during its working life. Scrolling through this chronology may help clarify such issues. For alphabetical listings please refer to the index.

1841 Deal Boats
The New Zealand Company expedition brought out these work-boats, a type built and used at Deal on the south-east coast of England (vessels possibly chosen by Captain Arthur Wakefield, being a practical sailor). They were open boats, yawl-rigged with lugsails and over twenty feet long to carry what they did. They functioned as the forerunners of the Blind Bay fleet, carrying people and supplies around the bays and tackling the seas outside at times too. One became the pilot/customs boat, but both dropped from sight after that.

1841 *Eliza*
Schooner, 11 tons, first entered Nelson (in ballast) as early as 6 November 1841 with Captain Ralph, thence probably to Motueka for a cargo of pigs and potatoes. Arrived Wellington 15 November, then back in Nelson (Captain Scanlon) with whale blubber in December. In Nelson again February 1842 (Captain Stenning) with general cargo, then she dropped from sight. An *Eliza* wrecked at Palliser Bay July 1845 was assumed to be a 35-ton ship of that name. Could it have been this one?

1842 *Erin*
Square-stern clincher schooner, 12 tons, 30ft.4in x 9ft.9in x 5ft.7in, with a 'woman figurehead'. Owners J Ralph of Aorere, shipbuilder, and Joseph Hoare of Nelson, licensed victualler. Built at the Aorere by Ralph (master of *Eliza*) and Ezra Blowers for the Bays trade. Daniel Sheridan master. Ralph was no longer alive in 1844 and ownership was transferred to Henry Brown, a Wellington butcher. *Erin* was lost 20 miles east of Cape Palliser on 22 April 1844, with Henry Brown as master. The helmsman was under the impression he was steering a course off-shore when she struck a rock and quickly broke up, but most of the cargo was saved.

1842 *Katherine Johnston*
Cutter, 10 tons, 31ft.5in x 9ft.5in x 4ft.4in, built in Sydney 1841 and made three Tasman crossings. In 1842 she was owned by Captains T B Taylor and W H Watt, traders out of Wanganui. She was driven ashore in Worser Bay, Wellington in March 1848 and extensively damaged, taking 9 months to repair. Re-registered at Wellington in 1849, she was driven ashore again coming out of Akitio near Castlepoint with a light breeze and heavy surf on 21 February 1856. For want of assistance she became a total loss.

1842 *Mana*
Probably the 21-ton 37 x 13.7 x 6 foot schooner built by Alexander and Thomas Fraser at Mana Island in 1841, master Thomas Barker. No record after 1847. An Auckland vessel of that name gets a passing reference in P A Eaddy's *Neath Swaying Spars*.

1842 *Mary Ann*
This modified ship's boat from *Fifeshire* and her captain, Frederick Moore, features throughout the early narrative. She fulfilled a hooker role at times. There is reference to her carrying window frames for a settler and also picking up an ill man. She would not have been *Fifeshire*'s only boat and the others would have

been in use too, but we have no record of them. (Various smaller vessels would be about, but the commonplace ones went unrecorded.)

1842 *Nelson Packet*
Square stern clincher schooner, 14-ton 34.7 x 11.3 x 5.3 foot, built on Te Awaiti beach, Cook Strait 1841, Captain James Jackson (James Jackson McKay on the registration). Based in Nelson for nearly a year from April 1842. Captain Arthur Wakefield's party used her in the visit to Massacre Bay in late 1842. In February 1843 Captain Jackson now married, returned to Te Awaiti and in mid 1844, under her new owner Captain Poppelwell, she foundered somewhere in the Cook Strait region. The crew eventually found their way back after being reported as drowned.

1842 *New Zealander*
Schooner, 16-ton 35.1 x 12.2 x 5.5 foot, built 1841 at Kakapo Bay by Captain John (Jack) Guard at the same time as *Nelson Packet* was being built. She is recorded as lost in Cloudy Bay in 1843, but the date is uncertain (Grady places it as 1844). She called at Nelson but was a regular trader between Cloudy Bay and Wellington, carrying both oil and produce. (Captain Guard then appeared on *Pickwick*.)

1842 *Nymph*
Schooner, 22-ton 42.5 x 13 x 7ft.3 in, built Kaipara 1840, registered in Auckland. She was lost, carried ashore by the current in light winds on (probably) Raglan bar December or January 1843. Owner George Birley, Auckland, master Captain Scanlon (mentioned on *Eliza*).

1842 *Pickwick*
Cutter, 38 tons, 39ft.3in x 14ft.8in x 8ft.9in, built at Port Sorell, Tasmania in 1838, registered by J Williams in Nelson April 1842 and purchased by Jack Guard August 1844. She was wrecked 29 June 1845 off Cape Palliser in a SW gale and Captain Guard (late of the *New Zealander*) and a boy were saved with great difficulty while two others were lost. A party of Maori, led by a European, plundered her of everything that could conveniently be carried away. A later report corrected the location from Cape Palliser to Castle Point.

1842 *Rory O'More*
Schooner, 22 tons, 41ft.5in x 12ft.9in x 6ft.1in, launched in 1841 and Auckland-owned. *Rory O'More* was the first vessel to be built at Great Barrier Island. In September 1842 she was wrecked at Palliser Bay carrying oil and whalebone, probably from Akaroa to Wellington. She was salvaged but lost again at Catherine Bay in October 1843 lightering manganese ore out to the *Tryphena*. Sank with 20 tons of ore on board.

1842 *Three Brothers*
Schooner, 33 tons, 45ft, built in Queen Charlotte Sound 1842 and registered in Wellington 1843. Owner J Thoms was married to a daughter of the chief Nohorua, and in 1843 *Three Brothers* carried Te Rauparaha, Te Rangihaeata and about a dozen armed warriors across Cook Strait to the Wairau. In 1844 she entered the

Buller River during a sealing voyage. She sank in Porirua Harbour in 1847 while in Maori ownership, and her registry was closed.

1843 *Carbon*
Square-stern carvel schooner, 12 tons, 33ft x 10ft.6in x 5ft.7in, built at Motupipi 1843 by J and B Lovell and William Andrews, owned by her builders and George Webster with John Bathe as master until 1845 when Nelson merchant Charles Empson took her over. She was the first little ship built at Motupupi and seems to have been in the general coastal trade. Lost 30 June 1850 sailing Wellington to Ahuriri, Napier, under Captain Lambert. A fore-and-aft schooner was seen tacking off the point at Castlepoint, but about midnight a gale blew from the southeast and the next morning wreckage was found near Tuirangi.

1843 *Enterprise*
Cutter, 9 tons, built at Nelson 1843 by George Edwards, Captain John Bathe master. Almost certainly owned by J S Cotterell, the surveyor killed at the Wairau. *Enterprise* was wrecked at Howlands Bay, Queen Charlotte Sound, on 30 March 1844 when she took shelter after beating about in Cook Strait for some time en route from Wellington to Nelson under Captain Sinclair. She was anchored 150 yards off but her chain cable parted and she went ashore.

1843 *Finetta*
Cutter, 10 tons, 29ft x 9ft.2in x 5ft, built at New Plymouth 1842 by the New Plymouth Company, registered Nelson 20 February 1843. (The New Plymouth Co looked at Blind Bay, turned it down for settlement and bought Taranaki land from the NZ Land Company with which it merged in April 1841 when its bank collapsed.) *Finetta* was owned by J B Wilkinson, Whangaroa, and skippered by Captain John Watson. She was wrecked at Cape Campbell May 1845 after being caught in a gale off Port Nicholson Heads and driven across Cook Strait.

1844 *Ann and Sarah*
Square stern clincher cutter with a running bowsprit 16-ton 34.1 x 11.9 x 5.8 foot, built 1844 by R A Allan, shipbuilder, at Motupipi (registered Nelson in July) and owned by Allan and W Sinclair until 1849, when Apera Pukenui's name appears. We know she was on the Taranaki coast between New Plymouth and Kawhia in mid-1845.

1844 *Hydrus*
Lugger, 11-ton 37 foot, built at Nelson by Thomas Graham Freeman, 1843, for W Claringbold. Registered January 1844. Traded out of Nelson until Claringbold took her to Auckland in June 1845, having previously sold her. Accused of feloniously running away with her, but after some months he was acquitted.

1844 *Lively*
Square-stern carvel cutter, 23 tons, 36ft.7in x 12ft.7in x 7ft, built Torbay, Western Australia, in 1839. Owned by general dealer George Charlton of Kawhia, she traded up the west coast of the North Island as far as the Manukau under Captain John Gill 1844–46. From 1845 she took Nelson beer to Auckland.

1844 *Mary*
Built by Askew brothers at Riwaka about 1844 to take firewood to Nelson, she capsized 4 miles outside the harbour. G (other records say J) Askew was drowned.

1844 *Moonraker*
Square-stern clincher cutter (or ketch according to the surveyor), 11 tons, 29ft.6in x 10ft x 5ft.2in, built by Henry Parnell and Ambrose Ricketts and launched by Saltwater Creek bridge, February 1844. Owned by Parnell, Ricketts and baker William Jennings, master William Sinclair, traded to Kawhia and North Island west coast ports. She last left Nelson 15 August 1846, ownership changed to Kawhia Maori.

1845 *Amelia*
Schooner, 9 tons, reportedly the second vessel built by Ambrose Ricketts, licensed by March 1845. Wrecked Worser Bay, Wellington, 13 August 1846.

1845 *Erena*
Square-stern clincher schooner, 12 tons, 34ft.9in x 10ft.8in x 5ft.7in, built at Motupipi 1845 by W Andrews for Tamati Pirimona Marino (Thomas Freeman), the Ngati Rarua chief at Aorere, and Samuel Strong. Last in Nelson June 1848, her registry was closed in December 1850. (Freeman is also noted in *Examiner* 12 November 1856 as owner of *Mio*, lost at Astrolabe 26 October 1856.)

1845 *Rovers Pride*
An extract from Customs Office, Port of Nelson, 17 March 1845 (in R Ricketts' scrapbook): "tonnage unknown, James Joss, Master, from the West Coast, with greenstone. Vessel has not yet received her register". Later, "...no further trace of this vessel". See also 1866: *Roving Bride*. Some records have confused the vessels.

1845 *Sarah Berry*
Ketch, square-stern clinker bottom with carvel topsides, 11 (or 18) tons, 32ft.4in x 10ft.6in x 5ft.1in, built 1845 by S Jacobsen for T R Berry. Registered February 1846, master Robert Porter. Driven ashore on the Whangaroa bar 27 June 1846 with two women, six children and ten men on board. Through the intervention of missionary Wallace, a number of Maori swam out to rescue the passengers. The vessel was considered a total loss but was salvaged and re-registered in Auckland 1848, last recorded at Nelson 1849.

1846 *Mary Ann*
Square-stern clincher schooner, 27 tons, 38ft.9in, built at Green Point, Nelson by owner William McKenzie, a ship's carpenter, in 1846. Wrecked in Tolaga Bay June 1847 when she was driven back while attempting to sail out of the river, but later salvaged. George Cooper master. Traded around Nelson until the 1860s, wrecked again Constant Bay November 1866. (Not to be confused with the 1842 *Mary Ann*).

1846 *Ocean Queen*
Square-stern clincher and carvel schooner, 16 tons, 37ft (builder's certificate says 42ft x 11ft.5in), built at d'Urville Island (Rangitoto) by co-owners J M McLaren,

who settled there 1836, and H Gates. *Ocean Queen* was about the Cook Strait area 1846–50. A small trawling schooner of that name owned by Eckford and Outram, Wellington, parted her cables and went ashore in Worser Bay 19 October 1884 to become a total loss, but the connection is unconfirmed.

1847 *Catherine*
Square-stern carvel schooner, 10 tons, 32ft x 9ft.1in x 4ft.8in, built by T G Freeman 1847 for G W Schroder and registered March that year for Bay and New Plymouth trade. Masters William Burdett (1847), Marion Kirby (1848), Henare (1849), John Duncan (1854). Owned by merchant William Schroeder until 1854, then Renata, Maka, Ruka and Pirimona. A vessel of that name bound from Lyttelton to the North Island under owner Captain J Taylor was lost some distance off Lyttelton in 1864. Known to be very shaky, she was overloaded with 21 tons of coal instead of 15 and her planks gave way. No direct connection established between the two vessels.

1847 *Emergency*
Square-stern carvel schooner, 26 (or 35) tons, 44ft.7in x 12ft.4in x 6ft.9in, built and owned by S Strong, master John Petrie. Timbers from the wreck of the *Fifeshire* were used in this vessel built for the coastal and Melbourne trade. Last reported on a Melbourne to Hobart run in July 1849, she was gone from the Nelson registry by 1854.

1847 *Emily*
Schooner, about 15 tons, master and owner B Phillips, probably built in Nelson 1847 and registered in Wellington. Wrecked Palliser Bay in a gale in June 1949 en route to Otago, three passengers and four crew drowned.

1847 *Karorina*
10-ton schooner, Mason master, at Nelson 1847. This is probably one of the vessels described as built for the Maori.

1847 *Lucinda*
Square-stern clincher schooner, 21 tons, 37ft x 12ft x 6ft.5in, built at Motupipi by B Lovell and W Andrews in 1847 for Hemi Kuka Matarua of Pakawau. She traded until 1852 then passed from sight, although still listed in 1854.

1847 *Old Jack*
Clincher schooner, 8 (or 10) tons, 36ft, built at Kakapo Bay, Port Underwood, in 1847 and licensed at Wellington 1848. Master John (Jack) Guard was co-owner with Robert Waitt and John Matthew Taylor of Wellington. She traded in Cook Strait, Nelson and the Wairau for at least 7 years (no record after that). Captain Guard died in 1857.

1847 *Supply*
Square-stern carvel ketch, later a cutter, with a running bowsprit, 15 tons, 33ft.7in x 11ft.3in x 5ft.8in, built and owned 1846 by S Strong, registered April 1847. Master James D Murphy and William Boyce. Earned the sobriquet *The Roaring Gimblet*. May have been altered and cutter-rigged in 1852 when storekeeper Thomas R

Berry owned her and John Sedcole was master. In 1853 Nelson merchant William R Nicholson was owner and Edward McNab master. From 1854 Captain John Walker was her master for some years. Well known in the coastal, Bays and West Coast trades, *Supply* ran a service to Collingwood in the 1860s. Wrecked inside Pencarrow Head, Wellington, on 6 December 1870 when her ground tackle parted in a strong NW gale and she was beached to save lives.

1848 *Elizabeth*
Square-stern carvel schooner, 10 tons, 33ft.6in x 9ft.1in x 4ft.1in, built at Nelson and registered June 1848 with owners T Askew, A Rankin and R McIsaac. Re-registered 1854 by W E Washbourn, master James Moore. Her fate is uncertain but a vessel of this name, described as a cutter, was working the Charleston run and wrecked in October 1868 after arriving off Hokitika from Charleston and suffering damage in a strong gale.

1848 *Old Man*
Schooner, 8 tons, registered by 1848, owned by J Maclaren and used mainly in the Sounds trade. In September 1870 William James Maclaren obtained a coasting trade licence for her. (Not to be confused with the Tasmanian ketch later trading out of Nelson.)

1848 *Triumph*
Square-stern clincher schooner with figurehead, 12 tons, 32ft.1in x 10ft.7in x 4ft.9in, built at Riwaka 1847 by Ambrose Ricketts for Captain H Fowler, registered January 1848. She was wrecked in the Wairau River mid-June 1849.

1848 *William and Horina*
Square-stern clincher schooner, 12 tons, 32ft, built 1848 by T G Freeman 1848 for master Arapata Te Ware and 14 other Maori owners. Last at Nelson April 1852.

1849 *Catherine Ann*
Cutter, 12 tons, 31ft.5in x 10ft.6in x 5ft, built at Wellington by Captain Salvator Cemino in 1848, bought by Captain Henry Fowler 1849. Damaged at Port Gore 22 August 1849 and wrecked at Lyttelton April 1850. Repaired and re-registered at Lyttelton, she was finally wrecked at Port Levy January 1856.

1849 *Maria Josephine*
Square-stern carvel sloop, 22 tons, 37ft.9in x 11ft.6in x 6ft.6in, built at Nelson 1849 by Siegmund Jacobsen for wine-dresser J Frank, master William Boyce. In the Wellington trade, wrecked in the harbour 11 June 1851 when her rudder became unshipped during a southeast gale.

1849 *Rapid*
Schooner, 15 tons, very shallow draft, built at Nelson 1849 by T G Freeman for the Wairau wool trade. Owned by merchant Charles Empson, then J Lukins 1862-65. She was lost 7 July 1867 out of West Wanganui, loaded with coal for Wanganui.

1849 *Rose*
15 tons, Captain Walker. At Nelson in 1849.

1850 Mary
Topsail schooner, 29 tons, 52ft.8in x 13ft.1in x 5ft.4in, built at Nelson by T G Freeman and registered August 1850 for merchant Charles Empson. Master, W Boyce. Owned by Thomas Askew from 1856; on the West Coast 1864. Wrecked while sheltering at Totaranui 26 July 1865 after getting into trouble off Cape Farewell, leaking seriously and with a broken boom. She missed stays and went ashore.

1850 William
At Nelson with Askew as master in 1850, no detail.

1850 Jubilee
(Circa) John Westrupp's first vessel, probably a cutter. No records remain for her (she was probably not formally registered) so she remains one of the near-forgotten small craft of Nelson's first decade. However a Westrupp tale survives of John taking his family a long way up the Moutere River aboard her to attend a boxing match, presumably in the 1850s, so she clearly was shoal drafted. There is a tenuous reference to her in Emily Host's book.

1851 Fairy
Schooner, 10 tons, 32ft.7in x 9ft.8in x 4ft.8in, built at Massacre Bay 1850, owned by Ezra Blowers and George Dougall. Owned and registered at Port Victoria (Lyttelton) by Christchurch Conveyance Co 1852–3, then other Lyttelton owners. The *Nelson Evening Mail* reported her trading to Onehunga and owned there by timber merchant E Gibbons in 1866, and she was at Constant Bay 1868.

1851 Flirt
Schooner, 10 tons, 33ft, built at Port Underwood 1849. At Nelson by 1851 and in coastal trade that year. She was still trading to Motueka in 1876, taking out cargoes of potatoes, and she worked Heathcote and Kaiapoi rivers so may have been Canterbury based.

1852 Necromancer
Schooner, 16 tons, irreverently known as 'Old Nick'. A well-known Bays trader owned by Thomas Askew who probably built her, registered 21 May 1852. Traded to the Buller in 1860s. Askew (then a storekeeper) was on the West Coast for a time and she may have been based there. Lost on Farewell Spit 14 May 1869 when she was run ashore heavily laden with West Wanganui coal and sinking.

1852 Seabird
Schooner, 15 tons, 43ft.3in x 12ft.4in x 4ft.9in, built at Nelson prior to 1852, re-registered Lyttelton 1859. Foundered Amuri Bluff 3 February 1868. This vessel, together with *Shepherdess* and *Alert*, was owned for some time by Sam Bowling (Marshlands) and Captain George Jackson (Robin Hood Bay), but was Lyttelton-owned when lost.

1853 Atalanta
Schooner, 10 tons, 36ft.3in x 10ft.5in x 3ft.5in, built in Nelson 1853 and owned by blacksmith John Watts. In the Bays until the 1860s.

1853 *Jessie*
Cutter, 12 tons, Captain Goddard, at Nelson 1853-55. Goddard was also the master on *Jackall*.

1853 *Mary*
Schooner, 14 tons, 36ft x 10ft.7in x 5ft.5in, built at Nelson 1853 for Hoeta, Paraone and Punupi Ohamaru.

1853 *Sisters*
Schooner, 13 tons, 40ft x 11ft x 4ft.1in, built Nelson 1853, sank near Awaroa Heads 25 October 1856 after sailing from Nelson with four cattle and general cargo. A bullock kicked or stamped hard enough to start a plank and she went down but was salvaged to trade on until the 1880s. On the Collingwood run for a time, she was owned in 1868 by Lukins (Nelson), John Charles (Motupipi) and others.

1855 *Alert*
Ketch, 15 tons, at Nelson 1855–56 (according to Allan). Captains Jackson and Shortt ran *Alert*, a schooner, at the Wairau after 1860 (according to Buick) with owners Beauchamp Suisted and Co. See *Alert* 1867: this vessel may be misdescribed. *Seabird* (foundered 1868) and *Shepherdess* (lost Constant Bay 1879) had the same owners in Wairau times. Another *Alert*, a 69ft schooner built in Whangaroa by Lane and Brown and based in Lyttelton, was lost at sea with all hands in 1897 after clearing Lyttelton for Waitapu.

1855 *Australian Maid*
Schooner, 17 tons, 42ft, built at Sydney and brought to Nelson by Dan Gilbertson March 1855. Well known in Wairau and Bays trade until wrecked at Croisilles 6 November 1886.

1855 *Mermaid*
Cutter (later a ketch), 9 (or 12) tons, 31ft x 9ft.6in x 3ft.6in, built 1855, in Nelson by 1870s. Bought from Antonia Rose by Robert McNabb and Peter Askew 22 October 1872, then owned by Adolphus Dodson (Riwaka) and Peter Askew. Was around until 11 May 1878 when, under Captain W Smith and loaded with limestone, her cable parted in a moderate gale and she stranded on North Tata Island, in the eastern corner of Golden Bay, to become a total wreck.

1856 *Ann*
Schooner or cutter, 15 tons, 33ft.7in x 11ft x 5ft.5in, owner and master Captain Eure, in the Bays trade 1856 until at least 1872. She ran very regularly to and from Waitapu. In 1875 Eure was master on *Midge*.

1856 *Gipsy*
Schooner, 17 tons, 44ft.7in x 13ft.6in x 5ft.4in, built at Nelson 1856. She traded widely and was the first vessel up the Opawa River, sustained the Buller settlement with supplies and was first to cross the Grey River bar, supporting an exploration and survey party. She was owned by Thomas Askew when she was wrecked on the

Grey River bar 19 September 1863 (Captain Jack McCann) after a protracted five week trip from Nelson because of bad weather. Surveyor Arthur Dudley Dobson and four assistants, two prospectors and her crew of four all got ashore.

1856 *Jackall*
10 tons, Captain Goddard, at Nelson 1856-57 (see also *Jessie*).

1856 *Mary Thomson*
Schooner, 49 tons, 61ft.3in x 17ft x 7ft.1in, built 1850 at Gleneagle, Scotland, by Robert Thomson. Registered in Auckland. At Nelson 1856 to 1860s and Washbourn mentions her at Collingwood. Wrecked 26 May 1874 at Omaha Bay, opposite Great Barrier Island, where she may have been working as a collier.

1856 *Pride of the Isles*
Fore-and-aft schooner, 28 tons, 60ft x 13ft.5in x 5ft.6in, built and owned 1856 by D Gilbertson with co-owners D Davidson, J Fraser, W Million. Traded Wairau, Bays and coast. Lost a few miles south of Raglan 22 July 1860; her four crew landed safely.

1857 *Augusta*
Schooner, 35 tons, at Nelson from 1857 until lost September 1865 at Melville Cove, Queen Charlotte Sound, 'during a fearful gale'.

1857 *Coquette*
Cutter, 26 tons, Captain Walker, recorded from 1857 until wreckage found at Banks Peninsula 22 March 1873. Damaged on a rock about a week earlier under owner and master Captain R de B Hawtrey, it was supposed that she leaked and foundered after inadequate repair work.

1857 *John and Matilda*
8 tons, Captain Brooks. At Nelson 1857 until the early 1860s.

1857 *Shepherdess*
Topsail schooner, 38 tons, 46ft.2in x 14ft.2in x 7ft.1in, built in Sydney 1842, owned Captains Jackson and Shortt. Worked the coasts and was the last vessel to enter Constant Bay, where she was lost under Captain John Bilby 16 September 1879 to heavy rollers breaking into the bay. Pilot Charles Craddock lost his life trying to help her. *Shepherdess* had at least two other major incidents, stranding on Barretts Reef out of Wellington in 1876, badly damaged at Kaikoura in May 1879. She worked the east coast for a number of years supplying stations and taking out the wool clip.

1857 *Thetis*
5 tons, owner and master Captain Elmslie. (Arthur Elmslie was a pre-1840s resident of Queen Charlotte Sound).

1857 *Water Fiend*
Cutter, 18 tons, Captain Pearce, at Nelson 1857.

1857 *Kate*
7 tons, Captain McNabb, in the Bays trade 1857. A schooner called *Kate* foundered after leaving Constant Bay 14 May 1875, having been badly damaged on the beach.

1857 *Sarah Elizabeth*
Schooner, 20 tons, Captain Heberley, at Nelson 1857–1861. Lost with a load of timber at the Whareama River, 10 miles south of Castlepoint, when the wind failed as she crossed the bar.

1857 *Three Brothers*
Cutter, 12 tons, 31ft.2in x 7ft x 3ft.6in, Captain John Westrupp, recorded from 1857. Licensed to owner John Edward (Jack) Westrupp, son of Captain John, from 17 April 1872. Well known in Bays trade and on Motueka and Collingwood gold rush runs, she was lost on the Nelson boulder bank 12 March 1881. (Reed offers an incorrect date and origin for this vessel.)

1857 *Wave*
Yacht/cutter, Captain Porter 1857. In Bays trade.

1858 *Auckland*
Cutter, 19 tons, Captain Porter, at Nelson 1858 to 1860s. Wrecked Godley Head 1863.

1858 *Esther*
Schooner, 7 tons, Captain Liddell. At Nelson from 1858, wrecked near Manawatu River 12 February 1866, four men lost.

1858 *Hope*
Barge, 20 tons, Captain Charles, used as a tender to the steamer *Tasmanian Maid* on the Wairau and Opawa rivers. At Nelson 1858–62, wrecked Jackson Head June 1862 on passage to Nelson with a cargo of wheat. Later at Constant Bay so she must have been salvaged.

1858 *Spray*
6 tons, Captain Hitchcock, at Nelson 1858 to 1860s.

1858 *Woodquest*
Cutter, later ketch, 12 tons, 40ft, built at Riwaka 1858, wrecked at Westport December 1870 but salvaged and later registered in Auckland as *Rose* (possibly still Westport-owned).

1860 *City of Nelson*
Schooner, 29 tons, 54ft.5in x 14ft.7in x 6ft.1in, built at Nelson 1860, owner and master Captain William Hooker. Advertised 1862 as freight and passenger service to the Buller River for the West Coast goldfields. She left Nelson for Wanganui in March 1867 but never arrived.

1860 *George Lorimer*
Schooner, at Nelson from 1860, Captain Sanderson.

1860 *Harriet*
Cutter, 15 tons, Captain Callaghan, in Nelson 1860–1870s.

1860 *Jane*
19 tons, 44ft.3in x 12ft.6in x 5ft.7in, described as a galliot (a small Dutch trading vessel, the hull built in barge fashion with a bluff rounded bow, fore-and-aft rigged on a single mast, often with a sprit). Also reported as a schooner. Built in Nelson 1860, owner J J H Jacobsen until 1863, John Charles and James Lovell 1863–1867/8, then B Franzen. Traded Bays and Havelock, regularly to the Buller before and during the gold rush. Wrecked 18 April 1871 at Kempe Point, 5 miles west of Jackson Head, Cook Strait, under Captain W Watts. Owing to a fresh south-easterly and heavy sea she was unable to weather the point. (If she were truly of galliot style, this is unsurprising in those waters.)

1860 *Mist*
5-ton, Captain Liddell, at Nelson from 1860.

1861 *Diana*
Ketch, 30 tons, Captain Smith, at Nelson 1861–69. She accidentally caught fire at West Wanganui Inlet 15 October 1869, under Captain Henry Hamilton, and was totally destroyed.

1861 *Grace Darling*
Schooner, 15 tons, 42ft.9in x 13ft.6in x 5ft.3in, built at Wahapu 1855 by W Brown and described as a cutter, owned by mariners Joseph Cousens and John Trigger of New Plymouth, registered in Nelson 25 March 1861. She was lost in the early hours of 1 June 1865 when leaving Nelson for Motueka with six passengers. With a heavy swell running she struck rocks in the Haven entrance; one side was stove in and considerable noise from the passengers alerted the pilot boat which successfully effected a hazardous rescue.

1861 *Mosquito*
Cutter, 23 tons, Captain Scott, at Nelson from 1861.

1861 *Oddfellow*
Cutter, 15 tons, Captain Dellow, at Nelson from 1861.

1861 *Onward*
Schooner, 17 tons, Captain Barbour, at Nelson from 1861. A schooner of this name, in the timber trade, was lost 24 July 1865 on the Shoe and Slipper Islands, Bay of Plenty, and the crew rescued after four days. No connection established.

1861 *Petrel*
12-tons, at Nelson from 1861.

1861 *Unity*
Cutter, 15 tons, at Nelson from 1861. Provided Collingwood service with *Venture*. William Akersten was agent and as he also owned vessels he may have owned this one (and perhaps *Eliza*, on the Waitapu run).

1862 *Emerald Isle*
Schooner, 28 tons, 51ft.3in x 15ft.6in x 6ft.2in, built 1854 in Mercury Bay by William Oakes (or Henry Lloyd), owned by S A Leech. Traded to Nelson from 1862, repaired after wrecking at Port Underwood 1865. Owned in Westport 1867 by merchant Robert Alcoil, capsized after leaving Constant Bay August 1867 under Captain Abe, four drowned.

1862 *Nautilus*
Topsail schooner, 31 tons, 51ft.7in x 17ft x 6ft.5in, built at Riwaka 1862 for J Greenwood and R Harrison for the timber trade. First wrecked September 1863 at Palliser Bay, recovered and partially wrecked again May 1865 at Greymouth. Finally lost Manawatu Heads 6 January 1869 under Captain S Bolt (owner Captain Robert Thompson). No warning was flown at the bar, but the flag was run up when she was only 300 metres off and committed to entering.

1863 *Clara*
Schooner, at Nelson from 1863. Sold by William Askew to butcher Francis Trask 20 August 1872.

1863 *Polly*
Cutter, 10 tons, 33ft x 9ft x 5ft.8in, owner and master Maclaren. At Nelson 1863–70, owned in 1867 by Benjamin Lovell, Fredrick Jones and John Kidson 1867. Owned 23 March 1872 by Thomas Shenton Woolf and John Mortimer, who bought her from Benjamin Lovell Jnr for £10 'including firewood'. The record notes 'vessel burnt at Sandy Bay'.

1864 *Venture*
Cutter, 15 tons, 37ft, built 1864 in Auckland by Thwaites, Henderson and Co for T Windover. Worked coast and Blind Bay, carried timber from Havelock and, with *Unity*, provided a Collingwood service. Struck Cape Campbell reef 10 August 1872, sailing from Wellington to Kaiapoi in thick and rough weather, and beached at Flaxbourne but had to be abandoned.

1865 *Thames*
Cutter, 17 (or 23) tons, 43 (or 54)ft, built Coromandel 1859. Owned by Captain John Garnes of Pelorus Sound. Re-registered *Nelson* as a ketch 1882 and wrecked North Head, Port Underwood, 27 June 1886.

1866 *Edith*
15 tons, Captain Cromarty, at Nelson 1866.

1866 *Midge*
Cutter, 16.57 tons, 41ft x 13ft.1in x 5ft.6in, built 1854 at Mechanics Bay by Henry Niccol. Bought by J Lukins (registered owner 1870–73) for the Bays trade 1866, and she ran a Collingwood service in conjunction with *Sisters*. In March 1867 both master (Captain Duncan) and mate drowned when they had an altercation and both fell overboard in heavy weather, leaving the lone crewman to sail her in to Patea. Was on the Waitapu run (Captain Eure, *Ann*) 1875, also recorded in Motueka 1878, and with owner and master Charles Maclean 20 April 1886. She

stranded on Haulashore Island 6 February 1887 through the master's failure to keep the leading lights in line, and became a total loss.

1866 *Pearl*
Ketch-rigged square-stern carvel 'barge', 33.59 tons, 49ft.5in x 15ft.8in x 5ft, built 1864 in Port Cygnet, Tasmania, by Alex Kerr. The *Nelson Evening Mail* March 3rd, 1866 noted her arrival from Hobart Town. On the West Coast, Sounds and Bays trade from 1866. Owned by R G Gibbons of Gisborne 21 April 1871 and Joseph Kennedy, Gisborne, 8 March 1878, master William Andrews. Wrecked on Arrow Rock, Nelson, 22 May 1874 and again at Long Point, Hawke Bay in a strong gale, 8 June 1879, when she parted one of her cables and went ashore. Captain Henry Hardwick.

1866 *Constant*
Ketch, 14 tons, very shoal draft (only 4ft 6in loaded). Built in Tasmania by Bennett and first registered at Hobart in 1862. Bought by Westport entrepreneur Reuben Waite under captaincy of Charles Bonner. In 1866 she was the first to enter Constant Bay. Constant worked the coast for four years before she was wrecked on the Grey River bar on 24 August 1870. Crewmen Peter Shields and James Kern were drowned but her master and part owner John Pascoe survived.

1866 *Roving Bride*
Cutter, 10 tons, reportedly built by Ambrose Ricketts, noted at Nelson from 1866 with Ricketts as master. She regularly shipped limestone from the Tata Islands, to Lukin's kiln in Nelson. F W Flowerday sold her 5 September 1871 to W Turner (Customs Department transfer). Flowerday was the Torrent Bay builder of *Wanderer* (1871) and *Kestrel* (1872).

1866 *Three Friends*
13-tons, Captain Welch, at Nelson 1866.

1866 *Eliza*
Cutter, 12 tons, Captain Wakely, at Nelson from 1866 when 'the fast sailing cutter *Eliza*' offered a service to Waitapu. Her agent was William Akersten who may also have owned her. See also *Unity*.

1867 *Alert*
Ketch-rigged 'barge', 40.91 tons, 64ft x 15ft.8in x 5ft.2in, built 1856 at Peppermint Bay, Tasmania, by James Norris and registered at Lyttelton in 1863. Owned by Beauchamp, Suisted & Co when she was trading between Pelorus Sound and Lyttelton, then registered in Nelson 1867 with J Watkins as owner. Arthur Smith was a seaman on her about 1871 under Captain George Smith, and when he left her she was carrying railway iron from Wellington to Foxton. In the coastal trade until 1875 and owned by Wanganui auctioneer A Beauchamp when she was wrecked on the Patea bar, master C H Smith. See *Alert* 1855, which may be this vessel wrongly described.

1867 *Emily*
Ketch, 17 tons, 45ft x 13ft.2in x 4ft.8in, built 1867 at Riwaka by James Stewart

(Reed says Peter Askew) for H and C Harwood. Under Captain J F McNabb she traded between Riwaka and Nelson and would load potatoes and other produce on the 'Stony Road' and from beaches by poling to the bank and using a horse and dray. She was owned and captained by Henry Hamilton (see Diana) when she sailed from Collingwood 18 August 1875 and was never seen again. (Some confusion attaches; Reed says she was laid up on the Riwaka mudflat, but her loss at sea seems conclusive.)

1867 *Heathcote*
Schooner, 21 tons, 42ft.2in x 14ft.8in x 5ft.7in, built January 1867 at Heathcote, Canterbury. In the Bays and West Coast (Constant Bay) trade; wrecked in heavy southeast weather when she dragged her anchors and stranded on the south head of West Wanganui Inlet, 20 February 1872, under owner and master James Moore.

1867 *Old Jack (II)*
Cutter, 10 tons, built 1867 of kauri in Kakapo Bay, Port Underwood, by McPhail and Budge for John and Edward Guard. Re-measured in June 1912 after an engine fitted, renamed *Kyra* by Tim Dakin of Port Underwood, later owned by Jim Thompson of Westport as *Marilyn*. She was still fishing (re-powered and re-framed) out of Westport a century later, laid up in 1967.

1867 *Waiotahi*
Schooner, 16 tons, 42ft, built 1853 at Opotiki, registered 1867 and laid up on the Nelson mudflats by 1900. She traded between Nelson and the Sounds under Captain George Robinson, whose three sons were also at sea and shipped with him at times. In the mid-1860s she carried timber from Havelock.

1868 *Collingwood*
Ketch, 15 tons, 45ft.9in x 11ft.7in x 3ft.8in, built in Nelson 1868 for ship chandler William Akersten, used in the Sounds and Wairau trade. Francis Gillard was master when she became a total wreck on the Waimea Sands, 24 August 1874. She was anchored off, on the ebb tide, when she parted her cable and her crew of two survived in the rigging for seven hours before being rescued by the pilot boat.

1868 *Cosette*
Cutter, 8 tons, at Nelson in 1867, master William Hadfield, with firewood from Awaroa. William Hadfield sold her to Morris Levy 7 May 1875.

1868 *Planet*
Cutter, 12 tons (probably greater), 47ft x 11ft.9in x 4ft.6in, built 1859 at Devonport by George Beddoes (his first vessel) and working in the Bay of Islands-Auckland area into the 1860s. Licensed 2 February 1867 by Charles Wise of Motueka and 1876 by Mary Wise, in service between Motueka and Nelson. She continued in this service for years, regularly maintaining the mail, passenger and cargo run with the steamer *Lady Barkly*. About 1900 she carried timber from Mace and Holland's mill, Okiwi Bay, when she was trading between Nelson, Croisilles and the Sounds under Captain Jack Johnson. Other masters included Westrupp (1896) and Harry

Johnson. *Planet* was at Riwaka in the 1900s and Reed reports elderly Neil Swanson owned and lived on her when she was laid up on Haulashore Island, Nelson, about 1909, intending alterations but could not afford them.

1868 *Sea Breeze*
Ketch, at Nelson from 1868. Burchard Franzen owner on 21 October 1870.

1869 *Mavis*
(Circa) Ketch, 12 tons. *Faris* mentions *Mavis* losing her rudder and being severely bumped on the Constant Bay beach 3 August 1869. A vessel of the same name (used by Captain Arthur Smith in the timber trade between Motueka and Marahau about the end of the 19th century) was very decrepit and was laid up on the Moutere mudflat.

1869 *Prospect*
Round-stern ketch, 21 tons, 52ft x 15ft.2in x 4ft.7in, built 1869 by R B Scott at Nelson for J S Cross jnr and J C Burford, who owned her 3 April 1882. On 7 February 1870 R B Scott was appointed master by the Waimea Road Board and licensed within Blind Bay. She traded around the Bay ports with regular visits to Motueka under Captains Henry Brown and John Westrupp (Arthur Smith served with Westrupp on Prospect for a year and remarked that he was a good captain). Under Captain Westrupp she was headed for Astrolabe oyster dredging on 14 May 1884 when a hard nor'easter blew up. She sought shelter, missed stays and stranded on the north end of Fisherman Island where she broke up. The crew was picked up the next day and the reef became known as Prospect Reef.

1870 *Waihopai*
43 tons, 64ft, built in Invercargill 1867 and entered the Bays and Sounds trade 1870. Owned by J S Cross Jnr, master Peter Curron. Lost beating into Wellington 10 November 1877 in a gale with a cargo of timber from Pelorus. Ingram reports she was originally a twin-screw wooden steamer.

1871 *Modest Boy*
(Circa) Half-decked cutter, 8 tons, the Huffam family's 'maid of all work' and reportedly built by them. Licensed 1877 with Timothy Huffam as owner.

1871 *Wanderer*
Schooner, 31 tons, 52ft.2in x 14ft.2in x 6ft.8in, later altered to ketch, built by owner F W Flowerday at Nelson (possibly Torrent Bay) in 1871. Stranded 27 August 1873 at Caroline Bay, Timaru, having too little cable for an open roadstead and unable to beat out. She became a total wreck a fortnight later.

1872 *Kestrel*
Ketch, 20 tons, 45ft, built 1872 by F W Flowerday for Bays, Sounds and Lyttelton trade. Reported to have been an early 'wheat vessel', conveying wheat probably for Manoy's flour mill at Motueka. First wrecked Port Underwood 10 September 1873 in a southeast gale under Captain F Mellor but salvaged. On 20 July 1883 she missed stays and stranded on the Lyttelton breakwater under Captain James

Cowan. Repaired, she was taken across to Diamond Bay to ballast but left with no-one aboard and insufficient cable. She lifted her anchor, went ashore and broke up.

1872 *XXX*
Ketch owned by Dodson, Fell & Co, merchants, at Wairau 1872–76.

1873 *Dart*
Cutter, square-stern, carvel planked, 15 tons, 41ft.2in x 13ft.2in x 5ft.4in, built 1859 by Robert Howie at Waiheke Island, entered Bays and Havelock trade in 1873. Painter T R Louisson sold her to farmers Robert and James Parker of Stoke 22 November 1880 and she was broken up at Bulwer Town, Pelorus, in 1896.

1873 *Dido*
(Circa) Cutter, 35.64 tons, 53ft.7in x 17ft.5in x 6ft.2in, owned by merchants Dodson, Fell & Co and working the Wairau. Lengthened to 74ft in Nelson, February 1879 (Ingram records her as 58 tons, 74ft x 18ft.2in x 6ft.3in). Owned by Nelson merchant Robert Levien when she was lost in Palliser Bay June 1881 in a Cook Strait gale while sailing from Lyttelton to Waitapu, her crew of five drowned.

1873 *Falcon*
Ketch, 66ft.5in x 17ft x 5ft.4in, built as a 37-ton schooner at Hobart Town in 1865; another Wairau vessel owned first by Captain Milo then Chas Redwood (master John Morrison) until 1873. Merchants Dodson, Fell & Co owned her until 1878. A schooner *Falcon* trading to Patea from the Sounds, owned by Kaiapoi merchants F Robins and H J Day and skippered by former owner Captain Peter Greig Leslie, was lost 26 February 1884. She struck the breakwater sailing out from Patea and the crew all jumped ashore to make her fast but the tide slewed her and she sailed merrily off on her own out to sea. Wreckage was later recovered.

1874 *Dauntless*
Cutter, 12 (or 17) tons, 37 (or 40)ft x 11ft.3in x 4ft.3in, built at Riwaka 1874 by J Ricketts for T Woolf and J Mortimer, master Thomas Shenton Woolf. Later owned by B Franzen, she frequently worked Motueka 1876-79 under Captain Robert Westrupp. Registry closed June 1900 when she was lying a wreck near French Pass.

1874 *Ruby* (Aka *Lily of the Wave*)
Ketch, 10 tons, 37ft.5in x 9ft.6in x 3ft.4in, Thomas Askew owner. Transferred from M Askew to Robert Mackay 9 March 1876 for £40. A note in the customs file September 1876 says 'now the *Lily of the Wave*', a vessel recorded the same year with Ricketts as master. Reed mentions Jack and Bill Reed fishing with her at the Croisilles. She had a well in which fish could be held alive, thus lengthening the time she could stay out. *Lily of the Wave* was wrecked on Arrow Rock 11 May 1878 after she was left anchored with no one aboard, master Hone Raniera (a transliteration of John Daniel).

1876 *Goldseeker*
Cutter, reportedly built by J J Ricketts at Nelson, trading to Motueka by 1876. She

foundered July 1889 at Walker's Bay, Croisilles, in a night-time squall and one man swam ashore but there was no trace of the other. Reed said Captain Charles Frost traded Nelson to Croisilles with her 'for a very long time'.

1876 *Maid of Italy*
Cutter, 14 tons, built at Auckland and traded at Thames before being brought to Nelson about 1876 by Captain Ponsonby, who reportedly then taught at Riwaka School (Murray). Coastal licence issued 29 February 1876 to the Riwaka & Nelson Navigation Company (B McMahon, C P Pattie, J Infield, E A Mackenzie). Captain Sam Clark took over the ship for many years and later R G (Dick) Tregidga of Torrent Bay was owner and master (Russ Ricketts served under him). Captain Tregidga's two sons were also masters and there were a number of others over the years. By March 1920 *Maid of Italy* was owned by James (Brimbo) Westrupp, son of George Westrupp. She was re-measured and described as a launch after an engine was installed and was still working Collingwood in April 1925, finally dismantled on Nelson mudflat in the 1920s after 50 years of service.

1876 *May*
Schooner, round-stern, carvel, 17 tons, 40ft x 12ft.6in x 5ft.5in, built 1876 by owner and master W H Glover at Frenchman's Bay. Glover was drowned off her in Tasman Bay May 1877, and Burchard Franzen, who held a mortgage for £171 over her when she was built, owned her 29 October 1877 with George Brett as master. Waikawa contractor John Hippolite owned her in 1884, O H Hope in March 1888. In 1891 she was wrecked in Admiralty Bay, parting her cable and driven ashore by a northwest gale.

1876 *Standard*
Ketch, 10 tons, worked Constant Bay and later at Nelson. Purchased from William Rawlings (Greymouth merchant?) by J C Burford on 28 May 1873 for £50. Masters included Turner, Westrupp and Ricketts (1881).

1876 *Uno*
Schooner, 28 tons, 61ft, built and owned by foundry owner J C Moutray in 1876 for the West Coast and Bays trade. Built of iron, she was broken up by 1893.

1878 *Lily of the Wave*
See 1874, *Ruby*, and 1878, *Wave* (*Lily of the Wave* seems to have been confused with her.)

1878 *Phoenix* (Aka *Ida*)
Cutter, 11 tons, originally a ship's boat built about 1843 and subsequently lengthened and raised (Allan: *Port*). Mentioned at Nelson by 1878 with Captain Westrupp; John and probably each of his sons took her to sea at various times and John Westrupp also used her dredging oysters; they may have owned her. Renamed *Ida* shortly before the steamer *Charles Edward* ran her down by Gilbertson's wharf, near the Haven entrance, at night on 11 March 1891. She sank and Captain Cockram Westrupp was drowned but the vessel was raised a few days later, but deemed a write-off.

1878 *Wave*
Cutter, 10 tons, reportedly built by J J Ricketts at Freeman's Bay and his first larger vessel. Owners December 1878 were John and Frank Ricketts with Captain Ricketts as master. George Williams was master in 1888.

1879 *Camellia*
Ketch, square-stern, carvel, with a scroll head to her stem, 20.4 tons, 48ft x 14ft.3in x 5ft.6in, built at Motupipi 1879 by A Wahlstrom for owner and master Captain Henry Young. A handsome vessel, she traded Motupipi, Waitapu, Motueka, and Nelson, laid up opposite the gasworks on the Nelson mudflats 1909.

1880 *Argus*
Schooner (later ketch), 36 tons, 61ft x 15ft x 5ft, built of iron in Melbourne 1854 and written off as a wreck in Lyttelton, where she had been used as a water tender, in 1871. J C Burford owned her 6 June 1879 and she was repaired and brought to Nelson the following year as a coal trader, co-owned with salesman Oliver Field. Arthur Smith served on her under Captain Frank Williams. Altered to ketch in 1891, sheathed with kauri in 1901 by J J Ricketts when Alf Wahlstrom owned her, traded under Captain Sam Westrupp from around 1896 to 1907 working Ferntown with Elizabeth for coal, then Riwaka and Nelson with timber. Owned by Usher and Green 1907, laid up on Nelson mudflats 1922. Her remains can still be seen off Queen Elizabeth Drive.

1881 *Pet*
Schooner (later ketch), 21 tons, 49ft.3in x 13ft.3in x 5ft, built on Haulashore Island 1881 by D G Gilbertson & Sons. Owned by David Gilbertson (who died 21 November 1890), J G Trevor 1893, F G Mace and J Holland 1895, Ambrose Ricketts 1895–1897, H W Johnson 1904, and various other Motueka owners. Altered to a ketch at some point, wrecked 10 October 1907 under Captain D Bonner in Cannibal Cove, Queen Charlotte Sound, when her steering gear carried away.

1882 *Mersey*
Cutter, 17 tons, 40ft.7in x 13ft.7in x 5ft.8in, built 1877 by Thomas Sharp in Onehunga, registered in Nelson 1882. Owners included Frederick Flan, timber merchants H & T Baigent (1881-83), teacher F E Bisley and Motueka auctioneer J S Edelsten until 1885, Motueka Shipping Co. Owned in 1888 by Thomas Carter of Motueka who was probably the master. Reed mentions Captain Harry Williams as owner and master in the Nelson-Croisilles-d'Urville Island trade 'for a long period' and George Williams was master for a few months in 1892. Wrecked at 'Warramanga' (i.e. Wharawharangi) just west of Separation Point 16th June 1893.

1883 *Comet*
Ketch, 22.45 tons, 48ft.8in x 14ft.9in x 5ft, built 1883 on the south shore of the lagoon at Torrent Bay by J J Ricketts, owned by J J, F and C A Ricketts. She had a yard on the foremast with a squaresail for running with the wind. At one time G H Reeves was owner/master, in 1896 W Caldwell in Collingwood owned her. She was sold to Lyttelton and returned to Nelson when George Williams bought

her in 1911. His son P C Williams served on her until 1915, and was later master, although George Williams was master in 1916. Engine fitted 1920 when she was altered to a cutter and worked the Bays and Lyttelton trade, broken up at Bluff in 1941.

1884 *Elizabeth*
Ketch, carvel 'barge', 33.07 tons, 62ft.8in x 17ft.9in x 4ft.6in, a typical Tasmanian ketch with a round stern, built 1866 on the Huon River, Tasmania. Registered in Wellington in 1869 and in Nelson 1884, owned by wood and coal merchant J C Burford, then on 26 July 1884 by Wellington widow and hotelkeeper Barbara Thompson. Stranded at Parapara 1886 under Captain John Edward Westrupp, worked the Ferntown coal trade. Total loss just south of West Wanganui Inlet 29 September 1891 under Captain Robert Porter Westrupp, owner J C Burford. The wind dropped as she was on the bar, carrying a flaxmilling plant being shifted from Ferntown, and her crew of three landed safely and stripped most of the gear off.

1885 *Felicity*
Ketch, 24 (or 27) tons, 49ft.8in x 15ft.5in x 4ft.7in, built 1885 by owner H M Burnard at Frenchman's Bay for the Bays trade, especially coal from Puponga. Laid up at Motueka for two years. Captain George Williams was owner and master from 1901, and had a centreboard fitted to her. Lost when she missed stays off Pencarrow (near Wellington Heads) 11th September 1910 under master John Anderson, who had bought her from George Williams a few months earlier. He had turned back because of a northwest gale and confused seas en route to the Sounds and Havelock to load timber.

1885 *Gannet*
(Circa) Cutter, 17 tons, 52ft x 14ft.2in x 4ft.9in, built and registered in Auckland 1881. Came to Nelson with owner Captain R Goldie, re-measured at 25 tons 4 July 1907 after she was lengthened and converted to a ketch by J J Ricketts. Owned by Capt R G Tregidga 1912–18, wrecked 28 April 1918. She had been laid up through lack of work and Captain William Reed borrowed her to pick up a load of pie melons. He put her ashore at Ngaio Bay to load when a strong northerly came up, drove her further up the beach, and wrecked her. (Russ Ricketts said there was much activity afterwards by local farmers gathering melons at the beach).

1885 *Transit*
Ketch, round-stern, 21 tons, 49ft.2in x 14ft.1in x 11ft.6in, built Marahau by J J Ricketts for the Bays trade. Her timber came from Tom Drummond's sawmill. Launched 30 October 1885, the day of a total eclipse of the sun. Owned by J J, F and C A Ricketts, she was in service about 35 years. Command shared in early years by Frank and Charlie Ricketts, Gus Burnard master about 1906. Made regular visits to Marahau to load timber at a jetty about 40 metres below the concrete bridge. Laid up on Nelson mudflats and later Russ Ricketts broke her up at the gasworks wharf.

1886 *Champion*
Ketch, square-stern, carvel, 27.16 tons, 49ft.6in x 15ft.8in x 6ft.5in, built at

Admiralty Bay 1886 by Edmond Hammond, owned by William Turner, Edmond and William Hammond, then William Robinson 25 October 1886. In Bays and Sounds trade and later owned by B Franzen until his death. At one stage she was pierced by her anchor after settling on it when grounding out between tides, and filled with water. Broken up or wrecked in Pelorus Sound and subsequently washed out to sea by April 1904.

1888 *Result*
(Circa) Ketch, (originally a paddle steamer registered as a schooner), 21 tons, 59ft.8in x 12ft.7in x 4ft.5in, long and narrow, built in Auckland 1872 by Lewis and Brown, registered to Captain John Samuel Riley of Westport until 1908. (Riley and Seaton also owned the steamer *Nile* from 1887, fitted with the engine and paddles from *Result*.) Both traded to the Nile River north of Charleston, *Result* to Charleston and no doubt elsewhere on the Coast. Superceded by road access to Charleston, *Result* lay for some years in the Buller lagoon then was converted into a 23-ton ketch and in Nelson from about the 1890s. Owned by Captain Samuel Westrupp 1908 to 1917, traded in the Bays and called regularly at Riwaka. She struck a rock (now Result Rock) in Torrent Bay under Captain Thomas Reeves and sank with a load of coal 5 December 1917.

1889 *Anatuero*
Cutter, 10 tons, built between 1887 and 1889 at Otuwhero Bridge, Sandy Bay, by J J Ricketts for John Woolf, timber supplied by Tom Drummond from his Marahau mill. Charles Gabrielsen was master for a number of years, and young Ted Reed started his sea career on her as a twelve year-old boy. Traded Nelson-Motueka-Riwaka-Marahau prior to 1900 and Ted Reed later ran her for several seasons in the oyster trade, as did Captain Raymond Taylor. Her last owners were Robertsons of Wainui Bay where she carried timber and was finally laid up.

1893 *Calyx*
Ketch, clinker, double-ended, 16 tons. Traded in the Bays and Croisilles. First noted at Motueka 1893 when Arthur Manuel Smith owned her and George Williams was master until mid 1894. In March 1895 W Caldwell was running her between Collingwood and other bays. Arthur Smith bought her semi-derelict, lying at Frenchman's Bay, for £15 and traded with her for a long period' before she came to rest on the Moutere mudflat. (Murray suggests she was sold to Maori at Okiwa Bay and laid up there.)

1895 *Turanga*
Cutter, 12 tons, built in Auckland. At Nelson by 1895 under Captain R G Tregidga and was a frequent caller at Riwaka. Reed reported she was also used for fishing under Captain John Reed who skippered her in the Croisilles-Nelson firewood trade. Loss unclear; may have been confused with a 28-ton auxiliary schooner of the same name wrecked on the Mokau River bar 30 April, 1921, or lost near New Plymouth 26 May 1903.

1896 *Asa*
(Circa) 20-ton 40 foot ketch rigged scow type hull, built about 1896 probably at

Frenchman's Bay, after *Felicity* (Bark Bay was mentioned by Russ Ricketts as the building place), and owned by Captain Gus Burnard. Traded Nelson-Riwaka-Motueka-Torrent Bay-Awaroa-Collingwood for many years. Later sold to Captain Tom Nalder who carried timber and firewood with her. Laid up on the mudflat in Torrent Bay.

1899 *Lizzie Taylor*
(Circa) Ketch, 82 ft 77 ton, built 1892 East Devonport, Nth Tasmania by Edward Higgs – registered at Launceston. (Higgs worked as a boatbuilder in NZ for a time as well as Tasmania.) Sold to NZ end of C19 owned by timber merchant John Jackson Timaru, retaining her Launceston registration. Carried various cargoes in NZ coastal trade – eg. 1901 48,000 ft timber load to Timaru return 120 tons flour for Wanganui. Grounded entering Wanganui River 1902 and successfully repaired. Regularly did the timber run between Pelorus Sound (Havelock & Nydia), Wellington & Timaru. Wrecked 1915 on Namuka reef (Tonga) under charter to a German company during WW1.

1900 *Morning Light*
(Circa) *Two vessels of the same name worked the Bays during this period.*

The first: Straight-stemmed cutter, 28 tons, 47ft, built by Holmes Bros and registered in Auckland 1863. Registry closed 13 March 1909, she was broken up.

The second: Topsail schooner with a raked stem, built in Australia, owned for a time by Captain Kirk of Takaka. Said to have been a Canterbury 'wheat vessel'. Regularly loaded timber at Waitapu and Collingwood, ending her days as a lighter at Wanganui according to Murray's account. The two-masted rig identifies this latter *Morning Light* as the Waitapu vessel, but there is confusion in Allan's account.

1900 *Orakei*
Schooner-rigged deck scow, 32 tons, 69ft.6in x 18ft x 3ft.2in, built 1882 by Sims & Brown, Auckland. Bought by Puponga Coal Company 1899 to set up coal mine and then laid up at Puponga, Golden Bay. Fred Hadfield and Will Winter of Awaroa bought her, made her seaworthy and reregistered her 12 August 1910. Worked timber Croisilles to Nelson. Registry closed in 1921.

1903 *Maritana*
Cutter yacht, 19 tons, 44ft, built Auckland 1887, registered at Nelson April 1903, owner C Y Fell. A deep V-sectioned hull, she was altered by J J and Russell J Ricketts. Engine fitted December 1915 when owned by R J Ricketts, traded as a launch. Sunk at entrance to Croisilles 13 February 1918, salvaged and later sold to a Wellington owner, Maritana spent most of her trading time as a motor-powered vessel. Reportedly wrecked at the Chatham Islands.

1903 *Southern Isle*
Three-masted schooner-rigged hold scow, 83 tons, 92ft x 22ft x 4ft.5in, built in 1901 by D Darroch, Omaha. Capsized off Cape Farewell between 28 and 31 May 1916, crew of five drowned. Bought by Nelson Harbour Board 1917 and began service as the grab dredge *Te Wakatu* in March 1927. Retired in 1942.

1903 *Oban*
Schooner-rigged hold scow, 39 tons, 68ft x 17ft.5in x 4ft.3in, built 1879 by D Darroch, Omaha. Registered Nelson 29 July 1903, owner A McNabb. Serious mishaps included five strandings, three capsizes, a fire and a foundering, with four drowned. In 1906 the Marine Dept required her to have masts shortened and hull altered. Returned to Auckland in 1924, renamed *Motiti* and finally laid up after 65 years of service.

1905 *Matakana*
Cutter, 17 tons, 45ft.3in x 15ft.5in x 4ft.9in, built 1872 by Henderson and Spraggon in Auckland (her early history is in Ted Ashby's book). Owned and commanded by Captain R G Tregidga 1903–11 in the regular Nelson-Motueka-Riwaka trade, and in coal from Puponga, she was a fast sailer and won the Coasters' Race in 1906. Capsized and sank 9 November 1911 in thick weather when she was struck by a squall eight miles east of Riwaka. The crew got ashore in her badly-damaged boat.

1906 *Venture*
Ketch-rigged centreboard square-stern carvel scow-style, (but with a conventionally-planked full bow), 18.65 tons, 46ft x14ft x 3ft, built at Awaroa by William W Hadfield and launched January 1906 for the Bays trade. Owned by F G Hadfield and W Winter. Captains Hadfield, Watchlin, G M Burnard and Tom Reeves were masters. Traded mainly timber, cattle and flax from Awaroa. Laid up at Awaroa and registry closed 1941.

1907 *Lily*
Ketch, 14 tons, 38ft.8in x 12ft.4in x 5ft, built at Plimmerton 1890 by Henry Berg. Owned by Wellington tailor Charles Hodgson 1892–1907 then sold to William (Bill) Westrupp who was owner/master in the Bays trade for nearly 20 years. Sank in Nelson harbour 7 October 1909 when a wind change as she entered the harbour caused the tide to carry her up against the mole. Raised a week later, she continued trading until she was laid up in1924 in the Collingwood estuary. (Bill died at Stoke 1 April 1927.) *Lily* appears to have the distinction of being the last of the purely sailing Blind Bay hookers.

1917 *Pearl Kasper*
Ketch-rigged deck scow, 53 tons, 77ft.3in x 22ft x 3ft.5in, built 1910 by Geo Niccol, Auckland. Registered Nelson 29 March 1917, and the engine from *Southern Isle* installed. Owner and master R G Tregidga, his son Albert succeeded him 1942. Owned by Pearl Kasper Shipping Co (A K Greenslade) in 1947, altered to twin-screw motor ship in 1949, returned to Kasper family in Auckland 1954.

1919 *Vindex*
Deck-loading ketch, 44 tons, 80ft.6in x 20ft.6in x 3ft.1in, round-bilged, longitudinally-planked, flat bottom with a keel, built 1897 by C & W Bailey, Auckland. Registered in Nelson 20 June 1919, owners C J H Slade and W J Tregidga. Sunk at the mouth of the Hutt River 1939 and became a total loss.

1920 *Echo*
Schooner-rigged hold scow, 104ft.2in x 25ft.5in x 6ft.1in, built 1905 by W Brown

& Sons, Auckland in 1905. Operated by Eckford Shipping Co 1920–1965, mainly on the Wellington to Blenheim run although she appeared in Nelson periodically. Now on the Picton foreshore.

1930 *Te Aroha*
Schooner (auxiliary engined), round-bilged, (although sometimes erroneously referred to as a scow), 104 tons, 86ft, built 1909 at Totara North, registered Nelson 29 May 1930 to the Anchor Co. Sold to Karamea Shipping Co 1936, she was retired in 1976 and converted by Tim Phipps for tourist use at Picton. In 1979 she was extensively altered and transferred to Auckland.

1930 *Talisman*
(Circa) Schooner-rigged hold scow, 99 tons, 94ft.5in x 24ft x 4ft, built 1897 by Lane & Brown, Whangaroa. Registered Nelson 11 September 1939 as auxiliary oil twin screw scow, owned Golden Bay Shipping Co. Survived as a trader until 1963, was a floating jetty at Nelson marina until 1983.

1932 *The Portland*
Schooner-rigged auxiliary hold scow, 81 tons, 72ft x 21ft.7in x 4ft, built 1910 by Geo Niccol, Auckland. Registered Nelson 1 October 1932 to the Puponga Shipping Co, sold to West Haven Shipping Co 1946 and converted to twin screw motor ship 1947. Holed near Tom's Rock off Karori Light, Wellington, in early 1970s and brought back to Nelson, sold 'as is, where is' and went to Owaka, Southland where she remains apparently still intact. The use of the article 'The' in her name is unusual – it was relatively common for vessels to be referred to as objects when speaking of them (eg '*The Maid*') but not in their formal name. Rob Williams (formerly Motueka's harbourmaster) refers in jest how locals called her '*The The Portland*', sometimes shortened to simply '*The The*'!

1947 *Kohi*
(Circa) Schooner-rigged deck scow (previously named *Caed-Mile-Failte*), 92ft.5in x 27ft.5in x 4ft.2in, built 1911 by Geo Niccol, Auckland. Captain Bob Goldie was her master at Nelson, the Nalder family father and sons all sailed on her when she was brought down. Working in the broader Cook Strait region in the 1920s and 1930s, owned by T Eckford & Co of Blenheim 1945–1947 then Parry Bros, Auckland and Sullivan Shipping, Wellington. After sinking at Picton she was salvaged but beyond repair and became a jetty with fish freezers at Westhaven where she is still.

1954 *Vesper*
Deck-loaded ketch, 76ft.6in x 21ft.1in.x.3ft.5in, round-bilged, longitudinally planked, flat bottomed with a keel, built 1902 by Bailey & Lowe, Auckland. When she came to Nelson is unclear, but the Karamea Shipping Co sold her to Sounds ownership in 1965 for use as a barge after it was deemed uneconomic to repair her. Still working in the 1980s as a mussel barge.

BIBLIOGRAPHY

Allan, Ruth M, Nelson: *A History of Early Settlement*. AH & AW Reed, Wellington, 1965.
Allan, Ruth M: *History of Port Nelson*. Nelson Harbour Board, Nelson, 1954.
Ashby, Ted: *Phantom Fleet*. AH & AW Reed, Wellington, 1975.
Ault, H F: *Centennial History of All Saints Parish*. Nelson, 1962.
Barber, Laurie: *New Zealand, a short history*. Century Hutchinson, Auckland, 1989.
Bassett, Sinclair and Stenson: *The Story of New Zealand*. Reed Methuen, 1987.
Brereton, C B: *Vanguard of the South*. A H & A W Reed, Wellington, 1952.
Broad, Lowther: *A Jubilee History of Nelson*. Capper Press, Christchurch, 1976.
Buckley, Barry: *Sails of Suffering, the story of the Lloyds*. Buckley, Napier, 1990.
Buick, T L: *Old Marlborough*. Capper Press, Christchurch, 1976.
Burns, Patricia: *Fatal Success, A History of the New Zealand Company*. Heinemann Reed, Auckland, 1989.
Clark, Charles R: *Women and Children Last*. Otago University Press, 2006.
Collins Atlas of World History, Guild Publishing, London, 1987.
Chambers, Wesley. A: *Samuel Ironside in New Zealand*. Fay Richards, 1982.
Dawber, Carol: *The Jacksons of Te Awaiti*. River Press, Picton, 2001.
Dawber, Carol and Wilson, Lynette: *Awaroa Legacy*. River Press, Picton, 1999.
Dawber, Carol and Win, Cheryl: *North of Kahurangi, West of Golden Bay*. River Press, Picton, 2001.
Dawber, Carol and Win, Cheryl: *Ferntown to Farewell Spit*. River Press, 2003.
Dickinson, B E: *Historic Tahuna*. Dickinson, Nelson, 1991.
Ell, Sarah (ed): *The Lives of Pioneer Women in New Zealand*. Bush Press, 1993.
Faris, Irwin: *Charleston, Its Rise and Decline*. Capper Press, Christchurch, 1980.
Field, A N: *Nelson Province 1642–1842*. A G Betts & Son, Nelson, 1942.
Fraser, Lyndon (ed): *Irish Migration and New Zealand Settlement*. University of Otago Press, Dunedin, 2000.
Frost, Lucy: *No Place for a Nervous Lady*. University of Queensland Press, 1984.
Grady, Don: *Guards of the Sea*. Whitcoulls, Christchurch, 1978.
Hardy, Elsbeth: *The Girl who Stole Stockings*. A.T.O.M Australia, 2014.
Hawkins, Clifford: *Out of Auckland*. Pelorus Press, Auckland, 1960.
Hodder, Edwin: *Memories of New Zealand Life*. Longman Brown Green Longman & Roberts, London, 1862.
Host, Emily: *The Enchanted Coast*. John McIndoe, Dunedin, 1976.
Hutching, Megan: *Over the Wide and Trackless Sea*. Harper Collins, 2008.
Ingram, C W N and Lambert, M: *New Zealand Shipwrecks, 195 Years of Disasters at Sea* (7th revised edition).Beckett Publishing, Auckland, 1990.
Johnston, Mike: *Nelson's First Railway and the City Bus*. Nikau Press, 1996.

Kennington, A L: *Awatere, a district and its people*. Marlborough County Council, Blenheim, 1978.
Kerr, Garry: *The Tasmanian Trading Ketch*. Mains'l Books, Victoria, 1987.
King, Michael: *The Penguin History of New Zealand*. Penguin, Auckland, 2003.
Lash, Max D: *Nelson Notables 1840–1940*. Nelson Historical Society, Nelson, 1992.
McAloon, Jim: *Nelson, A Regional History*. Cape Catley, 1997.
McGill, David: *The Pioneers of Port Nicholson*. A H & A W Reed Ltd, 1984.
McKinnon, Malcolm (ed): *Bateman's New Zealand Historical Atlas*. Bateman, 2003.
McLauchlan, Gordon: *Bateman New Zealand Encyclopedia*. Bateman, 1987.
Maning, Frederick: *Old New Zealand*, Creighton and Scales, 1863.
Mill, John Stuart: *Dissertations and Discussions*. G Routledge, London, 1903.
Millar, J Halket: *Beyond the Marble Mountain*. R Lucas & Son, Nelson, 1948.
Moon, Paul and Biggs, Peter: *The Treaty and its Times*. Resource Books, 2004.
Natusch, Sheila: *The Cruise of the Acheron*. Whitcoulls, Christchurch, 1978.
Neale, June E: *The Greenwoods*. General Printing Services, Nelson, 1984.
Neale, June E: *Landfall Nelson*. Anchor Press, Nelson, 1978.
Neale, June E: *Pioneer Passengers*. Anchor Press, Nelson, 1982.
Newport, J N W: *Footprints*. Whitcombe & Tombs, Christchurch, 1982.
Newport, J N W: *Collingwood*. Caxton Press, Christchurch, 1971.
O'May, Harry: *Wooden Hookers of Hobart Town and Whalers out of Van Dieman's Land*. Government Printer, Hobart, 1965.
O'May, Harry: *Hobart River Craft*. Government Printer, Hobart, undated.
Peart, J D: *Old Tasman Bay*. R Lucas & Son, Nelson, 1937.
Pratt, W T: *Colonial Experiences, or, Incidents and Reminiscences of Thirty-Four Years in New Zealand by an Old Colonist*. Chapman Hall, London, 1877.
Reed, Edward L and Fry, Pamela: *Ted, The Life and Times of Edward Louis Reed*. Donna Starkey, Motueka, 1997.
Reeves, William Pember: *The Long White Cloud*. Golden Press, Auckland, 1973.
Ricketts, I N: *From Wiltshire to Nelson*. I N Ricketts, Auckland, 1994.
Ross, John O: *Capt F G Moore*. Wanganui Newspapers, Wanganui, 1982.
Salmon, J H M: *A History of Goldmining in New Zealand*. Government Print, 1963.
Saunders, Alfred: *Tales of a Pioneer*. L M Isitt, Christchurch, 1927.
Sherrard, J M: *Kaikoura, A History of the District*. Kaikoura County Council, 1966.
Simpson, Tony: *Before Hobson*. Blythswood Press, Wellington 2015.
Soper, Frank: *The Little Ships, a Golden Bay anthology*. Soper, Golden Bay, 2001.
Spenser, W E: *A History of the Buller District*. Robert T Porter, Westport, 1986.
Sutton, Jean: *How Richmond Grew*. J Sutton, Richmond, 1992.
Temple, Philip: *A Sort of Conscience, the Wakefields*. Auckland University Press, 2002.

Turnbull, Michael: *The New Zealand Bubble: the Wakefield Theory in Practice.* Price Milburn & Co, Wellington, 1959.
Vidal-Naquet, Pierre (ed): *The Collins Atlas of World History.* Guild Publishing, 1987.
'Waratah': *Tales of the Golden West.* Capper Press, Christchurch, 1983.
Washbourn, H P: *Reminiscences of Early Days.* R Lucas & Son, Nelson, 1935.
Washbourn, H P: *Further Reminiscences of Early Days.* R Lucas & Son, 1935.
Watt, M N: *Index to the New Zealand section of the register of all British ships.* NZ Ship & Marine Society, Wellington, 1962.
Whiteside, Iva: *From Kent to New Zealand, the Huffam Story.* Manukau Printing Services, 1984.
Williams, Percy Charles: *Memoirs of a Shellback.* Motueka and District Historical Association, Motueka, June 2002.
Wright, Matthew: *Reed Illustrated History of New Zealand.* Reed Publishing, 2004.

Unpublished manuscripts and papers
Jollie, Edward: 'Reminiscences', ref qms-1071, Alexander Turnbull Library.
Murray, H N: research papers, Motueka and District Historical Association Inc.
Kidson and Ricketts Reunion Committee: papers from the reunion archive.
Ricketts, Russell: 'The Experiences of a Blind Bay Sailor', collected papers and photographs, courtesy Carol Thompson and Kerry Miller, Nelson.
Smith, Arthur Manuel: 'Memories of the Sea', Motueka and District Historical Association (1980) Inc.
Nelson Provincial Museum archives: Customs Department records.

INDEX OF VESSELS

Acheron, HMS, 106, 107, **107**, 119, 130
Ada, 174
Airedale, SS, 215
Alert, 121, 200, 277, 278, 283
Amelia, 129, 137, 274
Amelia Francis, 162
Amelia Simms, 194, **200**
Anatuero, 182, 237, 249, 256, 290
Ann, 169, 278, 282
Ann and Sarah, 273
Arahura, SS, 34
Argus, 112, **115**, 194, 201, 209, **235**, 239, 47, **256**, 257, 260, 288
Arrow, 23, 28, 29, 31, 41
Arthur Wakefield, 219
Asa, 186, 237, 243, 244, 249, 257, 290
Atalanta, 137, 144, 146, 277
Aurora, 219
Australian Maid, 139, 146, 149, 261, 278
Awaroa, 189
Beautiful Star, SS, 160
Betsy Douglas, 172
Bolton, 11, 12, 22, **28**, 77, 224, 235
Brothers, 114
Brothers and Sister, 172
Bruce, SS, 169
Brougham, **28**, 38, 54, 90
Calyx, **9**, 194, 238, 247, 252, 290
Cambria, **192**
Camellia, vii, **50**, **74**, 193, 232, 256, 288
Carbon, **46**, 79, 129, 143, 273
Catherine, 109, 137, 146, 149, 163, 279
Catherine Ann, 116, 126, 127, 129, 131-134, 276
Champion, 252, 289
Charles Edward, PS/SS, 159, 213, 220, 236, 239, 297
Cheviot, 248
City of Nelson, 137, 280
Clifford, 224
Clio, **192**, 194
Clyde, 194

Collingwood, 157, 284
Comet, 27, 137, **176**, **180**, 184, **204**, 237, 248, 252, **253**, 257, 288
Comfort, 129
Constant, 160, 167, 169, 174, 283
Coquette, 146, 279
Cossett, 219, 284
Croydon Lass, **192**, 200, 262
Cymraes, 172
Dart, 219, 286
Dauntless, 147, 157, 182, 219, 286
Despatch, 169
Dido, 121, 286
Dove, 161, 234
Eagle, 234
Echo, 122, 123, **124**, 125, 205, 206, 255, 292
Eclipse, 247
Elenor, 224
Eliza, **28**, 39, 51, 54, 128, 163, 271, 272, 281, 283
Elizabeth, 50, 57, 109, 114, 126, 137, 146, 164, 194, 200, **229**, 270, 276, 280, 289
Emerald Isle, 171, 172, 282
Emergency, 34, 111, 275
Emily, 129, 194, 275, 283
Emma Simms, 194, 204
Emu, PS, 158, 159
Enterprise, 65, 78, 80, 128, 273
Erena, 110, 274
Erin, 9, **12**, 39, 44-49, 51, 54, 57, 58, 59, 77, 128, 143, 145, 270, 271
Fairy, 136, 137, 170, 174, 277
Falcon, 121, **124**, 171, 286
Fancy, 174
Fawn, 200
Felicity, iii, **1**, **6**, **185**, **186**, 186, 237, 238, 245-6, **246**, 251-2, 254-6, 289, 291
Fidele, 100, 101, 103, 129
Fifeshire, **28**, 30, 31, 33, 34, 49, 56, 59, 60, 74, 87, 111, 271, 275

Finetta, 128, 273
Flirt, 136, 137, 219, 277
Flora McDonald, 174
Flying Cloud, 172
Flying Squirrel, 174
Gannet, **102**, 103, 112, **189**, 238, 256, **256**, 289
Gipsy, 116, 121, 155, 156, 161, 278
Goldseeker, **150**, 251, 286
Halcyon, 169
Harriet, 281
Harry, 146
Harry Bluff, 169, 172
Hawea, SS, 218
Henrietta, 60
Hermione, 248
Hero, 129
Hera, **223**
Hinemoa, NZGSS, **220**, 240
Hope, **28**, 52, 84, 114, 121, 280
Huia, 232
Huon Belle, 194, 199, 262
Huon Pine, 198, 199
Hydrus, 78, 79, 80, 81, 273
Ida, (see also Phoenix) 287
Indus, 78, 79, 94
Iona, 172
Jackall, 137, 278, 279
James, 128
Jane, 156, 172, 178, 188, **204**, 281
Jessie, 137, 278, 279
Jewess, 33, 42, 163
John Bell, 194, 201
John and Matilda, 279
John Graham, 228
John Renwick, 12
Joseph Paul, 169
Joseph Simms, 194, 201
Jubilee, viii, 186, 238, 277
Kaikoura, 172
Kaitoa, SS, 214, **256**
Kate, **28**, 40, 127,149, 170, 172, 280
Katherine Johnstone, 27, 40, 271,
Karorina, 109
Kennedy, SS, 160, 169, 213
Kestrel, 184, 255, 283, 285
Kohi, **165**, 202, 203, 266, **210**, 256, 293
Koi, SS, 256

Kyra, (see also Old Jack II), 284
Ladybird, 215
Lady Barkly, PS&SS, 193, 194, **214**, 214, 219, **220**, 284
Lady Elizabeth IV, (police launch), iii, 240
Lake Erie, 202
Lambton, 17
Liberty, 137
Lily, viii, **146**, **189**, 238, 239, 241, 242, 247, 249, 256, 282
Lily, SS, 246
Lily of the Wave, (see also Ruby), 286, 287
Lively, 131, 273
Lizzie Taylor, **180**, 199, 200, 291
Lloyds, 12, **28**, 31, 32
London, 79
Look-In, **28**, 226
Lord Ashley, SS, 215
Lord Auckland, **28**, 31
Lord Horsley, SS, 215
Lucinda, 110, 275
Lutterworth, 220
Lyttelton, PS **124**, 159, 194, 212, **212**
Maid of Italy, **135**, 184, **189**, **192**, 219, 238, 243, 244, 249, **250**, 255, **256**, 257, 259, 272, 287
Mana, **28**, 40, 271
Mana, SS, 193,219
Maori Chief, PS, 211
Maori, SS, **218**
Maria Josephine, 129, 276
Marilyn, MV, (see also Old Jack II), 119, 257, 284
Maritana, 257, **257**, 291
Mary, (3 vessels), 95, 109, 116, 121, 137, 139, 156, 160, 277, 278
Mary Ann, (barque), **28**, 31, 35, 77
Mary Ann, (Moore), 33, 34, **35**, 38, **60**, 89, 90, 114, 271
Mary Ann (schooner), 131, 137, 146, 171, 274
Mary Jane, 174
Mary Ogilvie, 219
Mary Thompson, 146, 279
Matakana, 180, 184, **189**, **197**, 238, **242**, 242, 243, 255, **263**, 292
Matangi, SS, 34
Matilda, 129

Matuku II, ix, x, 122, 126, 127, 130, 131, 185, 242
Mavis, 170, 174, 238, 285
May, 113, 185, 219, 238, 239, 287
May Queen (ketch), 198
May Queen (barque), 219
Mermaid, 137, 219, 278
Mersey, 252, 288
Midge, 219, 240, 278, 282
Mio, 110
Modest Boy, 187, 188, 219, **233**, 285
Moonraker, 52, 77-78, 189, 274
Morning Light (2 vessels), 190, 194, 201, 201, 272, 291
Motiti (see also *Oban*), 205, 292
Moutua, ps, 159
Mullah, 169
Murray, SS, 159, 160
Nautilus, 156, 171, 282
Necromancer, (aka *Old Nick*), 116, 121, 137, 146, 149, 171, 277
Nelson, PS, 124, 159, 169, 213, 215
Nelson Packet, 19, 38, 46, 57, 58, 77, 90, 272
Neta, vii, 257-259, **258**
New Zealand, 113
New Zealand Maid, **vii**, **50**, 130
New Zealander, 38, 40, **46**, 272
Nikau, SS, 214
Nymph, **28**, 40, 58, 272
Oban, 189, 205, 207-9, **209**, 239, 292
Ocean, 38
Ocean Queen, 274
Oddfellow, 139, 281
Ohau, SS, 218
Old Jack, 119, 120, 275
Old Jack II, 6, **7**, 9, **120**, **235**, 238, 257, 284
Orakei, 191, 205, 238, 291
Osprey, (aka *Puffing Billy*), 121
Owake Belle, 5, 194
Pearl, 157, 171, 200, 219, **226**, 283
Pearl Kasper, viii, 31, **106**, 184, 196, **204**, 205, **206**, 206, 240, 255, 292
Penguin, SS, **217**, 218
Pet, **98**, **189**, 237, 244, **245**, 256, 288
Petrel, 129, 184, 255, 281
Phoebe, 89
Phoenix (aka *Ida*), 129, 219, **236**, 239, 297
Pickwick, **28**, 39, 128, 272
Planet, **147**, 219, 237, 256, 284
Polly, 137, 282
Portland, see *The Portland*
Pride of the Isles, 149, 279
Prospect, 219, 285
Rattler, HMS, 158
Rapid, 121, 137, 146, 164, 171, 234, 276
Result, 169, 174, **204**, 228, **229**, 238, 239, 256, 290
Return, 116
Richard and Mary, 219, 240
Rock Lily, 194
Rory O'More, **28**, 40, 42, **46**, 272
Rosanna, 17
Rotorua, SS, 217
Rover's Pride, 274
Roving Bride, 189, 274, 283
Sandfly, HMS, (see also *Tasmanian Maid*), **158**
Sea Flower, 137
Seabird, 121. 137, 277, 278
Shepherdess, 121, **122**, **123**, 155, 161, 171, 173, **173**, 174, 201, 277, 278, 279
Sisters, **28**, 146, 157, 278, 282
Southern Isle, 202-205, **203**, 291
Spray, 280
St Pauli, 75, 111
Standard, 169, 170, 186, 219, 239, 287
Star of the Sea, 200
Sturt, SS, 160
Sudden Jerk, **76**, **91**
Supply (aka *The Roaring Gimlet*), **45**, 111, 112, 121, 137, 139, 144, 146, **147**, 149, 154, 155, 161, 170, 171, 193, 275
Talisman, 206, 207, 256, 293
Tam O'Shanter, SS, 211
Taranaki, SS, 215
Tasman, SS, 214, 220
Tasmanian Maid, PS, 121, 158, **158**, 159, 212, 286
Taupo, SS, **220**
Te Aroha, 176, 207, 261, 293
Te Wakatu (see *Southern Isle*), 204, 291
Thames, 287
The Portland, 207, 231, 255, **261**, 293

Three Brothers, (schooner), 38, 109, 155, 272
Three Brothers (cutter), 146, **147**, 149, 150, 193, 219, 226, 238, 280
Topa, 74
Tory, 17, 42, 55, 71
Transit, 182, 182, 189, 189, 194, 209, 237, 251, 257, 289
Triumph, 116, 119-121, 132, 270
Tryphena, 40
Turanga, 184, 243, 244, 249, **250**, 255, 256, 290
Turau, 237
Undine, PS, 159
Unity, 281, 282, 283
Uno, 219, 281
Venture, (cutter), 281, 282
Venture (ketch), 182, **189**, **190**, 191, 195, 238, 257, 292
Vesper, 206, 256, 293
Victoria, 62, 66, 67
Vindex, **178**, 184, 205, 206, 253, 255, 292
Waimea, SS, **204**, 215
Waihopi, 219
Waipara, SS, 169
Wairarapa, SS, 218
Wairoa, SS, 190, 193,194, 214, 231
Waitapu, SS, 193, 214
Waitohi, 219
Wallabi, SS, 159, 160, 213, **213**
Wakatipu, SS, 217
Wanaka, SS, 62
Wanderer, **183**, 184, 283, 285
Waterwitch, 116
Wave, 247, 280, 288
Waverley, SS, **204**
Wellington, SS, 215
Whitby, 23, **28**, 29, 31, 41, 52, 88, 114, 147
White Swan, SS, 215
Wild Wave, 172
Will Watch, 23, **28**, 29, 31, 41, 79
William, 116
William and Horina, 109, 276
XXX, 286
Zephyr, 199
Zingari, 215, 216

INDEX

A

Abe, Captain, 282
Abel Tasman National Park, 85, 94, 148
Acts and Regulations, 139, 142, 179, 195, 196, 208, 210, 227, 249
Addison's Flat, 167, 175
Adele Island, 29, 31, 41, 151, 183, 205, 222, 248
Akaroa, **vi**, 10, 27, 109
Akersten, William, 114, 281, 283, 284
Albion wharf, 151
Allan, Robert, 273
Altimarlock station, 122
America, 23, 202
Amuri Bluff, 106, 277
Anatori River, 157
Anaweka River, 154
Ancell, Thomas (Old Sharkie), 248
Anchor Foundry, 211, 213
Anchor Shipping Company, 159, 214, 232, 253,
Anderson, Captain John, 172, 252, 254, 289
Anderson, Mr, 43, 45
Anderson, Ivan, viii
Andrews, Captain William, 110, 273, 274, 275, 283
Annesbrook Rise, 80, **81**, 82, 224
Anthony, Harry (Father Wobutus), 248
Anzac Park, 221
Aorere
    goldfields, 146, 153-4, 156
    land purchases, 109
    River estuary, 111, **118**, 144-5, **146**, 192, 194, 256, 271
Apiko, 143
apple growing, 149, 257
Arapata, Captain te Ware, 276
Arrow Rock, *see* Fifeshire Rock
Askew family, 94
Askew, George, 95, 274
Askew, Peter, 278, 284

Askew, Captain Thomas, 94, 95, 116, 122, 147, 141-2, 76, 277, 227-8, 286
Askew, William, 94, 274, 282
Astrolabe Roadstead, 38, 41, 48, 110, 183, 185, 274, 285
Atua Stream, 90, 91, 96
Auckland Point, 29, 31, 49, 51, 78, 79, 102, 109-114, 143, 221, 222, 229, 233
Auckland
    early capital, **vi**, 36, 53, 57, 75, 77, 86, 107, 142, 155, 179, 215
    trade, 117, 131, 135, 273
    boatbuilding, ix, 39, 202, 295, 271, 272, 282, 290, 291, 292, 293
Australia
    colonies, 2, 12, 23, 26, 75
    gold rushes, 117, 119, 143, 145, 162
    shipping, 131, 148, 160, 200, 273, 291
    trade, 81, 89, 103, 119, 143, 190, 215, 224
Awaroa, 4, 13, 191, 182, 187, 188-191, 195, 257, 268, 284, 191, 292
Awatere, 100, 101, 103, 104, 114, 129, 137, 142, 162, 268

B

Baigent, Edward, 80, 178, 179
ballast, 11, 44, 48, 73, 101, 126, 172, 208, 209, 210, 242, 262, 271, 286
Banks Peninsula, ix, x, 134, 252, 279
Barbour, Captain, 281
barges, *see* boatbuilding
Baring Head, 101, 130,
Bark Bay, 4, 111, 186-188, 234,301
Barker, Captain, 40, 271
Barnicoat, John Wallis, **51**, **52**, 68, **81**, **84**, 110, 152
Barrett, Captain Dicky, 33, 38, 42
Bartlett, Samuel, 48
Bathe, Captain John, 273

Bay of Plenty, 130, 281
Beaver, Station, the, 119, 120
Beavertown, *aka* Beaverton, **118**
    (*see* Blenheim)
Beit, Johann,54, 75, 111
Beit's wharf, 54, 113
Bell, Francis Dillon, 103
Bennett, Captain, 40
Bensemann, Cordt, 111
Berry, Emily (Williams), 228
Berry, Thomas R., 274, 275
Big Bush, *see* Grovetown
Bilby, Captain John, 279
Black Stump, the, 81, 99, 224
Blackball, **180**, 181, *186*
Blackmore, George T, 184
Blake, Isaac, (storekeeper), 160
Blakestown, 160
Blenheim, 114, 118-124, 205, **212**, 214, 252, 293
Blenkinsop, Captain John, 42, 55
Blick, Bingo, 244
Blick, Thomas, 188
Blind Bay, naming of, 25, 26
Blind Channel, 223, 226, 243, 244, 248
Blowers, Ezra, 45, 271, 277
boatbuilding
    early, 11, 13, 32, **52**, 74, 94
    Nelson, 36, 72, 111, 136, 137, 189, **231**, 235
    remote, 181-188
    techniques, 10, 11, 197
Bolt, Captain S, 282
Bolton Hole, 35, 224
Boniarto, Antonio 248
Bonner, Captain Charles, 157, 283
Bonner, Captain D, 288
Boulder Bank, 26, 29-31, **30**, 34, 35, 49, 66, **81**, 119, **219**, 224, 226, 232, 233, 280
    the cut, 226-228, **228**
Bowler, Sam, 121
Boyce, Captain William, 275, 276, 277
Brett, Captain George, 279
breweries, 131
Bridge St, 53, 78, 113, 116, 221
Britannia Heights, 30, 114

Britannia, *see* Port Nicholson
Broad, Judge, 64, 86
Brook St, 70, 139, 188
Brooks, Captain, 279
Browett, Alf, 244
Brown, Captain Henry, 39, 271, 285
Brownlee, William, 178, 179
Brownlee's mill, **180**, **181**
Brunell, Jack, 244
Brunner, Thomas, 154
Buller gold, 153, 157, 162,
Buller River, 137, 145, 154-6, 161, 163, 174, 273, 277, 278, 280, 281, 290
Buller settlement, *see* Westport
Burdett, Captain William, 275
Burford, J C (Cocky), **115**, 201, 209, 214, 285, 287, 288, 289
Burnard, Captain H M (Gus), 184, 186, 243, 289, 291, 292
Burtt, H W, 80

C
Cable Bay, 108
Callaghan, Captain, 281
Caldwell, family, 144
Caldwell, Captain W.O., 205, 288, 290,
California, 137, 145, 162
Canterbury
    settlement, 20, 71, 106, 131-133, 140
    shipping, 117, 163, 211, 218, 291
    Canterbury Association, 106, 131
Cantwells landing, 125
Capes:
    East Cape, ix, 130
    Cape Campbell, 101-3, **118**, 122, 127-9, 133, 273, 282
    Cape Farewell, 26, 154, 160, 161, 163, 277, 291
    Cape Foulwind, 167
    Cape Jackson, *see* Jackson Head
    Cape Kidnappers, 130
    Cape Palliser, 39, 100, **118**, 126-128, 130, 254, 271, 272, 275, 282,
    Cape Stephens, 26
    Cape Terawhiti, 100, **118**, 126, 128
    Cape Turnagain, 130

cargoes, **27**, 40, 79, 117, 119, 134, 138, 189, 194, 205, **210**, 215, 258, 277, 291
Caroline Bay, 285
Carrington, F A, 38
Carter, Captain Thomas, 288
Castlepoint, 129, 130, 271, 273, 280
Catherine Bay, 40, 272
cattle, *see* livestock
Caverhill, Tom, 100
Cawthron, Thomas, 162
Cemino, Salvator, 116, 276
certification of seamen, 185, 195-6, 249, 251
Chaffers, Captain E M,, 55
chandleries, 11, 235, 284
Charles, Captain, 280, 287
Charleston, **vi**, 160, 161, **166**, 167-175, 276, 290,
charts, 26, **30**, **55**, **88**, 103, 126, 129, 192, **224**
Chatham Islands, 22, 291
Christchurch, **vi**, 20, 78, 111, 130-1, 139, 155
Church Hill, 70
Clarence River, 103
Claringbold, W, 79, 273
Clark, Captain Sam, 287
Clifford, Charles, 103
Clifton, John, 204
Cloudy Bay, (*see* also Port Underwood), 57, **62**, 65, 66, 68, 69, 80, 103, 110, 119, 125, 205, 248, 272
Coal Bay, **47**, 130, 142, 143, 158, 207
Coal extraction, 11, 33, 43, 48, 57, 58, 82, 136, 143, 163, 194, 205
Coal cargoes, 33, 39, 40, 48, 49, 50, 115, 153, 163-4, 194, 204, 209, **229**, **236**, 239, 243, 252, 256
Coal usage, 11, 43, 82, 112, 130, 143, 158, 207
Coal and Limestone Association, 47
Collingwood
    Settlement, 42, 43, **47**, **144**, 145, 192
    as Port of Entry, 146
    shipping, 112, 139, 146, **146**, 153, 156, 158, 194, 199, **201**, 214, **214**

Collingwood Argus, 247
Collins, Captain Des, 208
Constant Bay, 131, 156, 161, **166**, 167-169, 172-175, 274, 277-285, 287
convicts, 12, 73, 108
Cook, Captain James, 25, 26, 29, 44, **55**, 99, 107, 153
Cook Strait
    Region, **vi**, ix, 38, 42, 59, 106, 110, **118**, 272, 275, 293
    Waters, iii, 65, 119, 123, **123**, 125, 126, 179, 205, 206, 238, 240, 272
    Weather & tides, 63, 99, 100, 102-3, **102**, 123, 125, 128, 130, 133, 273, 286
Cooper, Captain George, 129, 274
Cooper, Dr, 105
copper mining, 113, 138, 139, 142
Corless, Mr, 184
Coromandel, 39, 40, 282
Cotterell, John Sylvanus, 59, 64, 65, 78, 80, 273
Cowan, Captain James, 285-6
Cowper, W, 42
Craddock, Charles, 173, **173**, 279
Crawford, James Coutts, 33, 42,
Crayfishing (see also fishing),3, 130, 165, 258
Croisilles, 38, 138, 178, **178**, 205, 238, 247, 248, 249, 252
Cromarty, Captain, 282
Cross, James (Pilot), iii, 29, 33, 60, **60**, **61**, **71**, 214
Cross, Captain James S, jnr, 193, 214, **220**, 285
Cross, Captain Des, 34
Cross, Linda, i, 1, 185
Culverden, 106
Curran, John Philpot, Judge, 102
Curron, Captain, 285
Customs officialdom, 36, 39, 53, 195, 196, 208, 222, 270, 274

D
Daken, Tim, 119
Daniel, Captain John *see* Hone Raniera
Darroch shipbuilders, 205, 291, 292
Davidson, Captain, 149, 279

Davis, Rock, 201
Deal boats, iii, 12, 29, 31, 41, 51, 60, **60**, **61**, 62, 65, 66, **70**, **71**, 79, 90, 114, 271
Dellow, Captain, 281
Devanny, Andrew, 184
Dillon, Mr, 105
Dinghy building, 9,10, 55, 94, 95, 187, 231, **232**, 254
Dinghy usage, 3, 44, 78, 95, 116, 132-3, **143**, **146**, 150, 156, 169, 181, 233, 241, 243, 248, 253, 259
Doctor's Creek, 88, 89, 114
Dodson, Arthur, 161
Dodson, Kath and Nell, 15
Dodson, Mr, 48
Dodson, Adolphus, 278
Dodson, Fell & Co., 286
Doig family, 231
dolomite,194, 205, 207, **261**
Dougall, George,277
Drummond family, 92, 208
Drummond's mill, 182, **182**, 183, 289, 290
Drummond, Tom, 182, 183, 290
Dun Mountain Copper Mining Co, 113, 138, 139
Duncan, Captain John, 149, 240-1, 275, 282
Dundas House, 116
Dunedin, **vi**, 131, 156, 181, 194, 215, 217, **219**, 282
Duppa, George, 105, 106, 108
D'Urville Island (Rangitoto), 13, 38, 40, 65, 99, **106**, 110, 129, 177, 238, 274
d'Urville, Dumont, 26, 29, 41, 120, 185

E

earthquakes
    Wellington 1848, 120
    Wellington 1855, 120, 122
East Cape, *see* Capes
East India Company, 96
Eckfords Shipping Co, 29
Eckford and Outram, 275
Edwards, George, 52, **52**, 78-9, 94, 95, 116, 273
Edwards, Mary (m Fowler), 133, 134, 212
Edwards, Nathaniel, 137, 159, 212, **212**, 213,
Nathaniel Edwards & Co, 159, 212, 213
Ekawa, see also Puakawa, 58, 59, 68
Ellis, John, 142, 144
Elmslie, Captain Arthur, 38, 279
Elterwater, Lake, 100
Emms, William, 'Billy the rat', 248
Empson, Charles, 116, 121, 273, 276, 277
England, Captain, 35, 195
England, Justice, 66
Enner Glynn, 79, 82
Eure, Captain, 278, 282
Everett family,231
explosives, 227, 232

F

Factory Rd, 92
Farewell Spit, 5, 11, **47**, 110, 143, 159, 163-4, 191, 204, 277
Farewell, *see* Cape Farewell
farming, 27, 56, 76, 81-3, 86, 89, 94, 99, 103-4, 117, 119, 137, 140, 149, 157, 253
Fell, Alfred, 60, 96
Fell, Charles Y, 291
Fergusson, Captain, 38
Ferntown, 11, 145, **146**, 164, 194, 239, 247, 288-9, 294
Ferrers Creek, 93
ferry boats, 80, 96, 247
Fifeshire Rock, (*aka* Arrow Rock), 29, 30, 150, 223, 224, **226**, 227, **228**
Fiji Jack, 248
firewood, 82, 138, 177-8, **178**, 184, 187, 234, 238, 247, 249, 255, 267, 274, 282, 290
Fisherman Island, 83, 188, 285
fishing, 2, 8, 13, 93, 119, 207, 239, 247, 249, 257, 284, 286, 290
FitzRoy, Governor, 71, 77, 101, 104
flax industry, 117, 212
Flaxbourne, 102, 106, 282
flour mill, 93, 111, 179, 285
Flowerday, Ann, née Stanton, 184
Flowerday, Francis William, 183-4, 186, 283, 285
Flowers, Frank, 183-6

Flowers, Job, 143
Foster, A, 204
Fowler family, 231
Fowler, Captain Henry, 84, 116, 126-7, 133-4, 276
Fowler, Hugh, 119
Fowler, John, 96
    Fowler, Mary, née Edwards, 133-4
Fox, William, 27, 41, 77, 103, 108
Foxton, 40, 283
Franzen's wharf, 222, **222**, **245**
Franzen, Burchard, 239, 240, 281, 285, 286, 287, 290
Freeman's Bay, 288
Freeman, Thomas Graham, 79, 109, 116, 121, 136, 273, 274, 275, 276
Freeman, Thomas, see Tamati Pirimona
French, Elizabeth, iii
French Pass, 65, 110, 133, 205, 238, 252, 286
Frenchman's Bay, 3, **7**, 113, 184, **185**, 186, 238, 287, 289, 290, 291
Frost, Captain Charles
Fyffe, Robert, 129

G
Gabrielsen family, 231
Gabrielsen, Captain Charles 'Gabriel', 249
Galway Bay hookers, 6, **7**, 8, 45, 197
Gardner, William, 82
Garnes, Captain John, 282
gasworks wharf, **102**, 112, 246, **246**, 289
German settlers, 22, 75, 111
Gibbons, E, 277
Gibbons, R G, 283
Gibbs, Mary Anne (m Huffam), 188, 197
Gibbs, William, 145, 147, 148, 192
Gibbstown, see also Collingwood, 145, 147
Gibson, Captain, 204
Gibson, Sandy, 89
Gilbertson family, 231
Gilbertson, Dan G, 149, 189, 278
Gilbertson, David, 279, 288,
Gill, Captain, John, 273
Gisborne, **vi**, ix, 130, 131
Glencoe Gardens, 139

Gloucester St, 221
Glover, Sarah, (née Westrupp), 113, 185, 238-9
Glover, William (Bill), 185, 238-9, 240, 287
Goddard, Captain, 278, 279
Gold rushes:
    Australian, 110, 117, 119, 143
    Golden Bay, 142, 144, 146-7, 149, 153-4, 234
    Motueka, 145
    Pelorus Sound, 153
    West Coast, 153-7, 160-3, 167-9
Golden Bay, **47**
    Maori, 26, 59, 192
    Trade, 40, 146, 148, 157, 192-3, 199, 205, 214
Golden Bay Dolomite Ltd, 207
Goldie, Captain Bob, 102, 204, 246-7, 289, 293
Goodall's Corner, 94
Goodman, Arnold, 176
Goodsir, J T, 42
Gore Brown, Governor, 155
Graham family, 231
Grassmere, Lake, 100
Green Point, **12**, 13, 30, 31, 35, 52, 54, 112-4, **113**, **135**, 189, 189, 221, 223, 234, 274
Green Tree Point, 93, 94
Greenem, Captain Wally, 207
Greenwood Dr J., 89, 292
Grey River (see also Mawhera), 116, 152, 154, 155, 159-161, 172, 278, 283
Grey, Governor George, 104, 130
Greymouth, **vi**, 160-2, 167, 169, 172, 213-5, 240, 282
grog shops, 39, 51, **52**, 53-4, 101, 105
Grossi family, 231, 248
Grossi's Island, 244, 248
Grovetown, 67, 120
Grubb, Mr, 89
Guard, Jack, 9, 38, 39, 42, 119, 235, 272, 275, 284
Gully, Mr, 60

H
Haast, Julius, 155

Hadfield family, 188, 189, 205
Hadfield, Captain Fred, 188, 195, 291, 292
Hadfield, Rev Octavius, 191
Hadfield, William, 189, 284, 292
Hadfield slipway, 223
Halifax St, 78, 221
Hamilton, Captain R, 240, 281, 284
Hamilton, Captain Henry, 281, 284
Harbour Board, Nelson, 227, 191
Harbour board, Motueka, 253
Hardwick, Captain Henry, 283
Haulashore Island, vii, 31, 224, 227, **228**, 244, **245**, 256, 258, 283, 285, 288
Hauraki Gulf, vii, 198, 201, 202, 205, 206, 211
Havelock, **180**, 181, 193, 206, 214, 252, 281, 282, 284, 286, 289, 291
Haven Rd, viii, **51**, 53, 78, 80, 94, 112, 113, **113**, 139, 185, **204**, 221, 222, **222**, **229**, 231, **231**, 233, 234, 259
Hawke Bay, 200, 283,
Hawke's Bay, 130
Hawtrey, Captain R de B, 279
Hayes, Bully, 162
Heaphy River, 154
Heaphy, Charles, **22**, **25**, **46**, **60**, **144**
Hemi Kuka Matarua, 110, 275
Henare, Captain, 275
Henia, Captain Joseph, 109
Henry family, 231
Hill, Alfred, 79
Hinds, Rev Dr, 24
Hitchcock, Captain, 280
Hoare, Joseph, 271
Hobson, Governor, 19, 71, 141
Hodder, Edwin, 135, 146, 148
Hoeta, 109, 278
Hokitika, **vi**, 108, 154, 157, 160-162, 169, 215, 276
Holyoake family, 94
Holyoake, Richard, 94, 95
Hooker, Captain William, 280
Hooper & Renwick brewery, 131
Hooper, Captain, 149
hop industry, 92, 138, 177, 183, 187, 197, 238
horses, tow, 93, 120, 121

Horse-drawn trams, 138, 139
Horton family, 231
Hough, William, 145
Howard, J, 58
Howlands Bay, 128, 273
Huffam family, 187-8, 234, 285
Huffam, Timothy, 187, 285
Huffam, Fred, 188, 193
Hutt River, 205, 292
Hutt Valley, *see also* Waiwhetu, 42

I
Infield, J, 287
iron ore, see minerals
Ironside, Rev Samuel, 57, 67, 69, **69**, 71, **72**, 110

J
Jackson Head, *see* Cape Jackson
Jackson, Captain James (Jimmy), 38, 42, 57, 77, 90, 136, 272, 278, 279
Jackson, George, 121, 277
Jackson, John, **180**, 291
Jacobsen, Captain J J H, 156, 281
Jacobsen, Siegmund, 274, 276
James, Ned, 143, 144
Jennings, William, 77, 274
Johansen, C, 62
Johnson family, 231
Johnson, Charlie, 231, 232
Johnson, Ernie, 232
Johnson, Harry, 285, 288
Johnson, Captain Jack, 284
Jollie, Edward, 111
Jones, Frederick, 282
Jones, Johnny, 217
Joss, Captain James, 274

K
Kaikoura, 56, 85, 121-2, **123**, 129, 131, 172, 279
Kaiteriteri, 29, 31, 32
Kakapo Bay, 38, 119, 272, 275, 284
Kapiti Island, 40, 65, 129
Karamea River, 154
Karamea Shipping Co, 206, 293
Kawhia, **vi**, 40, 65, 131, 273, 274
Kekerengu, 103

Kemp, George, 125
Kern, James, 283
Kidson family, 140, 191, 231, 234
Kidson, Eliza (m Ricketts), 191
Kidson, Harry, 209
Kidson, Jack, 176
Kidson, John, vii, 11-13, 32, 62, 65-70, **70**, **71**, **72**, 100, 119, 139, 235, 282
Kirby, Captain Marion, 275
Kirk, Captain, 190, 194, 291

L
Lacey, Captain, 88
Lambert, Captain, 273
land allocation, (see also scrip), 56, 63, 99
Land lottery, 17, 56, 57, 63, 87, 103, 113
Land Commissioner, 58, 71, 77, 79, 141
Land Proclamation 1840, 57, 59
land purchases, 42, 43, 57, 58, 64, 70, 140, 154, 155
laws, see Acts
Leech, Captain, 160, 282
Leslie, Captain Peter Greig, 286
Levien, J H, 161
Levien, Robert, 139, 162, 286
Liddell, Captain, 280, 281
lime burning, 48, 58, 59, 189, **189**, 234, 235
limestone, 40, 49, 58, 136, 143, 189, 205, 209-10, 234, 243, 283
Little Sydney Stream, 78, 92, 93, 94, 130
Little Wanganui River, 154, 163
Livestock cargoes, 35, 49, 81, 93, 99, 106, 110, 111, 158, 205, 224
Livestock farming, 89, 108, 167
Lodders Lane, 92, 93
lottery, see land
Lovell, Benjamin, 110, 273, 275, 282
Lovell, James, 147, 273, 281
Lukins family, 231
Lukins, Amelia, 235
Lukins' lime kiln, 189, **189**, 210, 234, 283
Lukins, E H (Ted), 209, 237
Lukins, James, 234, 235, 240, 276, 278, 282
Lukins' wharf, 189, **204**, 209, **222**, 237, 244
Lyell, 157

Lyttelton, (aka Port Victoria & Port Cooper), **vi**, 106, 132-4, 184, 190, 192, 215, **218**, **219**, 252

M
Mac see also Mc
Mackay, Alexander, 154
Mackay, James, 154-5
Mackay, Robert, 281
Mackenzie, W, 131, 274
MacKenzie, E A, 287
MacLean, Captain Charles, 282
Mahakipawa, 139, 181
Maitai River, 31, 49, **51**, **52**, 78, 82, **141**, 224
Maka, 109, 275
Malarmo, Joe, 248
Mana Island, 40, 99, 127, 271
Manawatu River, 40, 280, 282
Mangles, Ross, 23
Manuka Bush, 88
Maori trading, **12**, 13, **22**, 28, **46**, **51**, 54, 110, 247
Maori settlements (see others by name), 39, 88, 120, 155
Mapua, 85, 224, 257
Marahau (see also Sandy Bay), 13, 85, 181, 182-3, 185, 205, 285, 289, 290
Marble, 205
Marine Department, 195-6, 205, 207-8, 245, 292
Marlborough (see also Wairau)
    land sales, 96, 105
    sea access, 121, 123
    separation of, 99, 100, 103, 104, 119, 142, 213
Marlborough Sounds (see also Queen Charlotte Sound & Pelorus Sound), 13, 45, 206
Marsden Valley, 15, 82
Marshall, Tut, 244
Massacre Bay (see also Murderer's Bay, Coal Bay and Golden Bay): **47**
    early boatbuilding, 42, 79, 277
    early trade, 40, 45, **47**, 116, 138, **144**, 163
    land sales, 33, 42, 54, 57-8, 85, 109
    name changes, 47, 130, 142, **143**

Masonic Lodge, 167
Mason, Captain, 109, 275
Matarua, Hemi Kuka, 110, 275
Maungatapu, 153, 268
Mawhera, (*see also* Grey R, Greymouth), **152**, 154
Matakapi, Solomon, 109
Mc *see also* Mac
McCann, Captain Charles (Jack), 155, 279
McCormack, Jimmy, 184
McKay *see* MacKay
McLaren, Captain James L, 38, 274
McMahon, B, 287
McNab, Captain Edward, 276
McNabb family, 94, 231
McNabb, A, 205, 292
McNabb, Albert, 241
McNabb, Allan, vii, 242
McNabb, Captain, 280
McNabb, Captain J F, 284
McNabb, Captain W F, 241
McNabb, Ethel (m Tregidga), 191, 241
McNabb, Robert, 278
Mellor, Captain F, 285
Mill, John Stuart, 95, 96
Miller, Barney, 99
Miller, Kerry, ii
Millington, F, 154
Milnthorpe wharf, 207, **261**
Milo, Captain, 286
Minerals:
    Copper ore, 138, 142
    Iron ore, 194
    Manganese ore, 40, 272
Mission Hall, Port, 188, 234
Moetapu, 228, 251
Mokihinui River, 154
Molesworth, Sir William, 24
Monaco, 224. 248
Monteath, C, 204
Moore, Captain Frederick, 29, 31, 33, 35, 38, **60**, 89, 90, 114, 163, 271
Moore, Captain James, 276, 284
Morrison and Sclanders, 114
Morrison family, 231
Morrison, W, 62
Morrison, Captain John, 286

Morse, Mr, 105
Mortimer, John, 282, 286
Mosquito fleet, 146, 147, 148, 228, 238
Motueka:
    exploration, 54, 79
    gold mining, 145
    Maori, 106, 110
    commerce, 5, 105, 108, 111, 157, 177, 257
    shipping, 106, 114, 116, 145, 158, 182, 187, 193, 219, 245, 258
    settlement, 29, 31, 34, 39, 88-90, 92, 108, 253
    wharfs, 114, **200**, **206**, 212, 193
Motueka River, 88, **90**, 92, 93, 116
Motueka Shipping Company, 288
Motupipi:
    boatbuilding, 13, 110, 129,193, 273, 274, 275, 278, 288
    commerce, 11, 40, 48, 58, 130, 143, 144
    conflict, 58-9, 63, 66
    shipping, 45-8, **47**, 58, 79, 85, 130, 139, 143, **144**, 208-9
Moutere, 75, 82, 88
Moutere inlet, 41, 81, 224, 257, 277, 285, 290
Moutere Bluffs, **242**, 243
Mount Arthur, **90**, 168
Munro, David, 141
Murphy, Captain James D., 90, 275
Murton, Peter, **8**, 9

N

nails, (also trenails), 5, 6, 42, 197, 243
Nalder, family, 184, 293
Nalder, Gordon, 74
Nalder, Newton, 187, 234
Nalder, Ron, 234
Nalder, Captain Tom, 291
Napier, **vi**, ix, 50, 100, 125, 185, 242, 254, 273,
Napier Wharf, (Port Nelson), 222
Navigation aids: 127, 227
    Beacons, 30, 49, 233, 244-5
    Buoys, 30, 224, 233
    Charts, 26, 103, 129, 224-5,
    Leading marks, 30, 155, 233, 244-5

Light-houses, 126, 127, 234, 254
Signal stations, 30, 114, 167, 168, 174
Nelson:
    boatbuilding, 12, 13, 53, 79, 95, 109,111, 116, 121, **128**, 136-7, 159, 188, 252
    Port, vii, 34, 114, 138, 195, **218**, **219**, **220**, **233**, 253
    Haven, (Wakatu), 5, **9**, **25**, **30**, 39, 40, 48-9, **51**, 74, **91**, **107**, 113, **150**, 221, **222**, **225**, **226**, **229**, **235**, 268
    Province, 99, 104, 119, 139, 141-2, 145, 154, 156, 157, 177
    Provincial Council, 139, **141**, 156, 159, 168
    settlement, **vi**, ix, 1, 15-16, 24-5, 28, 32, **52**, 55-7, 71, 77, 82, 96, 139
    shipping, 7, 28, 34, 38, 39, 40, **60**, 99, 112, 114, 121, 146, 148, **149**, 158, 178, 211-5
    wharves, **147**, **176**, **189**, 207, **217**, 234, 239, **245**, **256**
Nelson Anniversary, 60, **60**, 61
Nelson Examiner & NZ Chronicle, the, 5, 27, 35, 47, 58, 64, 70, 79, 141, 177
Nelson Rope Works, 11, 92
Nelson Coast Steam Assn, 157-8, 211-12
Nelson, Lord, 24
New Plymouth, **vi**, 38, 40, 99, 163, 199, 211, 215, 219, 234, 273, 275, 281, 290
New Plymouth Company, *see* Plymouth Company of New Zealand
New Provinces Act, 142
New Street, 221
    New Zealand Association, (1837), 17
New Zealand centennial, ix, 15
New Zealand Company:
    agents, 27, 30, 41, 53, 54, 57, **72**, 75, 77, 99, 103, 108
    directors, ix, 15, 17, 22, 23, 27 32, 53, 57, 63, 69, 157
    exploration party, 13, 23, 30, 33, 38, 42, 88
    land claims, 22, 25, 36, 41, 54, 55, 57, 59, 64, 77, 82, 108-9
    land titles, 21, 22, 52, 57, 63, 82, 96, 104, 105, **113**,140
    scheme, 12-21, **14**, 23, 24, 28, 36, 56, 57, 86, 96, 109
    settlement, 24, 25, **35**
    surveys, 42, 61, 65, 80, 90
New Zealand Company (1825), 17
New Zealand Constitution Act (1852), 139
New Zealand Gazette, 36, 42, 72
New Zealand Land Company, ix, 13, 15, 17, 55 (*see also* New Zealand Company)
Ngai Tahu, 153-5, 268
Ngaio Bay, 102, 257, 289
Ngati (*also* Ngai), 268
Ngati Apa, 29, 143
Ngati Awa (*aka* Te Atiawa) 22, 65, 143
Ngati Koata, 22
Ngati Kuia, 29, 65
Ngati Raroa, 22, 65, 110, 143, 274
Ngati Tama, 22, 65, 143, 154
Ngati Toa, 22, 29, 43, 58, 64-7, 103, 104, 109
Ngati Tumatakokiri, 143
Nicholson, Port, *see* Port Nicholson
Nicholson, Captain, 112
Nicholson, Rev T D, 125
Nicholson, William R, 276
North Cape, 129
North Durham, Province of, **55**
Norton, 'Rock Cod' Tommy, 248
Nova Scotia, 39

O

Ocean Bay, 38
Oddfellows' Lodge, 168
Ohamaru, Punupi, 109, 278
Onekaka, 144, 194, 253-4, 268
Opawa River, 114, **118**, 119-124, 278, 280
Orr & Wright, 39
Otago,20, 117, 129, 131, 156, 159, 172, 207, 217,
Otterson's jetty, 49, 51
Owen, W, 241
Oyster beds, 185, 249-9, 285, 290

P
Packard, Joseph, 143
paddle steamers, (*also* Vessels Index, prefix PS), 80, **107**, **121**, 130, **152**, 153, **158**, 158, 159, 160, 172, 174, 193, 211, 212, 213, 215, 290
Painter, Richard,
Pakawau, 42, **47**, 110, 143, 275
Palliser Bay, 100, 101, **118**, 126, 128, 129, 130, 271, 272, 275, 282, 286
Palliser, *see* Cape Palliser
Parapara, **47**, 194, 207, 234, **261**, 289
Paraone, 109, 278
Parere St, 221
Parker's Cove, 81, 224
Parker, Margaret, (m Westrupp) 113, 238
Parkers Rd, 79
Partridge, Thomas, 23
Paru, 33, 34
Pascoe, Captain John, 283
Patea, 40, 193, 200, 211, 214, 241, 282, 283, 286
Pattie family, 94
Pattie, C P, 287
Pawson, 'Briny Jim', 248
Pearce, John, 90
Pearce, Captain, 279
Pearl Kasper Shipping Company, 292
Pelorus Sound, **70**, 139, 153, 178, 179, 181, 208, 228, 251, 282, 283, 286, 290, 291
Pencarrow, 126, 254, 276, 289
Pepin Island, 238,
Captain Perano, Frank, 248
Perano, Ron, 238
Perry, Alexander, 129
Persson, Jim, 5, 9
Petrie, Ellen, Petrie, 69
Petrie, Hon. Henry, 69
Petrie, Captain John, 275
Phillip, Governor Arthur, 108
Phillips, Captain B, 129, 275
Picton Lime & Cement Co, 210
Picton,(*see also* Waitohi), 10, 133, 138, 202, 206, 215, 234, 252, 293
Pig Valley, 145

pilot services:
    Charleston (Constant Bay), **166**, 172-3, 279
    Collingwood, 147
    early Cook Strait waters, 29, 38, 133
    Gisborne, ix
    Nelson, iii, vii, viii, 33, **60**, 61, **62**, **71**, **74**, 79, 173, 233, 238, 239, 240, 245, 246, 251
Pirimona, 109, 110, 274, 275
Pito, 29, 31
pitsawing, 2, **3**, 4, 133
Plimsoll Line, 195
Plymouth Company of NZ, *aka* Plymouth Co. 38, 273
Poorman's Valley, 15, 82
Poppelwell, Captain, 272
population analyses, 16, 23, 42, 75, 86, 105, 137, 147, 153, 162, 217
Porirua, 273
Porter, Captain Robert, 274, 280
Port Chalmers, (*see also* Dunedin), **vi**, 10, 215
Port Cooper, (later Lyttelton) **vi**, 71, 106, 132
Port Gore, 129, 132, 276
Port Misery (Australia), 12
Port Mission, *see* Mission Hall
Port Nelson, *see* Nelson
Port Nicholson, (*aka* Wellington harbour), **vi**, 11, 33, 39, 42, 57, 71, 99, 100, **118**, 125, 127
Port Underwood (**aka** Cloudy Bay), 38, 39, 68, 103, 105, 119, 121, 137, 163, 184, 275, 277, 282, 284
Port Victoria, (later Lyttelton), **vi**, 106, 277
Potts, Dave, 207
Poverty Bay, 130, 132
Pratt, William, 34, 52, 52, 75, 79, 94-6, 116, 126, 132, 134, 136,
Pratt, William Henry, 193
Princes Drive, 30
Puakawa (*aka* Ekawa), 58, 66
Puaha, David, 109
Public Works Act 1908, 179, 210
punts, 5, 6, **76**, **91**, 95, 201, 202

Puponga, 191, 194, 204, 205, 239, 243, 252, 289, 291, 292
Puponga Coal Company, 293
Puramahoi, 144

Q
Quarantine grounds, 224
Quarantine Rd, 79, 81
Queen Charlotte Sound, 38, 99, 109, 125, 128, 129, 138, 172, 273, 279, 288

R
Rabbit Island, 30, 81, 224, 226, 248, 258, 268
Raglan, 40, 272, 279
Railway line, 223, **223**, **229**, 233
Railway sleepers, 139, 179
Rainbow valley, 106
Rainier, Henry, 184
Ralph, Captain Joseph, 39, 43, 45, 51-54, 184, 271
Ramage, George, 230
Raniera, Captain Hone, 286
Rangihaeata Head, 248 (*see also* Te Rangihaeata)
Rangitoto, *see* d'Urville Island, 110, 274
Raoul Island, 249
Reed family, 248, **250**
Reed, Captain Edward Louis (Ted), iii, 94, 222, 247, 249, 252, 290
Reed, Ekaumoenga, 248
Reed, Jack, 286
Reed, James, 248
Reed, Captain John, 290
Reed, Captain William (Billy), vii, 239, 248, 249, 286, 289
Reeves List for Shipping, 32
Reeves family, 231
Reeves, Jack, 258
Reeves, Captain G H, 28
Reeves, Captain Johnnie, vii, 257, 258-9, **258**
Reeves, Captain Tom, 245, 256, 258, 290, 292
Reeves, William Pember, 20
Renata, 109, 275
Rhind, Captain, 162
Richards, Commander, 129

Richardson, Dr Ralph, 181
Richardson, George, 57
Richardson Street, 30, 31, **35**, 53, 221, 231
Richmond, 80, 81, 159, 224, 243
Ricketts Brothers, **98**, 112, **115**, 190, **231**, 235, 251, 252
Ricketts family, ix, 5, 78, 113, 183, 188, 193, 11, 231
Ricketts, Ambrose, 11, 12, 13, 77, 116, 188, 189, 274, 276, 283
Ricketts, Edward Ambrose (Jimmy), **231**
Ricketts, Captain Bill, 207
Ricketts, Charles Alfred (Charlie), 188, 231, **231**, 246, 252, 299, 289
Ricketts, Eliza, née Kidson, 191
Ricketts, Elizabeth, 12, 77
Ricketts, Captain Frank Perry, 194, 214, 231, 288
Ricketts, George, **231**
Ricketts, John James (Jack, JJ), **102**, 182, 192, 184,189, 191, **231**, 246, 252, 286, 288, 289, 290, 291
Ricketts, Maria, 12
Ricketts, Russell J (Russ), 111, 209, 230, **231**, **232**, 233, 244, 248, 257, 287, 289, 291
Ricketts, Thomas, 189
Ricketts, William, 12
Rigging, vii, 11, 44, 49, 123, 126, 191, 237, 246, 264, 284
Riley, John, 144
Riley, Captain John Samuel, 290
Riwaka:
    boatbuilding, 5, 13, 91, 94, 95, 116, 182, 274, 276, 280, 282, 283, 286
    farming, 82, **92**, 110, 143, 177
    flour mill, 93, 110
    land titles, 54, 79, 90, 91, 95, 96, **97**, 108
    settlement, 90, 116
    shipping, 94, 187, **197**, 241, 243, **258**, 284, 288, 290, 291, 292,
    wharfs, 93, **250**
Riwaka Hotel, 92, 96
Riwaka River, 88, **88**, 91, 92, 96, 116
Riwaka & Nelson Navigation Co. 287
road construction, 75, 76, **76**, 80, 82, 92,

94, 95, **113**, 175, 179, 193, 194, 221, 222, 223
Robertson family, 256, 290
Robinson, Captain George, 284
Robinson, Joe, 42
Robinson, John Perry, 77, 141, 144
Rochfort, John, 154
Rocks Rd, **25**, **76**, **80**, 91, 223,
Rogers, Sanders, 156
Roil family, 144
rope, 11, 44, 76, 82, 126, 149, 150, 240, 248
rowing, 3, 44, 48, 62, 80, 85, 100, 114
rowing, competitive, 34, 60, 122, 123, 136, 235
Rowling, E snr, 241
Ruatoki River, 154
Ruka, 109, 275
Russell St, 52, 113, **113**, **229**, 230, 260

S
Saltwater Creek, 31, 34, 39, 49, 53, 78, 158, 221, 222
Saltwater Creek Bridge, **52**, 53, 78, 80, 110, 113, 274
sand as cargo, 205, **210**, 234
Sandy Bay (*see also* Marahau), 143, 148, 182-3, 205, 258, 282, 290
Sanderson, Captain, 280
Sarau, 75
Saunders, Alfred, 56, 59,67, 68, 87, 89, 99, 100, 119
sawmills, 5, 144, 179, 181, 182, 183, 189, 193, 252, 289
Sawyers, Morrie, 206
Scanlon, Captain, 271, 272
Scantling, Captain, 39
Schroder, George William, 109, 275
Scott, Captain, 154, 281
Scott, Captain Richard B, 285
scows,
    (overview), vii, viii, 201-10
    capsizes, 202, **203**, 205
    cargoes, **106**, **178**, 196, 205, **206**, **210**, 253-4
    construction, 202, **203**
    hull form 6, 171, **189**, **190**, 202, **203**, **204**, 251-2

propulsion, 207, 242, 255, 213
tonnage & stability issues, 196, 198, **206**, **178**
vessels, 291-3
Screw steamers, (*also* Vessels Index, prefix SS), 158-60, **159**, 193, **214**, 285
scrip, *see also* land, 21, 24, 56-7, 82, 87, 89, 96, 104
Scully family, 231
Scully, Captain, 246
Sedcole, Captain John, 276
Seddon, 'King Dick' (PM), 240
Sellars, Ken, 123
Separation Point, 26, 45, **47**, 48, 85, 148, 155, 191, 192, 196, 242, 288
sheep, *see also* farming, livestock, 35, 40, 92, **98**, 99, 100, 103-6, 119, 132, 137, 159, 169, 178, 182
Sheridan, Captain Daniel, 39, 45, 48-51, 54, 271,
Shetland Islanders, 175
Shields, Peter, 283
shipping:
    agents, 156, 162, 212, 231
    early unregulated, 38-40, 54, 114
    investment, 77-8, 159, 193, 206, 212-8, 227
    newspaper reports, 78, 148, **149**, 239
    points, 81, 105, 112, 132, 148, 174, 224
    regulations, 32, 195-6
    steam, *see* steamship companies
    trans-shipping, 117, 121, 138, 157, 215
Shipping and Seaman Act 1877, 195
Shipping Companies (local) *also* Steamship Co's:
    Christchurch Conveyance Company, 277
    Eckford Shipping Co, 293
    Golden Bay Shipping Company, 293
    Karamea Shipping Company, 293
    Pearl Kasper Shipping Company, 292
    Puponga Shipping Company, 293
    Sullivan Shipping (Wgtn), 293
    West Haven Shipping Company, 293
Shortt, Captain, 278, 279

Sinclair, Captain William, 273, 274
Smallbone family, 231
Smith, Captain, 281
Smith, Captain Arthur, 282, 285, 288, 290
Smith, Captain C H, 283
Smith, Captain George, 283
Smith, Manuel, iii, 94
Smith, Captain William, 238-9, 278
Somes, Joseph, 64
Sorcenelli, Sandy, 248
South Durham, Province of, **55**
Spain, William (Land Commissioner), 58, 64, 65, 71, 77, 108, 109, 141
Stafford, Edward, 141
Stanley, Lord, 64
Stanton, Ann (nee Flowerday), 184
Staples St, 88
Steamships, *see* paddle and screw steamers
Steamship Companies
    Anchor Line, 159, 193, 211, **212**, 213-5, 218, **220**, 232, 251, 253, **256**, 257, 293
    Australian Steam Navigation Co., 213
    Canterbury Steam, 218
    Richardson and Co., 218
    Harbour Steam Co., 211, 217
    Holm Line, 218
    Huddart Parker Line, 218
    Manukau Steam Ship Co., 211
    Nathaniel Edwards and Co., 159
    Nelson Coast Steam Nav. Co., 157-8, 211-12
    NZ Steam Navigation Co., 211, 215
    Northern Steam Ship Co., 211
    Tasmanian Steam Navigation Co., 218
    Union Steamship Co., 217
    Waikato Steam Navigation & Coal Co., 211
    Waiuku Steam & Navigation Co., 211
    Wgton & Havelock Steam Shipping Co.,193, 204
Steamships, see paddle steamers, screw steamers
Stenning, Captain, 39, 271
Stephen, James, 16, 19

Stephens Island,129
Stephens, Cape, 26
Stephens, Samuel, 41, 79, 89, 90
Stepneyville, 228
Stewart, James, 283
Stiles, William, 39
Stoke, 286, 292
Stokes, Captain J L, **107**, **224**
Storekeeping, 34, **35**, **51**, 5, 58, 77, 80, 132, 145, 146, 147, 148, 156, 157, 160, 162, 235, 275, 277
Stony Rd, the, 85, 93, 96, 289
Stringer, Alfred, 239
Stringer, Dick, 239, 242
Strong, Samuel, 110, 111, 274, 275
Sunday Island (*aka* Raoul Island), 249
Supper Party, the, 63, 86, 104, 139, 141
surf boats, 121, 169, 173, 174
survey maps, **21**, **84**, 95, **97**, **225**
survey parties, 29, 38, 42, 43, 54, 59, 62, 65, 107, 114, 129
survey vessels, 23, 26, 38, 65, 107, 114, 129
surveys, marine, 195, 266, 274, 206
Swainson, William, 140
Swanson, Neil, 284, 285
Swamp Road, 92
Swinie, Captain, 40
Symonds 'Old Bogo', 248

T
Tahiti, 94
Tahunanui Beach, 223
Tainui, 155
Takaka:
    Hill, 143, 194, 205
    River valley, 57, 58, 109, 146
    Settlement, **47**, **144**, 145, 190, **192**, 193, 194
Tamati Pirimona Marino, 109, 110, 274, 275
Tarakohe, **144**
Taranaki, 29, 38, 40, 43, 159, 211, 273
Tarapuhi, 155
Tasman, Abel Janzoon, 26, **143**
Tasman Bay (*see also* Blind Bay), 26, 246, 249, 262, 287
Tasman Sea, 39, 75, 111, 112, 147, 157,

161, 168, 171, 172, 197, 200, 218, 232, 271
Tasmania, 108
Tasmanian vessels, 39, **124**, 162, 164, 167, 171, 177, **180**, 193, 194, 197-200, **198**, 199, 226, **229**, 272, 283, 289, 291
Tata Islands, 40, 45, **46**, **144**, 189, 209-10, 243, 278, 283
Taupo Pa, 57
Taylor, Captain J, 275
Taylor, Captain Raymond, 290,
Taylor, Captain T B, 271
Taylor, Rev Tommy, **232**
Te Awaiti, 38, 272
Te Matea Bay, 38
Te Puaha, 103, 109,
Te Rangihaeata, 64-66, 66, 68, 70, 72, 89, 272
Te Rauparaha, 22, 58, 64-8, 71, 80, 109, **143**, 268, **269**, 272
Te Wakatu, *see* Wakatu
Telegraph, 148, 193,
Tenths reserves, 22, 109, 140
Temple, Philip, 71
Terawhiti, Cape, 100, **118**, 126, 127, 128
Thames barges, 197, 202, 207
The Beaver, *see also* Beavertown, 119, 120
The Colonist, 141
The Times, London, 19
The Wood, **52**, 78
Thomas, R, 68
Thompson, Magistrate Henry Augustus, 58, 59, 63, 64, 66, 67, 68
Thompson, T J, 84
Thompson, Captain Robert, 282
Thoms, Joseph, 38, 42, 109, 155, 272
Thomson family, 231
Thorpe St, 88
Timaru, **vi**, **180**, **183**, 184, 285, 291
timber:
    boatbuilding, 1, 2, 4, 9, 79, **115**, 130, 160, 172, 181-191, **182**, **183**, **185**, 201, 232, 237
    industry, 3, 4, 58, 82, 89, 136, 143, 177-91
    rafting, **35**, 61, 80, 122, 178, 179, 188, 244

shipping, 39, 40, 49, 110, 117, 119, 122, 134, 153, 160, **176**, **178**, 179, **180**, 190, 194, 196, 197, **199**, **200**, 205-6, 209, **229**, 243-4, 252, 256, **261**, 267
Toi Toi Valley, 221
Tolaga Bay, 131, 274
Tonga Bay quarry, 205
Tonga Island, 181, 188
Tonkin, Tim, Captain, **230**
Tophouse sheep run, 105, 169
Tophouse route, 59, 65, 69, 105, 106
Torrent Bay:
    Anchorage, 48, 183
    boatbuilding, 13, **176**, **183**, 184, **253**, 283, 285
    quarry, 205
    shipping, 208, **210**, 255, 256, 291
Totaranui:
    Anchorage, 48, 183
    farming & forestry, 147, 181, 191, 192
trading stores *see* storekeeping
Trafalgar Park, 257, 259
Trafalgar St, 31, 53
tramways, 112, **113**, 138-9, 181, **192**, 205, **222**, 223, 234, **261**
Traveller's Rest Hotel, 96
Treaty of Waitangi, 22, 74
Tregidga family, 184, **250**, 255
Tregidga, Captain Albert (Albie), 205
Tregidga, Emily, 184
Tregidga, Ethel, (née McNabb), 241, 243
Tregidga, Mary, 255
Tregidga, Richard Gill (Dick), 184, 255, 287
Tregidga, Captain Richard Gill jnr (Sonny), vii, 191, **197**, 205, 243, 249, **250**, 255, 259, 257, 287, 289, 290, 292
Tregidga, Captain William (Bill), 205, **250**, 255, 287, 292
trenails, *see* nails
Tuamarina, 67, **69**, 71, 75
Tuckett, Frederick, 33, 41, 43, 59, 64, 65, 68, 75, 77, 99
Tucker, Captain Jon, iii
Tukurua, 194
Turnagain, Cape, 130

Turner, W, 283, 290
Turner, Captain, 287
Tytler, J S, 58

U
Union Steam Ship Company, 217

V
Valle, Philip, 76
Valparaiso, 54
van Diemen's Land, 18, 108
Victoria Rd, 70, 112, 255
voting franchise, 139-142

W
Wade, John, 100, 101
Wahlstrom, Alf, 193, 288
Wai-iti Valley, 105, 179
Waikanae, 33
Waikawa, 258, 287
Waimakariri River, i, 154
Waimea
    District, 35, 79, 80, 81, 179, 200, 223, 224
    estuary, 81, **81**, 99, 223, 239, 248
    plains, 31, 80, 81, 83, 223
    River, 79, 80, 81, 82, 178, 179, 200, 223
 Sands (*aka* The flats or Waimea bank), 29, 30, 80, 95, 223, 224, 226, 247, 284
Waimea West, 76
Waimea East, **81**, **84**, 226
Waimea Road, 80
Waimea Road Board, 285
Wainui Bay, **81**, **84**, 226, 256, 290,
Waipiro Bay, **122**, 130
Wairarapa, 100, 130
Wairarapa, Lake, 101
Wairau:
    conflict, 59, **62**, 64-6, **70**, 71-73, 269, 272
    farming (*see also* Marlborough) 103-5, 119, 137
    land, 55, 59, 64, **69**, **70**, 77, 80, 85, 104, 105, 117, 142
    shipping, 100, 105, 106, 109, 111, 116, 119-23, **124**, 132, 137, 139, 275, 276, 278, 278, 284, 286
Wairau River, 62, 65, 67, **118**, 119-23, 125, 276, 289
Wairoa (*sic* – Wairau), 138
Wairoa River (Tributary to Waimea), 80
Waitangi Tribunal (*see also* Treaty), 22, 30
Waitapu, **47**, 193, 194, 199, **202**, 203, 208, **229**, 262, 280, 278, 281-3, 288, 291
Waite, Reuben, 156, 167, 177, 283
Waitohi, (*see also* Picton), 138
Waiwhetu, 42
Waka, 13, **22**, 26, **46**, **51**, 54, **90**, 109, 110, 268
Wakamarina, 153
Wakapuaka, 66, 79, 110, 154
Wakatu, (*aka* Whakatu, te Wakatu), 29, 31, 41, 64, 110, 268
Wakatu Lane, 221
Wakatu Rowing Club, 136
Wakefield Quay, **14**, 54, 112, 113, 221, 223
Wakefield, Captain Arthur, 27, 29-33, 39, 41, 43, 54, 57, 58, 63-4, 66-8, 82
Wakefield, Colonel William, 17, 21, 42-3, 53, 55, 57, 63, 64, 71, 99, 108
Wakefield, Edward Gibbon, 1, 12-20, **14**, **18**, 23
Wakefield's scheme see New Zealand Company
Wakely, Captain, 283
Walker, Captain John, 111, 112, 144, 149, 154, 155, 193, 276, 279
Walker, G, 154
Walling, Captain Bob, 207
Wanganui (town), **vi**, 24, 39, 40, 163, 164, 180, 214, 234, 240-1, 259, 268, 271, 276, 280, 291
Wanganui River 391
Wangapeka, 145
Wapping Point, (*aka* Warping Point), 43, 46, 194,
Ward, Amelia, (née Kidson), 70, 235
Ward, John, 139, 140
Ward, Ruby, (m Westrupp) 70
Warping Point, see Wapping Point
Washbourn, Henry, 42, 43
Washington Valley, 34, 49, 53, 221, 224

Watchlin, Captain, 292
Watson, Captain John, 273
Watt, Captain W H , 271
Watts, Captain, W, 281
Watts, John, 143, 277, 281
Webster, Captain, 40,
Webster, George, 273
Welch, Captain, 283
Weld (town), 102
Weld, Frederick, 63, 100, 101, 103, 106, 129
Wellington:
    boatbuilding, 116, **118**, **120**, 132
    capital, 179
    harbour (*see also* Port Nicholson), 100, 102, 126, 127, 129, 208, 254, 271
    land, 25, 43, 57, 87, 108
    earthquakes see earthquakes
    settlement, **vi**, ix, 18,20, 21, 24, 27, 34, 39, 40, 53, 56, 57, 63, 69, 71, 80, 81, 163
    shipping, 95, 99, 111, 117, 121, 123, 130, 132, 137, 193, 205, 214, 215, **217**, 218, **219**
Wellington, Duke of, 24
Wells, Ken, 207
Wells, Hughie, 235
West Coast (*see also* Westport, West Wanganui, Greymouth, Charleston and Hokitika)
    goldfields, 145, 153-6, 162
    land purchase, 154
    Maori see Ngai Tahu
    settlement, 153, 155, 162, **168**
    Sealing, 42
    shipwrecks, 131, 161, 274
    Shipping, 39, 111, 121, 130, 137, 157, 159, **166**,167, 170, 171, 212, 213, 215, **218**, 276
West Wanganui, (*aka* Westhaven), 11, 33, 39, 42, **47**, 154, 157, 161, 163, 164, 268, 276, 277, 281, 284, 289
Westhaven, (*see also* West Wanganui), 42, **47**, 154, **164**, **165**
West Haven Shipping Company, 293
Westport, **vi**, 119, 141, 154, 156, 157, 159, 160-2, 167, 169, 173, 175, 257, 280, 282-4, 290, 295
Westrupp family, 131, 151, 186, **236**, 239, **250**
Westrupp, Albert, 174, 205, 241, 244
Westrupp, Allen, iii, vii, 5, 6, 9, 15, 34, 177, 231, 234, 240, 258, 259
Westrupp, Captain Bill (William), **146**, 165, 238, 241, 242, 247, 256, 292
Westrupp, Captain Barbara (m Tucker),
Westrupp, Captain Cockram (Cocky) **236**, 238, 287
Westrupp, Captain George (Kemo), 238, 239, 247, 259, 287
Westrupp, Captain James (Brimbo), 238, 257
Westrupp, Jocelyn, iii, ix, 10, 287
Westrupp, Captain John, **40**, 113, **113**, 150, 151, 185, **204**, 222, **223**, 226, **229**, 238, 239, 240, 248, 249, 277, 280, 285, 287
Westrupp, Captain John Edward (Jack), 113, 150, 193, 206, 214, **229**, 238, 280, 289
Westrupp, Catherine (Kate), (née Woolf), 183, 191
Westrupp, Margaret, (née Parker), 113, 238
Westrupp, Captain Robert Porter (Bob), 164, **229**, 239, 249
Westrupp, Ruby, née Ward, 70
Westrupp, Captain Sam, viii,165, 183, 191, 207, 208, **209**, **229**, **230**, 238, 239, 240, 248
Westrupp, Sarah Ann (m Glover) 113, 185, 238-9
Westrupp, Sid (Dick), Pilot-launch master, 173, 240, 255
Westrupp, Captain Willy, iii, 165
Wett, Antonio (Tony), 239, 248
Whakatu Drive, 81, 266
whaleboats, 13, **62**, 65, 69, 103, 105, 114, 121
whalers, viii, 17, 35, 38, 42, 55, 66, 94, 101, 105, 110, 125, 173, 264
whaling, 13, 22, 38, 65, 69, 103, 105, 106, 119, 248
whanga, 163, 268
Whangamoa, 138

Whanganui River (*see* Wanganui River)
Whangaroa (Northland), 273, 274, 278, 293
Wharf Rd, (now Beach Rd), 243
Wharves:
    Akersten, wharf-builder, 114
    Albion wharf, **151**, 213, 222
    Awaroa wharf, 190
    Beit's wharf, 113
    Blenheim wharf, **124**
    Bond Store wharf, 222
    Burford's wharf, 209
    Brownlee's wharf (Havelock), **180**, 181
    Collingwood wharf, 194, **201**
    Customs-house wharf, 114, 222
    Fishermans' wharf (Nelson), 239, 249
    Ferntown wharf, 194
    Franzen's wharf, 222, **222**, **245**
    Gasworks' wharf, 102, 246, **246**, 289
    Gilbertson's wharf, **236**, 287
    Lukins' wharf, 189, 204, 222, 234, 237-8, 244
    Main wharf (Nelson), 74, 246, **256**
    Marahau jetty, 289
    Milnthorpe wharf (Parapara), 194, 207, **261**
    Morrison & Sclander's wharf, 114
    Motueka wharf, **200**, 212
    Motupipi wharf, 209
    Napier wharf (Port Nelson), 222
    New Zealand Company's wharf, 54, 113
    Nicholson's wharf, 112
    Onekaka wharf, 194
    Otterson's jetty, 49
    Riwaka wharf, 91, 93, **250**
    Waitapu wharf, **192**, 193, 262
    Wapping Point wharf, 194
    Westhaven wharf, 165, 256, **261**
Whitwell, Captain, 121, 159, 160, 193
Wiesenhavern, O, 169, 170
Wilcox, F, 155
Wildman family, 94, 231
Wilkes timber yard, 244
Wilkinson, Mr, 106, 273
Williams, Charles, 251

Williams family, 94, 231, 251
Williams, Emily, née Berry, 228
Williams, Frank, 228, 252, 255, 288
Williams, Captain George Patrick, **62**, **186**, 228, 245, 247, **251**, 251-4, 288-90
Williams, Capt Henry (Harry), 246, 252, 253, 288
Williams, Howard, iii, 43, 207, 251, 258
Williams, Ivan, 228
Williams, Captain James (Jim), 39, 246, 249, 252
Williams, Jeff, 228
Williams, Captain Joseph (Joe), 252
Williams, Captain Percy Charles, iii, 232, 233, 237, 238, 251, 252, 253, 259
Williams, Rob, (harbourmaster) ii, iii, 254, 293
Williams, William, (Pilot) 147
Wilson family, 94
Wilson, Alfred, 143
Wilson, Lynette, ii, iii
Winstanley family, 231
Winter, Will, 291,292
Wood, The, **52**, 78
wood, *see* boatbuilding, timber
wool, see also sheep, 99, 100 104, 105, 107, 111, 117, 119, 121, **122**, 132, 137, 148, 177, 208, **212**, 276, 279
Woolf family, 94,183, 231
Woolf, Catherine (m Westrupp), 183, 191
Wolf, John, 183, 290
Woolf, Captain Thomas Shenton, 282, 286
Workman, John, 100
Workman, Rewhanga, 100
World War One, 240, 242, 255, 257
World War Two, 206
Worser Bay, 129, 271, 274, 275
Wright, Captain, 149
Wright, James, 99
Wright, Orr &, 39
Wright, William, 42
Wynen, James, 121

Y
Young, Henry, vii, **74**, 288
Young, William Curling, 72

COVER PHOTOGRAPHS

Front cover photographs, clockwise from top left:

Pearl aground on Fifeshire Rock (pg 226)
The *New Zealand Company*'s land claim, on Cook's chart of NZ (pg 55)
Ketch *Elizabeth* alongside the Haven Road seawall (pg 229)
Cutter *Matakana* running under improvised squaresail (pg 263)
New Zealand Company land sales poster, London circa 1839 (pg 1)
Ketch *Transit* (pg 182)
Calyx in Nelson Haven (pg 9)
Pet loading sheep (pg 98)
Comet aground near the Gas Works jetty (pg 176)
Wharf-boy at Albion wharf circa 1870s (pg 151)
Billy Reed, mending nets (pg 249)

Central painting: Captain Young's *Camellia* (refer pp vii, 74)

Back cover illustrations:

Top right: Author Fred Westrupp on the helm of ketch *New Zealand Maid*
Left: 1845 sketch of Company Store, Nelson Haven by Longueville (pg 35)
Right: *Felicity* under construction, Frenchman's Bay, by Linda Cross (pg 1)

www.ingramcontent.com/pod-product-compliance
Lightning Source LLC
Chambersburg PA
CBHW081202170426
43197CB00018B/2901